Facing Georgetown's History

Facing Georgetown's History

A Reader on Slavery, Memory, and Reconciliation

Edited by Adam Rothman
and Elsa Barraza Mendoza

GEORGETOWN UNIVERSITY PRESS / WASHINGTON, DC

The publisher is not responsible for third-party websites or their content. URL links were active at time of publication.

Library of Congress Cataloging-in-Publication Data

Names: Rothman, Adam, 1971- editor. | Barraza Mendoza, Elsa, editor.
Title: Facing Georgetown's history : a reader on slavery, memory, and reconciliation / [edited by] Adam Rothman and Elsa Barraza Mendoza.
Description: Washington : Georgetown University Press, 2021. | Includes index.
Identifiers: LCCN 2020044103 | ISBN 9781647120962 (hardcover) | ISBN 9781647120979 (ebook)
Subjects: LCSH: Georgetown University—History. | Georgetown University—History—Sources. | Jesuits—United States—History. | Jesuits—United States—History—Sources. | Slavery—United States—History. | Slavery—United States—History—Sources. | African Americans—History. | African Americans—History—Sources. | Racism—United States. | Reconciliation. | Memory—Social aspects—United States.
Classification: LCC LD1961.G52 F33 2021 | DDC 378.753—dc23
LC record available at https://lccn.loc.gov/2020044103

♾ This paper meets the requirements of ANSI/NISO Z39.48-1992 (Permanence of Paper).

22 21   9 8 7 6 5 4 3 2 First printing

Printed in the United States of America

Rachel McCarthy, Sienna Brancato, and Alejandra Rocha, Production Assistants
Cover design by Erin Kirk
Interior design by BookComp, Inc.

We dedicate this book to the men, women, and children who endured slavery on the Jesuits' Maryland plantations and at Georgetown.

CONTENTS

PART II: MEMORY AND RECONCILIATION

ESSAYS

THE WORKING GROUP

THE GU272 DESCENDANTS

RECONCILIATION AND REPARATION

ILLUSTRATIONS

FOREWORD

An accoumpt [*sic*] of my Negros
Dick bought of Thos. Linthicum —about 42 y³ old
~~Sambo~~ of Edward Diggs — — —about 32 y³ old dead
Tomboy of Coll. Darnall — — —abᵗ 23
Jack of ditto — — — — —— — abᵗ 21
. . .

> —Daybook of James Carroll, Catholic planter, merchant, and trader

19th June
1838.
Articles of agreement between Thomas F. Mulledy, of George Town,
District of Columbia, of one part, and Jesse Beatty and Henry Johnson,
of the State of Louisiana, of the other part. Thomas F. Mulledy sells to
Jesse Beatty and Henry Johnson two hundred and seventy two negroes, to
wit:—Isaac, a man sixty five years of age, Charles, his eldest son, forty years
of age, Nelly his daughter, thirty eight years of age, Henny, a girl thirteen
years of age, Cecilia, a girl eight years of age, Ruthy, a girl six years of age . . .

> —Contract signed by Fr. Thomas F. Mulledy, SJ, Provincial of the
> Maryland Jesuits and recent president of Georgetown College,
> and two Louisiana planters

Bought. Sold. Generations enslaved on Jesuit estates in Maryland. Georgetown University's origins reside here.

The past is not remote or resolved. It still wounds.

Confronting painful elements of this nation's history is difficult, but the
legacy of slavery—and the racism it fed and reinforced—remains malignant.
It influences who Americans think "we the people" are, as citizens and as
communities. Challenging this legacy requires recognizing the depths of its
roots and persistence of its reach.

Consider the reach of profit. The power of Manhattan's financial district
grew in no small measure from the trade of plantation-grown cotton. Two

precursor banks of JPMorgan Chase used thousands of enslaved human beings as collateral on loans to plantation owners. Aetna, among other companies, wrote life insurance policies on human "property." These are but a few examples of how a supposedly "sectional" economy bound North to South, the nation to overseas, and past to present.

So it should not surprise anyone that venerated institutions of higher education were built by the ill-gotten wealth that "slave trading" and "slave-holding" afforded founders, donors, trustees—before and after the American Revolution. It shouldn't surprise anyone that unknown numbers of enslaved workers erected campus buildings from mortar and bricks. Or that the daily operations of these institutions exploited the daily labor of those who could never enroll as students. Or that, within these halls of learning, theories of scientific racism would elevate an ideology of white supremacy.

The academy's entanglement with slavery and with race-making was never accidental or temporary. It was deliberate, invested, and committed.

In 2015 Georgetown University joined a growing number of US colleges and universities to acknowledge such ties. Convened by President John J. DeGioia, the Working Group on Slavery, Memory, and Reconciliation also faced the centrality of Catholic and Jesuit slaveholding to the school's origins and survival. The newly renovated Mulledy Hall on campus was a spark. Fr. Thomas F. Mulledy, SJ, served as the president of Georgetown College from 1829 to 1838, and again in the late 1840s. Praised for increasing student enrollments and promoting the institution, he also oversaw a college sinking into debt. In 1838 Mulledy coordinated a mass sale to two Louisiana planters of nearly three hundred persons of African descent enslaved on Jesuit plantations in Maryland. The deal was supposed to yield $115,000— well over $3 million in today's dollars. Jesuit leaders in Rome, Italy, had permitted the sale to proceed on condition that enslaved husbands and wives wouldn't be separated, that their religious needs would still be met, and that monies from the sale would be invested in capital and not used to satisfy debt. These conditions were not met.

Some colleges and universities have chosen to go beyond public acknowledgment of complicity to contend more fully with difficult, inconvenient truths. A few institutions are trying to take responsibility for the lasting toll of past injustices in the present.

Georgetown University has stated its commitment to "a long-term and ongoing process to more deeply understand and respond to the University's role in the injustice of slavery and the legacies of enslavement and segregation in our nation." The school has chosen to pursue "a path of memorialization and reconciliation in our present day" via "engagement with the members of the Descendant community, collaborative projects and new initiatives, and learning and research."[1]

But what is needed to reconcile such a past with the present? What forms of retrospective or reparative justice are necessary?

Facing Georgetown's History offers an important reader on slavery, memory, and reconciliation. Editors Adam Rothman and Elsa Barraza Mendoza have carefully selected essays, articles, and archival documents that not only reveal the university's foundational ties to slavery but provide crucial context to understand the meanings of this history today. Original and previously published pieces also shed light on steps toward reckoning—by the institution, by descendants of those enslaved and sold, and by the Society of Jesus. The volume explores what the efforts at reconciliation and repair thus far entail and what they could promise. Descendant voices and views inform many of these pages. So do those of various scholars and writers, including Georgetown faculty and students.

The editors aptly note that the university's origin and early decades are "a microcosm of the whole history of American slavery." Jesuits arrived in colonial Maryland in 1634 and had long participated in its tobacco economy before Pope Clement XIV suppressed the order in 1773. Ex-Jesuits continued their work until the Society of Jesus was formally restored in 1814. Many hundreds of people in bondage—if not more—toiled on Maryland estates, generation after generation, to sustain Jesuit-Catholic missions.

Archival materials included in the reader document this history, from a 1717 deed naming enslaved persons sold, to the mass sale in 1838, to the 1862 departure of the last man Georgetown College rented from an "owner." A contract at the end of the Civil War between a Louisiana plantation owner and newly freed men and women outlines an early experiment in which labor terms changed from forced to paid.

Seen another way these materials give stark evidence of the world inhabited by those enslaved. All but one of the documents present the perspectives of those who wielded power to extract labor without consent. The key exception is a 1791 petition for freedom filed, through his attorneys, by Edward Queen. His claim: that he was held unjustly because his grandmother had been enslaved unjustly. Queen won his case, and several (but not all) family members who filed petitions in turn won their freedom.[2] Other archival records indirectly present the voices and actions of those unfree. A "runaway" ad run for Isaac, placed by Georgetown College's clerk in 1814, reveals a man who tried to take his own freedom before he was captured and sold. And a priest who witnessed the removals accompanying the 1838 sale recounted the pleas of a "pious" woman, genuflecting before him: "If ever someone should have reason for despair, do I not now have it? . . . What will become of me? Why do I deserve this?" The priest's response: "Trust in God."

This history is personal. Paternal ancestors of mine were enslaved by Jesuit priests, they were sold by Jesuit priests, and via court petitions they found freedom from servitude to Jesuit priests. While I am not a direct descendant of those sold and shipped to Louisiana in 1838, some of them are family.

It's because of research on Maryland freedom suits by William G. Thomas III, because of the Georgetown Slavery Archive under curator Adam Rothman, and because of the Georgetown Memory Project's efforts, under Richard Cellini, to identify living descendants that I've learned how close this history is.

I first visited the Booth Family Center for Special Collections at Georgetown to search for forebears in the Jesuit Maryland Province Archives. After requesting the early 1700s daybook and will of Catholic planter James Carroll, plus Jesuit estate records, I was told that I'd have to share them with another patron. That the other patron was Adam Rothman was serendipity. He was pulling items to show some descendants of the Queen family who were visiting that day. By unexpected fortune I met cousins many generations removed from our common ancestor.

Jesuit papers two and three centuries old revealed more. On page after brittle page—at once meticulous, fragmented, and inconsistent—Africans and African Americans stood out, though never on their own terms. They are prominent in lists of tasks required on plantations, in lists of chattel itemized as economic units to be sold, in lists noting births, baptisms, deaths, and burials of these children of God. Records released odors of dust, mold, and age. Yet ink—handwritten so long ago—would still run under a drop of water, would still fade if exposed to sunlight.

The last page I touched and read that first day in the archives was penned in 1749 by Fr. George Hunter, SJ, of Venerable Memory, in his Spiritual Retreat:

> To the Greater Glory of God.
> Charity to Negroes is Due from all particularly their masters. As they are members of Jesus Christ, redeemed by his precious blood, they are to be Dealt with in a charitable, Christian, paternal manner, which is at the same time a great means to bring them to do their Duty to God, & therefore to gain their Souls.

What is needed to reconcile such a past with the present? What forms of retrospective or reparative justice are necessary? Perhaps no single response to either question is yet possible. Members of the descendant communities, of Georgetown University (from administration to students), and of the Society of Jesus are still working to define a path forward, together.

Facing Georgetown's History is an essential piece of that path, offering elemental respect and accountability in truth-telling. It acknowledges those long silenced, including the 272 women, children, and men sold to Louisiana in 1838—and the many hundreds more who toiled from the seventeenth century to the Civil War. This volume also contributes to the necessary public dialogue on the legacy of slavery today.

These thoughts find the page at a time of crisis, late summer 2020. A global pandemic and national protests inform them. This moment will have passed when you read these words. But the impact of this time and of how it fits within a larger, longer historical context will endure. The pandemic will reach an end before unjust and unjustified acts of violence ever will. The lives of those held in bondage against their will mattered—in 1715, in 1838, in 1865—as they matter today. As do the lives of those continuing to experience deeply rooted racial injustice.

In 1967 Fr. Pedro Arrupe, the Superior General of the Society of Jesus, sent a letter to every American Jesuit that spoke to the "gravity of the current racial crisis in the United States."[3] He believed that the "crisis involves, before all else, a direct challenge to our sincerity in professing a Christian concept of man" and that "*American Jesuits cannot, must not, stand aloof.*" More than half a century later, this moment calls on all who would heed it not only to bear witness but to work toward justice long denied.

—Lauret E. Savoy
Author of *Trace: Memory, History, Race, and the American Landscape*

Notes

1. Georgetown University's website on "Slavery, Memory, and Reconciliation" can be viewed at http://slavery.georgetown.edu/.

2. For details on freedom petitions filed by those enslaved on Jesuit-Catholic plantations in Maryland (including Edward Queen), see William G. Thomas III, *A Question of Freedom: The Families Who Challenged Slavery from the Nation's Founding to the Civil War* (New Haven: Yale University Press, 2020).

3. The 1967 letter from Fr. Pedro Arrupe, the Superior General of the Society of Jesus, can be found in "Interracial Apostolate," in *Justice with Faith Today: Selected Letters and Addresses—II*, ed. Jerome Aixala (St. Louis: The Institute of Jesuit Sources, 1980), 13–27. It is also available at https://jesuitportal.bc.edu/research/documents/1967_arrupeinterracial/.

ACKNOWLEDGMENTS

This book grows out of nearly five years of work on slavery, memory, and reconciliation at Georgetown University. However, the origins of this volume are older than that. We owe an intellectual debt to Emmett Curran and other Georgetown faculty and students who were part of the American Studies Program's Jesuit Plantation Project. We follow in their footsteps as we endeavor to reveal this past, making it accessible to the broader community.

This book was a collaborative effort. Our research for it would not have been possible without the expertise of the staff at Georgetown's Booth Family Center for Special Collections. Special thanks to Lynn Conway, the university archivist, who always helped us with our questions. Mary Beth Corrigan, too, has been a reliable guide to Georgetown's archival materials.

We also thank the many researchers who have worked with the Georgetown Slavery Archive. Particular thanks go to Julia Bernier, a past Georgetown and Andrew W. Mellon Fellow for the Study of Slavery; Claire Healy, who began the translation of documents in Latin; and Cory Young, a PhD candidate in the Department of History. Many of the undergraduate students who took American Studies 272: Facing Georgetown's History over the past few years contributed research and ideas that have shaped this volume. Genealogical research conducted by the Georgetown Memory Project has also been an important source of information about the GU272 and their descendants.

Georgetown University's president John J. DeGioia has been a consistent supporter of the work of the Georgetown Slavery Archive since it was launched by the university's Working Group on Slavery, Memory, and Reconciliation in 2016, and we are grateful to the President's Office for all their help.

Conversations with colleagues have strengthened this book in direct and indirect ways; thanks to Herbert Brewer, David Collins, Derek Goldman, Maurice Jackson, Sharon Leon, Chandra Manning, Laura Masur, Alondra Nelson, Josiah Osgood, Carlos Simon, Will Thomas, and Craig Steven Wilder, among others. Bernie Cook has been a constant partner in this work.

Several of the documents we present in this volume are reproduced with the permission of the Maryland Province of the Society of Jesus and the

Jesuit Archives in Rome. Many thanks to Thomas McCoog for facilitating the publication of this archival material. Jesuit stewardship of their archives is the reason why these materials, some centuries old, are available to historians today. Moreover, we are indebted to the work of the Jesuits' Slavery, History, Memory, and Reconciliation Project.

We have been honored to get to know members of the GU272 descendant community through our research and teaching, and we are grateful for the opportunity to include some of their voices and perspectives in this volume. Many thanks to Sandra Green Thomas and Cheryllyn Branche for permission to publish their words, and to Lauret Savoy for her moving prologue. Thanks as well to the Tilson family for their generosity and commitment to history; to Melissa Kemp, who introduced us to Louisa Mason's legacy in Maryland; and to the formidable Mélisande Short-Colomb.

This book is really the brainchild of Al Bertrand, the director of Georgetown University Press. We'd like to thank the anonymous readers for the press for their helpful suggestions, and Elizabeth Crowley Webber for her careful editing.

Finally, Adam would like to thank Marian, Frances, Roby, and Rita for their love and support. Elsa would like to thank her husband and her mother.

EDITORS' NOTE

This book contains a range of sources, essays, and articles dating from the eighteenth century to the present. The words and phrases used in these texts to describe people of African descent varies from era to era, and we have left the language as we found it, even when language from the original sources might be considered offensive or outdated today. The shifts in terminology from "Negro" and "colored" to "black," "African American," and "Black"— as well as a preference for "enslaved" over "slave"—are themselves historical markers of time and change. Nor have we standardized the method of citation found in the modern scholarly articles included in this anthology. The essays that come from the discipline of history use endnotes, while Alondra Nelson's essay, which comes from the discipline of sociology, uses parenthetical citations.

Facing Georgetown's History

Introduction

ADAM ROTHMAN

This volume is a collection of essays, articles, and documents intended to introduce readers to the history of Georgetown University's involvement in slavery and recent efforts to confront its troubling past. Georgetown's early history, which is closely tied to that of the Society of Jesus (Jesuits) in Maryland, is a microcosm of the whole history of American slavery: the entrenchment of chattel slavery in the tobacco economy of the Chesapeake in the seventeenth and eighteenth centuries, the contradictions of liberty and slavery at the founding of the United States, the rise of the domestic slave trade to the cotton and sugar kingdoms of the Deep South in the nineteenth century, the political conflict over slavery and its overthrow amid civil war, and slavery's persistent legacies of racism and inequality. Georgetown is also emblematic of the complex entanglement of American higher education and religious institutions with slavery. Copious archival materials—literally, "receipts"—document that history down to the sizes of shoes distributed to enslaved people on the Jesuit plantations that subsidized the school.[1] Today Georgetown's efforts at recovery, repair, and reconciliation are part of a broader contemporary moment of reckoning with that history and its legacies. Among the many institutions that are coming to terms with the past, universities are uniquely situated to conduct that reckoning in a constructive way through research, teaching, and the modeling of thoughtful, informed discussion. We hope that this volume will contribute to that effort at Georgetown and beyond.

PART I: HISTORY

The facts are not in dispute. Georgetown was founded in 1789 by a slave-holding Catholic elite in the new United States. The school anchored a web of plantations, churches, and schools managed by the Maryland Jesuits and their proxies.[2] Its first student, William Gaston, went on to become an acclaimed jurist and large slaveowner. The university's largest lecture hall is currently named after him. Enslaved men and women labored on campus for seventy years, from the 1790s to the 1860s, as teamsters, carpenters, cooks, and nurses. The school rented many of them from nearby owners who pocketed the wages—a common practice in the nation's capital. Some of these laborers are still buried beneath the campus in a church cemetery dating to the 1810s that was abandoned later in the century and then built over in the 1950s. The Maryland Jesuits' infamous sale of their human property—272 children, women, and men known as the GU272 who lived and worked on plantations across Maryland—helped to pull the struggling school out of a burdensome debt in 1838. The leaders who orchestrated the sale had few qualms about it. Catholic and Jesuit theologians had long defended the enslavement of Africans, and most American Catholics—including Georgetown's leaders—rejected abolitionism. The college community came largely from the southern states and sympathized with the Confederacy during the Civil War years. More than 80 percent of students and alumni who fought in the war fought for the Confederacy.[3]

After the war, the school's rowing club adopted the Blue and Gray as its colors to signify a new harmony between Northern and Southern students. Union blue and Confederate gray soon became the school's official colors, and to this day, Georgetown's alma mater proclaims, "Wave her colors ever." As Reconstruction ended, a Jesuit priest named Patrick Healy became president of Georgetown. The son of an enslaved woman and an Irish-born cotton planter from Georgia, Healy essentially passed for white, went to Catholic schools in the North, and rose in the ranks of the Society of Jesus to lead Georgetown. Although Healy is sometimes celebrated today as the first African American president of an American university, he concealed his ancestry and the Jesuits kept his secret. Georgetown did not enroll an African American undergraduate student until Samuel Halsey Jr. in the early 1950s, and the history of the school's African American workers in the modern era has yet to be told. Even after the abolition of slavery, Georgetown was a bastion of whiteness for nearly another century, slowly changing with the advent of the civil rights movement.

None of this history was purposely hidden—except for the secret of President Healy's ancestry, which was discovered by a biographer in the 1950s. Jesuit historians had written about the people owned by the Maryland Province in the *Woodstock Letters*, a Jesuit periodical, in the early twentieth century. The multivolume *Bicentennial History of Georgetown University*, published in 1993 by Robert Emmett Curran, a history professor at

Georgetown, remains an excellent resource for understanding the school's relationship to slavery. Led by Curran and other faculty, the university's American Studies Program developed a whole curriculum on the topic and even launched a pioneering website, the Jesuit Plantation Project, to make archival materials relating to Georgetown, the Jesuits, and slavery accessible to the public. More broadly, historians of slavery have written extensively about Jesuit slaveholding around the world. The hundreds of enslaved people owned by the Maryland Jesuits in the eighteenth century were the northern outpost of a vast Jesuit slaveholding complex in the Caribbean and Latin America, with thousands of slaves, before the order was suppressed and its property confiscated in the 1760s and 1770s.[4]

Yet outside of a relatively small number of scholars, Jesuits, and other students of history, few people knew about any of this until recently. It was far from common knowledge even at Georgetown, a venerable university that prizes its storied past. Just because knowledge is available within academia does not mean that it is accessible to or known by the broader public. That gap is part of what this volume is trying to rectify. To that end, part I takes a deep dive into Georgetown's history of slavery: its ties to Catholic and Jesuit slaveholding, the lives of enslaved people at Georgetown and on the Jesuits' Maryland plantations, and the fate of those sold to Louisiana and those who remained. It includes background essays by historians that explain the relationship between Georgetown, the Maryland Jesuits, and slavery in minute detail, as well as a sampling of archival documents that illuminate the world of the Maryland Jesuit enslaved community over time. It is our hope that this collection of essays and documents will help to preserve and publicize knowledge about Georgetown's history of slavery for the benefit of scholars, teachers, students, descendants, and anyone else who is curious and wants to learn in a deep and serious way. As Lauret Savoy's foreword suggests, this history is of more than academic significance. It has become a locus for the memory of the injustice of slavery and hope for repair and reconciliation.

PART II: MEMORY AND RECONCILIATION

This book has grown out of a five-year effort at Georgetown University to wrestle with the demons of our school's history. That effort has involved many different people: the school's leadership, administration, and staff; its students, faculty, and alumni; Jesuits and descendants of the people owned and sold by the Jesuits; and journalists and the media, who have amplified and broadcast the story of what has taken place at Georgetown. We, the editors of this book, have been involved in it ourselves as historians. If the first part of this book offers a survey of Georgetown's history of slavery, the second part looks closely at the recent effort to acknowledge that history and somehow make amends. We examine how memory and reconciliation has taken shape around Georgetown's history of slavery. This book is both a contribution to that project and a reflection on it.

At the beginning of the 2015–16 academic year, Georgetown's president John J. DeGioia appointed a Working Group on Slavery, Memory, and Reconciliation to research the school's historical ties to slavery and make recommendations about how to acknowledge that past. President DeGioia, who earned a PhD in moral philosophy at Georgetown, knew his school's history. Georgetown was reopening a newly renovated residential hall named after Fr. Thomas F. Mulledy, SJ, a Jesuit priest who had been president of the College in the 1830s and the mastermind of the Jesuits' sale of their human property in 1838. Was this a man who should be honored in Georgetown's landscape of memory? This relatively simple question led to many others.

President DeGioia did not appoint the working group in a vacuum. The United States had been shaken by the police killing of Michael Brown in Ferguson, Missouri, on August 9, 2014, and the horrific massacre of worshippers at Emanuel AME Church in Charleston, South Carolina, on June 17, 2015. #BlackLivesMatter was trending on social media and protests were erupting in city streets and on college campuses. At Georgetown during the 2014–15 academic year, undergraduate history major Matthew Quallen wrote a series of articles in the student newspaper that investigated the school's historical ties to Jesuit slaveholding, drawing the attention of a new cohort of students to the 1838 sale. Quallen and several other students would join the Working Group as members. The national crisis was spurring student activism against racism.

The formation of Georgetown's working group was not unprecedented. Under the leadership of Ruth Simmons, Brown University had investigated its historical ties to slavery and the slave trade a decade earlier, issuing its trailblazing report *Slavery and Justice* in 2006. Historians, archivists, and students at other universities (including the University of Maryland, Emory University, and Columbia University) had been researching, teaching, and learning about their own schools' ties to slavery as well. Moreover, historian Craig Steven Wilder's landmark book *Ebony and Ivy*, published in 2013, had shown that Georgetown's history was part of a larger pattern of entanglement between America's oldest, most celebrated universities and slavery.[5]

After the formation of the working group, two things happened during the 2015–16 academic year that elevated Georgetown's inquiry to national prominence. First, students stepped up their pressure on the university. They pushed forward the process of historical reckoning, linking it to present conditions on campus and the Black Lives Matter movement. Student activists staged a sit-in in President DeGioia's office late in the fall semester, demanding a set of reforms that included changing the name of Mulledy Hall. Two of the student leaders, Crystal Walker and Ayo Aruleba, also served on the working group. It was the social media–savvy students who came up with #GU272 to honor the enslaved people sold by Mulledy.

The second major development was the revelation of living descendants of the GU272. Richard Cellini, an alumnus of Georgetown, founded an independent nonprofit organization called the Georgetown Memory Project to conduct genealogical research to identify living descendants of the GU272. Cellini soon found Patricia Bayonne-Johnson, the president of the Eastern Washington Genealogical Society in the Pacific Northwest, who had worked with Louisiana genealogist Judy Riffel a decade earlier to trace her family history to Nace and Biby Butler, a married couple who were part of the Maryland Jesuit enslaved community sold to Louisiana in 1838. Cellini and Bayonne-Johnson caught the eye of reporter Rachel L. Swarns, who wrote a powerful story on the front page of the Sunday *New York Times* on April 17, 2016, that traced the search for GU272 descendants and asked what Georgetown owed them. The question of reparations was now on the table.

The working group submitted its report to President DeGioia in June 2016. The report summarized the historical research that had been done and the events on campus that had been sponsored by the working group to heighten awareness. It offered a series of recommendations, which included new names for the campus buildings that had been named after Mulledy and Fr. William McSherry, SJ, the architects of the 1838 sale; a commitment to research and teaching about Georgetown's historical ties to slavery; and engagement with the emerging GU272 descendant community as a vital dimension of the concept of reconciliation. Releasing the report to the public on September 1, 2016, President DeGioia announced that members of the descendant community who applied to attend Georgetown would be treated the same as the children of faculty, staff, and alumni—effectively granting them "legacy" status for purposes of admission to the university.

Since then, the GU272 descendant community has continued to grow, now numbering in the thousands. Descendants have enrolled in and graduated from Georgetown. Many have visited Georgetown's Booth Family Center for Special Collections to see the fragile archival documents, from baptismal records to bills of sale, that contain the names of their enslaved ancestors. This material (including the documents published in this volume) can be viewed online via the Georgetown Slavery Archive, a digital humanities research project launched by the working group in February 2016 to make original archival material accessible to the public. Genealogical research by the Georgetown Memory Project and by the descendants themselves has connected families who were divided long ago by the domestic slave trade and more recently by migration, distance, and generational drift. Members of the descendant community have organized and argued for Georgetown and the Jesuits to make not just symbolic gestures but to pay reparations.

Georgetown, the Jesuits, and the descendant community are still working out the meaning of reconciliation, and with it, the thorny problem of reparations. In an April 2017 Liturgy of Remembrance, Contrition, and Hope in Georgetown's Gaston Hall with GU272 descendants sharing the stage and in the audience, President DeGioia and Fr. Timothy Kesicki, SJ, the president of the Jesuit Conference of Canada and the United States, apologized for their institutions' complicity in slavery. Since then, leaders of Georgetown, the Jesuits, and the descendant community have been meeting regularly to work out the framework of a durable collaboration. In the meantime, Georgetown students took the initiative to call for material reparations. In a student election in April 2019, Georgetown undergraduates voted overwhelmingly in favor of a small student activity fee to create a reconciliation fund to benefit the GU272 descendant community in places like Maringouin, a small town in Iberville Parish, Louisiana, that is home to hundreds of descendants. The university did not approve the fee but pledged to create a fund through other means to fulfill the same purpose. That is where things stand now, in the summer of 2020, in a world disrupted by COVID-19 and electrified by revived protests over police killings and racist inequality in the United States.

Part II of this volume examines this more recent history of memory and reconciliation: the debates over the meanings and legacies of slavery in the present and the prospects for restorative justice in places like Washington, DC, and Maringouin, Louisiana. It can be difficult to discuss these controversial issues, but it's necessary. We have included a variety of perspectives in this part of the book: essays on historical memory by the distinguished historian Ira Berlin and sociologist Alondra Nelson; Ta-Nehisi Coates's influential 2014 argument for reparations from *The Atlantic*; the recommendations of Georgetown's Working Group on Slavery, Memory, and Reconciliation; Kesicki's apology on behalf of the Jesuits; and journalism and reflections by Georgetown students. The GU272 Descendant Association has a motto: "Nothing about us without us," and so this volume includes some of their voices as well. Perhaps that may be a small step toward reconciliation.

Ultimately, we hope that this book will help readers to understand Georgetown's history of slavery and why it matters to so many people today.

Notes

1. Distribution of shoes at St. Inigoes, March 1818, St. Inigoes Rent/Blacksmith Accounts Ledger [170 G]., 01/01/1804-12/31/1832, Maryland Province Archives, Booth Family Center for Special Collections, Georgetown University, http://slaveryarchive.georgetown.edu/items /show/228 (accessed July 6, 2020).

2. The Jesuits were formally suppressed by Pope Clement XIV in 1773. The Jesuits in the new United States transferred their property to a secular entity, the Corporation of Roman Catholic Clergymen, which retained formal ownership of the Jesuits' property after the Society was restored in 1814.

3. Robert Emmett Curran, *The Bicentennial History of Georgetown University* (Washington, DC: Georgetown University Press, 1993), 1:223.

4. For an overview of this global history, see Adam Rothman, "The Jesuits and Slavery," *Journal of Jesuit Studies* 8, no. 1 (2021): 1–10.

5. Craig Steven Wilder, *Ebony and Ivy: Race, Slavery, and the Troubled History of America's Universities* (New York: Bloomsbury Press, 2013).

PART I

HISTORY

ESSAYS

1

War and Priests:
Catholic Colleges and Slavery
in the Age of Revolution

CRAIG STEVEN WILDER

MIT historian Craig Steven Wilder examines the role of slavery in the establishment of the first Catholic colleges in the United States. This chapter was first published in Sven Beckert and Seth Rockman, Slavery's Capitalism: A New History of American Economic Development *(Philadelphia: University of Pennsylvania Press, 2016).*

I have been a faithful servant to the Society [of Jesus] going on 38 years, & my wife Molly has been born & raised in the Society, she is now about 53 years of age[.] Now we have not a place to lay our heads in our old age after all our service. We live at present in [a] rotten logg house so old & decayed that at every blast of wind we are afraid of our lives and such as it is it belongs to one of the neighbours—all the rest of the slaves are pretty well fixed and Father [Peter] Verhaegen wants me and my wife to live on the loft of one of the outhouses where there is no fire place nor any way to warm us during the winter, and your Reverence know it is cold enough here—I have not a doubt but cold will kill both me and my wife here—To prevent the evil, I am will[ing] to Buy myself & wife free if you accept of 100 dollars[,] 50 dollars I can pay down in cash, the rest as soon as I possibly can.

— Thomas Brown, enslaved, St. Louis University, 1833

In August 1797, shortly after the end of his final term in office, President George Washington rode horseback to the Catholic college in Georgetown, a settlement that the state of Maryland had ceded six years earlier to the federal district. In 1789 John Carroll had founded the college. Carroll was the nation's first Catholic bishop and a former Jesuit—Pope Clement XIV had suppressed the Society of Jesus in 1773, a proscription that lasted forty-one years. Georgetown president Louis Guillaume Valentin DuBourg and a small faculty of French and Creole Sulpicians (Order of St. Sulpice) and ex-Jesuits from the United States, the West Indies, Ireland, and continental Europe greeted the general. Washington spoke to the faculty and a larger body of students from the porch of Old North, the second academic hall on campus. Enslaved people completed the scene. Slaves belonging to the faculty and officers and slaves owned by or leased from local craftsmen and merchants labored at Georgetown during its first four decades. The Catholic clergy owned several Maryland slave plantations that funded their missions, including the college and St. Mary's Seminary (founded in 1791) in Baltimore. In fact, the college had an account with the local tobacco merchant Brooke Beall—who owned Yarrow Mamout—before it had a single student. The vice president governed the campus servants, and the records offer glimpses into the routineness of that business: In 1793 the merchant Thomas Corcoran received "Cash [for] 1 p[ai]r shoes for Negroe Nat." Two years later the officers paid "Cash for Negro[es] Jos[eph] & Watt for 3 days work." In December 1798 they agreed to board "4 Negro Children @ $20. Each" with Margaret Medley in town.[1]

If George Washington's visit to Georgetown confirmed the incorporation of Catholics into the United States, then the enslaved people on campus captured the economic forces binding the new nation. Georgetown was a product of the American, French, and Haitian Revolutions—exiles of the Atlantic uprisings dominated the college—and it was a beneficiary of the slave economies that excited this age of political transformation. Higher education in the United States rose with the slave trade and evolved with the westward expansion of plantation slavery and the dependent rise of the manufacturing and banking economies of the northeastern cities. Colleges had advanced the commercial development of the American colonies. Europeans had used colleges to supply colonial administrations, impose religious orthodoxy, facilitate trade, and wage cultural warfare against aboriginal nations. Americans founded at least seventeen new colleges—an average of one per year—between the end of the Revolution and the turn of the century to secure their economic and political interests. The commodification of black bodies also underwrote those developments.

Washington had financial links to the town and personal ties to the college. He was a founder of the Potomac Company, a commercial partnership that sought to develop Georgetown—"the gateway to the West"—a Potomac River port situated at the narrowest land passage from the Atlantic seaboard across the Appalachian Range and into the rich territories of the Ohio and Mississippi River Valleys. Bishop Carroll, a slave owner, located his college at the center of this region, on a cliff overlooking an active tobacco port. Father DuBourg and the faculty had corresponded with George and Martha Washington, and the professors and students had visited the Washingtons at Mount Vernon. A small group of Protestants studied at the college during its first decade, among them the president's nephews, Bushrod and Augustine Washington.[2]

Of the possible years that Georgetown's governors could have chosen as their founding moment, they eventually selected 1789, a relatively late date but one concurrent with the ratification of the constitution and the inauguration of George Washington. "It gives me Pleasure to hear G[eorge]. Washington is chosen President," the Reverend John Fenwick wrote from the Catholic college in Flanders to his cousin, the prominent tobacco merchant Captain Ignatius Fenwick of Carrollsburg, Maryland, for "he deserves that Post to be sure if merit has any Weight."[3]

The crisis of the American Revolution had allowed Catholics to escape their status as a persecuted and despised minority, and Washington was the symbolic guarantor of the fragile compacts unifying a diverse nation. Early in his presidency, he sent assurances of religious liberty to Quakers, the Reformed Dutch, Episcopalians, and Presbyterians. He replied to a plea from the nation's Roman Catholics—signed by John Carroll and several lay leaders, including the wealthy planter Charles Carroll of Carrollton, Maryland—with an affirmation of freedom of conscience and faith. (John Carroll and Charles Carroll were maternal cousins through the Darnall family.) A few months later, the president promised the Jews of Newport, Rhode Island, a government that "gives to bigotry no sanction, to persecution no assistance." His response to John Carroll acknowledged the sacrifices of Catholics, domestic and foreign, during the Revolution.[4] The inclusion of Catholics in the citizenry rewarded their wartime contributions, but commerce opened this era of interdenominational concord and undergirded this political confederation.

In late 1633, three English Jesuits—Fathers Andrew White and John Gravenor and Brother Thomas Gervase—set sail for Maryland aboard the Ark and the Dove. The ships landed first in Barbados, which had a population of English and Irish Catholics. The captains piloted the vessels through the Caribbean before venturing up the mainland coast to Virginia. On Lady Day 1634 the Jesuits officiated the first Catholic mass in Maryland and then turned their efforts to evangelizing Native Americans. Four other Jesuits arrived that decade. Reverend White opened an Indian academy near the Anacostia River. Father Roger Rigbie ministered to the Piscataway and translated the catechism into their language. By 1640 the Jesuits had plans for a college at the St. Mary's settlement to facilitate missionizing the Lenape, Anacostia, Nanticoke, Susquehannock, and other indigenous peoples.[5] At that time there was only one Protestant college in the Americas, Harvard (founded 1636), and it was constitutionally anti-Catholic.

Although Maryland was the most heavily Catholic of the English mainland colonies and the only Catholic proprietorship, Catholics were less than a tenth of the population. In 1649 the General Assembly and Cecil Calvert, Lord Baltimore, instituted religious tolerance in the colony, a modest protection that survived only a few decades. Following the outbreak of England's Civil War in 1642, Protestants arrested Fathers White and Copley and deported them in chains. They hunted the Reverends Roger Rigbie, Bernard Hartwell, and John Cooper and carried them to Virginia. Anti-Catholics gained strength after the Glorious Revolution of 1688—the overthrow of the Catholic James II, formerly the Duke of York, and the restoration of the Protestant monarchy—forcing the revocation of Baltimore's proprietorship. In 1692 the General Assembly established the Church of England. In 1704 it restricted the exercise of Catholic sacraments, prohibited Catholics from operating schools, limited the corporate ownership of property to hamper religious orders, and encouraged the conversion of Catholic children.[6]

Established churches in the English colonies were vigilant against Catholic infiltration, and colleges helped address these religious and political threats. During the English Civil War, Massachusetts banished Catholic clergy and assigned the death penalty for repeat trespassers. New England's proximity to New France fueled tensions. The colonists had a half dozen wars with New France, beginning with King William's War, the American theater of the Nine Years' War (1688–1697), and ending with the French and Indian War, the colonial arm of the Seven Years' War (1756–1763). Virginia established Anglicanism and forbade Catholics from voting, bearing arms, serving on juries, and testifying in court. In 1693, during King William's War, planters and ministers in Virginia organized the College of William and Mary under Anglican governance. Anti-Catholic literature filled the libraries at Harvard, William and Mary, and Yale (founded in 1701 by Connecticut's Congregationalists).[7]

The Glorious Revolution also swept New York, bringing the removal of Governor Thomas Dongan, a Catholic appointed by King James. As early as 1685 Governor Dongan had encouraged English Jesuits to establish a Latin school in New York City with hopes of raising a college. Many Protestants feared the Jesuit incursion. Jacob Leisler's 1698 rebellion sought to erase the vestiges of Catholic rule. After November 1, 1700, authorities could imprison for life any Catholic priest found in the colony, execute priests who were recaptured, and drag any persons who aided a Catholic cleric to the pillory.[8]

The colonial government's bloody response to the April 1712 slave revolt in Manhattan—during Queen Anne's War, the colonial arm of the War of the Spanish Succession (1702–1713)—fed in part on anti-Catholic rage. Following the revolt, the New York legislature assigned the death penalty for any slave who attempted or conspired to harm or kill any free Christian, and in 1730 it expressly broadened the law to punish slaves who assaulted "any Christian or Jew." By that time, Jewish merchants such as Rodrigo Pacheco, Jacob Franks, Moses and Samuel Levy, Nathan Simpson, Isaac Levy, and Mordecai and David Gomez were trading enslaved people and goods between the Dutch and British Caribbean, the North American mainland colonies, Africa, and Europe. They often partnered with leading Christian merchants, including Adolph Philipse, Robert Livingston, William Walton, Anthony Rutgers, Arnot Schuyler, Jacob Van Cortlandt, David and Matthew Clarkson, and Henry Cuyler.[9]

The 1741 slave conspiracy revealed how commerce was reshaping social relations. In April, as the investigations began, several Jewish merchants distanced themselves from the threats, domestic and foreign, by swearing loyalty to George II and acknowledging his absolute political and spiritual authority over the colonies. They then condemned as "impious & heretical" the "damnable Doctrine & position" of the Catholic Church that monarchs could be excommunicated, deposed, and "murthered by their Subjects." The authorities hanged John Ury, a suspected Catholic priest, and three other white people, and tortured, exiled, or executed scores of black people. Mordecai Gomez served as interpreter in the trial of several "Spanish Negroes," black captives from the Spanish colonies who claimed to be free men. The justices ordered death for a "Spanish Indian," a Native American prisoner from a nation allied to Spain.[10]

It was the violent expansion and integration of the Atlantic slave economies that created the financial and social conditions for the growth of higher education in the British colonies. In less than a quarter century, slave traders and other merchants in New England and the upper Mid-Atlantic and planters in the lower Mid-Atlantic, the South, and the West Indies funded six new colleges. In 1745 Anglicans in Barbados organized Codrington College, the only seminary in the British Caribbean. The following year, Presbyterians chartered the College of New Jersey (now Princeton University). About 1749, Anglicans, Presbyterians, and Quakers began the College of Philadelphia (the University of Pennsylvania). In 1754 the governing Anglican minority in New York City established King's College (Columbia University). A decade later, in 1764, Baptists founded the College of Rhode Island

(Brown University). In 1766 the Dutch Reformed leadership in New Jersey opened Queen's College (Rutgers University). In 1769 New Hampshire granted a charter to the Congregationalist minister Eleazar Wheelock for Dartmouth College.[11]

Jewish families had used tutors and small private academies to educate their children, but they gained some access to the new colleges. Donations from the slave traders Jacob Rodriguez de Rivera and Aaron Lopez of Newport, Rhode Island, and the planter and merchant Moses Lindo of Charleston, South Carolina, led the trustees of the College of Rhode Island to admit Jewish students. The colleges in New York City and Philadelphia also opened admissions.[12]

Catholics had no colleges in the British colonies. Ordered priests ran small academies and sent privileged youth abroad to complete their education. A number of colleges in continental Europe specialized in training English and colonial Catholics. The cousins John and Charles Carroll studied at the somewhat clandestine preparatory school at the Jesuits' Bohemia Manor plantation in Maryland. Eleanor and Daniel Carroll then sent John to the Jesuit College of St. Omer in northern France. Elizabeth and Charles Carroll of Doughoregan, Maryland, enrolled "Charley" at the College of Rheims. Robert Plunkett and Robert Molyneux—later the first two presidents of Georgetown College—journeyed from England to the seminaries at Watten and Douai, respectively. The young Louis Guillaume Valentin DuBourg—Georgetown's third president—left Cap François, Saint-Domingue (now Cap-Haïtien, Haiti), to attend St. Omer. Another future president of the college, Stephen Larigaudelle Dubuisson, sailed as a boy from Saint-Marc, Saint-Domingue, to study in France. "I shall never be able to repay the care & pains you [have] taken of my education," Charley Carroll wrote to his "Dear Papa" while studying law at the Inner Temple in London.[13]

African slavery afforded these Catholics significant personal freedom. Charley Carroll served as his father's business liaison while studying in Europe. "I shall keep my Estate in and nigh Annapolis, two large seats of Land containing each about 13[,]000 Acres, my Slaves and [the Baltimore] Iron Works to ye last, so that you may chuse," Carroll of Doughoregan promised his son. The family estate neighbored those of a number of wealthy plantation and merchant families, including the final generation of Quaker slave owners, such as the elder Johns Hopkins.[14]

African slavery enabled colonial Catholics to survive, and even prosper, in the British Atlantic. "I shall always have a great Regard for any of our Countrymen; so that if you know of any Gentlemen, who chuse to send their children to the College, I shall be glad to have them here at Bornhem," the Reverend John Fenwick appealed from the Dominican (Order of Preachers) college in

Flanders. Individual priests, including Father Henry Pelham, and lay leaders held the Jesuits' Maryland farms as personal property and bequeathed this real estate to other clerics and laypeople to evade the legal restrictions on religious corporations. The Jesuits were also among the first slave owners in the colony, and they used similar legal maneuvers to secure their titles to hundreds of enslaved people.[15]

By the eighteenth-century, the order owned plantations that reached from the northeast border with Pennsylvania and Delaware to the southwest boundary with Virginia. In 1637 the Calverts gave the Jesuits the St. Inigoes (Ignatius) plantation, which comprised 2,000 mainland acres and 1,000 acres on St. George's Island in the St. Mary's River. In the summer of 1640 William Britton acquired the Newtown plantation. In February 1670 Father Pelham received 4,000 acres, along the Potomac near Port Tobacco, where the Jesuits built St. Thomas Manor. By the eighteenth-century the Jesuit estates comprised more than 14,000 acres in Maryland—including St. Inigoes and Newtown in St. Mary's County, St. Thomas in Charles County, White Marsh in Prince George's County, and Bohemia in Cecil County—approximately 2,000 acres in Pennsylvania, and small parcels in other colonies.[16]

Visitors routinely documented the Catholic clergy's reliance on slavery. "Ten thousand acres of the best ground in Maryland forms at this hour, part of the property of the Jesuits," protested Patrick Smyth, an Irish priest who spent several months in Maryland and then published a treatise that accused the clergy of abusing enslaved people to support profligacy. He had ample evidence. Granny Sucky, a ninety-six-year-old enslaved woman, recalled that Father John Bolton of St. Inigoes beat her when she was a child, in the mid-eighteenth-century, for interrupting his self-flagellation. Violence was not the only form of abuse. Child mortality was high at St. Inigoes and the other Jesuit plantations. During the twenty-five-year period ending in 1780, when Jesuit superior George Hunter resided at St. Thomas Manor, only twenty-six of the forty-eight black children born on the plantation survived to maturity. The Jesuits "have a prodigious number of negroes, and these sooty rogues will not work, unless they be goaded, and whipped, and almost slayed alive," Smyth charged.[17]

Lay Catholics were no less dependent on bondage. Carroll of Doughoregan taught his son the businesses of plantation management and manufacturing, which involved lessons in the application of violence. The Carrolls used enslaved black laborers on their estates and at the ironworks, for which they also purchased European indentured servants. On his return to America, the younger Carroll took ownership of a share of the lands and more than 300 human beings. "Two of them have been well whipped," he assured his father after hiring a new overseer, "& Will shall have a severe whipping tomorrow—they are now quite quelled."[18]

At the outbreak of the American Revolution, Charles Carroll could not vote, hold public office, or serve in the militia. His coreligionists from Georgia to New Hampshire also faced restrictions on their civil liberties. When he journeyed to the Continental Congress, he came not as a member but as a mere adviser to the Maryland delegation. Carroll was a strident defender of political freedom who had described the tendencies of tyranny in the pages of the same colonial paper that had carried advertisements for the family's runaway slaves. In July 1776, Carroll of Carrollton became the only Catholic signer of the Declaration of Independence. That August, Marylanders affirmed the right to the free exercise of religion for professing Christians. Another fifty years passed before the legislature approved a constitutional amendment to enfranchise Jews.[19]

The American Revolution required a radical transformation in the status of Catholics. Although Protestants in Ireland displayed broad sympathy and support for the American rebellion, David Doyle concludes, they ultimately rejected models of independence that required "sharing political power with Catholics." In contrast, "Long Live the King of France" ranks among the more noteworthy chants of a colonial army that had acquired its military experience in wars against the Catholic empires. The United States accepted a peculiar dependence on the Catholic powers of the Atlantic world. Benjamin Franklin sailed for Paris to lobby the court of Louis XVI. Congress sent James Jay of New York and Arthur Lee of Virginia to plead its cause before the Spanish crown. In September 1777 it authorized Ralph Izard of South Carolina to appeal for funds and support in Italy, where there was significant interest in the American conflict.[20]

For a war between the Protestant king of Great Britain and his Protestant colonists, the American Revolution was a decidedly Catholic affair. Several French Catholic general officers advised George Washington and the new United States government, devised military strategies, and even commanded colonial troops, including: Jean-Baptiste Donatien-Joseph de Vimeur, Comte de Rochambeau; the young Marie Joseph Paul Yves Roch Gilbert du Motier, Marquis de Lafayette; François Jean de Beauvoir, Marquis de Chastellux; and Claude-Gabriel, Duc de Choisy. Casimir Pulaski, a Polish Catholic, raised the cavalry for the colonial army, and Thaddeus Kosciuszko, also a Polish Catholic, served as the American army's chief engineer.[21]

The Americans embraced their Catholic allies. Yale granted an honorary degree to Conrad Alexander Gerard, French minister to the United States, and the College of William and Mary paid the same tribute to Chastellux. The

Reverend John Carroll preached patriotism, and three of his nephews fought under Lafayette. Washington made camp at White Marsh, where General Thomas Conway, headquartered at the Jesuits' manor, sought Charles Carroll's advice on organizing Irish troops. The Catholic clergy set up a military hospital at Newtown. The United States commissioned a Catholic chaplain, and Abb. Claude Robin, a priest under Rochambeau's command, boasted of the enthusiastic crowds and extravagant official reception that greeted French forces in Philadelphia in early September 1781. The celebrants became even more raucous when they learned that French troops had also arrived in the Chesapeake.[22]

The French and Spanish crowns had given covert support to the American rebellion from its earliest stages. The colonists negotiated with Spain through the embassy in Paris, and Lafayette returned to France to appeal for direct military intervention in the American war. Spain attacked Britain's interests in South America and smuggled supplies to the colonists across the Alleghenies. In 1778, France officially recognized the United States, and the following year Spain declared war on Great Britain. In the summer of 1780, forty-six French vessels carrying more than 12,000 soldiers and sailors landed in New England. Jacques-Melchior Saint-Laurent, Comte de Barras, brought his fleet south from Rhode Island, and François Joseph Paul, Marquis de Grasse, sailed north from Saint-Domingue and Martinique to force the British general Charles Cornwallis's surrender at Yorktown. The Spanish naval officer Francisco de Saavedra de Sangronis served under the Marquis de Grasse, raised money in Cuba and Santo Domingo for the offensive, and helped design the campaign. General Washington and three French officers—Rochambeau, Barras, and Grasse—signed the October 19, 1781, capitulation on behalf of the victorious United States.[23]

In 1783, as the British evacuation continued, John Carroll called the clergy to White Marsh to draft a governing structure for the church. The Corporation of Roman Catholic Clergy—which the Maryland General Assembly incorporated in 1792—also administered its financial affairs and took ownership of its estates. Carroll's vision took shape as the slave economies recovered, and it focused on a region of the new nation with a long history of commercial and social interaction between Protestants and Catholics. The English invasion had disrupted slavery, and enemy troops had ransacked Newtown Manor. The British navy had blockaded and occupied the Chesapeake Bay and the lower Potomac, empowering thousands of black people to escape the plantations in St. Mary's County and Port Tobacco. In December 1784 Father James Walton ordered the slaves at St. Inigoes to begin raising a new church. The following year, Father Carroll laid the cornerstone. Francis Neale, a future president of Georgetown College, presided at the dedication.[24]

The American victory and the subsequent unraveling of the French empire set the conditions for the institutionalization of the Catholic Church in the United States. In April 1789, George Washington was inaugurated in New York City. That same month riots broke out in Paris, and within weeks, France was in the throes of revolution. After mobs stormed the Bastille on July 14, 1789, the Marquis de Lafayette sent the key to the breached prison as a souvenir to his friend and ally, George Washington. That year Pope Pius VI established a United States diocese that became a refuge for French clerics. Urged by Benjamin Franklin, the Vatican also elevated John Carroll to bishop.[25]

The ripples of the French Revolution quickly reached the United States. The tobacco merchant Joseph Fenwick had left for France after the American Revolution, a moment of great economic optimism. He soon encountered an Irish smuggler and Thomas Jefferson, and he received excellent advice from both. The smuggler convinced Fenwick to situate his business in Bordeaux, and Jefferson promised that French markets would be eager for American goods. After he became secretary of state, Jefferson appointed Fenwick consul in Paris. Fenwick's letters to his cousin and sponsor, Ignatius Fenwick of Carrollsburg, detailed the course of events. During the first year of the Revolution, the National Assembly abolished aristocratic titles and curtailed the authority of the church. The Sulpician John Dubois escaped from Paris in disguise.

In August 1791 Dubois landed in Virginia with letters of introduction from Lafayette. The Lees, Randolphs, Monroes, and Beverlys assisted the young priest, and Patrick Henry tutored him in English. By that time, enslaved people on the island of Saint-Domingue, France's most valuable colony, were in full rebellion, after months of isolated uprisings. White families fled the island. Hundreds of French and Creole families relocated to Maryland, with assistance from the state, to wait out their respective revolutions.[26]

The Atlantic revolutions allowed Bishop Carroll to create a network of colleges and seminaries that threaded Catholicism into the social fabric of the United States. After opening Georgetown in 1789, the bishop turned his attention to helping the Sulpicians establish a seminary. The antichurch and anticlerical thrusts in France threatened the order's Parisian academy, and the Sulpicians began fundraising and recruiting European students for a Maryland seminary. In 1791, as the first class was entering Georgetown, the French priests opened St. Mary's. "All our hopes are founded on the seminary of Baltimore," Carroll confessed. In 1792 Bishop Carroll dispatched a group of Dominicans, who had come to Maryland as refugees, to the rapidly growing territory of Kentucky. Catholics were not the only Americans to recognize the opportunities in Europe's instability. In 1795 George Washington and Thomas Jefferson briefly plotted to resettle the whole faculty of the College of Geneva, thrown into turmoil by the European revolutions, in the United States.[27]

Georgetown was the child of the Atlantic rebellions. Émigrés of the revolutions in France and Saint-Domingue filled the faculty and the student body. The first class included François and Antoine Cass, and students from France, Madeira, Martinique, St. Lucia, Guadeloupe, Cuba, St. John, and Saint-Domingue and Santo Domingo arrived in the following years. By 1798 the governors were publishing the college prospectus in English, French, and Spanish. Among the earliest presidents were Fathers Louis DuBourg and Stephen Dubuisson, born to slaveholding Creole families in Cap François and Saint-Marc, respectively—key sites of the slave unrest that matured into the Haitian Revolution. Reverend DuBourg traveled to Havana, Cuba, to open a college, and, when that effort failed, he recruited the children of the planters to St. Mary's Seminary and St. Mary's College (chartered in 1805), which the Sulpicians began under the presidency of John Dubois.[28]

"To American Commerce—May it ever derive greater pride from the distress it has relieved, than from the wealth it has accumulated," the guests toasted during a feast on the evening of January 9, 1809. "The concourse of French and American ladies and gentlemen was numerous and brilliant," the Maryland Gazette boasted. Creoles from Aux Cayes came to honor the West Indies trader Duncan McIntosh and other merchants and captains who had risked their vessels and money running rescue missions to Saint-Domingue. Father DuBourg presented McIntosh with an award for his humanitarianism. McIntosh was credited with saving more than 2,000 people. In an address to the Free School Society that same year, New York City mayor DeWitt Clinton praised "the Refugees from the [French] West Indies" who had established one of the city's early charity schools, an academy that was "patronized and cherished by French and American gentlemen, of great worth and respectability."[29]

Slavery accelerated the absorption of these refugees into the American church. The Corporation of Roman Catholic Clergy assigned Bohemia to the Sulpicians, who used the profits from the plantation to fund St. Mary's Seminary. "That the managers of St. Thomas [plantation] be allowed the sum of £75 for a Negro boy called Alexis in the service of the Bishop," read the March 1797 minutes. The clergy also voted to sell a parcel of land to raise $4,000 to complete the construction of Georgetown College. In the late summer of 1799, the Sulpicians protested that they had made major improvements to Bohemia farm and asked to be compensated with "the young negro girl, called Peg, and the small boy, called Jack, both now in the Service of the Seminary, and another boy also called Jack, now in the Service of Revd.

Mr. Maréchal, at Bohemia." (Ambrose Maréchal was the philosophy professor at Georgetown and the seminary.) A few months later the clergy voted to
allow the Sulpicians to keep Jack and Peg, "as long as they retain said negroes
in the Seminary."[30]

The bodies and the labor of enslaved people paid the Catholic Church's
debts, including the liabilities of Georgetown College, which was tuition-
free during its first forty years. In October 1799 the Roman Catholic Clergy
approved the sale of "Kate & her two Children now belonging to Bohemia
estate." In April 1804 the corporation resolved to satisfy its obligations by selling expendable slaves from their Deer Creek property "to humane and Christian masters." A couple of years later, John Ashton demanded that the clergy
give him "ye boy Davy . . . (Simon's son & now motherless)" from White
Marsh to meet a debt. "Whereas, permission . . . was heretofore granted for
two slaves of the estate of Bohemia to be sold for the benefit of Geo-town
College," began a March 1808 inquiry from the trustees. Money and people
flowed fluidly between the campuses, the churches, and the plantations. As
late as 1820, nearly two dozen Georgetown undergraduates vacationed at
the horse farm on Newtown plantation. The corporation typically held its
meetings at St. Thomas, Newtown, and White Marsh. Robert Plunkett,
Georgetown's founding president, began his ministry at White Marsh, and
at least two early presidents had managed Jesuit plantations—Leonard Neale,
St. Inigoes; and Francis Neale, St. Thomas—a duty that involved disciplining,
acquiring, and disposing of people.[31]

The treatment of enslaved people on the Jesuit farms was alarming. After
1805 the Jesuit brothers began supervising the plantations. "Some years ago
Blacks were more easily kept in due subordination and were more patient
under the rod of correction than they are now, because then discipline flourished, but now it is going to decay," complained Brother Joseph Mobberly,
manager of St. Inigoes. "The present white generation seems to lose sight of
the old observation, 'the better a negro is treated, the worse he becomes.'"
Mobberly hired five overseers in the four-year period beginning 1816. He
also served as the plantation doctor and only hired trained physicians for
emergencies.[32]

The declining profitability and deteriorating management of the Maryland farms created other crises. In 1820 the Irish priest Peter Kenney, official
visitor to the Maryland province, documented awful conditions. The super-
visors were providing insufficient rations to slaves, overworking servants,
and inflicting excessive violence on enslaved men and women. Father Kenney especially condemned the practices of whipping pregnant women and
beating women "in the priests own parlor, which is very indecorous." The
clergy paid little attention to the spiritual lives of the servants, and Kenney

suggested that the order begin looking toward a moment when it could "get rid of the slaves, either by employing whites or letting out their lands to reputable tenants."[33]

Rather than retreating from slaveholding, the bishops built their church by tracking the westward expansion of plantation slavery. The 1803 Louisiana Purchase had opened a vast and heavily Catholic missionary field. After being named bishop of Louisiana in 1812, Louis DuBourg recruited veteran Maryland priests—particularly a dozen Belgian Jesuits under Father Charles Van Quickenborne—to establish the Missouri province, manage its plantations, and elevate St. Louis Academy (founded 1818) into a university, the first west of the Mississippi River. Bishop DuBourg gave his Florissant farm and slaves to the Missouri Jesuits and empowered the future St. Louis University president Van Quickenborne "to sell any or all of them to humane and Christian masters" if they proved recalcitrant or immoral.[34]

"The Indian Mission was the chief object of the establishment of the Society [of Jesus] in Missouri," Father Van Quickenborne admitted in January 1830, just months before Congress passed the Indian Removal Act, which initiated the relocation of the eastern Native American nations west of the Mississippi River. Bishop DuBourg had donated Florissant on the condition that the Missouri Jesuits begin an Indian mission. The Belgians had also raised more than $3,000 in Europe for Christianizing Native Americans, and they staffed missions to the St. Johns and Kickapoo. "On the loftiest hill of the renowned Charbonniere (I do not recall whether you saw it) there is an Indian mound," Father Peter Verhaegen, another of the Belgian presidents of St. Louis University, wrote to Georgetown president William McSherry in 1838, "& this mound we undertook to explore . . . & found human bones, but no indian curiosities." Even weak religious missions could be used to legitimate expansion. "Our Belgians . . . have arrived safe," Verhaegen told McSherry of a new group of recruits in 1839, and "they wish to be remembered to their brethren at Georgetown."[35]

The enslavement of Africans and the dispossession of Native Americans had been tied together from the early years of European colonization, and assertions of the urgency of evangelizing Indians were routinely followed by declarations of the necessity of human bondage. In 1832, when Father Kenney had inspected the Missouri province, he complimented "the good conduct, industry, & Christian piety of all the coloured servants of both sexes." Despite the broad use of enslaved labor, Missouri was the only province in which Kenney registered no serious concerns. However, a year later, Thomas Brown, enslaved to President Verhaegen, strongly disagreed. Brown begged the Jesuit superior for permission to buy his and his wife Molly's freedom. He had served the society for nearly thirty-eight years, and Molly Brown, fifty-three years old, had been born enslaved to the Jesuits. He accused Verhaegen of confining them to an outhouse with neither heat nor insulation as winter approached. "Now we have not a place to lay our heads in our old age after all our service," he continued. Father Kenney's visit had exposed troubling issues. Kenney had to remind his brethren that it was beneath the dignity of priests to beat or threaten enslaved women. He recommended that they employ laypeople to punish women, and assigned the Jesuit brothers the duty of whipping enslaved men, while cautioning that they should all avoid "severe punishments."[36]

In 1832 Georgetown's governors conceded that the college had to impose tuition, a business decision that intensified the Corporation of Roman Catholic Clergy's discussion of dissolving the Maryland slaveholdings. Financial concerns rather than moral considerations brought an end to slavery in the Maryland province. The order had been violating commitments to maintain families and find suitable Christian masters. It was now seeking bids on hundreds of human beings, and apparently even attempted to sell the whole group to the Missouri Jesuits. In June 1838 the former Georgetown president Thomas Mulledy contracted the sale of 272 men, women, and children to Henry Johnson, a Catholic and the former governor of Louisiana, for $115,000. Beginning that fall, the Jesuits shipped their slaves to Louisiana in three cargoes. About 15 percent of the revenues went to pay down Georgetown College's construction debts.[37]

Clergy trained in Maryland spread across the nation. Belgian and French priests governed expansion into the regions opened by the Louisiana Purchase and Indian Removal. John Dubois left St. Mary's to become bishop of New York and was succeeded in that seat by one of his most famous students, the Irish immigrant, John Hughes, who had paid his tuition at St. Mary's by supervising servants in the college gardens. In 1841 Bishop Hughes founded the college that became Fordham University, the first Catholic college in New York. In 1843 Thomas Mulledy became the charter president of Holy Cross, the first Catholic college in New England. John McElroy, who also departed from Maryland, founded Boston College.[38]

Neither the Jesuits nor the antebellum Catholic Church disengaged from human bondage with the Maryland sale; rather, both followed the westward movement of plantation slavery in search of influence and affluence. African slavery had repeatedly rescued the Catholic community through a century and a half of oppression in the Protestant colonies. Catholics had used the slave economies to evade anti-Catholic laws and survive anti-Catholic violence. They embraced human bondage to secure their own liberty. The proslavery and anti-abolitionist tradition in the Catholic hierarchy began at the birth of the church in the Revolutionary era, when human slavery straightened and leveled the road to Catholic assimilation. The Atlantic slave economies laid the foundations of the Catholic Church in the United States and underwrote the creation of a national church that helped to integrate future waves of Catholic immigrants.

Notes

1. Yarrow Mamout was an African Muslim who eventually gained his freedom and became a landowner and businessman in Georgetown. Charles Wilson Peale and James Alexander Simpson painted portraits of Mamout, who, a biographer suggests, might be posing in both portraits in the blue uniform of a Georgetown student. One of Beall's sons attended the college, and Simpson taught art there. Georgetown was originally part of Montgomery County, Maryland. In 1814 Pius VII restored the Society of Jesus. Paul R. O'Neill and Paul K. Williams, *Georgetown University* (Charleston, S.C.: Arcadia, 2003), 9–16; John M. Daley, *Georgetown University: Origins and Early Years* (Washington, D.C.: Georgetown University Press, 1957), 94–96; Robert Emmett Curran, *The Bicentennial History of Georgetown University: From Academy to University, 1789–1889* (Washington, D.C.: Georgetown University Press, 1993), 1:46–48; Michael Pasquier, *Fathers on the Frontier: French Missionaries and the Roman Catholic Priesthood in the United States, 1789–1870* (New York: Oxford University Press, 2010), 25–31; Georgetown College, Expense Book, February 12, 1794–February 12, 1802, esp. the entries for April 22, 1795, December 14, 1796, December 21, 1796, October 24, 1796, January 3, 1797, and January 15, 1798; Georgetown College, Book of Expenses and Remittances, October 1796–December 1799, esp. 120; Georgetown College, Ledger A, Financial Ledgers, 3 vols., 1789–1799, esp. 1:78, 94, 99, 2:120, Special Collections Research Center, Georgetown University Library, Washington, D.C. Brooke Beall Ledger, 1790–1798, 112, MS 111, Furlong Baldwin Library, Maryland Historical Society, Baltimore (hereafter MHS); James H. Johnson, *From Slave Ship to Harvard; Yarrow Mamout and the History of an African American Family* (New York: Fordham University Press, 2012), esp. 98–99; Kathleen M. Lesko, Valerie Babb, and Carroll R. Gibbs, *Black Georgetown Remembered: A History of Its Black Community from the Founding of "The Town of George" in 1751 to the Present* (Washington, D.C.: Georgetown University Press, 1991), 1–11; Sylviane A. Diouf, *Servants of Allah: African Muslims Enslaved in the Americas* (1998; New York: New York University Press, 2013), 107, 119–20; see Peter Kenney, "Consultations" (1832), 7, box 126, folder 2, Maryland Province Archives of the Society of Jesus, Special Collections Research Center, Georgetown University Library, Washington, D.C. (hereafter GUSC).

2. William W. Warner, *At Peace with All Their Neighbors: Catholics and Catholicism in the National Capital, 1787–1860* (Washington, D.C.: Georgetown University Press, 1994), 7; Barbara Jeanne Fields, *Slavery and Freedom on the Middle Ground: Maryland during the Nineteenth Century* (New Haven, Conn.: Yale University Press, 1985), 13; John Carroll, "Last Will and Testament," November 22, 1815, in *The John Carroll Papers*, ed. Thomas O'Brien Hanley, 3 vols. (Notre Dame, Ind.: University of Notre Dame Press, 1976), 3:369–73; John Gilmary Shea, *Memorial of the First Centenary of Georgetown College, D.C., Comprising a History of Georgetown University* (Washington, D.C.: printed for the College, 1891), 9–10; *New-York Weekly Museum*, March 7, 1789; Georgetown College, College Catalogs, 1791–1850, box 1, vol. 1, GUSC; President and Professors of George Town College to George Washington,

March 1, 1797, and March 15, 1797, and Louis Guillaume Valentin DuBourg to Mrs. Martha Custis Washington, July 20, 1798, George Washington Papers, ser. 4, General Correspondence, Library of Congress.

3. The college was chartered to grant degrees in 1815. Edward B. Bunn, *"Georgetown": First College Charter from the U. S. Congress (1789–1954)* (New York: Newcomen Society, 1954); Thomas E. V. Smith, *The City of New York in the Year of Washington's Inauguration, 1789* (New York: Anson D. F. Randolph, 1889); John Fenwick to Ignatius Fenwick, June 12, 1789, Capt. Ignatius Fenwick Papers, MS 1274, Furlong Baldwin Library, MHS.

4. "The Address from the Roman Catholics to Washington," 1790, and "Washington to the Roman Catholics of the United States of America," March 12, 1790, in Peter Guilday, *The Life and Times of John Carroll: Archbishop of Baltimore* (New York: Encyclopedia Press, 1922), 1:363–67; George Washington to the Synod of the Dutch Reformed Church in North America, October 1789, George Washington to the Society of Quakers, October 1789, George Washington to the Presbyterian Ministers of Massachusetts and New Hampshire, November 2, 1789, and George Washington to the Hebrew Congregation at Newport, August 18, 1790, in *The Papers of George Washington*, ed. W. W. Abbot and Dorothy Twohig (Charlottesville: University of Virginia Press, 1987–), 4:263–77, 6:284–86; see also Fritz Hirschfeld, *George Washington and the Jews* (Newark: University of Delaware Press, 2005).

5. Thomas Hughes, *History of the Society of Jesus in North America: Colonial and Federal* (London: Longmans, Green, 1917), 1:247–93, 344–46; Andrew White, *A Relation of the Colony of the Lord Baron of Baltimore, in Maryland, Near Virginia; A Narrative of the First Voyage to Maryland* (Baltimore: Maryland Historical Society, 1847); Nelson Waite Rightmyer, *Maryland's Established Church* (Baltimore: Diocese of Mary land, 1956), 5; Margaret C. DePalma, *Dialogue on the Frontier: Catholic and Protestant Relations, 1793–1883* (Kent, Ohio: Kent State University Press, 2004), 5–6.

6. The Catholic community closed St. Mary's Chapel after that assault and reused the bricks for a manor house on the safer ground of St. Inigoes. Hughes, *History of the Society of Jesus in North America*, 1:562–64, 2:13–45, 155, 480; Rightmyer, *Maryland's Established Church*, 5–7; Joseph A. Agonito, "St. Inigoes Manor: Portrait of a Nineteenth Century Jesuit Plantation," 2–5, Dr. Lois Green Carr Research Collection, SC 5906-10-83, Maryland State Archives, Annapolis; Nelson Waite Rightmyer, *Parishes of the Diocese of Maryland* (Reisterstown, Md.: Educational Research Associates, 1960), 1–2; John D. Krugler, *English and Catholic: The Lords Baltimore in the Seventeenth Century* (Baltimore: Johns Hopkins University Press, 2004), 242–43; Thomas Murphy, "Jesuit Slaveholding in Maryland, 1717–1838: Real Poverty and Apparent Wealth on the Jesuit Farms," in *Studies in African American History and Culture*, ed. Graham Russell Hodges (New York: Routledge, 2001), esp. 37–39.

7. Arthur J. Riley, "Catholicism in New England to 1788" (PhD diss., Catholic University of America, 1936), esp. 180–93, in Catholic University of America, *Studies in American Church History*, vol. 24; DePalma, *Dialogue on the Frontier*, 6–11; Mary Peter Carthy, *English Influences on Early American Catholicism* (Washington, D.C.: Catholic University of America Press, 1959), 12–19.

8. Dongan received the Castleton estate on Staten Island. Although he returned to Ireland in 1688 to succeed his brother as Earl of Limerick, the Castleton grant lived into the next century as the largest single slaveholding on the island. Robert Emmett Curran, *Papist Devils: Catholics in British America, 1574–1783* (Washington, D.C.: Catholic University of America Press, 2014), 124–25; David S. Lovejoy, *The Glorious Revolution in America* (1972; Hanover, N.H.: University Press of New England, 1987), 282–84; William J. McGucken, *The Jesuits and Education: The Society's Teaching Principles and Practice, Especially in Secondary Education in*

the United States (1932; reprint Eugene, Ore.: Wipf and Stock, 2008), 55–56; D. P. O'Neill, "Liberation of Spanish and Indian Slaves by Governor Dongan," United States Catholic Historical Society, *Historical Records and Studies*, vol. 3, pt. 1 (January 1903), 213–16. John Fiske, *The Dutch and Quaker Colonies in America*, 2 vols. (Boston: Houghton, Mifflin, 1899), 2:289; DePalma, *Dialogue on the Frontier*, 7–8. Jacob Leisler's holdings were valued at 15,000 guilders in a 1674 tax assessment. See "Valuation of Property in New York in 1674," in *Ecclesiastical Records, State of New York* (Albany, N.Y.: James B. Lyon, 1901), 1:641–42. Also see Francina Staats, "Last Will and Testament," August 19, 1728, "Abstracts of Unrecorded Wills Prior to 1790," vol. 11, *Collections of the New-York Historical Society for the Year 1902* (New York: printed for the society, 1903), 186–88.

9. Kenneth Scott, "The Slave Insurrection in New York in 1712," *New-York Historical Society Quarterly* (January 1961), 47–67; New York Colony, *Census of Slaves, 1755* (New York, 1755); "An Act for Preventing Suppressing and Punishing the Conspiracy and Insurrection of Negroes and Other Slaves," December 10, 1712, "An Act for the More Effectual Preventing and Punishing the Conspiracy and Insurrection of Negro and Other Slaves; for the Better Regulating Them and for Repealing the Acts Herein Mentioned Relating Thereto," October 29, 1730, *Colonial Laws of New York, From the Years 1664 to the Revolution* (Albany, N.Y.: James B. Lyon, 1894), 1:761–67, 2:679–88; Elizabeth Donnan, ed., *Documents Illustrative of the History of the Slave Trade to America* (New York: Octagon, 1965), 3:462–508; New York Colony Treasurer's Office, Reports of Goods Imported (Manifest Books) to New York, esp. boxes 1–4, New York State Archives, Albany. See also Isaac Levy and merchant trade in Philadelphia. Darold D. Wax, "Negro Imports into Pennsylvania, 1720–1766," *Pennsylvania History* 32 (July 1965), 261–87.

10. Mordecai Gomez's slave, Cajoe (alias Africa), was also arrested. Colonists routinely searched for fugitive Spanish Indians and Spanish Negroes, and their advertisements betray the expansive geography of slavery. Spanish Indians had also participated in the 1712 revolt. Oath of Allegiance to George II by Jews in American Colonies, April 27, 1741, Papers of Jacques Judah Lyons, box 14, folder 35, American Jewish Historical Society Archives, New York; Daniel Horsmanden, *The New York Conspiracy*, edited and with an introduction by Thomas J. Davis (Boston: Beacon Press, 1971), esp. 178–87, 249–51, 260–62, and appendices; *American Weekly Mercury*, July 23, 1741. Scott, "The Slave Insurrection in New York in 1712"; *Boston Evening-Post*, April 9, 1739.

11. Craig Steven Wilder, *Ebony & Ivy: Race, Slavery, and the Troubled History of America's Universities* (New York: Bloomsbury, 2013); Donald G. Tewksbury, *The Founding of American Colleges and Universities Before the Civil War with Particular Reference to the Religious Influences Bearing upon the College Movement* (New York: Teachers College, 1932), 16–33, 55–60.

12. Catholic families in the British colonies routinely bypassed the colleges in New Spain and New France. Moses Lindo to Sampson and Solomon Simson, April 17, 1770, and corporation of the College of Rhode Island to Moses Lindo, January 1, 1771, Rhode Island College Miscellaneous Papers, 1763–1804, box 1, folder 1, Brown University. Jacob R. Marcus, *The Colonial American Jew, 1492–1776* (Detroit: Wayne State University Press, 1970), 3:1198–1211; Jacob Rader Marcus, *Early American Jewry: The Jews of New York, New England, and Canada, 1649–1794* (Philadelphia: Jewish Publication Society of America, 1951), 1:64–68, 79, 164; Oscar Reiss, *The Jews in Colonial America* (New York: McFarland, 2004), 175–77; Edwin Wolf and Maxwell Whiteman, *The History of the Jews of Philadelphia from Colonial Times to the Age of Jackson* (1956; reprint Philadelphia: Jewish Publication Society of America, 1975), 14–27.

13. J. Fairfax McLaughlin, *College Days at Georgetown* (Philadelphia: J. B. Lippincott, 1899), 17–20; Maura Jane Farrelly, *Papist Patriots: The Making of an Early Catholic Identity* (New York: Oxford, 2012), 181–85; Bernard Ward, *History of St. Edmund's College, Old Hall*

(London: Kegan Paul, Trench, Trübner, 1893), 50–95; Peter Guilday, *The English Catholic Refugees on the Continent, 1558–1795* (New York: Longmans, Green, 1914), esp. 1:63–120, 141–45; Ronald Hoffman, *Princes of Ireland, Planters of Maryland: A Carroll Saga, 1500–1782* (Chapel Hill: University of North Carolina Press, 2000), 99–101; Annabelle M. Melville, *John Carroll of Baltimore: Founder of the American Catholic Hierarchy* (New York: Charles Scribner's Sons, 1955), 8–12; Lewis Leonard, *Life of Charles Carroll of Carrollton* (New York: Moffat, Yard, 1918), 241–49; Thomas Murphy, *Jesuit Slaveholding in Maryland, 1717–1838* (New York: Routledge, 2001), 3–32; John Gilmary Shea, *The Catholic Church in Colonial Days* (New York: John G. Shea, 1886), 40–50; James Hennesey, "Neither the Bourbons nor the Revolution: Georgetown's Jesuit Founders," in *Images of America in Revolutionary France*, ed. Michèle R. Morris (Washington, D.C.: Georgetown University Press, 1990), 1; Cornelius Michael Buckley, *Stephen Larigaudelle Dubuisson, S.J. (1786–1864) and the Reform of the American Jesuits* (Lanham, Md.: University Press of America, 2013); Shea, *Memorial History of the First Century of Georgetown College*, 23, 69; Charles Carroll (son) to Charles Carroll (father), July 23, 1761, *Maryland Historical Magazine*, 11:177–78.

14. In 1776 the estate of the first Johns Hopkins, grandfather of the philanthropist, included six black men, twelve black women, and twenty-five black children in Anne Arundel County. Charles Carroll (father) to Charles Carroll (son), April 16, 1759, in *Unpublished Letters of Charles Carroll of Carrollton, and of His Father Charles Carroll of Doughoregan*, ed. Thomas Meagher Field (New York: United States Catholic Historical Society, 1902), 20, 29–32; Robert W. Hall, *Early Landowners of Maryland*, vol. 1, *Anne Arundel County, 1650–1704* (Lewes, Del.: Colonial Roots, 2003), 32–33; Betty Stirling Carothers, comp., *1776 Census of Maryland*, 12, Furlong Baldwin Library, MHS; Charles Carroll (father) to Charles Carroll (son), September 1, 1762, *Maryland Historical Magazine*, 11:272–74.

15. John Fenwick to Ignatius Fenwick, March 14, 1784, Capt. Ignatius Fenwick Papers; *The American Missions: Maryland Jesuits from Andrew White to John Carroll*, An Exhibit in the Special Collections Division, Georgetown University Library, Washington, D.C., September 27–November 29, 1976, entry 10; see Jesuit and non-Jesuit wills, Maryland Province Archives, box 25, folders 6–12; Hughes, *History of the Society of Jesus in North America*, 1:281–82.

16. *American Missions*, entry 9; Agonito, "St. Inigoes Manor," 2–3; lists of lands and acreage held by the Jesuits in Maryland and Pennsylvania, Maryland Province Archives, box 23, folder 9; James Walter Thomas, *Chronicles of Colonial Maryland* (Cumberland, Md.: Eddy, 1913), 218–19.

17. Patrick Smyth, "*The Present State of the Catholic Missions Conducted by the Ex-Jesuits in North America*" (Dublin: P. Byrne, 1788), 17–19; *American Catholic Historical Researches* (July 1905), 193–206. Joseph Mobberly, *Diary*, pt. 1, 20–21, Brother Joseph P. Mobberly, S.J., Papers, 1805–27, folder 1, GUSC: Agonito, "St. Inigoes Manor," 11–16. The births are recorded on the front inside cover of "Old Records," pigskin account book from St. Thomas Manor, Maryland Province Archives, box 3, folder 8. See also John Carroll to Cardinal Leonardo Antonelli, March 1, 1785, and John Carroll to John Thayer, July 15, 1794, in Hanley, ed., *John Carroll Papers*, 1:179–82, 2:122–23.

18. Thomas O'Brien Hanley, *Charles Carroll of Carrollton: The Making of a Revolutionary Gentleman* (Washington, D.C.: Catholic University of America Press, 1970), 175–82; Whitman H. Ridgway, *Community Leadership in Maryland, 1790–1840: A Comparative Analysis of Power in Society* (Chapel Hill: University of North Carolina Press, 1979), 327; Charles Carroll (son) to Charles Carroll (father), November 5, 1769, *Maryland Historical Magazine*, 12:285—86.

19. Farrelly, *Papist Patriots*, 220–57; *A Declaration of Rights, and the Constitution and Form of Government, Agreed to by the Delegates of Maryland, in Free and Full Convention Assembled* (Annapolis, Md.: Frederick Green, 1776), 11–14; Peter Wiernik, *History of the Jews in America, from the Period of the Discovery of the New World to the Present Time* (New York: Jewish Press, 1912), 125–27; H. M. Brackenridge, *Speeches on the Jew Bill, in the House of Delegates of Maryland* (Philadelphia: J. Dobson, 1829). The Carrollses advertised regularly in the *Maryland Gazette*, including an appeal on September 5, 1754, for the capture of the "New Negro," Caesar, and three indentured servants, Robert Cox, George Dale, and John Oulton.

20. David Noel Doyle, *Ireland, Irishmen and Revolutionary America, 1760–1820* (Dublin: Mercier, 1981), 167; James Breck Perkins, *France in the American Revolution* (Boston: Houghton Mifflin, 1911), 241–25; Martin I. J. Griffin, *Catholics and the American Revolution* (Philadelphia: privately printed, 1911), 233–52; *Connecticut Courant and Weekly Intelligencer*, May 4, 1779; David W. Robson, *Educating Republicans: The College in the Era of the American Revolution, 1750–1800* (Westport, Conn.: Greenwood, 1985), 110.

21. General Washington's personal secretary was an Irish Catholic. Thomas P. Phelan, "Colonel John Fitzgerald: Aide-de-Camp and Secretary to General George Washington," *Journal of the American Irish Historical Society* 18 (1919): 233–44.

22. Hennesey, "Neither the Bourbons nor the Revolution," 5; Griffin, *Catholics and the American Revolution*, 250; Thomas, *Chronicles of Colonial Maryland*, 218–20, 269–71; Doyle, *Ireland, Irishmen and Revolutionary America*, 51–76; David Lee Russell, *The American Revolution in the Southern Colonies* (Jefferson, N.C.: McFarland, 2000), 14–16; David T. Gleeson, ed., *The Irish in the Atlantic World* (Columbia: University of South Carolina Press, 2010); Maurice J. Bric, *Ireland, Philadelphia and the Reinvention of America, 1760–1800* (Dublin: Four Courts, 2008), 1–45; Thomas D'Arcy McGee, *A History of the Irish Settlers in North America, from the Earliest Period to the Census of 1850* (Boston: Office of the American Celt, 1851), 23–32; Chris Beneke, "The 'Catholic Spirit Prevailing in Our County': America's Moderate Religious Revolution," in *The First Prejudice: Religious Tolerance and Intolerance in Early America*, ed. Chris Beneke and Christopher S. Grenda (Philadelphia: University of Pennsylvania Press, 2011), 279; Thomas J. Fleming, *Beat the Last Drum: The Siege of Yorktown, 1781* (New York: St. Martin's Press, 1963), 102; Abbé Claude C. Robin, *New Travels through North-America: In a Series of Letters; Exhibiting, the History of the Victorious Campaign of the Allied Armies, under His Excellency General Washington, and the Count de Rochambeau, in the Year 1781* . . . (Philadelphia: Robert Bell, 1783), 44–47.

23. Robert Arthur, *The End of a Revolution* (New York: Vantage, 1965); Thomas E. Chávez, *Spain and the Independence of the United States: An Intrinsic Gift* (Albuquerque: University of New Mexico Press, 2002), 8–13; Lee Kennett, *The French Forces in America, 1780–1783* (Westport, Conn.: Greenwood, 1977), 7–36; Stephen Bonsal, *When the French Were Here: A Narrative of the Sojourn of the French Forces in America, and Their Contribution to the Yorktown Campaign Drawn from Unpublished Reports and Letters of Participants in the National Archives of France and the MS. Division of the Library Congress* (Garden City, N.Y.: Doubleday, Doran, 1945), 3–7.

24. Agonito, "St. Inigoes Manor," 7–9; Griffin, *Catholics and the American Revolution*, 252; Benjamin Quarles, *The Negro in the American Revolution* (Chapel Hill: University of North Carolina Press, 1961), 116–18; Warner, *At Peace with All Their Neighbors*, 3–5; Philip A. Crowl, *Maryland During and After the Revolution: A Political and Economic Study* (Baltimore: 1943); Ronald Hoffman, *A Spirit of Dissension: Economics, Politics and Revolution in Maryland* (Baltimore: Johns Hopkins University Press, 1973).

25. Carroll was installed in office on August 15, 1790, while in England. Frances Sergeant Childs, *French Refugee Life in the United States, 1790–1800: An American Chapter of the French Revolution* (Baltimore: Johns Hopkins University Press, 1940), 9–19.

26. Patrick Henry arranged for the small Catholic community to meet in the Virginia capitol. Joseph Fenwick, Bordeaux, to Captain Ignatius Fenwick, Maryland, March 21, 1787, May 31, 1787, October 11, 1788, December 8, 1790, Capt. Ignatius Fenwick Papers; "Return of the Consuls and Vice-Consuls of the United States of America," *New-York Magazine; or, Literary Repository*, August 1791, 487; John R. G. Hassard, *John Hughes, First Archbishop of New York* (New York: D. Appleton, 1866), 26; James Haltigan, *The Irish in the American Revolution and Their Early Influence in the Colonies* (Washington, D.C.: Patrick J. Haltigan, 1908), 270; *Maryland Gazette,* October 6, 1791–December 15, 1791; James V. Crotty, "Baltimore Immigration, 1790–1830: With Special Reference to Its German, Irish, and French Phases" (PhD diss., Catholic University of America, 1951), 22–23.

27. Charles G. Herbermann, *The Sulpicians in the United States* (New York: Encyclopedia Press, 1916), 16–23; John B. Boles, *Religion in Antebellum Kentucky* (1976; Lexington: University of Kentucky Press, 1995), 54–56; Alphonsus Lesousky, "Centenary of St. Mary's College, St. Mary, Kentucky," *Catholic Historical Review* (October 1921), 154n–157n; François D'Ivernois to Thomas Jefferson, September 5, 1794, in *The Papers of Thomas Jefferson*, ed. John Catanzariti (Princeton, N.J.: Princeton University Press, 1950–), 28:123–33; Thomas Jefferson to George Washington, February 23, 1795, in *The Writings of George Washington: Being His Correspondence, Addresses, Messages, and Other Papers, Official and Private, Selected and Published from the Original Manuscripts; with a Life of the Author, Notes, and Illustrations*, ed. Jared Sparks (Boston: Ferdinand Andrews, 1838), 11:473–76.

28. Georgetown College, College Catalogs, 1791–1850, box 1, vol. 1; *Georgetown University Alumni Directory* (Washington, D.C.: Georgetown University Alumni Association, 1957); *American Missions*, entries 69–70; Shea, *Memorial History of the First Century of Georgetown College*, 24; "An Account of the Foundation and Progress of the College of St. Mary's, Baltimore," *Companion and Weekly Miscellany*, August 16, 1806; Curran, *Bicentennial History of Georgetown University*, 1:54–56. On the chartering of St. Mary's College, see *Maryland Gazette,* January 3–24, 1805.

29. The rescues were dramatic. About 3 p.m. on July 9, 1793, several ships carrying hundreds of refugees had landed in Baltimore. Dozens of vessels followed with approximately a thousand white people and hundreds of enslaved black people. A relief committee of prominent Marylanders greeted the white passengers, and the state appropriated funds to aid their relocation. *Maryland Gazette,* July 11, 1793, January 18, 1809; Crotty, "Baltimore Immigration, 1790–1830," 22–25; DeWitt Clinton, "Address Before the Free School Society in the City of New York" (1809), in *The Life and Writings of DeWitt Clinton*, ed. William W. Campbell (New York: Baker and Scribner, 1849), 323.

30. The corporation retained the profits from any sale of enslaved people or increase of other capital stock at Bohemia. "Proceedings of the Corporation of Roman Catholic Clergy," August 25, 1795, March 29, 1797, August 22, 1799, October 9, 1799, Maryland Province Archives, box 23, folders 9–10.

31. Proceedings of the Corporation of Roman Catholic Clergy, October 9, 1799, May 24, 1803, April 25, 1804, and February 3, 1806, Maryland Province Archives, box 23, folders 10, 13; Georgetown College, Minutes of the Board of Directors of Georgetown College from 1797–1815, entry for March 29–31, 1808, in Minutes of the Board of Directors, September 1, 1797, through July 11, 1815, box 1, GUSC; Murphy, "Jesuit Slaveholding in Maryland, 1717–1838," 38. Father Joseph Moseley noted, "David arrived from ye White Marsh to St. Joseph's, ye 10th

of January 1767, formerly Mr. Neale's Negroe at Deer-Creek in Baltimore." Joseph Moseley, St. Joseph's Church Account Book, 1764–1767, Maryland Province Archives, box 49, folder 2. See also Father Neale's agreements for the training of women servants and his Register, 1827–1832, which records the births and baptisms of enslaved children, Maryland Province Archives, box 15, folders 17, 18; Curran, *Bicentennial History of Georgetown University*, 32; Newtown Ledger, 1817–1823, 80–81, Maryland Province Archives, box 46, folder 1.

32. Robert Emmett Curran, *Shaping American Catholicism: Maryland and New York, 1805–1915* (Washington, D.C.: Catholic University Press of America, 2012), 35; Mobberly, *Diary*, pt. 1, 14; Agonito, "St. Inigoes Manor," 11–13. See Mobberly's comments on the overseers: St. Inigoes Receipt Book, 1804–1832, 55–58, Maryland Province Archives, box 44, folder 1.

33. Peter Kenney, "Temporalities, 1820," 11, Maryland Province Archives, box 126, folder 7.

34. Gilbert J. Garraghan, "The Beginnings of St. Louis University," *St. Louis Catholic Historical Review*, October 1918, 85–101; Kenneth J. Zanca, ed., *American Catholics and Slavery: 1789–1866* (Lanham, Md.: University Press of America, 1994), 153–56; Joseph Aloysius Griffin, *The Contribution of Belgium to the Catholic Church in America, 1523–1857* (Washington, D.C.: Catholic University of America, 1932); Obituary for the Reverend Charles Felix Van Quickenborne, *Catholic Telegraph*, August 31, 1837.

35. "Reasons for giving a preference to the Indian Mission before any other. Given by F. Chas. C. Vanquickenborne," ca. 1831, in Peter Kenney, "Missouri Mission, 1831–32, Consultors Diary," and Peter Verhaegen to William McSherry, July 10, 1837, July 19, 1837, January 4, 1838, November 27, 1839, Maryland Province Archives, box 128, folders 2–4.

36. Brown added that Verhaegen's other slaves were treated far better. A year earlier, Verhaegen had presided at the opening of a church for people of color. Wilder, *Ebony & Ivy*, prologue; Curran, *Shaping American Catholicism*, 34–42; Thomas Brown, St. Louis University (probably to William McSherry, Georgetown), October 21, 1833, Maryland Province Archives, box 40, folder 5; Rev. Father Peter Kenney, "Extraordinary Consultation," August 20, 1832, and "Memorial, 1832," Maryland Province Archives, box 126, folders 2, 6; *Catholic Telegraph*, June 2, 1832.

37. Murphy, *Jesuit Slaveholding in Maryland*, 76–77, 203–4; Kenney, "Temporalities, 1820," 11, and Kenney, "Extraordinary Consultation," August 20, 1832, 20, Maryland Province Archives, box 126, folders 2, 7; Peter Verhaegen to William McSherry, February 9, 1837, Maryland Province Archives, box 128, folder 4; see the correspondence, mortgage certificates, 1838, and articles of agreement between Thomas Mulledy, S.J., and Henry Johnson and Jesse Batey, June 19, 1838, Maryland Province Archives, box 40, folders 9, 10.

38. Hassard, *John Hughes*, 23–24; George P. Schmidt, *The Old Time College President* (New York: Columbia University Press, 1930), esp. 32–33.

2

"Splendid Poverty": Jesuit Slaveholding in Maryland, 1805–1838

ROBERT EMMETT CURRAN

Georgetown historian Robert Emmett Curran provides a detailed examination of slaveholding by the Maryland Jesuits from the early years of the mission to the sale of 272 persons in 1838. Proceeds from the sale were used to pay the debts of Georgetown College. This essay was first published in Randall M. Miller and Jon L. Wakelyn, Catholics in the Old South: Essays on Church and Culture *(Macon, GA: Mercer University Press, 1983).*

"A PRODIGIOUS NUMBER OF NEGROES"

In 1788 Patrick Smyth, an Irish Roman Catholic clergyman who had recently returned from a brief ministry in Maryland, published a pamphlet on *The Present State of the Catholic Mission, Conducted by the Ex-Jesuits in North-America.* Smyth's conclusion was that any impartial observer could readily see why the mission was languishing. The ex-Jesuits, Smyth reported, were

> superbly lodged on the banks of the Potomack, or basking in the luxuriant climes of the Eastern Shore. . . . They have a prodigious number of negroes and these sooty rogues will not work, unless they be goaded and whipped, and almost flayed alive.

"Oh God of Heaven!" he melodramatically exclaimed,

> and is it thus your widely extended vineyard is neglected? . . . Are
> your very ministers become taskmasters? they, who should cherish
> the hapless African in their bosoms, and share the sad burden of his
> afflictions?[1]

John Carroll, one of the ex-Jesuits and the superior of the Church's missions in America, responded to Smyth in a pamphlet of his own, exposing the falsehoods and distortions that Smyth was spreading.[2] But the accusations and insinuations of the Jesuits as "Lords of the Land" persisted. They reached a climax with the mass sale of their slaves in 1838.[3]

Jesuit landholdings in Maryland by the nineteenth century *were* extensive, though small when compared to the former estates of their brethren in Latin America. In 1824 they amounted to something more than 12,000 acres, most of which consisted of four large estates in the southern counties of Prince Georges, Charles, and St. Mary's and two smaller plantations on the Eastern Shore. In addition, the order possessed two farms totaling more than 1,700 acres in eastern Pennsylvania.[4] It had acquired these properties from Lord Baltimore according to the conditions of plantation issued by the proprietor in 1636, by acquisitions, and by bequests from individual Catholics. From the beginning, the Jesuits depended upon their estates to support their ministries to settlers and indigenous Americans.

To work these lands, the Jesuits relied upon indentured servants, a practice they never completely abandoned. As this form of labor became increasingly difficult to secure and retain in Maryland, as elsewhere in the Chesapeake region, the Jesuit missionaries, like their secular fellow planters, turned to slave labor. Although there is explicit evidence of Jesuits' slaves only from 1711 on, it is highly probable that they were working the plantations for at least a generation by that time.[5] By 1765 there were 192 such slaves.[6]

THE CORPORATION AND
THE MARYLAND MISSION

At the suppression of the Society of Jesus by Pope Clement XIV in 1773, every bishop in the world was instructed to take possession of the order's property within his jurisdiction. Since no bishop in British America was closer than Quebec, the order was never carried out in Maryland.[7] The lands there remained in the control of the ex-Jesuits. To protect the property, they organized, in 1783, the Select Body of the Clergy, and nine years later received legal recognition from the state of Maryland as the Corporation of the Roman Catholic Clergymen. The charter empowered three to five trustees, elected by the members of the Select Body, to administer the property. With this authority the trustees appointed the managers of the several plantations, distributed the revenue accruing from them, approved expenditures, and oversaw the general business of the estates.

In 1805 five of the former Jesuits in Maryland received permission to affiliate with the Russian Province of the Society of Jesus, which Catherine the Great had protected from suppression. John Carroll, now bishop of Baltimore and head of the corporation, signed an agreement with Robert Molyneux, the Jesuit superior, allowing the society to reenter into possession of its old estates. The corporation, however, continued to be the legal owner and to control the operation of the land. Membership in the Select Body was limited to Jesuits after 1816, but the Jesuit superior had no direct authority over the corporation.

In the first three decades after the restoration of the Society in the United States, a majority of those in the Maryland mission were foreigners.[8] With two exceptions, all of the mission superiors during that period were foreign-born. Since only citizens could be members of the Select Body, the foreign superiors had no legal authority over the property.[9] Persistent tensions continued between the native Jesuits and their foreign brethren. The American Jesuits tended to regard the immigrants—particularly those from Russia, Italy, and Belgium—as "ignorant monarchists" who appreciated neither the republican traditions of this country nor the peculiar position of the Society of Jesus in Maryland as a large landowner. Superiors like Giovanni Grassi and Anthony Kohlmann were criticized for incurring large debts to promote what the indigenous Jesuits regarded as unrealistic plans for their colleges in Georgetown, New York, and Washington. Francis Dzierozynski, the superior from 1823 to 1830, struck many as a good religious who was more fit to "be governed than to govern."[10] The trustees of the corporation particularly resented the financial burdens placed upon the mission by the superiors' admission of novices from Ireland, Belgium, and elsewhere in Europe.

Many of the Jesuits from continental Europe, if not openly antidemocratic, were critical of American institutions and values. Dzierozynski wrote a young Maryland Jesuit in Rome that he hoped that the Marylanders studying there would shed their republican spirit.[11] Men like Dzierozynski, a native of Polish Russia, and Stephen Dubuisson, who had left Saint-Domingue with his parents during the revolution there, found the American Jesuits too independent, too materialistic, and too little observant of the rules of religious life. To Dzierozynski, Dubuisson, and others, the American Jesuits were too much the children of their culture.

THE STATE OF THE PLANTATIONS

These factions and the poor financial condition of the mission caused the general of the Society, Thaddeus Brzozowski, to send an Irish Jesuit, Peter Kenney, as his special visitor in 1820. One of Kenney's assignments was to examine the state of the farms. He found "splendid poverty... so much apparent wealth & real poverty... Complaints of bad management, unprofitable contracts, useless & expensive experiments & speculations" greeted Kenney on every plantation with the exception of the one at Newtown.[12]

Adam Marshall, the Jesuit charged with overseeing the plantations for the corporation, described them as "immense tracts of land resembling rather an Indian hunting ground than lands inhabited by men acquainted with the arts of civilized life."[13] Marshall reported to the superior general that St. Inigoes, St. Thomas, White Marsh, Bohemia, and St. Joseph's were all "in wretched condition." The dwellings for the slaves were "almost universally unfit for human beings to live in." Even the best farm within the mission, Conewago in Pennsylvania, was in debt. Everywhere accounts were incorrectly kept, if at all. In only two places could he reckon with any reasonable certainty the annual revenues and expenses. None of the estates were fulfilling the purpose for which they had been created—that of supporting the apostolic work of the mission. The tobacco the Potomac plantations grew was of an inferior quality.[14] White Marsh, potentially the most valuable property they possessed, had a debt in excess of $6,000, despite the large revenues it had brought in for the past several years.[15] The general debt of the mission was nearly $32,000.[16] Nor did Marshall think improvement a possibility. "We have no men capable of managing a farm."[17] During the Colonial period Jesuit brothers had been assigned this responsibility wherever possible, but their numbers were few so that priests, with the occasional assistance of lay overseers, most often served as managers. With the restoration of the Society in 1805, Jesuit brothers slowly were given charge of the farms by the corporation. By 1820 brothers managed five of the six plantations in Maryland, with the exception of St. Joseph's at Tuckahoe in Talbot County. Two years later four of them had either been removed or demoted to the status of assistant manager under a priest, the apparent victims of Kenney's and Marshall's devastating reports.[18] One aspect of the brothers' management that disturbed Kenney was their arbitrary treatment of the slaves. He had found general disaffection among the blacks. In some places the weekly ration of meat was only a pound and a quarter ("often this has not been sound"); pregnant women were being whipped; the behavior of the slaves was scandalous; and their practice of religion was virtually nonexistent. At the conclusion of his visit in 1820, Kenney instructed the mission consulters to issue regulations concerning the treatment of slaves with which the local procurators would have to comply strictly. "Great zeal, piety, prudence & charity with a regular system," he concluded, "are requisite to check the evils attendant on the possession of slaves."[19]

The Maryland Jesuits, one should note, did make conscientious, if not consistent, attempts, by word and example, to shape among their fellow Catholic slaveholders an appropriate Christian attitude toward the treatment of their human property.[20] As early as the 1760s a Maryland Jesuit chastised his congregation for regarding their slaves as "inferior species."[21] John Lewis, the last superior of the mission before the Jesuits' suppression, reminded his hearers of Saint Paul's warning that "he who takes no care of his domesticks is worse than an infidel and has denyed his faith." He urged them to regard their slaves as "Brothers in Jesus Christ."[22] The slaves, in the Jesuits' eyes, had certain basic rights: adequate food, clothing, shelter; proper care when they were old or sick; a Christian marriage in which the spouses were not separated.[23]

By the 1820s the living conditions for the slaves on most of the plantations were less than adequate. The hard times of the early years of that decade were partly responsible. By 1823 the novice Jesuits at White Marsh subsisted on a diet of little more than bread and water before the corporation closed the novitiate. Two years later the local superior had to sell a portion of the estate to buy winter clothing for the blacks.[24] The high percentage of slaves either too young or too old to work also compounded the pressures upon the estates to provide for all those dependent upon them. Thus, in 1820, only fourteen of the sixty-one slaves at St. Inigoes were working the land; twenty-three were under fourteen years of age.[25] At White Marsh a higher proportion was working: thirty-two out of sixty-eight. Twenty-six were under fourteen, and fourteen were over forty-five.[26] These exceptionally high percentages of underage or superannuated slaves may have been due to the general good care the blacks received. At any rate, by the early 1830s the material condition of the slaves seems to have improved significantly as conscientious priests like Joseph Carbery, Ignatius Combs, and Peter Havermans were assigned to St. Inigoes, St. Thomas, and Newtown respectively.

An immigrant Jesuit, Fidèle de Grivel, reported to Rome in 1831 that St. Thomas remained somewhat in a "delapidated state" but improvements were taking place, and all, including the slaves, had plenty to eat. Indeed, in their enjoyment of the rudiments of life, de Grivel thought that the blacks were "Lords" in comparison to the peasants of his native France.[27] White Marsh was still struggling to meet its basic needs, although by 1832 Father Samuel Mudd had paid off all its debts.[28] The most thriving plantation was St. Inigoes, where Carbery had instituted a system of dividing the estate into several farms. One farm he rented out to a white farmer. Another he worked himself with approximately half of the active slaves. The other five tracts of land he assigned to slave families at the annual charge of $1.25 an acre. These last families were responsible for providing for all their needs. By the mid-1830s, Carbery was claiming success for this free-enterprise project. The debt was paid off, the blacks had an incentive to produce for themselves, and their economic improvement led them to better moral and spiritual lives, as well.[29]

The Jesuits' slaves on most of the estates were routinely able to earn money, either by doing extra work for their owners or by selling products they had made, produce they had raised in their own gardens, or seafood they had gotten from the river. Joseph Mobberly, a Jesuit brother manager, estimated that the average family at St. Inigoes was able to earn from eighty to 100 dollars a year.[30] Carbery's experiment was the first attempt to increase productivity by giving at least some of the blacks the incentive of working their own fields exclusively.

The moral and spiritual condition of the slaves also was a concern in these years. Despite catechesis and required attendance at Mass, Kenney found their lives a moral wasteland and a scandalous reproach to the Society. At Bohemia he encountered illegitimacy: a *ménage à trois* involving a slave, a free black, and an abandoned married woman; another slave living with a prostitute; still another's house serving as a "tavern for selling whiskey &c to ours & our neighbour's servants." Except for an old woman, none had been to the sacraments for twelve years[31]—all this among a slave population of seven. Bohemia's slaves were particularly notorious, but Kenney received similar complaints at all the plantations in Maryland.[32]

Some Jesuits attributed this moral anarchy to the Society's own failure to discipline the slaves. To William Beschter in Baltimore the proverb "he is as bad as a priest's slave" was all too warranted. "Our slaves corrupt . . . with impunity," he wrote. Neither their moral offenses nor their laziness was punished. It was no surprise to Beschter that the farms languished, given this moral climate.[33] Brother Mobberly, who managed St. Inigoes from 1806 to 1820, shared Beschter's conviction that a lack of discipline lay at the root of the growing corruption and discontent among the slaves. "The better a Negro is treated," Mobberly wrote in his diary, "the worse he becomes."[34] Mobberly's own attempts to discipline his slaves had just the opposite effect. By the time Kenney visited the plantation in 1820, the blacks compiled a litany of complaints to cite against the brother. Kenney listened (as he had elsewhere), and the corporation removed Mobberly within a month.[35]

SEEKING CHANGE

Mobberly, a Maryland native, had given much thought to the place of "the peculiar institution" within the mission. He wrote a long tract in 1823 justifying slavery as a necessary good that provided for the forty percent of the human family that was "deficient in point of intellect . . . & know not how to take care of themselves."[36] Despite this pro-slavery position, long experience on the Jesuit plantations had convinced him that the present slave economy based on the raising of tobacco and corn was unprofitable and was destroying the soil. Furthermore, abolitionist activity in Maryland among the Quakers and Methodists was causing the slaves to grow more restive. Fears of insurrection were growing. In 1814 an abortive uprising had occurred within sight of St. Inigoes. As early as 1815 Mobberly was urging that the mission rid itself of its slaves and entrust the land to tenant farmers and the production of wheat.[37] The corporation was actually ahead of Mobberly. In the fall of 1814, the trustees raised the issue of not only changing from slave to free labor but also of freeing the slaves themselves. The following June they resolved "to dispose for a limited time of the greatest part of the blacks on the different plantations."

They intended to set a term of service for each black on their estates, after which he or she would be free. As John Carroll, one of the trustees, explained,

> since the great stir raised in Engld, about Slavery, my Brethren being anxious to suppress censure, which some are always glad to affix to the priesthood, have begun some years ago, and gradually proceeding to emancipate the old population on their estates.[38]

Such deferred emancipation was a policy of the corporation that predated the restoration of the mission in 1805.[39] Probably more common was the practice of allowing the slaves to purchase their freedom through their earnings. In 1801 the corporation censured Peter Brosius of Conewago for manumitting a slave on that estate. Such a precedent, the trustees noted, would prove "not a little injurious to that subordination, which ought to be preserved among the other slaves belonging to the Corporation." They advised Brosius to have the slave purchase his freedom, at least on a *post factum* basis.[40]

During the 1790s, when the Abolition Society in Maryland was fostering many slave petitions for freedom in the courts, several blacks on the estates at White Marsh and St. Thomas adopted this strategy of suing for their freedom through the aid of sympathetic lawyers. None apparently was successful, although one of the cases remained in the courts until 1811.[41]

The resolution passed by the corporation in 1814 was never carried out. At a meeting six years later the trustees repealed it with the explanation that "mature reflection" had convinced them that such a plan was "prejudicial."[42] By 1820 two things had happened: Kenney had been appointed visitor, and Ambrose Maréchal, Carroll's successor as archbishop of Baltimore, had initiated his claims against the Jesuit estates. Kenney agreed to support the Jesuits' desire to "part with the slaves" on the two conditions that the change be well planned and that they were certain that it would be for the better.[43] The archbishop's threats to go to court with his claim may also have caused the trustees to delay any mass sale of slaves.

As the debts of the mission grew in 1822, the trustees mortgaged White Marsh and its blacks.[44] A month later they authorized the agent, Adam Marshall, to sell as many as thirty slaves from that plantation, if he judged it could survive without their labor.[45] For whatever reason, no sales ensued.

In July 1823 the Holy See ruled in favor of the archbishop's claim and ordered the Maryland Jesuits to surrender White Marsh with all its slaves and equipment to Maréchal, but they refused to do so on the grounds that the incorporation of their property in Maryland gave it a civil character that a bishop could not touch. In that same summer the superior general, Aloysius Fortis, appointed another foreign superior, Francis Dzierozynski, to resolve the controversy and to break the power of the corporation as an independent authority. To Fortis the real cause of their impoverished state was that they loved property too much and obedience not enough. "Let them renounce the property," he exhorted Dzierozynski, and God would bless their work.[46] Within two years the trustees reluctantly renounced any right to administer the property without the consent of the superior general.

A NEW IMPETUS TO END
THE MARYLAND TRADITION

In the fall of 1830 Peter Kenney returned to America as visitor. A decade earlier he had been forced to cut short his first visit in order to attend the General Congregation in Rome that the Society had called upon the death of its superior general. Now a new general, Jan Roothaan, had instructed Kenney to make a thorough investigation of the question of whether or not to sell the plantations. Kenney found them in much better condition than they had been in 1820. Almost all were debt-free. Only St. Joseph's seemed a bad investment for the future.[47] But the estates were still not supplying revenue to the general fund of the mission to support the training of Jesuits or Georgetown College. Indeed, regarding the financing of education, a traditional major apostolic activity for Jesuits, Kenney concluded that the mission was "as perfectly destitute of means, as if it had not one acre of landed property."[48]

Before the visitor could complete his investigation of the estates, Father General Roothaan ordered that the Maryland Jesuits not sell, but continue their efforts to improve them.[49] The premature decision apparently was the result of the intervention of the former superior, Dzierozynski, who had informed the general in January 1831 that, contrary to reports, the farms were producing and the mission debts were practically gone.[50]

The superior general had said nothing about the slaves. A year later, in August 1832, Kenney's four appointed advisors in Maryland urged him to make clear to Roothaan "the State of public feeling on the subject of slavery & the other disadvantages of the system." Four of the five wanted Roothaan's permission to liberate in a gradual manner the mission from its slaves and to substitute free laborers in their place. Three of them, Fidèle de Grivel, Thomas Mulledy, and William McSherry, strongly supported the proposal. Dzierozynski was equally opposed to it; Stephen Dubuisson favored it with great reservations.[51]

In 1820 Kenney had already been of the mind that ridding the estates of the slaves would remove "an immense burden" from the mission and "the odium" that the survival of slavery on the Jesuit estates in Maryland cast upon the whole Society.[52] The thrust for change, however, now came from a new breed of American Jesuits with no particular loyalty to the Maryland tradition. Mulledy and McSherry were among six young Jesuits that Kenney had sent to Rome in 1820 for their philosophical and theological training. By 1830 Mulledy was already rector of Georgetown and McSherry the assistant to the mission superior. To some of the older Jesuits in Maryland they seemed all too ambitious. One had the impression that they were trying to take over the mission with "grand plans of selling the farms . . . putting the money in a bank . . . and manumitting the slaves, at least after some years of service."[53]

Mulledy and McSherry both came from northwestern Virginia, an area in which slaveholding was not so deeply implanted. Although the sons of slaveholders (McSherry himself had been raised on a large estate near Martinsburg with more than a score of slaves), both were convinced that the problems that plagued the Society in Maryland—pressing debts, lack of funds, struggling colleges, corrupt slaves—stemmed from the attempt of the Maryland Jesuits to be both priests and planters.[54] Of the two, Mulledy proved the more aggressive in urging the Society to abandon the "Maryland Way" that had prevailed since the 1630s. Shortly after he had returned from Rome in 1829 he petitioned Roothaan to reopen the question of selling the farms and slaves. By 1833 he was telling the superior general that it was impossible to maintain both the estates and the colleges at Georgetown and Frederick. "We can not have both flourishing colleges and flourishing missions," Mulledy warned Roothaan.[55]

In that year the Maryland mission was raised to the level of a province and McSherry named the first provincial superior. He made his headquarters at

St. Thomas Manor, where he had the opportunity to study closely the workings of that plantation, as well as those at St. Inigoes and Newtown. He is "verifying what I foresaw many years ago," Mulledy reported to Roothaan in March 1835, "that these farms were a curse on the Society in this region. The negroes behave abominably on many of them & the priests allow them to destroy soul and body. They are neither farmers nor priests, nor religious— but some bad combination of all."[56]

THE DECISION TO SELL

In 1830 Mulledy had suggested to the superior general that the slaves be sold on the basis of deferred emancipation in order that they might be prepared for their eventual freedom during their stipulated years of future service. The longer the Society kept the slaves, he went on, the more it would run the risk of being forced to sell some as their numbers grew or became more restless under the influence of abolitionists. "Wouldn't it be necessary to separate families?" he conjectured. "And isn't this a hideous thing in America?"[57]

The Maryland Jesuits had long been sensitive to the changing climate concerning slavery.[58] By the 1830s Jesuits like Mulledy and McSherry were becoming increasingly uncomfortable about their status as slaveowners. At the same time, new legislation in Maryland, triggered by the rampant fears among whites concerning the growing free black population, made it more difficult to pursue a policy of deferred emancipation.[59] Thus the declining status of the free black in Maryland was making emancipation less acceptable as a goal, while persistent financial pressures were making a mass sale more thinkable. Should the latter occur, it would almost certainly involve the removal of the slaves to the Deep South, since the plantations in the Chesapeake region were, on the whole, too small to absorb the nearly three hundred blacks on the Jesuit estates. Since the typical Maryland slaveholder had one slave and ninety percent held fewer than fifteen, the possibilities for a local sale of nearly three hundred slaves without breaking up families were clearly extremely limited.

In 1835 the Maryland Province held its first congregation. Out of the deliberations of the ten delegates came requests to the superior general to allow them to reduce the number of country missions, to sell the slaves and some of the lands, and to work the remainder with tenant labor. This would enable the province, so the delegates reasoned, to focus its limited resources on establishing colleges and a mission band in cities like Baltimore, Philadelphia, and Richmond.[60] Mulledy, McSherry, James Ryder, and George Fenwick (all Roman-trained) were persuaded that the future of the Society in

America lay in rapidly growing urban centers rather than the stagnant rural areas of southern Maryland and the Eastern Shore.[61] These four were joined by Stephen Gabaria, who had been in the United States less than two years, and Francis Vespre to form the majority that supported the *postulatum* to sell the slaves.

Aloysius Young, the provincial's assistant from an old Maryland family related to the Carrolls, wanted Roothaan to know that Mulledy, the dominant force in the congregation, and his supporters were biased against the rural tradition. Young claimed that Vespre, the province procurator, had succumbed to Mulledy's pressure but personally opposed the plan. He urged the superior general not to abandon the lands and institutions in Maryland, where Catholicism and the Society had flourished for over two hundred years, simply to appease the empty fears about an imminent division of the Union and a possible civil war (two reasons that had been given in the congregation for selling the slaves).[62]

Young spoke for other native Marylanders who remained committed to the estates. Most of the local superiors opposed the sale. They pointed to the profits they were beginning to realize at Newtown and St. Inigoes, and contended that the blacks on their plantations, far from being corrupt, were leading truly edifying lives in the practice of religion and in their general behavior. They were skeptical about the superior opportunities to be found in the cities. At least one local superior of an estate, Ignatius Combs at White Marsh, opposed slavery in principle, and much more the slave trading that such a sale would involve.

One delegate to the congregation pleaded that the general consult the opinion of some of the older men in the province who knew much more about slaveholding than most of those who were supporting the sale.[63] To Roothaan's query about seeking such wider advice, McSherry airily replied that he already knew what these older Jesuits thought and what weight to give to their opinion.[64]

It was the Europeans who were most vocal in opposing the sale. With the exception of Young, all those who had voted against the measure in the congregation were Europeans. Dzierozynski, the former superior, had wrestled as early as 1822 with the morality of selling the blacks in order to relieve the mission's financial pressures. By 1831 he was convinced that selling the lands and "our blacks" was "a dangerous . . . unjust" scheme.

> Lands are a patrimony from our Fathers . . . by what right can they be alienated? I consider the blacks under this respect only, that they are our sons, whose care and salvation has been entrusted to us by Divine Providence and are always happy under our Fathers.[65]

Peter Kolchin has pointed to the similarity in viewpoints that Russian noblemen and Southern planters exhibited toward serfs and slaves, respectively.[66] What is striking about the arguments used by the European Jesuits in Maryland is the manner in which they tend to imagine the master-slave relationship as an idealized master-serf relationship. They tended to see the slaves as innocent and pious, gathering as families to recite their rosaries, working hard when treated properly, bringing consolation to the missionary by their staunch faith despite their lowly position. In the Europeans' view the lot of the country slaves was a blessed one compared to that of the corrupt, impoverished free blacks in the cities.[67]

The European Jesuits regarded the estates not only as a sacred trust, but as a refuge from the cities and as a guarantee of their status in society. As Fidèle de Grivel observed to Roothaan in 1835, "The Protestants have, up to now, appreciated us only because of our large estates; if we sell them, they will consider us no better than Methodist preachers who crisscross the country to accumulate money."[68]

To Jesuits like Dubuisson and de Grivel a bond existed between the Society and its blacks that could be broken only for the most extreme reasons, such as incorrigibility, but not need of money. They argued that selling them would lead to the slaves' physical and moral ruin, and would give great scandal to Protestants and Catholics alike. Dubuisson informed Roothaan while in Rome in 1836:

> There is in general a great repugnance among the blacks of Maryland to being sold south. Without doubt [our slaves] . . . would despair when they should be dragged from their ancient manors and churches. Isn't the very idea of being forced to go with new masters a cruel one?

What it meant, Dubuisson concluded, was that in a state in which selling slaves south was virtually unknown (less than two percent of sales), the Maryland Jesuits would be collaborating with planters from the deep South to parlay the labor of their blacks into immediate financial gain. The abolitionists, he warned, would not miss the meaning.[69] Peter Havermans tried to explain to Roothaan what it meant for a slave to be sold south:

> As far as I can determine, they are to be sold to non-Catholics . . . in a non-Catholic area, more than a thousand miles away, which will surely give many an occasion of criticizing us. For no one does this sort of thing except evil persons, such as slave traders who care about nothing but money, or those who by necessity are so pressed by debts

that they are forced into such a sale. . . . I tell you this will be a tragic and disgraceful affair . . . especially since some of the slaves have been my personal responsibility.[70]

THE SALE OF 1838

Selling slaves was not new to the Maryland Jesuits. But the sales had usually taken place to keep families together or to punish refractory slaves, such as at Newtown in 1774 or at Bohemia in 1832. In 1835, however, McSherry began to sell blacks to meet financial needs. Fourteen were sold from St. Thomas, then eleven from St. Inigoes.[71] The latter were sold to Henry Johnson, the ex-governor of Louisiana, and Thomas Jameson, a Catholic planter from the same state. McSherry claimed, against the objections of Dubuisson and others, that it was not possible to sell them to neighbors, and that Johnson had promised to provide for their religious needs in the same manner the Jesuits themselves had cared for them.[72]

In October 1836 Superior General Roothaan finally approved the sale of the slaves, provided that their religious needs be met, that families not be separated, especially spouses, and that the money be invested for the support of Jesuits in training.[73] The Panic of 1837, with its deflationary effects upon the economy, delayed its execution. "We could not at the present time," McSherry wrote Roothaan in May 1837, "obtain one tenth part of what we could have obtained last year for them."[74] The onset of the cancer that would within two years claim his life forced McSherry to ask to be replaced as provincial. In October 1837 the superior general appointed Mulledy to succeed him.

Mulledy wasted little time making the final sale. In June of 1838 he agreed to sell 272 slaves from the four estates in southern Maryland to Johnson and a partner for $115,000. The pair made a down payment of $25,000 and were given ten years to complete the transaction. Eight thousand dollars went to the settlement of the archbishop's claims against the estates, and $17,000 was applied to the $30,000 debt Georgetown College had incurred through Mulledy's ambitious building campaign when he had been rector. The remaining $90,000 was to be invested for the support of the Jesuits in formation. "All the Catholics who live near our estates, with no exceptions," Mulledy assured Roothaan, "approve the sale. They say it should have been done twenty years ago." He admitted that the Jesuit superiors on the plantations were quite upset "because they no longer will be great lords." He hoped, however, that this would make them better Jesuits.[75]

Rumors of a mass sale had been circulating among the slaves since at least 1832. To give the local superiors no chance to encourage their blacks to escape, Mulledy arrived without notice, accompanied by Johnson and a sheriff. Thomas Lilly, stationed at St. Thomas Manor, was outraged. "They were dragged off by force to the ship and led off to Louisiana. The danger to their souls is certain," he wrote to Roothaan. "The buyers have promised they will be treated in a Christian fashion. But given the laws and customs of that region it will be very difficult to keep them." Lilly, a native of Pennsylvania, did not believe the superior general could have permitted such a scandal had he been properly informed, or had he consulted more of the members of the province. The majority, he reported, were appalled.[76]

One is tempted to wonder whether the sale would have happened had the corporation still been a semiautonomous body. Carbery, Combs, Dubuisson, Dzierozynski, and de Grivel all had the seniority that had normally meant membership on the corporation before it became subservient to the provincial.

The main body of the slaves was sent in a second ship in November 1838. This time there were runaways at White Marsh and St. Inigoes. Joseph Carbery at the latter plantation and (apparently) Ignatius Combs at the former warned their blacks to hide in the woods. At least nine did so at White Marsh and two at St. Inigoes. There is reason to believe that some escaped at St. Thomas, as well.[77] Most of these seem to have returned eventually to the farms.[78] By late November the only blacks who remained, except the elderly and runaways, were those who were married to spouses on other plantations or to free blacks. Mulledy wrote John McElroy on November 11, 1838, that Johnson had left behind these slaves in order to attempt to purchase their spouses as well.[79] It would seem at this point that Mulledy was already resigned to shipping them with or without their spouses. Four days later he was again at Newtown rounding up the remaining slaves. The Dutch Jesuit Peter Havermans, who was as disturbed as Lilly about the sale, recorded a particularly pathetic scene in which the slaves submitted to their fate with "heroic courage and Christian resignation."[80] At the end of November a third ship carried the last of the slaves south. The available evidence suggests that, despite the elaborate instructions of Superior General Roothaan, families were separated.[81]

"THE STOCK OF SLAVE TRADERS WHO VALUE NOTHING EXCEPT MONEY"

The scale of the sale created something of a sensation within the Catholic community along the East Coast of the country. Benedict Fenwick, the Bishop of Boston, thought it "extraordinary news. Poor Negroes! I pity them," he wrote his brother in September 1838. The bishop supposed that the antislavery party was ultimately responsible for forcing the Maryland Jesuits to resort to such an extreme measure.[82] Many others, however, did not share the bishop's judgment about where the blame lay. Stephen Dubuisson wrote the general from his parish in Alexandria that the sale had badly affected the Society's reputation, both in Washington and Virginia.[83] Havermans told Roothaan that Catholics and Protestants alike were scandalized. What Mulledy had done, Havermans charged, was "the stock of slave traders who value nothing except money," or the desperate recourse of those overwhelmed by debts.[84]

Dubuisson and Havermans' readings of the reaction were undoubtedly colored by their own convictions about the immorality of the sale. There is strong evidence, however, that other people were highly disturbed by what had happened, that some took their complaints to the Archbishop of Baltimore, Samuel Eccleston, and that Eccleston carried their charges to Roothaan. Eccleston had proposed to McSherry, in 1837, that the Province sell both its land and slaves in order to concentrate on urban missions and colleges, which he promised to help them found.[85] At that time he already knew about the slaves McSherry had sold to Louisiana. Although the complete Eccleston-Roothaan correspondence has apparently not survived, it would seem that the core of the charges he brought to the general was the separation of families.[86]

In the late fall Roothaan began a correspondence with the former provincial superior, McSherry, about the scandal Mulledy had created with the sale of the slaves.[87] Roothaan evidently was ready to remove Mulledy as provincial, but McSherry counseled delay.[88] By August, however, Roothaan became convinced that there no longer could be any doubt about what had happened and that greater scandal would be given if nothing were done. The general ordered McSherry to inform Mulledy to resign as provincial, at least until he could clear himself of the charges, which the general doubted he could. If he refused, he was to be dismissed. Roothaan concluded: "In some way it must be understood even in America, that men of the Society, unless they are motivated by the spirit of the society . . . and the observance of the Rules, not only will not be a great help, but will make for great ruin!"[89]

By this time, however, Mulledy was already on his way to Rome. In late June Eccleston and McSherry had persuaded him that, for his own sake, he had to step down as provincial superior and take his case to Roothaan himself. Within the week Mulledy was on his way to the Eternal City. Eccleston urged Roothaan not to dismiss Mulledy from the Society. The latter was in shock. He wrote in his diary: "No Mass (unwell). *Ave Crux. Spes Unica* [hail the cross, our only hope]."[90]

Peter Havermans congratulated the general for taking such decisive action. What Mulledy had done, Havermans pointed out, was "a sad example that many can follow: but decent men had now seen in Mulledy's removal that the Society did not approve of such things." They would see it even more clearly, Havermans suggested, should Mulledy not return from Europe.[91]

CHILDREN OF THEIR CULTURE

Four years later, in 1843, Mulledy was allowed home through the intercession of Bishop Fenwick, who needed a president for the new school he was founding in Worcester. In the year of his return, the debating society at Georgetown College invited him to give a public address. In his remarks Mulledy contrasted the peaceful liberty that America enjoyed with the conscription that was becoming the curse of Europe. The worst feature of conscription, he told them, was the cruel way in which it separated parents from children, wives from husbands. Prize liberty, he instructed them, and work to make right what is wrong in America. But be cautious, he warned, for "if special care be not taken in eradicating the vice you will root out the virtue too."[92] Mulledy would seem to have had more than conscription in mind.

Thus ended the Society's history in Maryland as a large slaveholder. The change to exclusive tenant farming eventually proved a profitable one by the late 1840s, as sharecropping was gradually introduced. Ironically, the Society abandoned its slave labor at the very time the estates were beginning to produce. In Carbery, Combs, Havermans, and Lilly, the Society finally had a set of effective managers. Had the alliance between the European Jesuits and these local managers had its way, there might well have been increasing efforts to make the Jesuits' estates models of Christian slavery, such as Christian evangelists like Charles Colcock Jones were attempting to create elsewhere in the South. Most Maryland Jesuits, including those on the farms, seemed to have perceived by the 1830s that slavery's days in Maryland were numbered. They might then have begun consciously to prepare the slaves for freedom, as Carbery was in effect doing at St. Inigoes. But few seemed prepared to go against the prevailing climate. For much of their history Maryland Jesuits had been outcasts, if not outlaws, but still very much the children of their culture who wanted to prove that they belonged. This tradition, economic expediency, and the urban vision of a younger American generation of Jesuits prevailed. The sale of 1838 with all its consequences was part of the price of progress and a morality play worthy of Harriet Beecher Stowe.

Notes

1. Patrick Smyth, *The Present State of the Catholic Mission, Conducted by the Ex-Jesuits in North-America* (Dublin: P. Byrne, 1788), 17–18.

2. "Response to Patrick Smith," in *The John Carroll Papers,* ed. Thomas O'Brien Hanley, 3 vols. (Notre Dame, IN: University of Notre Dame Press, 1976), 1:337–46.

3. In May 1839, for instance, an official of the Society for the Propagation of the Faith, who had been supporting the Maryland Jesuits for years, confided to the treasurer of the Maryland Province of the Society of Jesus that the SPF kept getting reports of the great wealth in land and slaves that the Maryland Jesuits possessed; Francis Vespre to Jan Roothaan, New York, May 30, 1839, *MD* 7-I-13, *ARSI.*

4. Thomas Hughes, S.J., *The History of the Society of Jesus in North America: Colonial and Federal Documents* (London: Longmans, Green, 1908), 1:379–80.

5. Hughes, *History of Society,* Documents, 1:222. Andrew White, the first Jesuit in Maryland, brought two mulattoes to Maryland, in 1633 and 1635, but there is no evidence they were slaves; see Peter Finn, "The Slaves of the Jesuits in Maryland" (master's thesis, Georgetown University, 1974), 6; Whittington B. Johnson, "The Origins and Nature of African Slavery in Seventeenth-Century Maryland," *Maryland Historical Magazine* 73 (1978): 236–45. Joseph Zwinge, S.J., speculated from ex-slave reminiscences that two servants working on the plantation at St. Inigoes in 1644 were slaves; "The Jesuit Farms in Maryland," *Woodstock Letters* 41(April 1912): 204.

6. Zwinge, "Jesuit Farms," 204.

7. Richard Challoner, the vicar apostolic of the London District, to whom fell the task of carrying out the Holy See's orders regarding Jesuit property in territory controlled by Great Britain, ruled out any American confiscation as being impractical (Hughes, "History: Text III" [unpublished redaction of 1933], 209, in Georgetown University Libraries Special Collections [hereafter GULSC].

8. The catalogue of the mission in 1819, for instance, showed that of the 53 members, only 19 were Americans. Irish (16), Belgians (8), Germans (4), and French (3) Jesuits made up most of the foreign majority.

9. The corporation's trustees, for instance, acknowledged in 1817 that with the death of Archbishop Leonard Neale, an ex-Jesuit, spiritual jurisdiction of the estates had now passed to the superior of the mission. It was understood that the trustees retained temporal jurisdiction (GULSC, Maryland Province Archives [hereafter MPA], Corporation Minutes, October 11, 1817).

10. George Ironside to Aloysius Fortis, Washington, D.C., October 10, 1825, *MD* 3-I-31, *ARSI.*

11. Peter Kenney to John McElroy, Tullahey, June 28, 1822, MPA, GULSC. Kenney reported in 1833 that a story was making the rounds in Ireland that during the War of 1812 one of the foreign Jesuits in Maryland "sallied out of the house & abused a number of American soldiers who were drawing cannon through our grounds, Calling them rebels to their King, & wishing that the fate of rebels might attend them." John England, Bishop of Charleston, was the bearer of the tale and his source, according to Kenney, was Benedict Fenwick, the former Maryland Jesuit and then Bishop of Boston (Kenney to Stephen Dubuisson, Dublin, October 28, 1833, MPA, GULSC).

12. Kenney, "Temporalities," 1820, MPA X-T-1, GULSC.

13. Adam Marshall to Enoch Fenwick, August 14, 1820, MPA 205-G6, GULSC.

14. Marshall to Luigi Fortis, Georgetown, February 6, 1821, *MD* 2-II; Marshall to Fortis, March 5, 1821, *MD* 2-I-32, *ARSI.*

15. Marshall to Fortis, White Marsh, February 5, 1822, *MD* 2-II-26, *ARSI.*

16. Charles Neale to Fortis, Portobacco, November 27, 1822, *MD* 6-II-1, *ARSI.*

17. Marshall to Fortis, February 5, 1822, *MD* 2-II, *ARSI.*

18. Joseph Heard remained in charge of Bohemia, which Marshall had found recovering under Heard's careful management (Marshall to Fortis, March 5, 1821, *MD* 2 II-6, *ARSI*).

19. Kenney, "Temporalities," 1820, MPA X-T-1, GULSC.

20. See Peter Finn, "The Slaves of the Jesuits," 45–74; Thomas Murphy, S.J., *Jesuit Slaveholding in Maryland, 1717–1838* (New York and London: Routledge, 2001), chap. 4.

21. The hand seems to be that of John Boone; the date 1765–1770, American Catholic Sermon Collection (hereafter ACSC), GULSC.

22. John Lewis, before 1761, ACSC, GULSC.

23. Finn, "The Slaves of the Jesuits," 50–51; Brother Joseph Mobberly's Diary, 1820, 142–43, GULSC.

24. Dzierozynski to Fortis, Georgetown, January 29, 1825, *MD* 3-I-19, *ARSI.*

25. Census of 1820, Prince Georges County, Maryland, National Archives and Records Administration (hereafter NARA).

26. Census of 1820.

27. De Grivel to Jan Roothaan, Georgetown, January 26, 1831, *MD* 4-II-9, *ARSI.* According to de Grivel, forty of the sixty slaves were female. Peter Kenney echoed de Grivel's conviction about the relative position of the slaves in comparing the latter with the peasants in Ireland; Kenney to McElroy, March 30, 1822, McElroy Papers, MPA, 206-Z-10a, GULSC.

28. De Grivel to Nicholas Sewall, White Marsh, May 30, 1832, MPA 4-5-6, GULSC.

29. De Grivel, "*Memoire Sur la Congregation Prov. du Maryland commences le 3 Mai le 8 Juillet 1835*" [1835] *MD* 5-I-21, *ARSI;* Carbery to Stephen Dubuisson, St. Inigoes, April 25, 1838, MPA, GULSC.

30. Mobberly Diary, 1:132–33, GULSC.

31. Kenney, "Temporalities," 1820, MPA X-T-1, GULSC; "Observations made by R. F. Visitor at the Residence of St. Francis Xavier Bohemia Cecil Co., Mar., June 1831," MPA, X-P-5, GULSC.

32. "Memorial Left with the Superior of the Mission, S.J. in Missouri by the Rev. F. Peter Kenney, Visitor of the Society in the United States, N. Amer. 1832," MPA, X-S-1, GULSC.

33. Beschter to ?, Georgetown, March 27, 1829, *MD* 3-IV-18, *ARSI.*

34. Mobberly Diary, 1:143, GULSC.

35. Corporation Minutes, April 20, 1820, MPA, GULSC; Kenney, "Temporalities," 1820, MPA X–T-1, GULSC. As Finn notes, the slave of the Jesuits had the unique opportunity of voicing his complaints and problems to a superior higher than his local master; Finn, "The Slaves of the Jesuits," 81.

36. Mobberly Diary, 2:1–87, GULSC.

37. Mobberly Diary, 1:74–77, 139–41, GULSC; Mobberly to Giovanni Grassi, St. Inigoes, February 15, 1815, MPA 204-K-3, GULSC.

38. Corporation Minutes, June 14, 1814, MPA, GULSC; John Carroll to John Troy [1815] in *Carroll Papers,* 3:313.

39. John Carroll to Francis Neale, Baltimore, October 3, 1805, MPA 203-T-8, GULSC.

40. Corporation Minutes, Newtown, 1801, MPA, GULSC.

41. Proceedings of Representatives, Select Body of the Clergy, St. Thomas, June 3, 1795, MPA, GULSC; see Jeffrey Brackett, *The Negro in Maryland: A Study of the Institution of Slavery* (Baltimore: Johns Hopkins University Press, 1889), 54–155.

42. Minutes of Corporation, St. Thomas, August 22, 1820, MPA, GULSC.

43. Kenney to Louis De Barth, April 24, 1820, MPA 205-H-3, GULSC.

44. Corporation Minutes, St. Thomas Manor, October 16, 1822, MPA, GULSC.

45. Corporation Minutes, St. Thomas Manor, November 20, 1822.

46. Fortis to Dzierozynski, Rome, March 25, 1824, MPA 500 39b, GULSC.

47. Kenney to McElroy, St. Joseph's, July 2, 1832, MPA, GULSC.

48. "Instructions given by Revd. F. Kenney to Revd. F. McSherry Procurator" [1833] MPA X-M-2, GULSC.

49. Kenney to Dubuisson, July 20, 1831; MPA 210-T-8, Kenney to McElroy, August 4, 1831, MPA 210-T-E, GULSC.

50. Dzierozynski to Roothaan, January 28, 1831, *MD* 4-I-5, *ARSI.*

51. August 28, 1832, *MD* 4-I-23, *ARSI.*

52. Kenney, "Temporalities," 1820, MPA X-T-1, GULSC.

53. Beschter to Roothaan, February 15, 1830, *MD* 3-IV-23, *ARSI.*

54. Mulledy to Roothaan, Georgetown, January 7, 1830, *MD* 3-IV-20, *ARSI.* This concept of the hyphenated priest first appears in a letter from Richard McSherry to his Jesuit brother. It was a theme that both William McSherry and Mulledy repeated often in the next several years.

55. Mulledy to Roothaan, Georgetown, October 28, 1833, *MD* 5-III-4, *ARSI.*

56. March 8, 1835, *MD* 5-III-6, *ARSI.*

57. Mulledy to Roothaan, January 7, 1830, *MD* 3-IV-20, *ARSI.*

58. This heightened concern among Jesuits survived John Carroll. Two years after his death in 1815, the corporation sold five troublesome blacks at the Bohemia estate to a slave trader with the understanding that he would transport them to Louisiana. A local magistrate, a Methodist opposed to slavery, intercepted the stage carrying the blacks out of the state and charged the Jesuit superior at Bohemia with kidnapping. The charge was dropped, but the corporation bought back the blacks to avoid scandal (Mobberly Diary 1:111–17, GULSC).

59. Ira Berlin, *Slaves Without Masters: The Free Negro in the Antebellum South* (New York: Pantheon Books, 1974), observes that "nowhere was the sense of crisis greater than in Maryland" (210ff).

60. *Acta Primae Congregationis, Provinciae Marylandiae Societatis Jesu,* 1835, MPA, GULSC.

61. Even Augustine Bally, a Jesuit missioner in rural Pennsylvania who was so successful during his long tenure at the province's church/farm in Goshenhoppen that the village was renamed for him, had to admit that Catholicism was advancing much more rapidly in the cities than in the country places; Bally to Roothaan, Goshenhoppen, January 31, 1842, *MD* 7-VII-3, *ARSI.*

62. Young to Roothaan, Georgetown, October 1835, *MD* 5-II-2, *ARSI.*

63. Dubuisson Memorial, 1836, *MD* 5-II-4, *ARSI.*

64. McSherry to Roothaan, Georgetown, August 30, 1836, *MD* 5-II-3, *ARSI.*

65. Dzierozynski to Fortis, Georgetown, April 12, 1822, *MD* 2-I-51, *ARSI.*

66. Peter Kolchin, "In Defense of Servitude: American Proslavery and Russian Proserfdom Arguments, 1760–1860," *American Historical Review* 85 (October 1980): 809–27.

67. *Memoire du Pere Stephen Langaudelle Dubuisson de la Campagnie de Jesus, missionarie aux Etats unis d'lAmerique Septentrionale, Mai 1836, MD* 5-IX-7, *ARSI.* Dubuisson told of

blacks with Protestant masters who had stoically suffered whipping for converting to the Catholic faith. Giovanni Grassi, born in Parma and educated in Polish Russia, had written in 1818 about "the very great consolation which the negroes bring to the missionary; for among them, although they are poor slaves and so abject in the eyes of the world, are found chosen souls filled with such beautiful sentiments of true piety, that they move one to tears"; Grassi, *Notizie varie sullo stato presente della repubblica degli Stati Uniti dell'America settentrionale scritte al principio del 1818* (Milano: 1819).

68. De Grivel, *Memoire Sur La Congregation* [1835], *MD* 5-I-21, *ARSI.*

69. Dubuisson Memorial, *MD* 5-II-4, *ARSI.* The one European to support the sale, Gabaria, was merely concerned about the persons to whom they would be sold. He judged the sale itself would cause little stir; Gabaria to Roothaan, Georgetown, January 20, 1837, *MD* 5-III-13, *ARSI.*

70. Havermans to Roothaan, Newtown, October 20, 1838, *MD* 7-I-9, *ARSI.*

71. De Grivel claimed that one of the slaves sold at St. Thomas was actually exchanged for a horse, and that the trade had given great offense to the Catholics in the area. "They were saying," he reported to the general's assistant, "even priests engage in the business of human flesh." "After a month," he added, "the horse died and the Catholics rejoiced"; de Grivel to Aloysius Landes, October 24, 1835, *MD* 5-II-1, *ARSI.*

72. McSherry to Roothaan, Georgetown, August 30, 1838, *MD* 5-II-3, *ARSI.*

73. Roothaan to McSherry, October 27, 1836, MPA F-3-A[2]-F5-E, GULSC.

74. Georgetown, May 13, 1837, *MD* 5-I-39, *ARSI.*

75. Mulledy to Roothaan, Fredericktown, August 9, 1838, *MD* 7-I-5, *ARSI.*

76. Lilly to Roothaan, St. Thomas Manor, July 2, 1838, *MD* 7-II-1, *ARSI.*

77. Zwinge, "Jesuit Farms," 195; in the census of 1840 fourteen slaves were listed for St. Inigoes, six at White Marsh, and seventeen at St. Thomas.

78. The census of 1840 listed fourteen slaves at St. Inigoes, six at White Marsh, and seventeen at St. Thomas, many of whom were not elderly; NARA, Census of 1840, Charles, Counties of Charles, Prince Georges, and St. Mary's.

79. Mulledy to McElroy, Georgetown, November 11, 1838, MPA 212-M-16, GULSC.

80. According to Havermans, one old woman sought his blessing on her knees and begged to know what she had done to deserve this. "All the others came to me seeking rosaries . . . If ever any one had reason to despair, it was I," he told Roothaan; Newtown, October 20, 1838, *MD* 7-I-9, *ARSI.*

81. According to Fidèle de Grivel, all the blacks married to spouses not belonging to the Society were sold to their spouses' masters or to those nearby. Some children, however, had been separated; de Grivel to Charles C. Lancaster, Georgetown, May 4, 1839, MPA 212-G-9, GULSC). But de Grivel, who was at Georgetown, seems to have underreported the fragmentation of families that the sale had incurred. The sale records indicate that at least some of the couples were separated; Newtown Account Book, MPA 112-W-O, GULSC. Some complex situations could exist. One father at White Marsh reportedly escaped to Baltimore with his three children. The wife was nonetheless willing to leave without him because the husband was living with another woman; de Grivel to C. C. Lancaster, Georgetown, November 11, 1838, MPA 212-M-5a, GULSC.

82. Benedict Fenwick to George Fenwick, Boston, September 1, 1838, MPA 212-N-2, GULSC.

83. Dubuisson to Roothaan, Alexandria, June 24, 1839, *MD* 7-I-14, *ARSI.*

84. Havermans to Roothaan, Newtown, October 20, 1838, *MD* 7-I-9, *ARSI.*

85. McSherry to Roothaan, Georgetown, March 13, 1837, *MD* 5-II-5, *ARSI.*

86. The Jesuit historian Thomas Hughes, who knew intimately the Roman Archives, wrote in 1907 that "it was Eccleston ... who ... when people threw up their hands highly scandalized, ... ran forward and denounced Mulledy to the General"; Hughes to E. I. Devitt, Rome, January 29, 1907, GUA, GULSC.

87. In the Roothaan-McSherry corresponse, there is never any explicit identification of the "scandal" Mulledy had given. However, in a letter to a Maryland Jesuit at the end of 1839, the superior general admitted that the scandal was connected to the sale of the slaves; Roothaan to Francis Vespre, December 31, 1831, 169, Register of Responses of the Superior General, *ARSI.*

88. Roothaan to McSherry, Rome, February 14, 1839, MPA 500-84b, GULSC.

89. Roothaan to McSherry, Rome, August 3, 1839, MPA, 500-84c, GULSC. It is clear from Roothaan's letter that Eccleston's testimony had been crucial. In December 1839 Pope Gregory XVI issued an apostolic letter in which he denounced the slave trade in which blacks "as if they were not men, but mere animals, howsoever reduced into slavery, are ... contrary to the laws of justice and humanity bought [and] sold." He condemned any ecclesiastic or lay person who "shall presume to defend that very trade in negroes as lawful under any pretext or studied excuse"; Pope Gregory XVI, *In Supremo Apostolatus fastigio,* English translation in *Letters to the Honorable John Forsyth on the Subject of Domestic Slavery,* by John England (Baltimore: John Murphy, 1840). Benedict Fenwick later thought that the Maryland Jesuits might have had advanced notice of this papal letter and thus accelerated their efforts to sell their slaves before it was promulgated; Fenwick to Eccleston, Boston, March 11, 1840, Eccleston Papers, AAB 24-U-1, AASMUS. There is no evidence that Mulledy or any of the Maryland Jesuits knew that such a letter was coming. But it is quite likely that Roothaan was aware of it.

90. Eccleston to Roothaan, Georgetown, June 27, 1839, *MD* 7-I-15, *ARSI;* Mulledy Diary, June 27, 1839, GUA, GULSC.

91. Havermans to Roothaan, Frederick, February 14, 1840, *MD* 7 VI 7, *ARSI.*

92. Address to the Philodemic Society (1843), Mulledy Papers, GUA, GULSC.

3

Catholic Slave Owners and the Development of Georgetown University's Slave Hiring System, 1792–1862

ELSA BARRAZA MENDOZA

Elsa Barraza Mendoza uses evidence from Georgetown University's financial records to examine the place of enslaved laborers in the founding and operations of the school. Distinguishing slaveholding at the school from the Jesuits' Maryland plantations, the essay argues that the school used its position as a provider of education services to rent enslaved laborers from parishioners, parents, and students. This essay was first published in the Journal of Jesuit Studies *8, no. 1 (2021): 66–80.*

In January 1792, Thomas Corcoran (1754–1830), a prominent merchant with a storefront in Georgetown, received an order for eight pairs of shoes from the newly founded Georgetown College. Among the recipients of these pairs of shoes made or resoled by Corcoran were William Gaston (1778–1844), the first student enrolled at the college; Jean Edouard de Mondésir (1770–1844), a Sulpician seminarian recently emigrated from France and Georgetown College's first teacher; Francis Neale (1756–1837), a secular priest from the diocese of Baltimore; and four enslaved people who labored and most probably resided on campus: Byrne, Suckey, Joseph, and Nat.[1] Since beginning operations in 1792, Georgetown College owned or hired enslaved people to work on campus in areas such as the kitchen, the classrooms, the refectory, the infirmary, and the gardens.[2]

This article examines the place of enslaved laborers in the founding and operations of the university and its community. Through research in the university's administrative and financial records; the archives of the Maryland Province of the Society of Jesus; and manuscript collections in Maryland and Washington, DC, it proposes three key arguments: first, the school used its position as a provider of education and religious services to obtain enslaved laborers from two types of Catholic slaveowners: priests and parents—women in particular—who sent their children to Georgetown. Second, the school itself never owned many individuals, favoring renting laborers over owning them. Georgetown did not own more than five people in any given year from 1792 to 1862. Finally, the school's dependence on enslaved labor was not mitigated by the Jesuit order's sale of 272 people from its plantations in 1838. Indeed, the last enslaved man left campus in March of 1862, only a month before the passage of the Compensated Emancipation Act of the District of Columbia.

Georgetown University's written histories are silent on Byrne, Joseph, Nat, and Suckey, and the many others whose names are lost to us. But enslaved laborers kept the school operating for decades. Slavery as an economic force that dominated the republic is invisible in interpretations that sought to create a wide-ranging account of the life and growth of the US's first Catholic university. The main characters of Georgetown's histories are archbishops, Jesuits, and prominent people. In accounts informed by archival work in the Jesuit Roman Archives (ARSI), slavery appears only in observations such as that students "even used slaves to pay for tuition," or that "there were never more than a few slaves at Georgetown college."[3] As a result, the slaveholding that was crucial to the neighborhood, city, and region in which Georgetown found itself appears irrelevant to the school's existence. Nothing could be further from the case.

Local archives—such as the school's own financial and academic records—offer a different perspective than the bureaucratic exchanges with Rome. Here we find how enslaved people were essential to the school's daily operations. Men and women held in slavery cooked and cleaned for the school. They did the laundry and worked the farm. They even cared for the sick, including on at least one occasion the school's president and treasurer. The profits from their sale gave a financial lifeline to the school.[4] Men and women leased to Georgetown by Catholic slaveowners appear in balance sheets that span multiple financial ledgers. The occupations of some of them, as well as significant events in their lives, can be traced in cashbook and daybook entries, along with transactions for whiskey, sugar, and meat. Their ceaseless presence is a testament of slavery's grip on college life.

This dependence on enslaved laborers was widespread in American colleges. As historian Craig Steven Wilder argues, "it was the violent expansion and integration of the Atlantic slave economies that created the financial and social conditions for the growth of higher education."[5] The Chesapeake was full of religious, educational, and lay institutions with significant entanglements to slaveholding. As Jennifer Oast has shown in her study of universities and slaveholding churches in Virginia, institutions of higher education were prolific owners or hirers of enslaved people.[6] Thus, Georgetown's entanglement with slaveholding can be examined as a microcosm of the rampant exploitation that spread across the nation. Its hires of enslaved people are an example of how leasing people allowed for the persistence of slavery in cities, and Georgetown's use of enslaved laborers is a reflection of how Catholic education depended on the enslavement of others.

1. TO HIRE OR BUY?

Two factors defined Georgetown's relationship with slavery: its location and its ties to the Roman Catholic Church. The practice of hiring enslaved people thrived in many southern cities and Georgetown was no exception.[7] The city possessed a thriving slave market.[8] In the 1790s, the first decade of the college's operation, around twenty-eight percent of the city's population were enslaved people.[9] Among the first families with children enrolled in the college, seventy percent owned at least one person. In short, the culture of slavery on campus mirrored that flourishing right outside its gates.

The American Catholic Church was at the heart of Georgetown's reliance on enslaved labor. After the suppression of the Society of Jesus in 1773, Maryland's twenty-one Jesuits—the region's only Catholic priests—organized with the purpose of governing their religious affairs and "preserving in the same hands the property of the Houses of the Society."[10] This attempt at episcopal governance produced two results: Georgetown College and the Corporation of Roman Catholic Clergymen (henceforth CRCC). Founded in 1792, the corporation consolidated many of the properties that the Jesuits had controlled in the Maryland colony but had lost upon the suppression. Among its properties numbered about 323 people on nine plantations, encompassing about thirteen thousand acres across Maryland.[11] Georgetown's founders and several members of its board of directors were stakeholders in this organization that held their assets in a trust.[12]

The priests who founded Georgetown and the corporation were also individual owners of properties, which in many cases included enslaved people.[13] While not every priest left a record of his attitudes toward slavery, many did, and these indicate no moral qualms with human ownership.[14] Georgetown's founders were known as slavers. They were even accused of trafficking enslaved people by two Dominican priests who visited from Europe in

1813.[15] Slaveholding enhanced their social status and provided revenues to their education mission.[16] The school's founders had a contentious relationship with those they enslaved. At least twenty people sued members of the CRCC for their freedom on the basis that they were illegally enslaved. The priests involved in these suits were a member of Georgetown's initial board of directors and a future president of the school.[17]

The choice of using enslaved laborers at Georgetown College was an extension of Catholic slaveholding in Maryland. Catholic farmers, including Jesuit priests, were indistinguishable from their Protestant neighbors in using enslaved laborers in their plantations after the arrival of the first enslaved Africans in Maryland in 1642.[18] Before the suppression of the Jesuits, priests enslaved men and women in their plantations and their first schools. However, Maryland's clergy counted on the generosity of the lay elite to provide them with enslaved laborers through gifts and bequests, and thereby had little initial need to visit the slave markets for plantation laborers.[19] After the foundation of Georgetown College, there was no significant exchange of enslaved laborers between these plantations and the school.[20] In fact, as labor became increasingly necessary on the campus, the college's leadership turned not to ownership but to renting people.

Leasing enslaved laborers—with the proceeds of their salaries benefiting their owners—was typical for the region. In the Chesapeake, the market to hire enslaved people was competitive. The region's economy depended on hiring to satisfy the temporal needs of its planters, manufacturers, and households.[21] Hiring gave enslavers flexibility, steady revenues, and it allowed them to meet changing labor demands.[22] This system suited the needs of an urban environment, where households and businesses did not require the same labor to operate as plantations.[23]

At Georgetown, economy and the priests' conceptions of manual labor guided the hire of enslaved people. Under the circumstances envisioned by the founder of the Jesuits, Ignatius of Loyola (c.1491–1556), Jesuit fathers formed to be engaged in apostolic activities would not be distracted by practical labors. These priests would dedicate themselves to missionary tasks and would only engage in manual work "when there [were] no others who do the work."[24] Thus, within the order it was foreseen that the "lowly and humble positions" such as "cook, steward, buyer, doorkeeper, infirmarian, launderer, gardener, and alms gatherer"[25] would be the responsibility of lay brothers within the order, who were not ordained priests.[26] However, from 1758 to 1809, the Maryland mission had no lay brothers.[27] Thus enslaved laborers worked in plantations, clergy's households, and schools.[28]

The school's founders had privileged access to the labor of enslaved persons. Hiring enslaved people for the members of the CRCC was not a business arranged at the slave market or through correspondence with strangers, as was common in the region. Instead, it was part of parish business since the early years of Maryland's Catholic Church.[29] Professors, parents of students, and women leased out enslaved laborers to Georgetown College. Beyond its economic benefits, hiring enslaved people was a social practice that connected the school's leaders to a community. It was the basis for the school's labor system, and a means that made both the expansion of Catholic education and Catholicism itself possible.

2. THE HIRE OF ENSLAVED PEOPLE DURING GEORGETOWN'S FIRST DECADES, 1792–1814

During Georgetown's first three decades, the school hired up to twelve enslaved people per year to work in crucial activities for its construction, maintenance, and operation.[30] Every level of the school's administration profited from enslaved laborers. For example, a lay professor, Charles Boarman (1751–1819), rented four enslaved people on a yearly basis: Lewis, Sam, Polly, and Sucky. He also rented two enslaved carpenters for the expansion of one of the college's buildings. Boarman used the funds he received for their labor to finance the education of his two children enrolled at the school.[31]

The school's religious authorities also profited from the people they enslaved. Leonard Neale leased eight people to the school between 1792 and 1802, during his tenure as coadjutor bishop of Baltimore (1795–1815) and president of Georgetown (1799–1806). Regis, George, Suckey, Stashy, Jenny, Nace, John, and Jack were brought by Neale from Prince George's County to the city of Georgetown.[32] Neale received on average $16 for each of them on his accounts.[33] Neale's brother, Francis, a professor and the college's fourth president (in office 1809–12), also hired out two people to the institution, Henrietta Edelen and an unnamed man. Edelen labored at the washhouse while Francis Neale resided at the college as convener of the residence.[34]

Diocesan priests were not the only clergymen who participated in the slave trade at Georgetown. From 1796 to 1799, members of the Society of the Priests of Saint Sulpice, commonly known as Sulpicians, held the offices of president, vice-president, and multiple professorships at the school.[35] These priests arrived in the United States after fleeing the French and Haitian revolutions. Their presence at Georgetown was integral to the school's slave hiring system. The Sulpicians connected Georgetown to slave hiring markets within Maryland's French community.[36] During their years on campus, creole students paid servant attendance fees and used enslaved people to pay school costs. A Sulpician priest kept an enslaved woman born in Santo

Domingo on campus, other Sulpicians used enslaved men to carry their bags, and a widowed woman who fled the Haitian revolution resided at Georgetown hiring out people she enslaved to the school.[37] This eclectic group of *emigrés* leased at least seven people in their three years at the school. Their names were Maria Louisa, Joseph, Nicholas, Zeelam, Isely, Desiré, and an unnamed child. Isely passed away at Georgetown. The rest disappeared from the school records after the Sulpicians left in 1799.[38]

After the Sulpicians' departure, the numbers of students from the West Indies decreased.[39] However, the practice of using enslaved labor to defray school costs did not end. Slave hiring to finance education expenses was a prevalent practice among Maryland families as well.[40] These families often liquidated their outstanding debts with Georgetown using goods such as coffee, muscovado sugar, red wine, meat, lambs, horses, and Louisiana cotton, along with the labor of enslaved people.[41] Thus, Georgetown's slaveholding system became tied to Maryland's Catholic community—who became the majority of its students—and its main source for enslaved laborers.

The hire of enslaved laborers did not prevent the school from purchasing and selling people. In a span of three decades, Georgetown sold a woman named Liddy to a lay man and purchased five people: George, David, Len, Wat, and an unnamed woman. In 1801, the College acquired a man named George from John Llewellin, a student indebted to the college. Georgetown credited Llewellin's account with $67, which was more than one year of board.[42] Another transaction between Georgetown and its lay community was the 1810 sale of Liddy to Phillip Bussard for $220. For this sale Georgetown received $70, one barrel of whiskey, and sugar.[43] However, most of Georgetown's forays in the slave trade involved the CRCC. In 1802, Leonard Neale purchased the aforementioned Wat for $400. Afterwards, Neale sold him to St. Inigoes plantation—one of the estates of the corporation—with a profit for the college.[44] Six years later, Francis Neale purchased a woman "for the use of the college," and a man named Len from the same plantation.[45] From the White Marsh plantation, Georgetown's clergymen purchased David for $707, although after a dispute they only paid $500 to that estate.[46]

These transactions occurred in spite of a regulation from the CRCC that banned the "sale of slaves for life."[47] In practice, Georgetown's priests saw people as capital. Transactions involving them were one of their preferred modes of payment for settling debts. Even after the corporation decided in 1813 to "dispose of the whole or greatest part of the slaves on their estates, for a term of years, after which they should be entitled to freedom," the priests at Georgetown kept hiring and using enslaved people on campus and their plantations. Enslaved people were fundamental to their finances, and they admitted as much. In 1820, for example, the CRCC repealed their decision to sell the people enslaved at their plantations, as they "on mature reflection considered the measure prejudicial."[48] The discussions concerning this repeal are a mystery to us. However, it is not a secret that enslaved people were integral to Georgetown's growth during its first decades.

3. THE HIRE OF ENSLAVED PEOPLE
UNDER THE JESUIT ORDER, 1814–38

Under the fully restored Jesuit order, the university and its dependence on enslaved labor did not change.[49] However, the school's hiring system transformed from one dependent on immigrants from the French Caribbean to one dominated by women slaveowners connected by faith or family connections to the school's priests and students. After 1814, women hired out more than seventy percent of the people enslaved on campus. Female parishioners probably found Georgetown's priests to be reliable business acquaintances. In many cases, women refrained from the practice of using male intermediaries in their business dealings. These women acted independently as owners, arranging for the rental and prices of the people they enslaved. As a group, they created a community of slaveholders who provided a constant supply of labor to the college and who often bankrolled Georgetown's projects by loaning money.[50]

Women from the Fenwick family, for example, leased at least sixteen people in the early nineteenth century, including a man named Phil, who died during his time laboring at the school.[51] One of the most recurring hirers was Margaret Fenwick (1760–1829), the mother of the future bishop of Boston and founder of the College of the Holy Cross, Benedict Fenwick, S.J. (1782–1846). Fenwick rented to Georgetown at least six people counted among her property: Michael, Harriet, Gabe, Hillary, and two unnamed men. She also leased to the Jesuits a property that served as a boarding house for students and professors.[52] Many of these arrangements stood for periods longer than five years.[53] While boarding at the school, her sons were often charged with "servants and commissions fees," and on one occasion, two of her sons, Benedict and Francis (1785–1825), hired an enslaved person for two days.[54]

During this period, Georgetown also increased its use of enslaved laborers in construction projects. In its early years, the school had used enslaved laborers for one of its first buildings, Old North.[55] To expand the college in 1816, the Jesuits at Georgetown hired people from neighborhood slaveowners who were not part of the college's usual business acquaintances. Prominent slave owners from the neighborhood provided an enslaved workforce that focused on different aspects of Georgetown's expansion.[56] Daniel Bussard (d.1830), a land developer and builder who lived steps from campus, hired out four of his enslaved masons for the construction of the infirmary and a smoke-house.[57] George B. Magruder (d.1817), a merchant, tobacco planter, hired out an enslaved man named George along with a group of unnamed men to "lay 13,000 bricks" and build arches and chimneys. Georgetown also paid the mayor of the city, John Cox (in office 1823–45), for the labor of a man named Richard and for a group of carpenters whose activities included "lay-ing 254,888 bricks, building a 188-ft fire wall, walling up a well for privy, and building 1 window in servants' room."[58]

This construction project demonstrated the reliance of the college Jesuits on enslaved labor for the existence of the school. This expansion was a sorely needed enterprise for an institution that had issues boarding students and creating a living space similar to European boarding schools.[59] Several groups of unnamed men were hired for periods of days. Besides the men enslaved by Cox, Daniel Bussard, and Magruder, Georgetown also hired groups of men from James Harvey (1795–1867) and George Athee (dates unknown). Har-vey hired out, for periods of twenty-two days, at least six enslaved men named Edward, Isaac, Ben, Charles, Tobias, and Sam. Some of their activities included the construction of "a vault in the academy," "building ovens in the smoke-house," and hauling stone and sand. Athee received $181 for 103 days' work by Isaac, who was involved in the building of ovens for the infirmary and topping the chimneys at the church. There was not an aspect of this project in which slavery was not involved. Enslaved people delivered the construction materials, were carriers of notes for their payment, and even delivered the food to main-tain the working crews and the college during this expansion.[60]

These enslaved laborers represented a temporary addition to the school's enslaved community, bringing the total of enslaved people at the college close to twenty between 1815 and 1816. However, the school's expansion along with administrative problems, and the poor management of the plantations held in trust by the CRCC, precipitated a crisis at Georgetown that decreased its revenues and labor force. As the 1820s came to an end, Georgetown had less income flowing from the Jesuit plantations and saw decreasing revenues from their base of slaveholders. The college did not receive fees from parents, even when these fees had been reduced. More than half of the boarders were in debt to the college.[61] Moreover, the barter economy that allowed parents to exchange enslaved labor with school fees had stopped as the majority of the hirers were now widowed women whose children had already graduated. Georgetown's main source of enslaved labor on campus was coming to an end as Maryland's slaveholders considered selling people to "Georgia-men."[62]

The Jesuits who led Georgetown were part of this transformation of Maryland slaveholding. After discussions that began as early as 1810, they initiated a plan to sell the majority of the people they enslaved at their Maryland plantations.[63] They also explored the possibility of sending them to Liberia.[64] The arrival of a Jesuit visitor from Rome increased the pressure to divest the slaveholdings of a mission that was known as "the deceased limb of the Society."[65] Georgetown was the neural point of this plan. The Jesuits used the school to identify possible buyers. They discussed, lobbied, and wrote about the issue on school grounds.[66] Georgetown's president, Thomas Mulledy (in office 1829–38), networked within the school's acquaintances in search of a buyer.[67] At least three times, they tried to sell their enslaved community to parents of students enrolled at the school, including the newspaper publisher Duff Green (1791–1875).[68]

In 1838, after postponing the sale for a year because of the panic of 1837, the Jesuits settled on two buyers, the Louisiana politician Henry Johnson (1783–1864) and Dr. Jesse Batey (d.1852).[69] A nephew of Johnson would soon enroll at the school.[70] Part of the principal of the sale directly benefited the coffers of the institution.[71] Georgetown University was the place where the Jesuits conceived, planned, and executed the sale of 272 people they held in bondage. But the Jesuits did not sell a single individual who labored at their school, since they rented most of them.[72] At Georgetown, the Jesuits actually bought people to labor on campus at the same time that they orchestrated the mass sale of people from their plantations.[73]

4. THE DECLINE AND FALL OF GEORGETOWN'S SLAVEHOLDING SYSTEM, 1838–62

The sale of 272 enslaved people in 1838 did not transform Georgetown's enslaved labor force. From 1840 to 1850, at least ten enslaved men and two enslaved women labored at the college.[74] These men cleaned dormitories, cooked for students and priests, took care of Georgetown's president, and cleaned the school during vacations. As the school's properties grew, they toiled in newly constructed vineyards, a college farm, and the Jesuits' vacation villa.[75] Women labored at the washhouse, cleaning the clothes of over a hundred students and twenty priests. They battled unhygienic conditions that saw some of them ravaged by fevers.[76] Nearly fifty years after its opening, Georgetown College still ran on the labor of the enslaved.

However, the Jesuits' ways of obtaining enslaved laborers adapted as the number of students who used enslaved people to pay school fees diminished precipitously after 1840. There were two separate reasons for this development. First, there was a concerted effort by the school's bookkeeper, Br. Sylvester Clarke (1820–68), to limit specie payments.[77] Only families with long histories with the school were allowed to use this mode of payment.[78] Second, after 1840, Georgetown transitioned from being the school of choice for Maryland's old Catholic families to an institution dominated by students from the Deep South.[79] With this transformation the number of enslaved laborers available from students decreased substantially, as hiring a person from them would have potentially required importation into the city. The banning of the slave trade in the District of Columbia in 1850 further restricted Georgetown's option of using students to obtain enslaved laborers.

As the number of students who used enslaved people to defray tuition decreased, geography became the determinant factor in Georgetown's hiring market. More than half of the enslavers who rented people to the school lived in the city of Georgetown. Wealthy, well connected residents hired out people to the school for months. For example, Bladen (1810–70) and James Forrest (d.1868), two of the richest men in the city, leased Georgetown three men from 1846 to 1849. Aaron, Jim, and an unnamed man labored at Georgetown after being rented by the Forrests to labor in dormitories and the grounds.[80] The Forrests were benefactors of the college and parents of students, and their ties to the Jesuits were such that some family members converted to Catholicism during the period when they rented people to the school.[81]

Women continued to be crucial to the perpetuation of slavery at Georgetown. Arrangements that spanned years were common between the Jesuits and their female business partners. For example, Mary Fenwick (1787–1866) rented out a man named Joseph Edelin to the school for more than ten years. The school's authorities often deferred the payments owed Fenwick for Edelin's labor. In October of 1845, the Jesuits discharged Edelin from campus, paying Fenwick only half of the money owed to her. However, their lack of payment does not appear to have been an obstacle between her and the Jesuits, as two months later, on December 3, 1845, the Jesuits rehired Edelin, this time to labor at the college farm for $8 a month.[82]

Another woman with business dealings with the Jesuits was Eliza Jenkins (1787–1859), the aunt of the college's treasurer. Jenkins hired out a man named Charles Taylor for a number of years to the school. Taylor labored at the college since 1836, at a time when his enslaver was Ralph Semmes (1809–77), a Georgetown resident.[83] Semmes sold Taylor to Jenkins in 1840 and the new enslavers continued to rent Taylor to the college. In 1842, Jenkins sold Taylor to Georgetown for $300, where he remained for many years.[84] This transaction, along with the sale of a man named Aloysius in 1844 for $635 were the only two forays in the slave trade by the school after 1840.[85]

Georgetown's limited incursions in the slave trade, along with the decrease in leases by students, heightened the importance of religious and professional communities as providers of enslaved laborers to the institution. Medical practitioners with long histories with the college rose as an important group of providers of laborers in this period. Such were the cases of Dr. Benjamin Bohrer (d.1862) and Dr. Nicholas Worthington (1788–1849), two men who had provided medical services to the college and who complemented the income from their medical practice with an active participation in the slave trade.[86] Bohrer hired out to the Jesuits an enslaved man named Salvadore, who labored primarily in the kitchens.[87] Worthington, on the other hand, was an old acquaintance of the Jesuits. His father, Dr. Charles Worthington (1759–1836), had been the school's doctor during Georgetown's first decades and had often hired out his laborers to the Jesuits.[88] His son preserved his relationship with the school. From his property in Charles County, Nicholas Worthington purchased an enslaved person as the Jesuits sold the majority of their enslaved community in 1838.[89] He also offered his medical services to the school and hired out a man by the name of Frank Butler.[90]

Butler labored at the school's kitchens from 1843 to 1848 for an average of $7 a month plus clothing, all paid in monthly installments to his enslaver. In 1846, after a change in the school's treasury office, Worthington negotiated an increase of $2 a month for the revenue he received from Butler's labor. In exchange for this raise he released the Jesuits of the obligation of furnishing Butler with clothes.[91] With this new agreement in place, Worthington continued to receive payments for two years, after which the Jesuits cordially informed Worthington that Butler's "services would be dispensed," even if there was not a "motive or any complaints."[92] However, Butler's dismissal from the college did not mark the end of his time as a laborer at Georgetown. His stay spanned nearly ten years and outlasted his status as an enslaved person. In July of 1849, Worthington passed away, leaving in his will a provision allowing Butler's family to purchase his freedom for $200.[93] Two months after Worthington's death, Frank Butler appears to have registered as a free man with the city, and Br. William Smith (dates unknown) hired him to labor in the dormitories of the college on a salary of $10 a month.[94]

Butler's life at the school and his transition from slavery to freedom over the course of his hire at Georgetown reveals the dynamic nature of the school's labor force during the 1840s. The presence of free laborers at the college continued to increase over the years, particularly after 1845. However, the majority of them were not free people of color. They were Irish men who had recently immigrated into the area.[95] As the numbers of immigrant laborers increased in cities, the spaces for enslaved laborers and free workmen changed. Once involving all areas of the college, the presence of enslaved men on campus became constrained to student dormitories and the kitchen.[96]

The number of enslaved men fluctuated from a high of eleven at the beginning of the 1840s to less than five in 1850. In this period, only three enslaved people remained in the college on a yearly basis. Jesuit lay brothers—whose numbers had increased over the years—often hired cooks and day laborers for shorter periods of time during the school term, acquiring only temporary relief for their labor needs. This hiring system increased the fluctuation of the school's labor force, particularly in peak times such as the harvest season.[97] As the numbers of enslaved men laboring in the college decreased, the number of Irish laborers grew considerably. Irish men labored in the gardens, the priests' dormitories, and the priests' kitchens alongside the French and Italian cooks hired for Georgetown's president. With salaries of $10 a month, and no obligations concerning meals, health care, and lodgings, they appear to have been a more competitive option to the cost-conscious Jesuits, who decided in 1844 to start decreasing their enslaved labor force.[98]

A crucial factor that precipitated the decline in enslaved laborers at the college was the actions of enslaved men who purchased their freedom. After 1850, as the landscape of slavery changed in the nation's capital, Charles Taylor and James Henry Young followed Frank Butler in purchasing their freedom while they labored at Georgetown. Young began laboring at Georgetown University intermittently since 1843, when his enslaver Mary Bronaugh Hook (1811–96), rented him to the Jesuits, using her brother Jeremiah Bronaugh as an intermediary.[99] After nearly ten years of labor at Georgetown, by 1852 Young appears to have negotiated his freedom with Hook and Bronaugh. On November 11, 1852, Georgetown loaned Young $119.50 to purchase his freedom as well as his mother's.[100] In this arrangement, the school advanced Young money for his freedom papers under the condition these "would remain in the possession of Georgetown College's authorities" until he paid off his debt. Young labored as a slave who was actually free under the law for nearly a year, until November 29, 1853, when he settled his debt with the Jesuits and took possession of his papers. Once in possession of his freedom documents, he did not leave the school; he continued to labor cleaning dormitories, having arranged with the president of the college, Bernard Maguire (in office 1852–58), a salary of $12 a month.[101] He received an extra salary during summer break and used the Jesuits as a bank, usually depositing with them a percentage of his salary as savings. He labored under these conditions for more than a decade.[102] Young left campus as a free man on the morning of May 5, 1864.[103]

Young's labor at the college for more than ten years and his transition from slavery to servitude is only surpassed by Charles Taylor's twenty-five years as an enslaved and free man at Georgetown. After Taylor became property of the school in 1842, he continued to labor cleaning dormitories, painting, and occasionally working during the harvest on the college farm.[104] On March 9, 1853, his financial account registered the payment of freedom papers and an increase in his wages within the college. After seventeen years of laboring under slavery at the school, Taylor became a free man. He remained at the school until his death in 1861, at age forty-one.[105] Most of his life had been lived under slavery at Georgetown College.[106]

At the time of Taylor's death, only one enslaved person labored at Georgetown, Aaron Edmonson. Edmonson arrived at the school in 1859 as a servant in the student dormitories. Like Young, he had been hired to the school on more than one occasion.[107] He lugged coal during the winter, painted halls during the summers, and cleaned after students during the school term.[108] His enslaver was Ann Forrest Green (1797–1870), a prominent Catholic woman whose children attended Georgetown college. She had inherited Edmonson and his two sisters from her mother, Rebecca Forrest (1764–1843). She received $12 a month for Edmonson's labor, which was collected by her son Osceola Green.[109] Edmonson labored for three years at the school, with a brief interruption between May and June of 1861. During his time at Georgetown, Union troops took over the school, students left to join the Confederacy, and the school's labor force continued to diversify as the establishment of a Union encampment demanded more laborers. Edmonson left the school on March 3, 1862, with one pair of shoes, a suit, and one pair of gloves.[110]

Edmonson achieved his freedom one month later, on April 16, 1862, with the passage of the Compensated Emancipation Act of the District of Columbia. He was thirty years old at the time. On June 28, 1862, Green petitioned the government for a compensation of $500 for the loss of his labor. She received $109.50.[111] Although Edmonson labored for years at Georgetown, the archival record recognizes Green as his owner, hiding the ways in which the Jesuits profited from his labor. Five months after Edmonson became free, the Greens continued to profit from his labor, as the school reimbursed them with nearly $40 of back wages. Green described Edmonson in her compensation claim as "tall, black, rather straight, very active, and capable."[112] He was the last man who labored under slavery at Georgetown College.

5. A DEFINING FORCE IN SCHOOL HISTORY

Slavery was one of the defining forces of Georgetown University's history. The school's relationship with slavery and the fruits of enslaved labor was like the many-headed hydra: strong, powerful, and resilient, and enveloping nearly all areas of college life. Enslaved labor was one of the pillars upon which the former Jesuits of Maryland built their academy and the US's first Catholic college. The university's land, its buildings, agents, professors, and founders, as well as many of its students, were entangled with slavery

in varying degrees. Revenues derived from slavery filled the college's meager coffers, and its list of creditors and debtors often read as a ranking of
Maryland's top planters. The clean clothes the students and priests wore, the
buildings they occupied, the classrooms and chapels they filled, the gardens
they enjoyed, and the food they ate were all areas touched by slave labor.
Georgetown's first seven decades of operation, its growth, the composition
of its student body, and its financial management are unexplainable without
understanding its relationship with slavery.

Priests, parishioners, and patrons united through the bonds of religion
formed the core of Georgetown's slaveholding community. All of the owners
who hired enslaved people to the school were related to the institution. More
than three quarters of them were parents of students and alumni. The majority
of them were women, who were integral to the persistence of slavery on campus. The rest had a legacy of providing services to the Jesuits or were parishioners at Catholic churches. This dynamic put Catholicism at the center of
Georgetown's slaveholding world. Hiring enslaved people from their fellow
Catholics was a social practice that allowed school leaders to use the education
services they provided as a means to acquire the labor they sorely needed.

Slave hiring enabled Georgetown's priests to reap the economic benefits
of slaveholding without purchasing people or transferring individuals from
their plantations. As a result, the sale of 272 people in 1838 did not change
slavery at the school. In fact, the funds from the sale helped strengthen the
school's position, benefiting its financial footing, and increasing its demand
for enslaved laborers. After the sale of 1838, Georgetown became the center of the Jesuits' participation in the slave trade. In America's first Catholic
college, enslavement persisted for decades, connecting the school over the
years to faraway places in the Caribbean and to closer locations, such as its
community in the District of Columbia.

Georgetown University was an active participant in the slave trade for
nearly seventy years. Its choice to hire enslaved people was an economic
decision that fit its leaders' attitudes towards manual labor as well as the
precarious financial standing of the school. Hiring gave the school financial flexibility, allowing it to operate with lower costs. Georgetown hired,
bartered, bought, and sold people since its first years. Its involvement with
slavery began when it opened its doors, and no history of the college can
be complete without recognizing the presence and labor of enslaved people
on campus. Byrne, Suckey, Joseph, Nat, Stephen, Tempey, Lewis, Sam, Polly,
Sucky, Nicolas, Wat, Harriet, Michael, Gabe, Hillary, Joseph, Frank Butler,
James Henry Young, Charles Taylor, and many more whose names are lost to
us are already in the College's financial records. It is time for them to be part
of Georgetown's history as well.

Notes

1. Thanks to Fr. David J. Collins, S.J., Adam Rothman, and the *JJS* editors for their feedback. The research for this article owes much to Lynn Conway, Mary Beth Corrigan, the rest of the staff at the Booth Family Center for Special Collections at Georgetown University, and fellow Georgetown Slavery Archive collaborators Julia Bernier and Cory Young. Ledger A1 [henceforth LA1], 1789–1793 (I.A.1.a), Georgetown College Financial Records: Vault Collection, Georgetown University Archives [henceforth GUA], Booth Family Center for Special Collections, Georgetown University. The *Journal of Jesuit Studies* requires biographical dates for all historical figures, but the birth and death dates for most of the enslaved people named in this article are unknown and cannot be included. This is itself a lingering effect of slavery.

2. Georgetown University was founded in 1789, the year when Bishop John Carroll (1735–1815), a former Jesuit, acquired the deed for the school's land. Classes began on January 2, 1792. See Robert Emmett Curran, *The Bicentennial History of Georgetown University* (Washington, DC: Georgetown University Press, 1993), 1:23–24, here 34. For examples of activities of enslaved people on campus during its first years, see Ledger A3 [henceforth LA3], 1796–1799 (I.A.i.c), GUA; Journal C [henceforth JC], (I.A..2.a) 1808–1813, GUA; Journal D [henceforth JD], 1813–1821 (I.A.2.b), GUA; Infirmary Ledger [henceforth IL], 1816–1830, Box 1, Folder 1, Infirmary Collection, [henceforth IC], GUA.

3. Curran, *Bicentennial History*; Joseph Thomas Durkin, *Georgetown University: The Middle Years, 1840–1900* (Washington, DC: Georgetown University Press, 1963); Durkin, *Georgetown University, First in the Nation's Capital* (Garden City, NY: Doubleday, 1964). On the use of enslaved people for tuition payments and the presence of enslaved laborers, see Curran, *Bicentennial History*, 36, 361n27.

4. 191A Ledger [henceforth 191AL], Box 68, Addenda to the Maryland Province Archives [henceforth AMPA], Booth Family Center for Special Collections, Georgetown University; Washington Lots, House Ledger [henceforth WLHL], 1846–1862 (I.AA.i.f), GUA; Journal G [henceforth JG], 1838–1873 (I.A.2.e.), GUA; Various Accounts, Students, Workmen, Societies [henceforth VASWS], 1837–1846 (I.AA.1.h.) GUA; Ledger F [henceforth LF], 1838–1842 (I.A.1.h.), GUA.

5. Craig Steven Wilder, "War and Priests: Catholic Colleges and Slavery in the Age of Revolutions," in *Slavery's Capitalism: A New History of American Economic Development*, ed. Sven Beckert and Seth Rockman (Philadelphia: University of Pennsylvania Press, 2016), 227–42, here 231–32.

6. Jennifer Oast, *Institutional Slavery: Slaveholding Churches, Schools, Colleges, and Businesses in Virginia, 1680–1860* (New York: Cambridge University Press, 2016).

7. Kathleen Menzie Lesko, Valerie Babb, and Carroll R. Gibbs, *Black Georgetown Remembered: A History of Its Black Community from the Founding of the Town of George in 1751 to the Present* (Washington, DC: Georgetown University Press, 1991), 2–3; Chris Myers Asch and George Derek Musgrove, *Chocolate City: A History of Race and Democracy in the Nation's Capital* (Chapel Hill: The University of North Carolina Press, 2017), 39–46; Mary Beth Corrigan, "Imaginary Cruelties?: A History of the Slave Trade in Washington D.C.," *Washington History* 12, no. 2 (Fall/Winter 2001–2): 4–27, here 6; Jonathan D. Martin, *Divided Mastery: Slave Hiring in the American South* (Cambridge: Harvard University Press), 161–63.

8. See Lesko, Babb, and Gibbs, *Black Georgetown Remembered*, 2–3; David Mould and Missy Loewe, *Remembering Georgetown: A History of the Lost Port City* (Charleston, SC: The History Press, 2009), 30–32.

9. Lesko, Babb, and Gibbs, *Black Georgetown Remembered*, 2, 6.

10. "John Carroll's plan for organizing the mission," Box 2, Folder 2, Maryland Province Archives [henceforth MPA], Booth Family Center for Special Collections, Georgetown University. On the Maryland Jesuits' organization after the suppression, see Ronald A. Binzley, "Ganganelli's Disaffected Children: The Ex-Jesuits and the Shaping of Early American Catholicism, 1773–1790," *U.S. Catholic Historian* 26, no. 2, Catholics in the Colony of Maryland and the Early Republic (Spring 2008): 44–77, here 59; Robert Emmett Curran, "Ambrose Maréchal, the Jesuits, and the Demise of Ecclesial Republicanism in Maryland, 1818–1838," in *Shaping American Catholicism: Maryland and New York, 1805–1915*, ed. Curran (Washington, DC: Catholic University of America Press, 2012), 13–29, here 14–16; Catherine O'Donnell, "John Carroll and the Origins of an American Catholic Church, 1783–1815," *William and Mary Quarterly* 68, no. 1 (January 2011): 101–26.

11. During the suppression of the Society of Jesus, the former Jesuits did not write reports on the state of their property. The number of people is an estimate done by reviewing the number of people enslaved on each estate according to the 1790 Federal Census. For their properties, see Liber JC, No. 3, fol. 285, General Court Land Record Books for the Western Shore of Maryland, "Properties," Box 23, Folder 14, MPA; "List of properties," Box 23, Folder 9, MPA.

12. Not every clergyman who taught at Georgetown was a member of the CRCC. For membership regulations, see "Membership in the Select Body of the Clergy, 1793(1816)," in Thomas Hughes, *History of the Society of Jesus in North America: Colonial and Federal (Documents)*, Volume 1, Part 2 (London: Longmans, Green, and Co., 1908), 1:768–69.

13. Proceedings of the General Chapter, October 11, 1784, Box 2, Folder 5, MPA; John Ashton, "On his personal property at the White Marsh," Box 35, Folder 6, MPA; Valuation of John Ashton's Negroes, Box 35, Folder 6, MPA; Will of Charles Sewall, Box 25, Folder 12, MPA; Will of Notley Young Box 25, Folder 8, MPA, Will of John Ashton, Box 25, Folder 9, MPA.

14. Eighteenth-century sermons from the Maryland mission reflect some of their attitudes toward slavery. Fr. John Boone (1735–85) thought slavery was an instrument to teach Christianity and implored masters to teach enslaved people to be good Christians, since their time "would be made up […] in interest, by the interest with which they would learn to labor for your service." See Boone, "*Medius vestrum stetit, quem vos nescitis.* St. John. c.l. v.25 There stands (or: stood) one among you, whom you know not—[1,26]" ACSC, Box 2, Folder 32; John Lewis (1720–88), the superior of the Maryland mission, in a sermon at Annapolis, described slavery as a vehicle for Christianization, "Tu quis es/Who art thou?" St. Jo.1.19, ACSC Box 4, Folder 32.

15. Robert Emmett Curran, "Rome, the American Church, and Slavery," in Curran, *Shaping American Catholicism*, 92–110, here 96–100.

16. Thomas Murphy, *Jesuit Slaveholding in Maryland, 1717–1838* (New York, NY: Routledge, 2001), 26–30; Edward F. Beckett, "Listening to Our History: Inculturation and Jesuit Slaveholding," *Studies in the Spirituality of Jesuits* 28, no. 5 (1996): 1–48, here 6–9.

17. Members of the Queen and Mahoney Families sued John Ashton, Francis Neale, and Sylvester Boarman for their freedom. Their claim for freedom was that they descended from a free woman. In Maryland, slavery followed *partus sequitur ventrem*, where the status of children followed that of their mother. See Eric Robert Papenfuse, "From Recompense to Revolution: Mahoney v. Ashton and the Transfiguration of Maryland Culture, 1791–1802," *Slavery & Abolition: A Journal of Slave and Post-Slave Studies* 15, no. 3 (1994): 38–62, here 38–47; Will G. Thomas III, "The Timing of Queen v. Hepburn: An Exploration of African American Networks in the Early Republic," *O Say Can You See: Early Washington D.C., Law & Family*,

http://earlywashingtondc.org/stories/queen_v_hepburn (accessed May 30, 2020). John Ashton was one of the first directors of Georgetown College, and Francis Neale was president of the college 1808–9 and 1809–12.

18. The oldest record of Jesuit slaveholding in Maryland dates from 1717. For the Jesuits' turn to slavery, see Murphy, *Jesuit Slaveholding*, 3–33.

19. From 1717 until 1773, the Jesuits of Maryland received in bequest at the very least fifty-two enslaved people through the legacies of Catholic planters such as James Carroll, who left the Jesuits more than 2,500 acres of land and at least thirty people. On Carroll's bequest and his properties, see "White Marsh: Devise of James Carroll," in Hughes, *History of the Society of Jesus in North America*, 1:248–50; "Codicil to James Carroll's Will, February 17, 1728," in Hughes, *History of the Society of Jesus in North America*, 1:250–51; Murphy, *Jesuit Slaveholding in Maryland*, 16, 35; and Charles Flannagan, "The Sweets of Independence: A Reading of the 'James Carroll Daybook, 1714–21'" (PhD diss., University of Maryland, 2005).

20. St. Inigoes accounts, kept by Fr. Francis Neale, 1805–1808, Box 43, folder 3, MPA; Neale to Joseph Marshall, December 1, 1817, Box 26, Folder 2, MPA; DB [henceforth DB], 1812–1814 (I.A.4.d), GUA; DB, 1814–1817 (I.A.4.e), GUA.

21. Martin, *Divided Mastery*, 27–28; Peter Way, *Common Labor: Workers and the Digging of North American Canals, 1780–1860* (New York: Cambridge University Press, 1993), 25–34; Barbara Jeanne Fields, *Slavery and Freedom on the Middle Ground: Maryland During the Nineteenth Century* (New Haven, CT: Yale University Press, 1984), 5, 27–28.

22. Martin, *Divided Mastery*, 165–94; John J. Zaborney, *Slaves for Hire: Renting Enslaved Laborers in Antebellum Virginia* (Baton Rouge: Louisiana State University Press, 2012), 10–27.

23. Richard C. Wade, *Slavery in the Cities: The South 1820–1860* (New York: Oxford University Press, 1964), 21; Midori Takagi, *"Rearing Wolves to Our Own Destruction:" Slavery in Richmond, Virginia, 1782–1865* (Charlottesville: University Press of Virginia, 1999).

24. Ignatius of Loyola, *The Constitutions of the Society of Jesus*, trans. George E. Ganns (St. Louis, MO: Institute of Jesuit Sources, 1970), 433 [henceforth *Constitutions*].

25. *Constitutions*, 148.

26. *Constitutions*, 13, 148, 305.

27. *Catalog of Members of the Maryland Mission of the Society of Jesus, 1634–1806* (Woodstock, MD: Ex Typis Collegii Ss. Cordis, 1887); *Catalogus Sociorum Missionis Federatae Societatis Jesu, 1807* (Woodstock, MD: Ex Typis Collegii Ss. Cordis, 1887).

28. Authors have overlooked the connection between the number of lay brothers and the use of enslaved laborers. See Murphy, *Jesuit Slaveholding*, 3–32, 129–35; Beckett, "Listening to Our History," 5–11. Maryland's use of enslaved laborers was similar to other Jesuit missions in the Atlantic, such as sixteenth-century Brazil. The Jesuit superior there, Manuel da Nóbrega (1517–70), declared that the Jesuits could not "live without some slaves to hew wood and draw water and bake our daily bread and perform other duties that cannot be carried out by lay brothers since they are so scarce." See Manuel da Nóbrega to Simão Rodriques, August 9, 1549, cited in Alida C. Metcalf, *Go-Betweens and the Colonization of Brazil: 1500–1600* (Austin: University of Texas Press, 2005), 180.

29. George Hunter's book for memoranda 1770–1785 172d, Box 46, Folder 6, MPA; St. Thomas Account Book, Box 47, Folder 2; St. Thomas Manor Account book, Box 46, Folder 6, MPA. On region's hiring practices, see Martin, *Divided Mastery*, 85; Zaborney, *Slaves for Hire*, 98–102.

30. DB, 1814–1817 (I.A.4.e), GUA; IL, 1816–1830, Box 1, Folder 1, IC, GUA; "Fr. Ripetti's Notes on the History of Gervase," Old Archives-Buildings, Box 3, Folder 4, GUA;

Ledger C [henceforth LC], 1803–1813 (I.A.i.e), GUA; Robert Molyneux to Charles Neale, October 1st, 1806, Box 93, Folder 2, MPA; LA3, 1796–1799 (I.A.i.c), GUA; JC (I.A..2.a) 1808–1813, GUA, JD, 1813–1821 (I.A.2.b), GUA.

31. Ledger B1 [henceforth LB1], 1800–1803 (I.A.i.d), GUA; LC, 1803–1813 (I.A.i.e.), GUA; JC, 1808–1813 (I.A.2.a.), GUA; JC, 1808–1813 (I.A.2.a.), GUA; DBLC, 1803–1808 (I.A.A.i.b), GUA; Expense Book [henceforth EB], 1802–1808 (I.A.3.b), GUA; IL, 1816–1830, Box 1, Folder 1, IC, GUA. This Sucky should not be confused with the Suckey enslaved by Leonard Neale.

32. "Leonard Neale, Certificate of Slaves," March 2, 1802, Liber H. No. 8, 1802, RG 351, NARA–DC.

33. LA1, 1789–1793 (I.A.1.a), GUA; JC, 1808–1813 (I.A.2.a), GUA; LA3, 1796–1799 (I.A.i.c.), GUA; LB1, 1800–1803 (I.A.i.d.), GUA; LC, 1803–1813 (I.a.I.e), GUA; DBLC, 1803–Nov. 1808 (I.A.A.1.b.), GUA; DB, 1809–1812 (I.A.4.c.), GUA.

34. F. Neale, Cash Book, 1818–1823 (I.A.3.e.), GUA; *Catalogus Sociorum Missionis Federatae Societatis Jesu*, 1818 (Woodstock, MD: Typis Collegii Ss. Cordis, 1893) 3. Before Henrietta Edelen, the Neales hired out an unnamed woman to Georgetown's washhouse. See EB, 1794–1802 (I.A.3.a.), GUA.

35. The Sulpicians were invited by Bishop John Carroll to lead Georgetown University and to build a seminary in Baltimore. Their presence at the college was a magnet for students from the West Indies who were fleeing the French Revolution, until the Sulpicians left in 1799. See John Carroll to Lord Arundell, October 4, 1790, Box 3, Folder 6, MPA; R. Nagot to the crcc, August 22, 1799, Box 23, Folder 9, MPA; George M. Barringer, "They Came to Georgetown: The French Sulpicians," *Georgetown Today* (July 1977): 7–8; Curran, *Bicentennial History*, 47–51; Kyle Roberts and Stephen R. Schloesser, eds., *Crossings and Dwellings: Restored Jesuits, Women Religious, American Experience, 1814–2014* (Leiden: Brill, 2017), 381–84.

36. For the relationship between Sulpicians and creoles in Maryland, see Annabelle M. Melville, *Louis Dubourg: Bishop of Louisiana and the Floridas, Bishop of Montauban, and Archbishop of Besancon, 1766–1833* (Chicago, IL: Loyola Press, 1986), 1:42; Peter Condon, "The Church in the Island of San Domingo," *United States Catholic Historical Society: Historical Records and Studies XIII* (May 1919): 11–61, here 36.

37. On student fees, see LA3, 1796–1799 (I.A.i.c.), GUA; LB1, 1800–1803 (I.A.i.d), GUA. For the Sulpicians' use of enslaved laborers, see Students Sundry Accounts [henceforth SSA], (I.I.A.A.i. a), 1796–1798, GUA; LB1, 1800–1803 (I.A.i.d.), GUA. For women slaveowners, see LA3, 1796–1799 (I.A.i.c.), GUA; Book of Expenses and Remittances [henceforth BER], 1796–1799 (I.A.4.a), GUA.

38. For their names, see LA3, 1796–1799 (I.A.i.c.), GUA; LB1, 1800–1803 (I.A.i.d); SSA, (I.A.A.i.a), 1796–1798, GUA; DB 1798 (I.A.4.b), GUA; BER, 1796–1799 (I.A.4.a), GUA; Certificates of Freedom, 1806–1851, C290–1, Baltimore County Court, Maryland State Archives.

39. The Sulpicians departed Georgetown after conflicts with the CRCC over revenues from the slave trade at Bohemia plantation. See John Carroll to Charles Plowden, July 7, 1797, *John Carroll Papers*, 2:218; John Carroll to Charles Plowden, December 11, 1798, *John Carroll Papers*, 2:248; Proceedings of the CRCC, December 3, 1798, Box 24, Folder 1, MPA; Proceedings of the CRCC, September 4, 1797, Box 24, Folder 1, MPA; Proceedings of the CRCC, October 9, 1799, Box 23, Folder 10, MPA; Curran, *Bicentennial History*, 50–52, 56; Thomas R. Ulshafer, "Slavery and the Early Sulpician Community in Maryland," *U.S. Catholic Historian* 37, no. 2 (Spring 2019): 1–21, here 14–15.

40. Curran, *Bicentennial History*, 36.

41. LA1, 1789–1793 (I.A.1.a), GUA; Ledger A2, 1793–1796, GUA; LA3, 1796–1799 (I.A.i.c.), GUA; LB1, 1800–1803 (I.A.i.d), GUA; LC, 1803–1813 (I.A.i.e), GUA. Curran makes a note of this process but does not explain how often families used enslaved people to pay their debts. See Curran, *Bicentennial History*, 36.

42. LB1, 1800–1803 (I.A.i.d), GUA.

43. JC, 1805–1813 (I.A..2.a), GUA; LC, 1803–1813 (I.A.i.e.), GUA.

44. "Bill of Sale," Georgetown College Financial Records Vault Collection (unbound), Box 1; EB, 1802–1808 (I.A.3.b.), GUA; Agent's Cashbook 1802–1820, Box 69, AMPA.

45. LC, 1803–1813 (I.A.i.e), GUA; DBLC, 1803–1808 (I.AA.i.b), GUA. These transactions from 1808 are possibly related to the policy of the CRCC to identify "supernumerary slaves" to "dispose of them to good and Christian masters." See "Proceedings of the CRCC, May 12, 1808," Box 24, Folder 1, MPA.

46. DB, 1818–1821 (I.A.4.f), GUA.

47. Carroll to Francis Neale, October 3, 1815, Box 57.5, File 15, MPA; "Proceedings of the CRCC, May 18–19, 1813," Box 24, Folder 1, MPA.

48. "Proceedings of the CRCC, May 18–19, 1813," Box 24, Folder 1, MPA; "Proceedings of the CRCC, September 14, 1813," Box 24, Folder 1, MPA; "Proceedings of the CRCC, June 14, 1814," Box 24, Folder 1, MPA; "Proceedings of the CRCC, August 22, 1820," Box 24, Folder 1, MPA.

49. The ex-Jesuits in the United States renewed their vows to the Jesuit order in 1805 by joining the group of the Society that continued to exist in Russia under the protection of the Russian monarchs. After this period, Jesuits began to slowly take control of the school from the CRCC. The full restoration of the order occurred in 1814. See Curran, *Bicentennial History*, 1:57–58, 64–65.

50. For women's participation in the slave market see Martin, *Divided Mastery*, 85; Zaborney, *Slaves for Hire*, 98–102; Marie S. Molloy, *Single, White, Slaveholding Women in the Nineteenth-Century American South* (Columbia: University of South Carolina Press, 2018); Stephanie E. Jones-Rodgers, *They Were Her Property: White Women as Slave Owners in the American South* (New Haven, CT: Yale University Press, 2019). For donations and loans by women slave owners, see LA3, 1796–1799 (I.A.i.c), GUA; JC (I.A..2.a) 1808–1813, GUA; Ledger D, 1814–1830 (I.A.i.f.), GUA; WLHL, 1846–1862 (I.AA.i.f), GUA; Brother Sylvester Clarke's Memoranda Book, Miscellaneous Ledgers Box 1 [henceforth BSCMB], GUA; Notes and Bills Receivable, 1841–1892 (I.A.6.h.), GUA.

51. LB1, 1800–1803 (I.A.i.d.), GUA; LC, 1803–1813 (I.A.i.e), GUA; DBLC, 1803–1808 (I.A.A.b.), GUA; EB, 1802–1808 (I.A.3.b), GUA; JC (I.A..2.a) 1808–1813, GUA.

52. Ledger D, 1814–1830 (I.A.i.f.), GUA; JC (I.A..2.a) 1808–1813, GUA; LC, 1803–1813 (I.A.i.e), GUA; JD, 1813–1821 (I.A.2.b), GUA; George Fenwick's Day Book, Box 42, Folder 1, MPA. On the Fenwick Family boarding students, see Curran, *Bicentennial History*, 46; William W. Warner, *At Peace with All Their Neighbors: Catholics and Catholicism in the National Capital, 1787–1860* (Washington, DC: Georgetown University Press, 1994), 240n44.

53. See JC (I.A..2.a) January 1808–September 1813, GUA; JD, 1813–1821 (I.A.2.b), GUA.

54. BER, 1796–1799 (I.A.4.a).

55. Before the construction of the infirmary in 1816, there is little information on the use of enslaved laborers to construct Georgetown's oldest buildings. See DB, September 14, 1814–February 5, 1817 (I.A.4.e.), GUA. For the construction costs of Georgetown's first building, see "Construction estimate for Academy," Box 19, Folder 4, MPA; "Estimate of Carpenters work to be done at Geo.town," Box 19, Folder 4, MPA; Curran, *Bicentennial History*, 1:24.

56. While most of the owners of Georgetown's enslaved community were Catholic, the majority of the owners of the slaves who expanded the college were Protestant businessmen. On the posts and dealings of these men, see "Georgetown Journals, 1751–1802," and "Board of Aldermen Journals," Box 1, Reel 1 and 2, Georgetown, Washington, DC. Corporation Government Records, Manuscript Division, Library of Congress, Washington, DC.

57. IL, 1816–1830, Box 1, Folder 1, IC, GUA. On the Bussard residence, see William P. Thompson, "Bussard Newman House–HABS no. DC–196," Historic American Buildings Survey, Office of Archeology and Historic Preservation, National Park Service, June 1968. The relationship between David and Philip Bussard is unknown.

58. IL, 1816–1830, Box 1, Folder 1, GUA.

59. Curran, *Bicentennial History*, 46, 67. The construction is also mentioned by Fr. John McElroy in his diary. See Diary 1, Vol 2, 1818, Box 1, Folder 2, JMcP.

60. IL, 1816–1830, Box 1, Folder 1, IC, GUA.

61. Adam Marshal to Francis Neale, January 5, 1821, box 59, Folder 4, MPA; Neale to the Luigi Fortis (1748–1829; in office 1820–29), March 1824, Box 60, Folder 8, MPA. On Georgetown's financial outlook, see "Report on the Financial Condition of the Province, 1820," Box 60, Folder 7, MPA; "Relations of students owing Money," Box 19, Folder 5, MPA; Curran, *Bicentennial History*, 98.

62. The Jesuits also considered selling their enslaved community for a term of years. See Enoch Fenwick (1780–1827) to Francis Neale, May 24, 1816, Box 59, Folder 17, MPA.

63. "Proceedings of the CRCC, May 18–19, 1813," Box 24, Folder 1, MPA; "Proceedings of the CRCC, September 14, 1813," Box 24, Folder 1, MPA; "Proceedings of the CRCC, June 14, 1814," Box 24, Folder 1, MPA; Peter Kenney (1779–1841) to Louis DeBarth (d.1822), April 24, 1820, Box 59, Folder 7, MPA.

64. Will Erkead (dates unknown) to William McSherry (d.1839), October 17, 1834, Box 13, Folder 4, MPA; Murphy, *Jesuit Slaveholding*, 193–94.

65. Charles Plowden to Kenney, June 12, 1819, cited in Cornelius Michael Buckey, *Stephen Lariguadelle Dubuisson, SJ and the Reform of the American Jesuits* (Lanham, MD: University Press of America, 2013), 94. On the importance of the arrival of the visitor, Fr. Peter Kenney, see Curran, *Bicentennial History*, 89–90; Curran, "Peter Kenney: Twice Visitor of the Maryland Mission (1819–21, 1830–33) and Father of the First Two American Provinces," in *With Eyes and Ears Open: The Role of Visitors in the Society of Jesus*, ed. Thomas M. McCoog (Leiden: Brill, 2019), 191–213; Thomas Morrisey, *Peter Kenney, S.J., 1779–1841: The Restoration of the Jesuits in Ireland, England, Sicily, and North America* (Washington, DC: Catholic University of America Press, 2014), 296–99.

66. Thomas Mulledy to John McElroy, June 12, 1838, Box 66, Folder 5, MPA; Mulledy to McElroy, November 11, 1838, Box 66, Folder 3, MPA; Fidelis Grivel to C.C. Lancaster, November 6, 1838, Box 66, Folder 3, MPA.

67. Mulledy to McElroy, June 12, 1838, Box 66, Folder 5, MPA.

68. Kenney to McElroy, August 19, 1832, Box 63, Folder 18, MPA; Kenney to Francis Neale, September 10, 1832, Box 63, Folder 17, MPA; Duff Green to Joseph Rosati (1789–1847, as bishop of St. Louis, 1826–43), February 7, 1838, Archdiocese of St. Louis Office of Archives and Records, "Duff Green plans to purchase the Maryland Jesuits' slaves and relocate them to Arkansas, February 7, 1838," Georgetown Slavery Archive http://slaveryarchive.georgetown. edu/items/show/480 [accessed May 30, 2020].

69. At the time of the sale, Johnson was serving in the US House of Representatives. He had previously served as governor of Louisiana (1824–88). On the sale, see Articles of Agreement Between Thomas F. Mulledy of Georgetown, Jesse Batey, and Henry Johnson of the State

of Louisiana, June 19, 1838. Box 40, Folder 10, MPA. On the sale of 1838, see Robert Emmett Curran, "'Splendid Poverty': Jesuit Slaveholding in Maryland, 1805–1838," in *Catholics in the Old South: Essays on Church and Culture*, ed. Randall Miller and Jon Wakelyn (Macon, GA: Mercer University Press, 1983), 125–46; Murphy, *Jesuit Slaveholding*, 187–214; Adam Rothman, "Georgetown University and the Business of Slavery," *Washington History* 29, no. 2 (Fall 2017): 18–22.

70. For the terms of the sale, see Jan Roothaan (1785–1853, as in office 1829–53) to McSherry, December 27, 1836, Box 93, Folder 9, MPA; Francis Vespre, *Provincia di Maryland–Intorno alla vendita di nostri servi*, 1836, ARSI, Maryl 5-II 6. On Joseph Johnson's enrollment at Georgetown and the use of remittances from the sale to defray the costs of his tuition, see Vespre to Johnson, March 29, 1840, Letter Book 1, 163, Box 77, AMPA; DCB, 1845–1848 (I.A.3.l), GUA.

71. DCB, 1839–1860, 190E, Box 68, AMPA; Bill Book 1840–1846 (I.A.6.g), GUA; 191AL, Box 68, AMPA.

72. The actual number of people sold in 1838 remains unclear. Historian Sharon M. Leon notes that "although the articles of agreement specify that 272 people are being sold, the 1838 census document lists 278 people." See Leon, "Re-presenting the Enslaved Community Sold by the Maryland Province Jesuits in 1838," September 30, 2016 (http://www.6floors .org/bracket/2016/09/30/re-presenting-the-enslaved-community-sold-by-the-maryland -province-jesuits-in-1838/) [accessed May 30, 2020]. Leon, Jesuit Plantation Project (https:// jesuitplantationproject.org/s/jpp/page/welcome/) [accessed May 30, 2020].

73. DB, 1830–1836 (I.A.4.g), GUA.

74. VASWS, 1837–1846 (I.AA.1.h.), GUA.

75. 191AL, Box 68, AMPA; WLHL, 1846–1862 (I.AA.i.f), GUA; VASWS, 1837–1846 (I.AA.1.h.), GUA; LF, 1838–1842 (I.A.1.h.), GUA; Ledger G, 1841–1845 (I.A.1.i), GUA; EB, 1841–1845 (I.A.3.k.), GUA.

76. See DB, 1837–1854 (I.A.4.h), GUA; JG, 1838–1875 (I.A.2.e.), GUA; LF, 1838–1842 (I.A.1.h), GUA; CB, 1845–1853 (I.A.3.m.), GUA. For washhouse conditions, see "Infirmary Book, 1840–1857," Box 2, Folder 3, IC, GUA; Consultation of December 9, 1840, Georgetown University's Consultors Books, Box 6, Folder 1, GUA.

77. For enrollment numbers, see Curran, *Bicentennial History*, 397.

78. For enrollment, see Curran, *Bicentennial History*, 397. For specie payments, see Bill Book, 1840–1846 (I.A.6.g), GUA. On the use of enslaved laborers to pay fees, see Ledger G, 1841–1845 (I.A.1.i.), GUA; VASWS, 1837–1846 (I.A.A.1.h.), GUA; Ledger E, 1830–1838 (I.A.1.g.), GUA.

79. Curran, *Bicentennial History*, 161.

80. On the Forrests' wealth, see Mary Mitchell, *Divided Town* (Barre, MA: Barre Publishers, 1968), 27–29, 36; Georgetown, DC City Directory, 1834. For their hires, see VASWS, 1837–1846 (I.A.A.1.h.), GUA; WLHL, 1846–1862 (I.AA.i.f), GUA.

81. Warner, *At Peace with All Their Neighbors*, 200.

82. DCB, 1845–1848 (I.A.3.l.), GUA; VASWS, 1837–1846 (I.A.A.1.h.), GUA.

83. EB, 1829–1836 (I.A.3.g.), GUA.

84. See EB, 1841–1845 (I.A.3.k.), GUA; VASWS, 1837–1846 (I.A.A.1.h.); BSCMB, GUA.

85. For Aloysius sale, CB, 1841–1845 (I.A.3.j.), GUA. In this period, the Jesuits also purchased one person in the plantations. See Bill of Sale for Len, September 4, 1843, Box 6, Folder 5, Maryland Province Collection, Georgetown University; Vespre to Woodley, April 16, 1844, Letter Book 2, Box 77, AMPA.

86. On Bohrer and Worthington's medical services at the College, see EB, 1809–1822 (I.A.3.c.), GUA; Day Book Drs. Bohrer and Magruder, 1835–1836, Box 1, Folder 8, IC, GUA. For Bohrer's practice with the enslaved community of Georgetown's neighborhood, see Medical Visits Bohrer and Magruder, 1831–1832–1833, Box 1, Folder 6, IC, GUA.

87. WLHL, 1846–1860 (I.A.A.1.f.), GUA.

88. IL, 1817–1819, Box 1, Folder 1, IC, GUA; LA1, 1789–1793 (I.A.1.a.), GUA; LA3, 1796–1799 (I.A.1.c.), GUA; JC, 1808–1813 (I.A.2.a.), GUA; LB1, 1800–1803 (I.A.1.d.), GUA.

89. DCB, 190E, Box 68, AMPA.

90. VASWS, 1837–1846 (I.A.A.1.h.), GUA; WLHL, 1846–1860 (I.A.A.1.f.), GUA; DCB, 1845–1848 (I.A.3.l.), GUA.

91. Vespre to Dr. N[icholas] W. Worthington, June 22, 1846, Georgetown Treasurer's Letter Books, 1840–1858, Box 2, GUA.

92. Vespre to Nicholas Worthington, August 31, 1847, Georgetown Treasurer Letter Books, 1847–1849, Box 2, GUA; DCB, 1845–1848 (I.A.3.l.), GUA.

93. Nicholas Worthington Will, July 16, 1849, Wills, Boxes 0019 D'lagnel, Julian A-022 Baines, Hanson, 1847–1854, 340–44.

94. WLHL, 1846–1860 (I.A.A.1.f.), GUA. Butler's manumission record was registered with the city of Washington according to the financial ledgers of Georgetown University. However, volume 4 (1846–55) is missing.

95. Multiple accounts show arrival dates from Ireland for the laborers hired by the college, the purchase of postage for letters sent to Ireland, prayer books, and pew rents. For examples, see WLHL, 1846–1860 (I.A.A.1.f.), GUA; VASWS, 1837–1846 (I.A.A.1.h.), GUA.

96. DCB, 1845–1848 (I.A.3.l.), GUA; WLHL, 1846–1860 (I.A.A.1.f.), GUA.

97. See EB, 1841–1845 (I.A.3.k.), GUA; DCB, 1845–1848 (I.A.3.l.), GUA; WLHL, 1846–1860 (I.A.A.1.f.), GUA.

98. See DCB, 1845–1848 (I.A.3.l.), GUA; VASWS, 1837–1846 (I.A.A.1.h.), GUA. On the boarding of Irish laborers, see WLHL, 1844–1862 (I.A.A.1.f.); GUA. On foreign cooks for the College president, see EB, 1841–1845 (I.A.3.k.), GUA; WLHL, 1846–1860 (I.A.A.1.f.), GUA.

99. VASWS, 1837–1846 (I.A.A.1.h.), GUA; WLHL, 1844–1862 (I.A.A.1.f.); Ledger H, 1845–1849 (I.A.i.j.), GUA; DCB, 1845–1848 (I.A.3.l), GUA.

100. WLHL, 1844–1862 (I.A.A.1.f.), GUA. The reasons for this sale are unclear. One possibility is the fact that Hook was about to move to Texas with her younger brother, Dr. John Mitchel Bronaugh. See J. M. Bronaugh, 1860 Federal Census, Census Place: Jackson Texas, Page 369; J. M. Bronaugh, 1870 Federal Census, Census Place: Jackson Texas, Page 476A.

101. WLHL, 1844–1862 (I.A.A.1.f.); CB, 1842–1852 (I.A.2.n.), GUA; CB, 1852–1856 (I.A.3.o), GUA.

102. WLHL, 1844–1862 (I.A.A.1.f.); CB, 1856–1858, (I.A.3.p.), GUA; CB, 1859–1865 (I.A.3.q.), GUA.

103. JG, 1838–1875 (I.A.2.e.), GUA.

104. EB, 1841–1845 (I.A.3.k.), GUA; CB, 1831–1841 (I.A.3.h.), GUA; VASWS, 1837–1846 (I.A.A.1.h.), GUA; DCB, 1845–1848 (I.A.3.l.), GUA.

105. WLHL, 1844–1862 (I.A.A.1.f.), GUA; CB, 1852–1856 (I.A.3.o), GUA; CB, 1856–1858 (I.A.3.p.), GUA; CB, 1859–1865 (I.A.3.q.), GUA; JG, 1838–1875 (I.A.2.e.), GUA; "September, 1861," Holy Trinity Church Deaths, 1818–1867, 109, Digital Georgetown.

106. For important events in Charles Taylor's life, see September 22, 1836–Marriage of Charles Taylor and Mary Boarman, Holy Trinity Church Archives, Sacramental Registers,

"Marriages (1806–1871)," 43, Digital Georgetown; March 4, 1838–Baptism Charles Francis Taylor, Holy Trinity Church Archives, Sacramental Registers "Baptisms (1835–1858)," 60, Digital Georgetown; March 1, 1840–Baptism Theodore Agustin Taylor, Holy Trinity Church Archives, Sacramental Registers, "Baptisms (1835–1858)," 100, Digital Georgetown; "September, 1861," Holy Trinity Church Deaths, 1818–1867, 109, Digital Georgetown.

107. Edmonson's first hire at the school was from May to September of 1849. See WLHL, 1844–1862 (I.A.A.1.f.), GUA. His whereabouts between 1849 and 1859 are unknown. It is possible that he served as a valet or servant in "Rosedale," Green's renowned house in Georgetown along with other members of his family.

108. JG, 1838–1875 (I.A.2.e.), GUA.

109. Ann Forrest Green, *The 1861 Diary of Ann (Forrest) Green of Rosedale*. James Nicholas Payne (sl: sn, 1991); "Rebecca Forrest Will," 1843, Wills and Probate Records Washington, DC, Boxes 0014, Quinlin, Tasker C–0018 Degges, John, 1837–1847"; CB, 1859–1865 (I.A.3.q.), GUA; DB, 1859–1864 (I.A.4.i.), GUA. On Osceola Green's relationship to the college, see Ainsworth R. Spofford, *Eminent and Representative Men of Virginia and the District of Columbia of the Nineteenth Century* (Madison, WI: Brant & Fuller, 1893), 161.

110. JG, 1838–1875 (I.A.2.e.), GUA. On Georgetown during the Civil War, see Curran, *Bicentennial History*, 220–48.

111. "Petition of Ann Green, 28 June 1862," Records of the Board of Commissioners for the Emancipation of Slaves in the District of Columbia, 1862–1863, Record Group 217, Records of the United States General Accounting [henceforth RG217]. NARA-DC; Ann Green, Commission's Valuations for Petitions, Records of the Board of Commissioners for the Emancipation of Slaves in the District of Columbia, 1862–1863. NARA Microfilm Publication M520.

112. DB, 1859–1864 (I.A.4.i.), GUA; "Petition of Ann Green, 28 June 1862," RG217, NARA-DC.

4

Passing:
Race, Religion, and the
Healy Family, 1820–1920

JAMES M. O'TOOLE

Boston College historian James M. O'Toole explores how religion and race shaped the life of Fr. Patrick Francis Healy, SJ, the twenty-ninth president of Georgetown University. Healy is known as the first Black man to become president of a major American university. While he was born into slavery in Georgia, however, he navigated his world by "passing" as white. This essay was first published in the Proceedings of the Massachusetts Historical Society *108 (1996): 1–34.*

In the summer of 1849, a college student confided his thoughts to his diary. He was a popular and bright young man, graduating first in his class. Three of his younger brothers were students at the same school, and they formed a protective circle for one another now that they were nearly a thousand miles away from the comforting surroundings of home. The diarist was also devout. Reared as a child without any religious practice, he was placed while a teenager in a Catholic college. There he had an intense religious experience and was baptized into the Roman church. As he wrote, he was about to embark on further studies which led him to a career in the priesthood. In a few short sentences on that August day, he summarized his life. "Today 5 years ago," he said, "I entered this college. What a change. Then I was nothing, now I am a Catholic."[1]

We may be tempted to dismiss that stark contrast—between a particular denominational affiliation on the one hand and "nothing" on the other—as merely the enthusiasm of an overly pious adolescent. These may just be the words of one who, after five years of schooling at the hands of Jesuits, knows how to use a stylized religious language that will win the approval of adults. This diarist, however, may have had more reason than his fellows to distinguish his previous condition as "nothing" from his present improved circumstances and brighter future prospects. He was James Augustine Healy, born in April 1830 and as he wrote a member of the first graduating class of the College of the Holy Cross in Worcester, Massachusetts. He would leave Worcester the following month for clerical studies in Canada and then in France, would become a priest in Boston, and would finally serve for twenty-five years as bishop of Portland, Maine, until his death in 1900. In the little world of nineteenth-century American Catholicism, that career would surely mark him as "something."[2] The source of his self-description as an erstwhile nothing was his unusual family background: he was the son of a white Irish immigrant planter in Georgia and a woman who was at once his father's African-American slave and his wife. For James Healy, as for his eight equally remarkable siblings, it was the Catholic church, perhaps the least likely of allies, that helped overcome the penalties society would have exacted from persons of such unorthodox racial heritage. An examination of their lives suggests the need for a more nuanced understanding of race and for an appreciation of other powerful forces, including religion, in the shaping of personal identity.

The story of James Healy and his family is a picturesque tale that leads from backcountry Georgia to Civil War Boston to Reconstruction Washington, D.C., to the political and religious turmoil of Rome in the 1870s, and even to the icy waters of the Arctic Ocean. It is not sheer romance, however, that attracts our attention to the Healys. Rather, an attempt to understand them brings us face to face with the central enduring dilemma of the American experience: the dilemma of race. For, in racial terms, who and what were the Healys? In a society, then as now, in which it seemed essential to be able to answer that question, their answer was anything but clear. Were they white? Were they black? Were they "mulattoes," a word susceptible of all sorts of imprecise meanings, many of them derogatory? Was their identity fixed by birth, or could they play a role in deciding it for themselves? How did one know what they were? Could one tell by looking at them, and what if one could not? That they faced these questions through the span of the nineteenth century, shattered across its center by the Civil War, compounded the problem. In the years before the war, the twisted logic of slavery depended on the maintenance of clear racial divisions or it depended on nothing; even slavery's stoutest defenders knew that. Slaves were black, they maintained, and blacks were slaves. If nuances were permissible, nothing about the peculiar institution could be sure. In the years after the war, as Jim Crow legislation took hold in the South and strict racial codes solidified North and South, to be black was to be rendered inferior by definition and increasingly marginalized. In that context of slavery, discrimination, and violence, James Healy's view of himself as nothing represented perhaps the best he could hope for.

Moreover, the answer to the question "what were the Healys?" was one that contemporaries thought had in fact, had to have a clear, unambiguous, even scientific answer. What one was depended on one's blood. What ran through one's veins and from whom it had come determined who one was, and that biological fact was immutable. Blood might be diluted, but its essence could not be altered. Culture, history, and science all seemed to prove that race was an essential fact of nature. As Winthrop Jordan, George Frederickson, and others have shown, by the nineteenth century both learned and popular American opinion agreed that the question of racial identity was really a simple one. Adhering to what came to be called the "one-drop rule," a single drop of ancestral Negro blood was considered sufficient to define one as a Negro. Given the right combination of unusual circumstances, some black people might break through the class barriers that white Americans thought the necessary concomitants of blackness, but their inner nature was thought to be unchangeable. They were simply exceptions that proved the rule. Given light enough complexions, some might even be able to deceive others, to "pass" as something they were not, but their inner reality would in the end, most thought, be exposed, leaving behind debilitating psychic scars in the process.[3]

Such theories of clear racial dividing lines always had difficulty explaining persons of mixed heritage. In the first place, the very existence of such people was visible proof that a powerful taboo, that proscribing interracial sexual contact, had been violated—and not just occasionally, but persistently. While early colonial attitudes may have been more tolerant of black-white sexual activity, American opinion had by the nineteenth century solidified into a uniform denunciation of so explicit a challenge to the orderliness of domestic racial arrangements. Though the extent of "miscegenation"—a mocking word, coined in the heat of the presidential campaign of 1864— was unknown at the time and has been debated by historians and sociologists since, fear of it was everywhere. The exploitation of black female slaves by their white male masters was condemned in theory while tolerated in practice, but the prospect of sexual relations between black men and white women was too shocking for most to contemplate. Antebellum Southerners and other Americans decried racial "amalgamation," legislated against it, and hid the evidence of it as much as possible, but it remained a dirty little secret that everyone knew.[4]

And what of the offspring of this racially subversive practice? What was their nature, and what place could there be for them in American society? Denoted by a bewildering variety of terms ("quadroon," "octoroon," and many others) that tried to specify more precisely than was possible the exact degree of racial mixture, American mulattoes were the objects of morbid fascination and constant speculation. At first, most white Americans were disposed to think them superior to full-blooded blacks; after all, they had some white blood in them, and that had to have an upward, civilizing effect. By the middle of the nineteenth century, however, the opposite view had come to seem more persuasive: blackness corrupted more powerfully than whiteness improved, and the result was a downward spiral for those of mixed race. Popular science concluded that mulattoes were biologically weak, morally corrupt, psychologically troubled, and even incapable of reproduction, just like the animals (mules) from which the word derived. Before the Civil War, some evidence suggests, whites had favored lighter-skinned mulattoes for being "less black," but after the war such distinctions among African Americans mattered less and less to the white community. In contrast to other countries, the United States produced no distinct interracial social class, and American mulattoes remained an anomaly.[5]

The absence of a clearly defined place for mulattoes in society inevitably reinforced another fear: that some of them had found a way to violate the American racial code, successfully pretending to be white instead of black. Black and mulatto passing as white was taken not only as a contravention of the natural order; it was also a sin made more grave by the deception that lay at its core and the nagging suspicion that inferiors were putting something over on their betters. The apprehension that a person one knew, a man one's daughter might literally marry, would turn out to be black instead of white was a haunting one. Anecdotal evidence, supported by later sociological studies, recognized that passing could take a variety of forms. Sometimes it might be inadvertent, as whites simply assumed a light-skinned black to be "one of their own." Occasionally, intentional passing might be opportunistic, as those with fairer complexions used that genetic accident to secure better jobs or to enjoy public accommodations otherwise reserved to whites. For this reason, whites often supposed that all blacks would pass if they could get away with it. Most serious of all was permanent passing since, if successful, it implied that the racial classifications on which so much seemed to depend had no real meaning at all.[6]

Whites consoled themselves, however, with the belief that passing always exacted a terrible price. If all African Americans had to live with the double consciousness that W. E. B. Du Bois described, the pressure toward what Du Bois called "self-questioning, self-disparagement, and lowering of ideals" was felt all the more forcefully by those of mixed heritage. A mulatto seemed quintessentially to be a "marginal man" of the kind described by Everett Stonequist, and the tensions of life on the margins were only heightened when some mulattoes crossed over to where they were thought not to belong. Though passing was not uncommon, Stonequist argued in his highly influential study in 1937, "bitter frustration and mental conflict" were its unavoidable fruits, making it "a doubtful form of adjustment." Only a few scholars dissented from this conclusion, and the idea lodged in popular belief that no one could ever pass permanently and be, at the same time, stable and well adjusted. In literature, passers were usually depicted as mercurial, unhappy, and destined for a bad end. The murderously inclined Joe Christmas wanders through Faulkner's *Light in August* (1932), unable to know who he really is, and Clare Kendry, a seemingly happy-go-lucky society woman in Nella Larsen's *Passing* (1929), throws herself out a window when her racial deception is revealed. The light-skinned narrator of James Weldon Johnson's *Autobiography of an Ex-Coloured Man* (1927) watches helplessly as a man is lynched and then feels himself turning black under the gaze of his white fiancé when he tells her his secret.[7] Better that one knew one's place and kept to it, these views agreed, than to try to be something one was not. If nature had made one black, even by the presence of only "one drop," better to accept that fact and its consequences than to struggle vainly against them.

Today, scholars in several disciplines have come to view race not as a natural category but largely as a social and intellectual construction. The meanings we assign to racial differences, like those we assign to gender differences, are rooted not in biology but elsewhere. Racial ideas may derive from the perception of physical distinctions, but those ideas are better understood as an assemblage of attitudes, science and quasi-science, class interest, outright prejudice, and other factors. Identity depends as much on consent as on descent, in Werner Sollors's now famous pairing: ethnicity and race are as much conditions which one achieves as conditions with which one is born. Physical appearance matters, Barbara Fields has argued, but only because of the historical and ideological context that assigns meaning to what we see. The popular language of race and ethnicity as hereditary things, determined once and for all by blood, has proved remarkably durable, but the social production of identity (by ourselves and others) is now seen as more significant than any essentialist view in which biology is destiny. Group boundary lines are more fluid than we often suppose, and individuals may have more of a role in choosing their identity than earlier racial theories thought possible. A number of case studies have shown this process at work: the so-called Colored Creoles of Louisiana, who evolved a complex interracial community, and the northern Cape Verdean immigrants, who lived on the borderline "between race and ethnicity," offer examples of groups in which racial selections were made from several available options. Even whiteness is constructed, Ruth Frankenberg and others have argued, correcting the unconscious assumption that somehow only blackness had to be explained. An active if not always conscious process of "race formation," supported in countless unfelt "everyday" ways, is at work in human society rather than the operation of immutable laws of nature.[8]

In trying to sort out these and other aspects of the dilemma of race in America, the Healy family offers not just a good story but an important challenge to the assumption that racial categories are fixed and unchanging. Just as important, the Healys illuminate the means by which choices of racial identity may be made. If society has defined you as black, it will not easily permit you to declare yourself white; the transit across the racial boundary will be difficult, if not impossible, without mitigating factors and intervening institutions. In any given case, these may derive from particular circumstances, and we need to know more about the operation of those circumstances. How one comes to understand the racial options that are available, how one determines which of these are more likely to prove successful than others, how one selects among them, and how one uses societal structures and personal opportunities are all critical decision points.

What is more, James Healy and his siblings reward study because the answers they gave to the questions of identity may seem surprising, or even disappointing, to us. Where they are remembered today, it is as African Americans: several of them are celebrated as the "first black" achiever in their field.[9] They themselves, however, recoiled from such an identification. All the rules of law and custom in their society demanded that race be their only identity, but they resisted such a conclusion, choosing instead to find something else to be. The historical literature has given us some portraits of blacks who could have passed but did not; we know very little, however, about those who made the opposite choice. For the Healy family, race was not a given, biological or otherwise, but a series of decisions that they made. They sought other bases for self-definition.

Primary among these alternatives for most of them was religion, and the choice is both expected and unexpected. During slavery and afterwards, religion offered African Americans an important source of cultural self-expression and a measure of independence from white dominance. We should not, therefore, find it unusual that religious identity provided the Healy family with a way around the uncertainties of their background. For most of their black contemporaries, however, the religions of choice were various forms of American Protestantism. The Healys took another path. When the young college student had to find a polar opposite to his "nothing"-ness, it is significant that what he chose to say was that he was a Catholic. Only a few years later, Frederick Douglass would describe his own transition in similar, though more secular, terms: "I was nothing before," Douglass remembered of his successful fight with a slave-breaker, "I was a man now."[10] For James Healy, the newly achieved status was not free, autonomous manhood but Catholicism, and he acted on that choice by pursuing a life in religion. That five of his brothers and sisters made the same decision presents us with a weight of evidence that demands exploration. By choosing this religious identity, they were also able to confirm a second and more difficult choice: to be white instead of black. Thus, the history of the Healy family illuminates the interplay of race and religion in American life.

The story of the Healys is long and full of vivid detail, but it may be briefly told. Michael Morris Healy was born in County Galway, Ireland, in 1796 and immigrated to America through the port of New York in 1815. Settling in Georgia three years later, he arrived just in time to participate in the land lotteries that were redistributing to white settlers' lands recently dispossessed from the Cherokees, the Creeks, and other tribes. He eventually owned 1,500 acres in Jones County, just across the Ocmulgee River from the market town of Macon, in the heart of what became cotton country. There he prospered: at his death more than thirty years later he owned forty-nine slaves. The average owner in the county had only fourteen; in Macon's Bibb County, the average was eight. Possession of that many chattels ranked him number 18 among the 453 slaveowners in Jones County; his land holdings placed him at number 36 of the 412 property owners there.[11]

At some point in the late 1820s, Michael Healy acquired a slave named Eliza Clark, who has since then always been described as a mulatto. Like most slaves, her immediate origins were not considered important enough to record anywhere, though there were later suggestions that at least one of her parents had been a refugee from the turmoil in Haiti during the 1790s. We know, of course, that it was not uncommon for owners to establish long-term sexual unions with their slaves and to father children by them, and this Michael Healy did with Eliza Clark. What was unusual in their case was that neither of them ever married anyone else and that they lived faithfully together until their deaths within a few months of each other in 1850. Only the rudeness of Jones County, still very much on the frontier, permitted an arrangement so contrary to convention. Georgia law made it impossible for this "marriage" ever to be sanctioned by the state and, as there were few churches in the area, no religious ceremony was ever provided either. Nor could Michael Healy grant Eliza Clark her freedom, for manumission had by then been restricted to exceptional cases and could be done only by special act of the state legislature. Notwithstanding these legal obstacles—not to mention the cultural horror that decried racial amalgamation—the two were husband and wife in everything but law.[12]

Ten children were born to this couple with clockwork regularity, and eight of these lived to adulthood. They did so in the North, for in Georgia as everywhere in the South, children took the condition of their mother: a mother's slavery made her children slaves too. Michael Healy could not legally emancipate them any more than he could his wife, so instead he followed what appears to have been a deliberate plan of removing them from conditions in which their enslavement was always a possibility. Local tradition told a story that he once turned his dogs on neighbors who suggested that he sell his own sons. He might not entertain that notion, but the prospect of it would, he knew, become dangerously real once he was no longer alive to protect them. Thus, as each of the children reached school age, Michael Healy sent them north into freedom; at the time of his death in August 1850, three months after the death of his wife, he himself was apparently planning to liquidate his holdings in Georgia and join them there.[13]

In the North they managed to achieve a level of security and success that would have been impossible for them at home. Hugh Clark Healy (1832–1853), the next oldest boy to James, attended Holy Cross with his brother and was later setting himself up in business in New York City when he died in a freak boating accident at the age of twenty. Patrick Francis (1834–1910) joined the Society of Jesus after his graduation from Holy Cross, studied at the best universities of Europe, and returned to America, where he eventually became the president of Georgetown University. Alexander Sherwood (1836–1875) also chose a career in the priesthood, studied music and canon law in Rome, was made rector of the Catholic cathedral in Boston, and seemed destined like James for the episcopacy before chronic ill health ended his life just shy of his fortieth birthday.

The oldest sister, Martha Ann (1838–1920), spent time as a novice in a community of French-speaking nuns in Montreal, but she left the order, married, and settled into a life of middle-class respectability in suburban Boston. Michael Augustine (1839–1904) was more volatile than his religiously inclined brothers. He kept running away from whatever school he was in, but during the 1860s he managed to find himself by enlisting in the Revenue Cutter Service, the nineteenth-century precursor to the Coast Guard. Rising to the rank of captain, he earned fame as commander of the great ice ship Bear, which enforced law and order off the coast of Alaska in the 1880s and 1890s. A baby named Eugene (1842) who died in infancy was followed by two more girls, both of whom persevered in the religious life their older sister had only sampled. Amanda Josephine (1845–1879) spent her short adulthood as a nursing sister of the Hospitallers of Saint Joseph in Montreal, while Eliza

Dunamore (1846–1919) joined the Congregation of Notre Dame, also in Montreal. In that order she achieved a prominence comparable to that of her brothers, serving as superior of several convents attached to the schools that the sisters maintained in Canada and the United States. Only the youngest, a second Eugene (1849–1914), seemed to fail, drifting from job to job, always asking his brothers for money, and occasionally landing in jail.

The mixed racial origins that their society took as natural obstacles to success obviously did not stand in the way of this group of brothers and sisters. Opposition may even have been a spur to achievement, for they look like nothing so much as classic overachievers, compensating for disadvantage with unremitting effort and a resolve to beat society at its own game. But how did they confront the enduring questions of who and what they were? What was it like for them, in Du Bois's well-known phrase, to be a problem? What identities did they construct from the disparate elements available, and what tensions did that process create? The evidence, assembled from more than a dozen archives around the country, permits some preliminary conclusions.

However much they might wish it so, the matter of race could not be avoided, for it was all around them in American life. Their constant pattern, however, was to separate themselves from African Americans, refusing to identify with them. Elsewhere in his student diary, for example, James repeated with neither commentary nor outrage the offhand stories of fellow students, many of them, like himself, the sons of slave owning parents in the South, about the "niggers" on the farms at home. The word came to him easily, even though it was uncommon usage among upper-class planters before the war and to resort to it carried lower-class connotations. He mimicked supposed Negro dialect with no indication that he thought it peculiar to do so. He and several classmates celebrated their graduation from Holy Cross by walking into town on the evening after their commencement to attend a blackface minstrel show starring the famous Ethiopian Serenaders, the foremost troupe of their day, who had played the White House and were just back from a tour of Great Britain. Though "there was too much noise" in the performance, he noted with more critical hauteur than the occasion called for, and "the words were not pronounced distinctly enough always to be understood," he admitted that he "laughed a great deal." So deliberately had he separated himself from the black part of his heritage, so comfortable was he with the choice of a white identity, that he found nothing remarkable either in the availability of racially charged entertainment or in his own enjoyment of it on what may accurately be described as the most important night of his life so far. He gave no thought to the possibility that the racial group being lampooned on the stage might include himself.[14]

Nor did he have any particular sympathy for abolitionists like William Lloyd Garrison, whom he dismissed as "a fool." He was delighted that a Garrison rally in Worcester, seeking to raise money for the purchase of a slave from the South, had managed to collect only $1.37.[15] Hostility toward abolitionists was, of course, normal respectable political opinion during the 1840s and 1850s, held by Northerners and Southerners alike, but the ironies of James Healy's stance toward slavery were more pointed. His own mother was legally a slave and technically so was he: should he ever return to Georgia—he never did—the law demanded that he be apprehended and sold. That possibility made him no more disposed to sympathize with slaves or those agitating for their emancipation.

More important, the profits from slavery had become essential to the well-being and advancement of his family. The successful cotton plantation in central Georgia depended on slaves, and the revenues from it continued even after his father's death, by which time James was a student at the Grand Seminaire in Montreal and the rest of the children were safely north of the Mason-Dixon Line. The land and personal property of Michael Healy were auctioned off immediately, but, in line with the common practice, his nearly fifty slaves were hired out to neighboring farms. The cash they generated—about $1,500 per year between 1851 and 1853—was sent to a trustee in New York City, who managed it for the surviving children. When most of the slaves were finally sold off in 1854 and 1855, they brought in just under $34,000, the rough equivalent of half a million dollars today. (The sale represented a tidy appreciation in value, for the executors had appraised the slaves at only $22,000.) This impressive sum, too, was invested in New York, where it became the foundation for the financial security of the family for the rest of their lives. Even more achingly ironic, acting on behalf of James and his siblings, the executors went to court in January 1856 to contest the suit of one of their slaves, a woman named Margaret, for her freedom. They won the case, and Margaret was immediately sold, together with three of her children, each of them to a different master, yielding an additional profit of $3,000.[16]

Neither free black nor absentee ownership of slaves was unknown in the antebellum South. These phenomena tended to concentrate in the lower South and in major urban centers throughout the region, such as New Orleans, Charleston, and Baltimore, but they could be found almost everywhere. The pioneer black historian Carter Woodson counted more than sixty free black slaveowners in Georgia in 1830, for instance, and more than three hundred absentee owners of Georgia slaves. More recent scholars, too, have identified significant instances in which free blacks and mulattoes used the ownership of slaves to secure their own tenuous positions in society. Embracing white values, free blacks who owned slaves sent an important message to the dominant white community, reassuring it that, while they violated the expected equation of blackness with slavery, they did not offer a more generalized challenge to the racial structure of the South. Adele Logan Alexander has described the interracial family of Nathan and Susan Hunt Sayre, who lived in Sparta, Georgia, only two counties away from Michael and Eliza Healy. Nathan Sayre even constructed their house in such a way that he could appear to be living the life of a respectable white bachelor while still providing for his African-American wife and their children. Susan Hunt Sayre supervised the household's slaves, who probably included half-brothers and sisters of her own children. Michael Johnson and James Roark, recounting the life of William Ellison, a manumitted slave in South Carolina, have suggested that mulattoes like him found it easy to justify slave ownership. Sharing the widespread contemporary opinion that, through the intermixture of white blood, mulattoes were morally superior to full-blooded blacks, they could look on slavery as the same benign, patronizing work of civilization as white slaveowners. In this way, Ellison could "broadcast his orthodoxy," satisfying whites that he, like them, was "motivated by safe, mundane, and thoroughly acceptable acquisitive instincts."[17] So it was, apparently, with the Healys.

In later life, formed successively in the conservative opinions of a priest, diocesan chancellor, and bishop, James Healy found no more commonality with blacks than he had as a young man. Generally supportive of the Union during the Civil War, he looked with a jaundiced eye on Radical Republican plans for Reconstruction. Shocked like most of the nation by the assassination of Lincoln, he worried that congressional overreaching would impede restoration of national harmony in the name of "the protection, the equalization + the super-elevation of the negro." For him, "the negro" was obviously someone else, and the "super-elevation" (the unusual word itself rings of skepticism and contempt) of that other was a dubious political and social goal. Once in Portland, he still found little reason to associate himself with the interests of African Americans. He served briefly on the committee of the American Catholic hierarchy that oversaw the so-called Negro and Indian Missions, but he put more emphasis on the latter half of that combination. Stepping down in 1892 after only a short tenure, he suggested that he be replaced by a bishop from the West, who presumably would have more interest in those he took to be the real objects of the effort.[18]

Similarly, he rejected the offer of a black seminarian from Ohio who sought admission to parish work in the Portland diocese in 1890, explaining that there were so few black Catholics in Maine "that it would be idle for me to think of adopting you as a subject."[19] The young man's request indicates that Healy was well enough known, at least within church circles, to be partly of African-American heritage. Seminarians were ordinarily prepared for service in the places where they had been born; there would have been no reason for this one to apply to a bishop so far from home if he did not think that, as a "fellow black," Healy might have been particularly sympathetic to him. The opposite proved to be the case. Apart from Healy's apparent assumption that a black priest could serve only in a black congregation—had he consulted his own experience of parish work in Boston, he would have known that this was not necessarily the case—his response underlines his unwillingness to be identified with the religious needs of blacks in post–Civil War America.

Other members of the family also had to address the question of race, and like James they showed no desire to identify themselves as black. Throughout his academic career, Patrick Healy did little to discourage student rumors that he may have had some "Spanish blood," a conveniently vague explanation for his appearance, which was still white enough so that his passport described his complexion as "light." Such descriptions were always notoriously imprecise: they depended entirely on what a particular passport agent saw (or thought he saw) when he looked at the applicant. Passport descriptions often employed an extensive vocabulary for designating blacks and mulattoes "yellow," "copper," "high brown," "blue," and many other terms, but none of those was used in this case. The description of Patrick as light would thus seem to indicate that he was taken as a light-skinned white man, not a light-skinned black man; if he were the latter, some other word would probably have been used. That identification was consistent throughout his life and is confirmed by surviving photographs. It would have been virtually impossible, for instance, for him to serve as president of Georgetown from 1873 to 1882—at that time, the school still depended for its enrollment largely on the sons of Southern Catholic parents—were the details of his family widely known.[20]

Most of his fellow Jesuits had known the whole story from the beginning but, contrary to what we might expect of them, they chose not to let it matter. No more eager in theory than other white Americans to grant public opportunities to blacks, they were privately willing to make exceptions when presented with this particular case. When Patrick traveled from Holy Cross to Georgetown in the fall of 1850 to become a Jesuit novice, one of his former teachers wrote a colleague there of the "family difficulties" in the case but recommended acceptance of the young man anyway. Patrick himself worried that "my irregularities" would tarnish the good name of the Jesuits. The real "difficulties" in question were canonical, deriving as much from the fact that his parents had never been legally married as from the interracial nature of their union. Under a strict construction of the canon law, his parents' non-marriage rendered him illegitimate and, without formal dispensation, that constituted a barrier to ordination to the priesthood. No such dispensation was ever sought, and thus it seems that the Jesuits simply agreed to look the other way on the matter.[21]

Back at Holy Cross a few years later, now as a teacher, Patrick had a brief personal encounter with racial animosity. Though generally content at his alma mater and fond of his pupils, he confessed to a Jesuit mentor that he sometimes had trouble in supervising "boys who were well acquainted either by sight or hearsay with me + my brothers." As a result, "remarks are sometimes made (though not in my hearing) which wound my very heart. You know what I refer," he added, reluctant to commit his secret to paper. This had only happened once, however, allowing him to hope "that all this will wear away" as time brought newer students who did not know his family.[22] Later on, Patrick found that, like James, he could look on blacks as "other." Crossing the Isthmus of Panama on his way to California during a generally unsuccessful fundraising tour for Georgetown in 1878, he recorded a few brief observations about the natives he encountered. Dismissing the Indians as "pagans" and objectifying blacks as his brother had, Patrick noted that some of "the negroes" were "intelligent" and even "able to read and write"; others were simply "lazy." That he was not one of them was happily reinforced farther up the Mexican coast when he was approached on the streets of Mazatlan by a fellow American who, he said, "detected my Irish accent."[23] The phrase says as much about how Patrick Healy saw himself as it does about how this new acquaintance perceived him. His father may have retained some of the brogue of his homeland, but Patrick had grown up in Georgia, Massachusetts, Maryland, and Europe. Just what sort of accent emerged from that widely traveled life cannot now be known, but it was unlikely to have been accurately characterized as "Irish." It mattered little. Being Irish in nineteenth-century America was not without problems of its own, but for Patrick Healy and his family it was certainly better than the alternative.

Sherwood, too, had to confront the problem of race, and his difficulties were more serious because, in comparison to his siblings, he had the darkest skin and the most evident negroid features. Unlike his "light" brother, Sherwood was described on his passport as having a "dark" complexion.[24] Given his appearance, there was little chance that he could pass as readily as his brothers, and this was apparent from the beginning of his career. Leaving Holy Cross before graduation, he pursued seminary studies and eventually a doctorate in canon law in Montreal, Rome, and Paris; he was ordained amid the splendor of Notre Dame Cathedral in 1858. This made him far better educated than the average Roman Catholic priest in America at the time, but that education only prepared him for a prominence that could be impeded by the color of his skin. When the bishops of the United States prepared to open a seminary in Rome specifically for the purpose of training a domestic clergy, Sherwood Healy's name came up in the discussion of candidates for its rectorship. Boston's Bishop John Fitzpatrick, a friend and genuine promoter of the Healy brothers' interests, thought Sherwood "admirably qualified" for the job, but even he acknowledged a problem. "It would be useless to recommend him," Fitzpatrick told New York's Archbishop John Hughes in 1859, noting Healy's relative youth. "There is also another objection," Fitzpatrick went on, "which, although in reason less substantial, would in fact be quite as stubborn. He has African blood, and it shews distinctly in his exterior." With the American boys, some of them from southern and border states, who would be students at the Roman college, the bishop feared that this "stubborn" reason would "lessen the respect they ought to feel for the first superior in a house."[25] A man with African blood might make his way in American society on the eve of the Civil War, but only if it did not "shew" too "distinctly."

Sherwood himself expressed a preference not to return to America at all—"for reasons I cannot condemn," Fitzpatrick told an official at Rome—but he did so, joining the faculty of a newly opened seminary at Troy, New York. Amid sometimes primitive living conditions he taught theology and church law, and he drilled his unpromising and mostly unwilling students in the intricacies of Gregorian chant. He even took a progressively responsible part behind the scenes in managing the shaky finances of the place, an expanded role in which Fitzpatrick urged him to "be cautious + slow."[26] This injunction toward caution, delivered orally, was recorded in the official diary that Boston's bishops kept of their activities. In fact, responsibility for actually writing the diary entries had by then fallen to Fitzpatrick's chancellor and secretary: James A. Healy. Given his own experience, James could readily second the bishop's concern that his brother not attract undue attention to himself.

Returning to Boston from Troy in 1866, Sherwood flowered under the patronage of a new bishop, John J. Williams. Named rector of the cathedral parish, he oversaw construction of a huge new church building for it, tending both to fundraising and to the supervision of the workmen. His canonical expertise also made him indispensable on a wider church stage: he and Williams attended a general council of the American hierarchy at Baltimore in 1866, and Williams also took him to Rome as an adviser during the First Vatican Council, which formally proclaimed the doctrine of papal infallibility, in 1869–1870. Episcopal patronage and his education acted as shields against what his brother Patrick had once called "useless questions" about Sherwood's origins. The aristocratic bearing he seems to have cultivated was also helpful. Father Hilary Tucker, an often-grumpy curate who served in the cathedral parish, complained that Sherwood had "too much of an opinion of himself," and acted as though he had been "ordained priest sub tit[ulo] patrimonii." Use of the latter phrase is very significant: it was a reference to the European practice whereby rich young men could be ordained outside the normal channels because of their family's wealth.[27] Sherwood might not have been able to pass as a white man like his supposedly Irish-accented brother, but with his siblings he shared a substantial financial patrimony. That allowed him to transcend the class boundaries which, most Americans thought, kept blacks inevitably inferior and to fill instead a public role that would otherwise have been closed to him.

For Capt. Michael Healy, one of only three of the surviving siblings who chose not to enter the religious life, the problem of race was less acute. To begin with, work on the sea offered unusual opportunities for African Americans throughout the nineteenth century: aboard ship, raw ability and level-headedness in a crisis simply mattered more than skin color. Beyond that, the captain had several advantages: a light complexion, a white wife who frequently accompanied him on his voyages, and an Irish family name which seemed to confirm the other two factors in identifying him as white. Thus, he was able to pass completely and permanently. The surviving documentation from his forty-year career in the Revenue Cutter Service indicates that most of those he came into contact with were unaware of his racial background. The evidence for this is largely negative but nonetheless clear. Nowhere does anyone, friend or foe (and his brusque, no-nonsense approach to law enforcement in Alaska made him controversial enough to have many foes), ever refer to him as being black or of mixed heritage. Two incidents from the 1890s are particularly telling. Healy was tried by court martial twice during his career for harsh treatment of his men—acquitted once, convicted once—and witnesses at the trials described the heated exchanges that had provoked the captain's severity. In the manner of sailors everywhere, the language was rough and direct, though it seems tame to modern ears. On one occasion a seaman refused a direct order, insulting Healy by calling him a "son of a bitch"; a few years later, a mutinous subordinate sneered that the captain was nothing but "a God damned Irishman."[28] Assuming that these sailors were blurting out the worst thing they could think of in the heat of the moment, the absence of racial insult is striking: Healy was a "son of a bitch," not a "black son of a bitch"; he was a "God damned Irishman," not a "God damned nigger."

Like his brothers, Captain Healy demonstrated that his own identification was with the white community. In his view, there were only two kinds of people in Alaska: "natives" and "white men." He used the latter term to denote anyone who was not a native, including himself. As an officer of the government who combined the duties of customs agent, rescue organizer, policeman, and judge, he knew that his official responsibility was primarily to the interests of the white settlers of the vast land. He worried that small parties

of whites, whom he referred to as "our people," might be subject to depreda-
tion by the native groups. "It is true," he wrote an official in Washington, that
so long as his ship was nearby "the Natives are . . . gentle and peaceful; but I
believe they would not hesitate to take advantage of a small number of white
men" in isolated camps. More often, however, his concern ran in the other
direction. The conduct of too many settlers had been "outrageous," he said;
"white men in this country . . . seem to think that the law was not intended
to apply to them, only to Indians. . . I try to convince them to the contrary."
For Michael Healy, there were whites and there were natives; like most of his
fellow citizens, he found no intermediate racial categories. He even passed
his racial identity to his son. When the teenager sailed into the Arctic Ocean
with his father in 1883 and set foot on a previously undiscovered island, he
proudly proclaimed himself the first "white boy" ever to do so.[29]

The evidence for elucidating the racial attitudes and self-perceptions of
the three Healy sisters is much more fragmentary than that for their brothers.
Very little documentation (in the form of letters or diaries) about them has
survived. Nor are there any extant photographs to support speculation about
the relative ease or difficulty they may have had in passing. The problem is
compounded because all of them were, for greater or lesser periods, members
of Catholic women's religious orders, in which the deliberate subordination
of individual personality to the collective identity of the community was
expected and enforced. In understanding them we must, therefore, work by
indirection and inference.

There were two communities of black Catholic nuns in the United States
at this time, the Oblate Sisters of Providence (Baltimore) and the Sisters of
the Holy Family (New Orleans), but the Healys never had any contact with
or interest in either of them. Nor did they seek admission to white American sisterhoods, which were less open to the idea of black members than
the Jesuits had proved to be with Patrick. Instead, they joined religious
orders that were not only all white but also foreign: in them, the normal
language of discourse and instruction was French. In 1855 Martha became
a novice in the Congregation de Notre Dame, a teaching order in whose
Villa Maria school in Montreal she and her two sisters were educated, but
she left it in 1863; two years later she married Joseph Cashman, a white store
clerk in Boston, with whom she had four children. Eliza joined that same
order in 1874 and remained a part of it until her death in 1919. Josephine
entered a nursing community, the Religious Hospitallers of Saint Joseph, in
1873 and contributed to their work at the Hotel Dieu in Montreal until her
death in 1879 at age thirty-four.[30] Canada had often served as a refuge for
blacks from the United States, but in this case it was family and religious
factors that were determinative. Both James and Sherwood had studied at a

seminary in Montreal, which happened to be adjacent to the property of the two women's communities. It was that physical proximity and the familiarity it provided that decided the choice of convents for the girls. No more than their brothers did these women think of themselves as African Americans: on Martha's death certificate in 1920, the space for her "color or race" bore the simple, unambiguous word "white."[31]

The career of Eliza Healy, known in her community as Sister Saint Mary Magdalen, shows that, like her clerical brothers, she chose for herself a religious, white identity. The Notre Dame congregation had been founded in Canada in the seventeenth century; by her day it taught young girls in parochial schools, mostly in Quebec and Ontario but increasingly in the United States as well. In addition to the Three Rs, the schools of the Notre Dame sisters stressed the refinement of their pupils. Music and drawing lessons were always offered, and drilling in ladylike penmanship was also emphasized. The nuns taught French to American working- and middle-class children, and English to French Canadians. They trained their charges in home economics, emphasizing not so much the practicalities of food preparation as the planning and execution of proper culinary events. The young ladies were instructed to devote as much time to writing the correct kind of invitations and planning the seating arrangements at table as to actual cooking.[32] This upper-class understanding of her role was apparently as congenial to Eliza Healy as it had been to her brother Sherwood. She held a succession of assignments in the order throughout the 1880s, negotiated with her brother James for the opening of a convent in the diocese of Portland, and served as the superior of four separate establishments, including fifteen years as administrator of a large convent in Vermont.[33] By throwing herself into this identity as a religious, irrespective of her race, she, like so many nuns in the nineteenth and twentieth centuries, had the chance to do what women outside the convent walls could do only with more difficulty: assume the leadership of large, complex institutions and shape a life of her own beyond the bonds of "true womanhood."

Eliza Healy's life as a professed religious sister draws our attention again to the choices she and her siblings made about who and what they would be. If only one or two of them had entered the religious life, we might attribute their decision to individual disposition alone, a choice with no larger or collective meaning. But five of the eight Healy children pursued religious careers; before taking the more conventional route of marriage and family, a sixth had also explored that option. Thus, religion, and Catholicism in particular, seems to have offered them a path through the complicated problem of identity, a path clearer than the alternatives.

There were other options to which they might have resorted. Identification of the Healys as Irish, for instance, would have been plausible enough given their surname. People who met them, like the expatriate who heard an Irish accent in Patrick's voice, often perceived them, especially those with light skin, as part of America's largest nineteenth-century immigrant population. Their religious vocations could reinforce this Irishness, since most contemporary Americans assumed (incorrectly) that all Irish were Catholics, and devout ones at that. James spent two weeks in Ireland in the summer of 1878 on his return from a trip to Rome and Paris, places that held greater attraction for him, but his Irish heritage appealed to him only up to a point. He had been scandalized to see nothing but whiskey featured in the Irish display at the Paris Exposition of that year—the American entries were not much better: "no taste in the arrangement," he sniffed—and he passed up the opportunity to kiss the Blarney Stone, satisfying whatever Celtic urges he felt by simply poking it with his umbrella. Still, at home he could sometimes take more interest in ethnic matters, writing to Boston's Irish-American mayor, Patrick Collins, from Portland in 1885, seeking aid in mediating a patronage squabble among Irish Democratic voters in Maine. Michael Healy, too, was often taken as an Irishman and not just by sailors interested in insulting him. He even joked to a longtime friend that his occasionally gruff manners were attributable to "my irish [*sic*] disposition," which he was always trying to control.[34]

Occasionally, the Healys might be identified primarily as southerners, especially since they lived their adult lives outside that region, making their origins sufficiently distinctive to attract attention. The first official notice taken of James by Boston's Bishop Fitzpatrick in 1849 had identified him simply as "James Healy of Georgia." The young man himself noted in his diary whenever classmates used certain "Yankee" expressions (as he called them) instead of the idioms he had brought with him from home. Later, living among the Yankees as a priest, he had apparently been on the receiving end of sectional suspicion often enough to warrant some defense of his origins, especially during and after the Civil War. Commenting on the widespread cries for vengeance after the assassination of Lincoln, he expressed a hope that "real southerners" would "clear themselves" of complicity in the crime by affirming their loyalty to the Union, thus putting the lie to a view of "all the South + Southerners as traitors." To those outside the South among whom the siblings lived, the precise geographical details could sometimes blur: the obituary for Eliza Healy, prepared by an officer of the Notre Dame sisters and circulated to their convents, identified her as coming from "a family of rich [and, by implication, white] planters in Texas."[35]

Neither of these alternative identities was as important to the Healys or as consistently applied by them as their Catholicism. On the face of things, it was an unlikely choice. The regular resurgence of anti-Catholic nativism in the nineteenth century meant that a deliberate decision to be a Catholic might represent for them at best a jump from the fire back into the frying pan. In the decade before the Healy brothers' arrival at Holy Cross, for example, a riot had destroyed the convent and school of the Ursuline Sisters at Charlestown, Massachusetts, and the leaders of the mob, identified at the scene by eyewitnesses, were acquitted at trial. In the 1850s, the state legislature authorized a "smelling committee" to sniff out the lurid details of sexual and other transgressions which, they were sure, were rampant at other convents in the state. Holy Cross itself was for twenty years unable to secure a legal charter from the state to grant academic degrees, partly on the grounds that the college was engaged in spreading the dangerous anti-republican ideas of popery. The Hotel Dieu in Montreal, where Josephine Healy was to spend her short adulthood tending the sick, had become a favorite setting for novels of nativist pornography: Maria Monk's gothic best-seller, *Awful Disclosures* (1836), was set there and offered fanciful but detailed floor plans of the secret chambers where wicked priests had their way with unsuspecting young nuns.[36]

More seriously, the record of the American Catholic church on questions of race was decidedly unimpressive. Patrick Healy's own Jesuit order owned slaves until the very outbreak of the Civil War, and slavery had its vigorous defenders among the Catholic clergy and laity until the very end. Papal statements had denounced the slave trade as early as the seventeenth century, but church leaders consistently found no incompatibility between religion and slave ownership. Two key figures in the American hierarchy gave explicit sanction to that moral distinction as a way of tolerating slavery itself. In the 1840s, Charleston's Bishop John England admitted that abuses of the slave system were always possible, but he echoed contemporary Protestant arguments that, so long as slaves were treated with "Christian principles," there was nothing wrong with the institution as such. Archbishop Martin Spalding of Baltimore sent the Vatican a long "dissertation" on the subject in 1863, pointedly assigning the blame for American slavery to "Protestant England" and arguing that African Americans were likely to become "miserable vagabonds, drunkards, and thieves" if freed; thus, they were better off as slaves. Lay Catholics shared these views. "We cannot alter the fact of negro inferiority," Orestes Brownson wrote in the middle of the war, and he expressed his hope that, once free, American blacks would simply "drift away" to Central and South America. He also remained certain that mulattoes were both "intellectually inferior to the white man" and unequal to blacks in brute animal strength. His own sons had been friends and college classmates of the Healy brothers, but Brownson did not on that account deviate from American racial orthodoxy.[37]

Officially, the church showed little more interest in African Americans after the Civil War than before it. With emancipation, the bishops paid lip service to the notion of helping American blacks, but real effort was lacking.

Assembled at Baltimore for two weeks in October 1866 for a national council, the hierarchy quickly dismissed a proposal from Rome that a special
bishop be appointed, one whose sole responsibility would be to evangelize
and assist freed slaves. Archbishop John McCloskey of New York flatly
rejected any suggestion that the American church as a whole had a duty
in this regard, saying that "in no way was the conscience of the bishops of
the North burdened in regard to the black." The council spoke nobly but
vaguely about the "new and most extensive field of charity" that the former
slaves presented, but it also expressed regret that "a more gradual system of
emancipation" had not been attempted. Sherwood Healy was present at this
council as an aide to Bishop Williams of Boston, but he was in no position
to influence the outcome of the deliberations even if he had wanted to. He
had himself once defended the proposition that "slavery is not an evil in se,"
and he acknowledged only the most general of responsibilities "to console
& civilize the negro." Twenty years later, his brother James, by then a bishop,
attended another meeting of the national hierarchy and raised no objection
to the policy of continuing effectively to ignore "the negro." On that occasion, another bishop had spoken patronizingly of the need to instill morality
in the former slaves, warning that it would be difficult to "make them honest
men, chaste women, obedient, [and] law-abiding citizens." Continuing what
had by then become his regular pattern of non-involvement with African
Americans, James Healy took no role in these discussions.[38]

That the Healys went along so readily and completely with their church's
failure to promote work on behalf of black Americans underscores the delib-
erateness with which they used Catholicism to separate themselves from that
part of their own heritage. Religion offered them an unexpected haven from
a self-definition that would have been predetermined for them by race alone.
How they came by that alternative depended, as many things do, on unusual
circumstances and even on luck. Michael Morris Healy may have been baptized a Catholic as a child in Ireland, but he lived as an unchurched backcountry planter in Georgia: there was no Catholic church in Macon until
late in his life, and he seems to have had nothing to do with it. His decision
to enroll his sons in a Catholic college far from home resulted not from any
denominational loyalty but, apparently, from a chance encounter he had with
Bishop Fitzpatrick on a steamer sailing between Washington and New York
in 1844.[39] His children's baptism into the Roman church, one after another
once they were out of Georgia, followed from this happenstance, and it was
in that church that most of them decided to make their way. The family's
financial security, of course, was critical. Without the wealth supplied initially by the slaves and the cotton plantation, they might never have had the
chance to define themselves as anything other than slaves or former slaves.

But, unexpectedly, Catholicism took them in. The church was traditional and conservative, unwilling to rock the nation's racial boat, but it also had leaders who could in private look the other way and accept these capable, if anomalous, siblings. At first, the Jesuits saw to the education of the boys, and they in turn looked after their sisters by placing them under religious instruction. The small social circle of Catholic Boston welcomed these exotic newcomers, perhaps because it was itself isolated in an otherwise cool social and religious climate. Feeling beset by hostile nativists, Boston's Catholics were disposed to embrace anyone who chose voluntarily to join them. James spent his school vacations living with the families of priests in Boston and Cambridge, and he celebrated Christmas of his senior year playing parlor games with a group that included Boston's bishop. Martha, coming north in 1848, boarded in the home of Bishop Fitzpatrick's sister. When the Healys proved themselves at ease in these closely-knit surroundings and eager to advance in them through vocational commitment, the mutual connection was reinforced. Conversion to the Roman church was a powerfully countercultural statement in nineteenth-century America, and the Healys' transition from "nothing" to Catholicism was perhaps a way of countering several different cultures all at once.[40]

They may even have found in this extended religious family a welcome substitute for—or at least a supplement to—their biological family. The siblings remained close throughout their lives, perhaps too much so: in 1863 Father Hilary Tucker complained that it was "very silly and undignified" for James Healy to allow his sisters "on almost every occasion . . . to kiss and fawn on him as they do." Worse, he was "perfectly blind with regard to his brother Eugene," only fourteen at the time, "who deserved twenty li[c]kings when he never got one." This affection notwithstanding, the large family of Catholicism exerted an even stronger hold on them, one that may have predominated over the ties of their natural parentage. In all the surviving documentation, James recorded but a single memory of his father (whom he called "Father"), a formulaic and probably apocryphal story of his being comforted as a child during a thunderstorm. Only once, when as a student he received a daguerreotype of her, did he ever refer to his mother and, interestingly, on that occasion he felt compelled to note that he even "recognised" her "after so long an absence from home." Knowledge of their parents' unusual marriage seems to have been kept from the children for as long as possible. Just after his mother's death in 1850, the short-lived Hugh Healy told a former professor that his younger siblings had at last been "informed of their situations in life." In marked contrast to this separation from their biological family, the brothers always opened their letters to Father George Fenwick, their teacher at Holy Cross and Patrick's patron among the Jesuits, with the salutation "Dear Dad."[41] A Catholic priest had become their only "Dad."

They responded to the reception that Catholicism gave them by internalizing religious sentiments and tying themselves closely to the church that had provided a place for them. Sherwood, for example, found in religion the only means to keep "pure from the defilement of a lower world," a phrase that resonates with fear of the "defilement" of interracial sexuality, the dread of which was all around him in society and in which he and his siblings may have shared.[42] We cannot reliably psychoanalyze the Healys from this historical distance, but their religion seems to have offered them escape from many forms of "defilement." Undertaking vocations as Catholic priests and nuns meant, of course, committing themselves to celibacy. Apart from the religious context in which they understood it, that deliberate turning away from sexual activity may have been appealing as a way to avoid altogether reenacting the cause of their racial dilemma, the problematic sexuality of their parents.

Only three of the surviving siblings married, each of them to a white spouse, and only two of those had children of their own, all of whom completed their parents' passage into the white community. These three who stayed "in the world" maintained varying degrees of commitment to religion. Martha lived the life of a conventional lay woman, attending mass at her parish church and seeing to the religious instruction of her children. Michael described himself as "not much of a Christian," but he supported Jesuit missionary work in Alaska and enrolled himself in a Catholic total abstinence society in an effort to control a recurring problem with drink. A hostile fellow officer in the Revenue Cutter Service, apparently sympathetic to the political nativism of the 1890s, had even told him, he reported, "that as a Catholic I had no place as an officer of the U. S. government"—another instance in which his racial identity, if known, would have provided both a clearer disqualification and a sharper insult. Eugene, who for a time made his way in life as a professional gambler, was the only sibling who seems to have remained largely apart from religion.[43]

To a greater or lesser extent, these three lacked the stability that the institutional church provided their vowed brothers and sisters. Martha, for instance, remained something of a cause for concern throughout her life: James criticized her as a spendthrift and for being unreliable. Michael was subject to moodiness and depression, especially when confined to shore for any length of time, and he even attempted suicide in 1900. Eugene proved to be nothing but trouble. In 1876 James visited Boston only to find him in jail—"left him there until repentance should come," he remarked coldly—and a few years later the bishop told his youngest brother that if he came to Maine a notice would be published in the newspapers disclaiming "any connection or responsibility" for him.[44] Intrafamily tensions are to be expected everywhere, and these should not be taken as support for the assertions of Stonequist and others that blacks who attempted to pass were destined for unhappiness. Still, among the Healys, those who identified closely with religion found more certainty and acceptance than those who did not. By attaching themselves to the intermediary institution of Catholicism, they clarified both the means for establishing themselves and the standards for what constituted success.

More specifically, their conversion was not to religious practice generally but to a particular denominational loyalty. Sherwood proclaimed his Catholicism "a badge, an ensign, a standard," dismissing all dissenters as merely "going back to the old paganism." James found Protestantism "hollow, unreal, and disjointed, . . . the merest shred of Christianity." Patrick, encountering a self-described Anglo-Catholic on a transatlantic voyage, found him "too sensible to be duped by the foolish arguments of Protestantism" but calmly told the man that he would go to hell if he did not "go the whole hog" and join the Roman church. During his episcopal career, James brought the convert's zeal to his view of religion. He aligned himself with the conservative wing of the American hierarchy, favoring the condemnation of labor unions as masonic "secret societies" and telling an official in Rome that Catholic liberals like James Gibbons and John Ireland were overly optimistic about the possibilities for reconciliation between their church and the American Way of Life.[45]

Though they defined their Catholicism in distinction to the other denominational options available, their choice of religious careers was sincere, at least insofar as we are able to judge individual motivation in such matters. Patrick approached his ordination in 1864 with some trepidation but a "solid conviction" that his calling was genuine. After the event, he felt like "a new man," and he attached particular emotional significance to a scriptural passage used in the ordination ceremony: "I no longer call you slaves but my friends."[46] The phrase probably meant something to every ordinand, evoking the imagery of leaving behind slavery to sin. For Patrick Healy, this transition would also have had a more literal meaning.

James was scrupulous in his religious observance as a student and in later life resorted increasingly to Marian devotion, declaring the apparitions at Lourdes "authentic + undoubted." Returning to Holy Cross in 1865 for an address, he proclaimed proudly that, in the sixteen years since his graduation, "I have never to my recollection delivered a discourse of any kind except as a mouth-piece of the Holy Church." He was, he had once admitted to a Jesuit mentor, "a poor outcast," placed "on a throne of glory" by his vocation; that made him "safe" from all challenges, personal or otherwise.[47] Even Josephine, about whom so little is known, threw herself wholeheartedly into the religious life. Entering the Hotel Dieu at twenty-eight, she rejected what her official memorialist remembered as a "natural independence and the delicate culture of his past"—this latter phrase an allusion to the family's wealth—in favor of a life of "more and more a perfect religious." Eliza (who, Josephine said, had had "a pretty hard struggle" in leaving home for the convent) was remembered with her community's highest compliment: a "distaste for the world" and "a desire to do something for God."[48]

Thus, Catholicism became the means for defining the selfhood of the Healy family, representing the decisive step in the formation and confirmation of their identity. The reasons not to be black in their society were perhaps so obvious as to need no elaboration, but the transition from black to white was difficult and risky at best. In other circumstances, those whom they encountered, particularly those who knew their background, might not have been as willing as they apparently were to let the Healys, in effect, get away with passing. In Catholicism, however, they managed to secure an intermediate position, something they could be and use in their transition from one race to another. Such a course was not supposed to be possible, for the question of race was understood to be settled by that unalterable matter of blood. Their racial identity, however, became a matter of their own choice.[49]

The attempt to find larger historical meaning in the Healys must also confront the problem of their exceptionality. By almost any measure, these were not typical people; they were so unlike their contemporaries that it might seem vain to look for any broadly applicable conclusions. We should not, however, dismiss them on this account. They offer a particular case of passing with which to test and revise the generalizations that have been made of that phenomenon. Perhaps passing was neither so difficult nor so personally costly as we have thought it. Perhaps, if other circumstances made the deception seem acceptable, whites were more willing to go along with passers than we have supposed. Moreover, their lives demonstrate the means by which racial choices are made and the important role of intermediate structures and identities such as religion in mitigating the predeterminative power we are disposed to assign to race alone. In finding a third "thing" to be—by their own decision, they were Catholics—they could at least partially escape the effects of the stark polarity of black and white.

Notes

1. Student Diary, Aug. 14, 1849, James A. Healy (JAH) Papers, Archives, College of the Holy Cross (ACHC).

2. The fullest account of Healy's life and career is Albert S. Foley, *Bishop Healy: Beloved Outcaste* (New York, 1954); see also William L. Lucey, *The Catholic Church in Maine* (Francestown, N.H., 1957), 209–242. Foley also published short biographical vignettes about James Healy and two of his brothers in *God's Men of Color: The Colored Priests of the United States, 1854–1954* (New York, 1955).

3. The classic studies of white American perceptions of the nature of black people are Winthrop D. Jordan, *White Over Black: American Attitudes Toward the Negro, 1550–1812* (Chapel Hill, 1968), and George M. Frederickson, *The Black Image in the White Mind: The Debate on Afro-American Character and Destiny, 1817–1914* (New York, 1971). See also Thomas F. Gossett, *Race: The History of an Idea in America* (New York, 1965).

4. For American attitudes toward interracial sexuality, see Jordan, *White Over Black*, 145–147 and 469–470; Catherine Clinton, *The Plantation Mistress: Woman's World in the Old South* (New York, 1982), 204–214; David H. Fowler, *Northern Attitudes Towards Interracial Marriage: Legislation and Public Opinion in the Middle Atlantic and the States of the Old Northwest, 1780–1930* (New York, 1987); and John D'Emilio and Estelle B. Freedman, *Intimate Matters: A History of Sexuality in America* (New York, 1988), 101–104. On the powerful fear of "amalgamation," especially that involving white women, see Peggy Pascoe, "Race, Gender, and Intercultural Relations," *Frontiers 12* (1991):5–18. The origins of the word "miscegenation" are described in Julius M. Bloch's curious but still useful *Miscegenation, Melaleukation, and Mr. Lincoln's Dog* (New York, 1958).

5. The fullest study of American mulattoes is Joel Williamson, *New People: Miscegenation and Mulattoes in the United States* (New York, 1980). See also Winthrop D. Jordan, "American Chiaroscuro: The Status and Definition of Mulattoes in the British Colonies," *William and Mary Quarterly* 3d ser., i9 (1962):183~200; John G. Mencke, "Mulattoes and Race Mixture: American Attitudes and Images from Reconstruction to World War I" (Ph.D. diss., Univ. of North Carolina, 1978); Leonard R. Lempel, "The Mulatto in United States Race Relations: Changing Status and Attitudes, 1800–1940" (Ph.D. diss., Syracuse Univ., 1979); and Patricia Morton, "From Invisible Men to 'New People': The Recent Discovery of American Mulattoes," *Phylon 46* (1985): 106–122. The perceived connections between interracial sexual activity and class are discussed in Donald L. Horowitz, "Color Differentiation in the American System of Slavery," *Journal of Interdisciplinary History* 3 (1973):519–541. Carl Degler, *Neither Black Nor White: Slavery and Race Relations in Brazil and the United States* (New York, 1971), offers an important comparative study on the position of persons of mixed heritage. For a glossary of the complicated language of interracial identification, see Salme Pekkala, et al., "Some Words and Terms Designating, or Relating to, Racially Mixed Persons or Groups," *Race: Individual and collective behavior*, ed. Edgar T. Thompson and Everett C. Hughes (Glencoe, Ill., 1958), 52–57.

6. For a general discussion of passing, see Williamson, *New People*, 101–106; and Paul R. Spickard, *Mixed Blood: Intermarriage and Ethnic Identity in Twentieth-Century America* (Madison, 1989), 335–336. Edward Reuter's 1918 study, *The Mulatto in the United States*, a dissertation bearing many of the racial attitudes of its time but not published until 50 years later, expresses the common belief that all blacks would pass if they could: *Mulatto in the United States* (New York, 1969), 315. Among the sociological attempts, all of them containing a degree of methodological uncertainty, to measure the extent of this phenomenon are: Louis Wirth and Herbert Goldhamer, "The Hybrid and the Problem of Miscegenation," *Characteristics of the American Negro*, ed. Otto Klineberg (New York, 1944); John H. Burma, "The Measurement of Negro 'Passing,'" *American Journal of Sociology* 52 (1946):18–22; James E. Conyers and T.H. Kennedy, "Negro Passing: To Pass or Not to Pass," *Phylon 24* (1963):215–223.

7. W.E.B. Du Bois, *The Souls of Black Folk* (New York, 1990; orig. pub. 1903), 13; Everett V. Stonequist, *The Marginal Man: A Study in Personality and Culture Conflict* (New York, 1937), 112, 194; Spickard, *Mixed Blood*, 336–337. Wirth and Goldhamer in "The Hybrid and Miscegenation," 317, run counter to this scholarly consensus, arguing that passers can indeed be well adjusted, but theirs was a distinctly uncommon opinion in its day. On the literary presentation of mulattoes and the phenomenon of passing, see Judith R. Berzon, *Neither White Nor Black: The Mulatto Character in American Fiction* (New York, 1976).

8. The literature on this subject is large and still growing. See especially: Werner Sollors, *Beyond Ethnicity: Consent and Descent in American Culture* (New York, 1986); Barbara J. Fields, "Ideology and Race in American History," *Region, Race, and Reconstruction: Essays in Honor of C. Vann Woodward*, ed. J. Morton Kousser and James M. McPherson (New York, 1982), 143–177; Noel P. Gist and Anthony Gary Dworkin, *The Blending of Races: Marginality and Identity in World Perspective* (New York, 1972), 1–23; Ruth Frankenberg, *White Women, Race Matters: The Social Construction of Whiteness* (Minneapolis, 1993); Donald L. Horowitz, "Ethnic Identity," *Ethnicity: Theory and Experience*, ed. Nathan Glazer and Daniel P. Moynihan (Cambridge, Mass., 1975), 111–140; Michael Omi and Howard Winant, *Racial Formation in the United States: From the 1960s to the 1980s* (New York, 1986); Noel Ignatiev, *How the Irish Became White* (New York, 1995); and Jordan, "Note on the Concept of Race," *White Over Black*, 583–585. For the reinforcement of racial attitudes in everyday life, see Thomas C. Holt, "Marking: Race, Race-Making, and the Writing of History," *American Historical Review* 100 (1995):1–20. Studies of communities in which the process of racial construction has been at work include Sister Frances Jerome Woods, *Marginality and Identity: A Colored Creole Family Through Ten Generations* (Baton Rouge, 1972); Virginia R. Dominguez, *White by Definition: Social Classification in Creole Louisiana* (New Brunswick, N.J., 1986); and Marilyn Halter, *Between Race and Ethnicity: Cape Verdean American Immigrants, 1960–1965* (Urbana, 1993).

9. It is also the case that, even among sympathetic observers, several of the Healys may be conflated into a single person. Mabel Smythe, ed., *The Black American Reference Book* (Englewood Cliffs, N.J., 1976), 454, for example, manages to attribute aspects of the lives of James, Patrick, and Sherwood to Patrick alone. Kathy Russell, et al., *The Color Complex: The Politics of Skin Color Among African Americans* (New York, 1992), 32–33, also confuses James and Patrick.

10. Frederick Douglass, *My Bondage and My Freedom* (New York, 1994; orig. pub. 1855), 286.

11. Foley, *Beloved Outcaste*, 3–16, and Albert S. Foley, *Dream of an Outcaste: Patrick F. Healy* (Tuscaloosa, Ala., 1976), 1–11, outline Michael Morris Healy's life. For an understanding of Healy's economic and social surroundings, see Joseph P. Reidy, *From Slavery to Agrarian Capitalism in the Cotton Plantation South: Central Georgia, 1800–1880* (Chapel Hill, 1992); see also William T. Jenkins, "Ante Bellum Macon and Bibb County" (Ph.D. diss.: Univ. of Georgia, 1966), and Donnie D. Bellamy, "Macon, Georgia, 1823–1860: A Study in Urban Slavery" *Phylon* 45 (1984):304. I have reconstructed Healy's land and property holdings using the estate records of the Jones County Court of Ordinary, microfilm copies of which are in the Georgia Department of Archives and History (GDAH) Atlanta. His naturalization petition, Apr. 3, 1818, is in Deed Book K: 144, Jones County Courthouse, Gray, Georgia. Tabulations and comparisons of his slave holdings have been made from the enumeration of slaves that was part of the U.S. census of 1850, a copy of which is in GDAH.

12. Foley provides confused and speculative accounts of Eliza Clark Healy's origins, which cannot now be known with certainty. On the common practice of slave concubinage, see, for example, Elizabeth Fox Genovese, *Within the Plantation Household: Black and White Women*

of the Old South (Chapel Hill, 1988), and Deborah Gray White, *Ar'n't I a Woman? Female Slaves in the Plantation South* (New York, 1985). Slave law is described generally in Mark V. Tushnet, *The American Law of Slavery, 1810–1860: Considerations of Humanity and Interest* (Princeton, 1981); the slave law of Georgia is outlined in W. McDowell Rogers, "Free Negro Legislation in Georgia Before 1850," *Georgia Historical Quarterly* 16 (1932):27–37, and Ira Berlin, *Slaves Without Masters: The Free Negro in the Antebellum South* (New York, 1974), 139–140. Ralph B. Flanders, *Plantation Slavery in Georgia* (Chapel Hill, 1933), 271–272, has identified another case of a stable planter-slave marriage in rustic central Georgia.

13. Foley, *Beloved Outcaste*, 9–10, and *Dream of an Outcaste*, 6, tells of Healy's violent reaction to the idea of selling his children. This story still lives and was repeated to me by a Macon local historian, Kate Henry, in a telephone conversation on July 28, 1994. Michael Healy's plans to leave Georgia were noted by his son: "Father will be on in the fall of the year and will leave Georgia next spring"; Student Diary, July 25, 1849, JAH Papers, ACHC.

14. Student Diary, Feb. 21, Mar. 5, Apr. 19, and July 16, 1849, JAH Papers, ACHC. On the uses and connotations of the word "nigger," see Eugene D. Genovese, *Roll, Jordan, Roll: The World the Slaves Made* (New York, 1974), 436–438, and Willard B. Gatewood, *Aristocrats of Color: The Black Elite, 1880–1920* (Bloomington, 1990), 170. The history and racial meanings of antebellum minstrelsy are discussed in Robert C. Toll, *Blacking Up: The Minstrel Show in Nineteenth-Century America* (New York, 1974), 25–103.

15. Student Diary, Aug. 19, 1849, JAH Papers, ACH.

16. The appraisal, hiring out, and sale of the Healy slaves are accounted for in Jones County Court of Ordinary: Inventories, Appraisements, Sales, and Returns, GDAH, M: 393; N: 282–283; O: 249–250; P: 1, 5–6, 552; and Q: 268–269. The suit involving Margaret is ibid., Q: 440; her sale is in Q: 268–269. On the practice of hiring slaves out, see Clement Eaton, "Slave-Hiring in the Upper South: A Step Toward Freedom," *Mississippi Valley Historical Review* 46 (1960):663–678. Useful in determining the contemporary equivalents of historical dollar amounts are John J. McCusker, "How Much Is That in Real Money? A Historical Price Index for Use as a Deflator of Money Values in the Economy of the United States," *Proceedings of the American Antiquarian Society* 101 (1992):297–373, and Scott Derks, ed., *The Value of a Dollar: Prices and Incomes in the United States, 1860–1989* (Detroit, 1994). McCusker says that one 1860 dollar was equivalent to $14.83 in 1989.

17. Carter G. Woodson, *Free Negro Owners of Slaves in the United States in 1830* (New York, 1968; orig. pub. 1924); Adele Logan Alexander, *Ambiguous Lives: Free Women of Color in Rural Georgia, 1789–1879* (Fayetteville, 1991); Michael P. Johnson and James L. Roark, *Black Masters: A Free Family of Color in the Old South* (New York, 1984), esp. 66 and 141–142. Berlin, *Slaves Without Masters*, 247–248, also discusses free black ownership of slaves.

18. Bishop's Journal, Dec. 4, 1865, Archives, Archdiocese of Boston (AAB); JAH to Gibbons, Jan. 29, 1892, Letterbooks, Archives, Diocese of Portland (ADP).

19. JAH to Reed, May 9, 1890, Letterbooks, AD.

20. Passport, Dec. 19, 1885, Patrick F. Healy (PFH) Papers 2:4, Archives, Georgetown University (AGU). For some terms commonly used to designate mulattoes, see Melville J. Herskovits, "The Color Line," *American Mercury* 6 (1925):204–208. For Healy's career as the "second founder" of Georgetown, see R. Emmett Curran, *The Bicentennial History of Georgetown University: From Academy to University, 1789–1889* (Washington, D.C., 1993), ch. 11; see esp. 291–292 for a discussion of Healey's gradual reorientation of the student body from southerners to northerners.

21. Early to Brocard, Sept. 9, 1850, Maryland Jesuit Province Archives 71:10, AGU; PFH to Paresce, Oct. 1864, ibid., 77:10. On the origins of the long-standing canonical prohibition

against the priestly ordination of illegitimate sons, see James A. Brundage, *Law, Sex, and Christian Society in Medieval Europe* (Chicago, 1987), 216–223; the canon law of this problem is discussed fully in Gilbert J. McDevitt, *Legitimacy and Legitimation: An Historical Synopsis and Commentary* (Washington, D.C., 1941), esp. 34–44 and 56–58. The question of illegitimacy also arose in the ordinations of James and Sherwood Healy. In these cases, too, their ecclesiastical superiors apparently resolved the problem by ignoring it; see Thomas H. O'Connor, *Fitzpatrick's Boston, 1846–1866: John Bernard Fitzpatrick, Third Bishop of Boston* (Boston, 1984), 155–156.

22. PFH to Fenwick, Nov. 23, 1853, Maryland Jesuit Province Archives 74:1, AGU.

23. California Diary, Dec. 9 and 16, 1878, PFH Papers, ACHC.

24. Passport #3071, Sept. 18, 1869, State Department Passport Files, National Archives Microfilm #M-i37i, reel 3. I have been able to locate photographs of only four of the Healy siblings: James, Patrick, Sherwood, and Michael. There are no images of the parents, who lived in the earliest years of photographic technology, nor of any of the sisters. Some 20th-century anthropometric research has suggested that female children of interracial couples may tend to be lighter-skinned than male children; see Caroline Bond Day, *A Study of Some Negro-White Families in the United States* (Cambridge, Mass., 1932), and Pierre L. van den Berghe and Peter Frost, "Skin Color Preference, Sexual Dimorphism, and Sexual Selection: A Case of Gene Culture Co-Evolution?" *Ethnic and Racial Studies* 9 (1986):87–112.

25. Fitzpatrick to Hughes, July 10, 1859, John Hughes Papers, Archives, Archdiocese of New York, A-9.

26. Bishop's Journal, Oct. 20, 1865, AAB. See also Fitzpatrick to Bedini, July 5, 1859, Congressi: America Centrale, 18 (1858–1860), Archives, Congregation de Propaganda Fide, Rome. On the Troy seminary, see Thomas J. Shelley, "'Good Work in Its Day': St. Joseph's Provincial Seminary, Troy, New York," *Revue d'Histoire Ecclésiastique* 88 (1993):416–438.

27. PFH to Fenwick, Mar. 7, 1854, Maryland Jesuit Province Archives 74:15, AGU; Hilary Tucker Diary, Aug. 15, 1863, AAB. Tucker had complained that James Healy suffered from the same inflated sense of importance; ibid., May 1, 1863. On Tucker, see James Hitchcock, "Race, Religion, and Rebellion: Hilary Tucker and the Civil War," *Catholic Historical Review* 80 (1994):497–517. On the practice of ordaining priests on their own patrimony, see James T. McBride, *Incardination and Excardination of Seculars: An Historical Synopsis and Commentary* (Washington, D.C., 1941), 131–138.

28. Testimony of Michael A. Healy (MAH), Mar. 20, 1890, in "Charges Against RCS Officers: Capt. M. A. Healy," Records of the Revenue Cutter Service, RG 26, National Archives, Box 11; Address of the Official Prosecutor, January 1896, ibid., Box 12. See Leon F. Litwack, *North of Slavery: The Negro in the Free States, 1790–1860* (Chicago, 1961), 163, for a brief discussion of the hierarchy of racial and ethnic insults in early 19th-century America. The cultural significance of strong language among sailors generally is treated in Greg Dening, *Mr. Bligh's Bad Language: Passion, Power, and Theatre on the Bounty* (Cambridge, 1992). On the opportunities available to blacks in seafaring, see James Farr, "A Slow Boat to Nowhere: The Multi-Racial Crews of the American Whaling Industry," *Journal of Negro History* 68 (1983):159–170; Martha S. Putney, *Black Sailors: Afro-American Merchant Seamen and Whalemen Prior to the Civil War* (New York, 1987); and W. Jeffrey Bolster, "'To Feel Like a Man': Black Seamen in the Northern States, 1800–1860," *Journal of American History* 76 (1990):1173–1199. A reasonably accurate fictional portrayal of Michael Healy appears in part VII of James Michener, *Alaska* (New York, 1988).

29. MAH to Commissioner of Education, Dec. 17, 1894, Alaska File, Revenue Cutter Service, National Archives Microfilm #641, reel 3; MAH to Shepard, Apr. 2 and July 4, 1893,

ibid. See also his comments on native-white relations in his *Report of the Cruise of the Revenue Marine Steamer Corwin in the Arctic Ocean in the Year 1885* (Washington, 1887). On his son's perception of himself as white, see Fred Healy Diary, July 25, 1883, Healy Collection (HM #47577), Huntington Library, San Marino, Calif.

30. The lives of the Healy sisters have been generally overlooked by those who have investigated the family. Foley (*Beloved Outcaste and Dream of an Outcaste*) gives only fragmentary and often contradictory accounts of them. Cyprian Davis, *The History of Black Catholics in the United States* (New York, 1990), 148, describes them briefly. The outlines of their religious careers have been provided to me by the Archives of the Congregation de Notre Dame, Montreal, and the Archives of the Religieuses Hospitallieres de Saint-Joseph, Montreal. Unfortunately, the Notre Dame archives, which contain (I believe) a great deal of material relating to Eliza Healy/Sister Mary Magdalen, have not granted me access to their collections; accordingly, I have been able to consult only such materials as a former archivist has selected and copied for me. I have traced Martha Healy Cashman's family through the vital records available in the Archives of the Commonwealth of Massachusetts, Boston.

31. On the 19th-century work of the Notre Dame sisters, see *Histoire de la Congregation de Notre Dame* (Montreal, 1969), vol. 10. The record of Martha Healy Cashman's death on May 18, 1920, is in the Registry of Vital Records and Statistics, Commonwealth of Massachusetts, Boston; she was the last of the Healy siblings to die. The death certificate for the ne'er-do-well brother Eugene, who died in Boston on Mar. 26, 1914, also in the Vital Records Registry, Boston, likewise identifies him as white.

32. On the music and drawing lessons, see the accounts for Eliza and Josephine Healy's own student days in the 1860s, Archives, Congregation de Notre Dame, Montreal, #326.000-44. The stress on penmanship may be seen in one of Eliza's copybooks from that period, which is in JAH Papers, ADP. For the upper-class approach to home economics, see the textbook the congregation used in its schools: *La Cuisine Raisonee* (Quebec, 1961; orig. pub. 1926), esp. 69–88.

33. Sister Mary Magdalen's assignments have been summarized for me by the archivist of the Congregation de Notre Dame, Montreal. Descriptions of the various religious houses where she served may be found in Histoire de la Congrégation de Notre-Dame, vol. 10, passim, and Sister Saint Francis of Rome Baeszler, "The Congregation of Notre Dame in Ontario and the United States: The History of Holy Angels Province" (Ph.D. diss., Fordham University, 1944). On Eliza Healy's negotiations to open convents in Maine, see Episcopal Diary, Aug. 8, Aug. 11, and Oct. 10, 1881, ADP. Some recollections of her time as superior of the convent in Saint Albans, Vermont, are recorded in Henry G. Fairbanks, "Slavery and the Vermont Clergy," *Vermont History* 27 (1959):310–312.

34. European Diary, May 20, May 16, and June 24, 1878, JAH Papers, ACHC; JAH to Collins, Apr. 7, 1885, Letterbooks, ADP; MAH to Jackson, Dec. 19, 1890, Sheldon Jackson Papers, Presbyterian Historical Society, Philadelphia.

35. Bishop's Journal, Sept. 18, 1849, AAB; Student Diary, Aug. 18, 1849, JAH Papers, ACHC; Bishop's Journal, Apr. 17 and 19, 1865, AAB; "Annales de la Maison More," Sept. 13, 1919, Archives, Congregation de Notre Dame, Montreal.

36. Nineteenth-century anti-Catholicism has been widely studied since Ray Allen Billington, *The Protestant Crusade, 1800–1860: A Study of the Origins of American Nativism* (New York, 1938), and John Higham, *Strangers in the Land: Patterns of American Nativism, 1860–1925* (New York, 1963). For an imaginative recent treatment, see Jenny Franchot, *Roads to Rome: The Antebellum Protestant Encounter with Catholicism* (Berkeley, 1994). Hostility toward Catholicism in Boston is treated at length in vol. 2 of Robert Howard Lord, et al., *History of the Archdiocese of Boston in the Various Stages of Its Development, 1603–1943* (Boston,

1944). On the struggle to secure a charter for Holy Cross, see Walter J. Meagher and William J. Grattan, *The Spires of Fenwick: A History of the College of the Holy Cross, 1843–1863* (New York, 1966), 51–55 and 103–105.

37. For studies of Catholic attitudes toward slavery, see the older work of Madeleine Hook Rice, *American Catholic Opinion in the Slavery Controversy* (New York, 1944), and the more recent Randall M. Miller, "Slaves and Southern Catholicism," *Masters and Slaves in the House of the Lord: Race and Religion in the American South, 1740–1870*, ed. John B. Boles (Lexington, 1988), 127–152. See also Joseph Butsch, "Catholics and the Negro," *Journal of Negro History* 3 (1917):33–51; Cuthbert Allen, "The Slavery Question in Catholic Newspapers, 1850–1865," *Historical Records and Studies* 26 (1936):99–169; and Benjamin J. Blied, *Catholics and the Civil War* (Milwaukee, 1945). On Spalding, see David Spalding, "Martin John Spalding's 'Dissertation on the American Civil War,'" *Catholic Historical Review* 53 (1966):166–85. For Brownson's views, see "Abolition and Negro Equality," *Brownson's Quarterly Review, National Series* 1 (April 1864):186–209.

38. The best summary of the failures of American Catholicism before and after the Civil War is Davis, *History of Black Catholics*, esp. 116–136. See also Edward J. Misch, *The American Bishops and the Negro from the Civil War to the Third Plenary Council of Baltimore (1865–1884)* (Rome, 1968), and Stephen J. Ochs, *Desegregating the Altar: The Josephites and the Struggle for Black Priests, 1871–1960* (Baton Rouge, 1990). McCloskey is quoted in James Hennesey, *American Catholics: A History of the Roman Catholic Community in the United States* (New York, 1981), 161; for Gross's address, see "The Missions to the Colored People," *The Memorial Volume: A History of the Third Plenary Council of Baltimore, November p-December 7, 1884* (Baltimore, 1885), 71–74. Sherwood Healy's remarks on slavery are in his undated notes, "The Church + Negro Slavery," Alexander Sherwood Healy (ASH) Papers 1:2, ACHC.

39. Foley, *Beloved Outcaste*, 19, and *God's Men of Color*, 2, says that Healy and Fitzpatrick met aboard ship in March 1844 as the former was traveling to New York on business and the latter was returning from his episcopal consecration in Washington. Since Foley's works were published without footnotes, it is impossible to verify his sources for this story, which is repeated in O'Connor, *Fitzpatrick's Boston*, 63–64; nor have I been able to locate specific documentation for it in Foley's own papers, which are in the Josephite Fathers Archives, Baltimore. Healy seems to have traveled north fairly frequently in the 1840s, often taking some of his children with him, so the story is at least plausible.

40. Student Diary, Dec. 25, 1848, and July 5, 1849, JAH Papers, ACHC. Foley, *Dream of an Outcaste*, 291, makes the same argument: "the Healys simply . . . identified with the group that accepted them, raised them, cherished them, and sheltered them." Franchot, *Roads to Rome*, 280–281, discusses the countercultural nature of antebellum Catholic conversion.

41. Tucker Diary, May 1, 1863, AAB; Tucker repeated his complaint about familial affection on Aug. 16, 1864. James's recollection of his father is in his New Orleans Diary, Mar. 10, 1885, JAH Papers 3:7, ACHC; his recognition of his mother in the long-since lost daguerreotype is in his Student Diary, Mar. 14, 1849, JAH Papers, ACHC. Hugh's note on explaining "their situation" to the children is in his letter to Fenwick, July 6, 1850, Maryland Jesuit Province Archives: Varia 71:13, AGU. For the use of "Dad" with George Fenwick, see that letter and also JAH to Fenwick, June 10, 1850, Maryland Jesuit Province Archives 71:14, AGU, and PFH to Fenwick, Oct. 2, 1853, ibid., 74:1.

42. ASH Commonplace Book, May 9, 1859, AAB.

43. Martha's religious activity may be traced in the parish sacramental registers held by AAB. Michael's religious sentiments are expressed in MAH to Jackson, March 1893, Alaska

File, Revenue Cutter Service, National Archives Microfilm #641, reel 3, and Jackson to MAH, Nov. 5, 1900, Sheldon Jackson Papers, Speer Library, Princeton Theological Seminary, the encounter with the anti-Catholic fellow officer is in MAH to Shepard, Dec. 14, 1892, Alaska File, Revenue Cutter Service, National Archives Microfilm #531, reel 2. On the elusive Eugene, see Foley, *Dream of an Outcaste*, 275, 293.

44. For the sometimes strained relations between James and Martha, see JAH to "Mrs. J. Cash man," Sept. 11, 1883; same to same, Feb. 4, 1884; and JAH to Pelletier, Dec. 4, 1885; all in Letterbooks, ADP. Michael's suicide attempt is described in PFH Diary, July 15–25, 1900, PFH Papers 1:4, AGU. On Eugene's troubles, see Episcopal Diary, Jan. 17, 1876, ADP, and JAH to Eugene Healy, Oct. 4, 1884, Letterbooks, ADP.

45. ASH sermon, "On the Creed," ASH Papers 1:3, ACHC; Hilary Tucker Diary, Apr. 24, 1864, AAB; JAH Diary, Jan. 10, 1886, JAH Papers 3:9, ACHC; PFH Diary, Oct. 1, 1863, PFH Papers 1:1, ACHC; JAH to Cardinal Mazella, Jan. 5, 1893, Letterbooks, ADP.

46. PFH to Paresce, Sept. 5 and October 1864, Maryland Jesuit Province Archives 77:10, AGU. The phrase in the ordination rite is from John 15:15.

47. JAH address on Holy Cross charter, April 1865, JAH Papers 1:4, ACHC; JAH to Fenwick, Mar. 22, 1855, Maryland Jesuit Province Archives 74:15, AGU. For his observations on Lourdes, see JAH Diary, Mar. 1–4, 1878, JAH Papers 3:3, ACHC; for examples of his youthful religious scrupulosity, see Student Diary, Dec. 28, 1848, and Jan. 1–4, 1849, JAH Papers, ACHC.

48. Circular on the death of Sister Josephine Healy, RHSJ, July 23, 1879, Archives, Religious Hospitallers of Saint Joseph, Montreal (original in French); Motherhouse Annals, Sept. 13, 1919, Archives, Congregation de Notre Dame, Montreal (original in French). In both cases these obituary notices have a formalized quality, but since they speak of the faults as well as the virtues of the deceased they cannot simply be dismissed on those grounds. Josephine had spoken of Eliza's early vocational struggle in a letter to Patrick, Apr. 16, 1874, PFH Papers 2:2, AGU.

49. Other instances of racial choice deserve study. Du Bois examined the case of another Georgian, Henry Hunt, who, though able to pass as white, chose to identify instead with the black community, see his "The Significance of Henry Hunt," *Fort Valley State College Bulletin* 1 (October 1940):5–16; the original speech from which this essay was derived is in the W.E.B. Du Bois Papers, Archives and Special Collections, University of Massachusetts-Amherst. See also Mary C. Waters, *Ethnic Options: Choosing Identities in America* (Berkeley, 1990).

DOCUMENTS

5

Enslaved People Named
in a Deed, 1717

This document is the earliest slaveholding record by the Maryland Jesuits. It registers a sale of goods at Brittons Neck, an early settlement that became Newtown plantation. The deed names fifteen persons enslaved by the Jesuits, eight adults and seven children—Will, Jack, Kitt, Pete, Mary, Teresa, Clare, and Peggy and Jack, Clemm, Tomm, James, Betty, Cate, and Susan. Their names are listed beside church property and household goods. This transaction between the head of the Jesuit mission and a layman was intended to protect the Jesuits' property from anti-Catholic regulations in Maryland. The Jesuits recovered their property years later.

Why did the Maryland Jesuits become slaveholders?

Know all men by those psent yt I William Hunter of Charles County Gent for and in Consideration of the summ of Tenn Shillings to me ye sd William Hunter in hand pay'd By Thomas Jameson senr of Charles County Gent the receit wherof I do hereby acknowledge and of every part thereof do acquitt and discharge him ye sd Thomas Jameson his Executrs admrs & assigns and for diverse other good causes and considerations me there to moving have Given granted bargain'd and sold and By those presents do give grant bargain and sell unto ye sd Thomas Jam[eson] all and Every ye Goods Church stuff Plate Household stuff negros horses mares neat cattle Hoggs Sheep Husbandry Implements Tobacco Corn & all other grain and all other things whatsoever now on or Belonging to [?] Dwelling Plantation of Britton's neck and ye Quarter on ye bottom [?] ye sd neck mentioned in a schedule hereunto annexed to have an[d] hold all and every ye sd Goods Church stuff Plate Household stuff negros horses mares neat cattle Hoggs Sheep Husbandry Implements Tobacco corn and other grain and all other things in ye sd schedule mentioned unto sd Thomas Jameson his Executrs administrrs and assigns for ever t[o] and their only benefitt and proper use and behoof. In witness [there?] of I have hereto sett my hand and seale this thirteenth of January in ye year of our Lord one thousand seven hundred and seventeen.

Sign'd Seal'd & Delivered
in presence of us William Hunter

    his
Jonathan + Walker
    mark

    his
Daniell + Riordan
    mark

Memorandum the thirtieth day of January one thousand seven hundred & seventeen in ye presence of this subscriber of above nam'd Wm Hunter deliver'd into ye hands and possession of ye. above nam'd Thomas Jameson one bay gelding ye [same?] being one of ye geldings in ye schedule to this pro[?] mention'd and in parts and lieu of ye whole in ye sd schedule mentioned & express'd and in token of possession of ye whole

his
Jonathan + Walker
mark
his
Daniell + Riordan
mark

[Page 2]

A Schedule exhibiting ye particular Goods of Church S[tuff] Plate Household stuff Negros Horses mares neat Cattle Hoggs [ripped page] Given & sold by ye above named William Hunter to the above named Thomas Jameson in ye above Deed viz——

| Church Stuff & Plate | 1 Ciborium, 2 Chalices and pateris, 2 Small Candlesticks some little boxes All of them sliver, 1 brass Crucifix, 4 brass Candlesticks, 6 Vestments stoles & manifolds, 5 Alts, 3 amiers, 4 veils, 4 Palls, 2 Surplices, 3 Corporalls, altar Cloths several purificators [?] 1 Comunion Cloath, 3 painted pictures with frames, mass book |

Negro Servants 15	4 Men, Will, Jack, Kitt, Peter. 4 Women, Mary, Teresa, Clare, Peggy, 4 Boyes, Jack, Clemm, Tomm, James, 3 Girles, Betty, Cate, Susan
Household stuff & Furniture	Lower Rooms 4 Prints with frames, 1 Striking Clock [?] 4 bedsteds 5 Leather chairs 7 do flagg. 4 do wood, 1 long table, 1 do round, 4 do square, 1 small falling table. 2 Trunks 2 [ripped page] 1 Cask of 7 bottles each 3 pints, 3 pairs tongs, 3 fire shovels, 2 large [ripped page] Books of severall sorts att most 500. Upper Rooms kitchen & out houses 1 long table, 3 square do 3 b[ed]steds, 3 Chests, 1 Close-stool, 1 prebellows, several cider [?].
Brass, Copper, Bell * [?] all	1 Great Bell, 2 do small, 1 large copper, about 2 gallns 2 brass kettl 1 skillett, 1 warming pann, 3 Candlesticks, 3 still and [? ripped and burned page]
Iron	6 potts, 2 pottracks, 2 spitts, 4 frying panns, 4 preand iron [ripped page] 2 Crosscutt saws, 2 hand saws, 3 broad axes, 1 Gunn, 2 Chafting [ripped page]: [?] saws, awls, chisels, files, and other tools.
Pewter & Tinn	Dishs good 7. Do old 3. do deep 3. Basons 4. Plates good 22. 24 [ripped page] standish 5 bed pann, 2 Lanthorns, milkpanns, saucepans, biskett molds.
Earthenware	Butterpotts, milk pans, Juggs, cupps etc.—
Bedding	8 feather beds, Bolsters, pillows, 4 flock beds, Bolsters, pillows [ripped page] white sheets good. 2 pre very poor do 3 pre do old 4 pre speckl'd [ripped page] 1 silk quilt 1 pre Curtains and vallene new 2 pre do old, 3 pre good [ripped page] 3 other pairs 6 pr narrow course new pillow cases
Table Linen	5 Table cloaths, 32 napkins new & old, 14 Towells.
Stock	Neat Cattle 28 Steers young & old, 24 milk Cows, 2 yeare old Hors[ripped page] yearlings 3, Calves 19, Bulls 3, Hoggs old 44, Young 17, Piggs 14, Sheep 75, Horses 5 for ye plough, 2 Riding Geldings, 2 Mares 1 young Gelding not broke. 1 Waggon old, 1 Cart old, 3 new ploughs ploughshares 8 Coultors etc—

[Page 3]
30 Jany 1717
The Deed of gift
to Mr Thomas Jameson by Revd W. Hunter.

6

A Sermon on the Treatment
of Slaves, 1749

The Jesuits justified slavery, claiming that it was a lawful way to Christianize Africans and include enslaved people in Catholic ritual and community. Jesuit priests baptized, married, buried, and catechized enslaved persons in the Chesapeake beginning in the eighteenth century. While leading a spiritual retreat in 1749, Fr. George Hunter, the head of the Jesuit mission, reflected on the duties that enslavers had toward the persons they held in bondage. He described enslaved persons as part of the body of Christ, suggested to his fellow Jesuits catechizing methods, and chastised Jesuits for focusing on the economics of their plantations instead of the progress of their religious mission.

How did the Jesuits justify slavery?

To the Greater Glory of God.

Charity to Negroes is Due from all particularly their masters. As they are members of Jesus Christ, redeemed by his precious blood, they are to be Dealt with in a charitable, Christian, paternal manner, which is at the same time a great means to bring them to do their Duty to God, & therefore to gain their Souls.

Much talk of temporals shews the mind too much bent upon such things, & therefore must be disedifying in persons of our calling. Our discourse ought to be chiefly of the progress of our Missions, how to make greater progress; how to serve God in a more decent, handsome, pompous manner as a thing that helps to the interiour, by striking an awe; respect & reverence; where &

how greater good may be done, more conversions be made, what methods to be taken for the catechising of children & Negroes, as well as instructions for others by more familiar Discourses in lieu of formal Sermons, which generally are not so beneficial as more familiar instructions.

Revd Father George Hunter, Soc. Jes., of Venerable memory, in his Spiritual Retreat, at Portobacco,

December 20. A. D. 1749.

7

Edward Queen Petitions
for Freedom, 1791

Enslaved people wanted to be free and pursued a variety of strategies to attain that goal, from running away, to self-purchase, to suing in court. In 1791 Edward Queen, a man held in bondage at White Marsh plantation, sued Fr. John Ashton—one of the founders of Georgetown—on the basis that he was descended from a free woman named Mary Queen. Ashton, the manager of White Marsh, held eighty-two persons in bondage at that estate, including several members of Queen's family. In 1794 the court ruled in favor of Queen, who gained his freedom and joined the growing ranks of free people of color in Maryland.

How did Edward Queen establish his claim to freedom?

To the honorable The Judges of the General Court.

The petition of Edward Queen humbly sheweth that he is held in slavery by the Revd. John Ashton altho he is informed he is entitled to his freedom being descended from a freewoman, viz, being the son of Phillis who was the daughter of Mary Queen commonly called Queen Mary, a freewoman. He therefore prays your honours to direct Summons to issue against the said John Ashton returnable immediately to answer the premises; & that your honours, the facts being found, will adjudge your petitioner to be free. And he will pray & so forth.

G Duvall

P.B. Key

for Petr.

Witnesses

Revd. Thos. Digges, PG.

Plummer Liams, AA.

8

Isaac Runs Away from Georgetown College, 1814

On February 1, 1814, the Daily National Intelligencer *published an advertisement for Isaac, an enslaved man who ran away from Georgetown College days earlier. Isaac had lived at the school since 1807, when the Jesuits purchased him for $300. According to the advertisement, Isaac was twenty-three years old and literate. It was suspected that he would try to get to Pennsylvania, but he never made it. Isaac was captured and thrown in jail in Baltimore and sold by the Jesuits to a man in Hartford County, Maryland. Isaac was one of dozens of enslaved people who labored at Georgetown College in its early decades.*

What does this newspaper advertisement tell us about Isaac's life as an enslaved person and the policing of slavery?

Thirty Dollars
Reward
Ranaway from Georgetown College, on Saturday night the 29th inst a Negro Man named ISAAC, about 23 years old quite black complexion, about 5 feet 8 inches high; had on when he went away a short coat of drab cloth, pantaloons of the same kind, fur hat & great coat made of thick drab coating and bound with ferreting—he carried with him a pair of blue cloth trowsers, [t]wo Russia linen shirts, an old hat and other articles of clothing not recollected, it is probable he may change his clothing - he has learned to read tolerably well, and it is likely he may have procured a written pass. It is supposed that he is gone to Pennsylvania; he was raised at Mrs Johnson's near Bryantown, Charles County. The above reward will be

paid if secured in any Jail more than 50 miles from the District, and reasonable expenses paid if brought home, or twenty dollars if a shorter distance, by the subscriber Clerk of Georgetown College, District of Columbia.
John McElroy
February 1—d/m

9

A Jesuit Overseer Calculates
the Cost of Slave Labor, 1815

As overseer at the Jesuits' St. Inigoes plantation in southern Maryland, Br. Joseph Mobberly wrote to the president of Georgetown, Fr. John Grassi, to explain that slavery did not pay. He calculated that the Jesuits' Maryland mission would save more than $300 per year by employing hired workers rather than slaves. The enslaved community at St. Inigoes accused Br. Mobberly of extreme violence, including the beating of pregnant women. In 1820 he was dismissed from his post and sent to Georgetown University as a teacher. At the school he wrote a treatise lauding slavery and defending violence as a means of control.

Why did Br. Mobberly believe that "free" labor was cheaper than slave labor?

Feb 5th 1815
Revd & Dr F. in Xst
It is better to sell for a time, or to set your people free——1st. Because we have their souls to answer for—2nd Because Blacks are more difficult to govern now, than formerly—and 3rd Because we shall make more & more to our satisfaction.—The two first propositions are evident—I therefore proceed to prove the third. The shortest way to prove this, is to calculate our annual expenses in regard to our people. Having done this with as much exactness as I could, the amount stands thus
Bread for 43 Blacks = 630 Bush. corn @ 80 cts. per bush . . . .$504..00
Meat = 3468 lbs. Bacon @ 17cts pr. lb . . . .589..56

68 lbs. Hog's lard @ 15 cts. Pr lb $10..20 cts—34 prs shoes @$1..10cts each—47..60

419 Yds linen @ 30 cts. Pr yd $125..70 cts.—34 prs. Stockings @ $1 each 159..70

206 yds. Cloth @ 40 cts pr. Yd. $82..40 cts. Making up cloth & linen $34=116..40

mending 34 prs. Shoes $17—Hire of Mrs. Fenwick's 3 men @ $40 each $120....137.00

Medicine & contingent expences [*sic*] $20—120 chord of wood @ $2 pr. Chd. $240–280..00

————————

$1834..26

Now let us suppose we had 14 hired hands and no others on the land to maintain—no slaves—suppose we give those hands $80 each, they finding their own clothes; our expences would then be as follow

Bread for 14 hands 190 Bush. @ 80 cts pr. Bush ... ... $152..00

1340 lbs. Bacon @ 17 cts pr lb. $227..80 cts = ...227..80

10 Laborers @ $80 each $800—Gardener $80—milk maid $40...920..00

House cook $40—cook for workmen $40 ... .80..00

————————

$1379..80

60 chord of wood @ $2 pr chd $120

————————

$1499..80

Total expences [*sic*] of the Blacks ... ... $1834.26 cts

Total expences [*sic*] of the white Laborers 1499.80

————————

Saved + $334.46

Thus by adopting the plan of hiring we save from our annual expenses the sum of $334.46 cts. according to this calculation which I think is pretty correct. But I know that much more can be saved, for there are the county and direct taxes on slaves which I have not included—Besides, suppose we make as large crops with the 14 hands as we have with the slaves, in this case there will be more corn & a great deal of meat for sale. We have made 400 Bbls. corn and 6000 lbs pork & there is no doubt but that the same can be made with the 14 hands. Then I calculate thus

If we make 400 Bbls with the 14 hands, 238 Bbls will serve the Laborers & all the stock plentifully—There will therefore be left for sale 152 Bbls @ $4 per Bbl ... ... $648..00cts

Again, if we raise 6000 lbs pork, 1340 llbs as said above will feed the 14 hands, in this case I can sell 4660 lbs . . . . = 466..00
I then bring down what has been saved above +.......334..46

Saved & gained . . . .$1448..46
We have about 15 fires burning, most of them consuming wood all day & all night—Thus all our Blacks during the winter can do scarcely any thing else besides the procuring of wood &c. But if we had the 14 hands mentioned above, 6 fires to burn during the day only, would be sufficient, in which case we could manure the land, make fences & do many other things during the winter besides the procuring of wood. . . . Thus you see Dr. Father we are in the dark as long as we keep slaves. Should any objections be offered, I can give satisfactory answers—I have weighed the matter pro & con. As to our Smiths work and mill, there will be no difficulty as our gain is equal Zero—

Our smith's shop & wind mill gain nothing, all expences considered. They are only good for convenience sake. I hope your Reverence will take this matter into consideration & let me know your mind. I know the resolve made by the Board concerning slaves, & the sooner that resolution is executed, the better it will be. We had no mail last monday—Old Nacy is ill—I sent this day to New Town for Revd. Mr. Moynihan. His complaint is the gravel.
A curious fact
This Christmas last past a young man of good meaning (a protestant) went to the protestant meeting house for the purpose of Receiving what they call the sacrament or Lord's Supper—On examination he refused to receive, because he discovered that the parson instead of distributing Bread & Wine, was handing round nothing more than Bread and cider! This fact was related the other day by the young man himself in a company of Catholics & protestants. It happened in our settlement.
By your silence you leave me to conclude that you are either much engaged in the council assembled, or that I have tired you out with my repeated letters—We now want the clover seed to sow. I hope to hear from your Reverence ere long—meanwile pray for yours in Xst.
Jos. P. Mobberley
Br. Barron & I have had a few charity quarrels in which he has been defeated & now seems rather ashamed of his visions, dreams, and prophetic sayings. He now tires us with his farming principles & various opinions. In our last quarrel he said he should go to Baltimore in the spring to consult the Archbp. His difficulty is (from what I can learn) that God commanded him to go to the College and remain there in the Society, but wishes however to be freed

from his vows without sin. Answer this difficulty who can—He and I are friends yet.

Revd. Jno. Grassie President
Of Geo. Town College
Dist. Columbia

10

Baptism of Sylvester Greenleaf
at Newtown, 1819

Sylvester Greenleaf was born at Newtown plantation on February 12, 1819. Nearly four months later, he was baptized in the presence of his parents John and Esther and two sponsors. Nineteen years later, the Jesuits sold the Greenleafs to Henry S. Johnson, a congressman and former governor of Louisiana. The family was shipped to Louisiana on the Katherine Jackson and ended up on Johnson's Chatham plantation in Ascension Parish, Louisiana, a thousand miles from Newtown.

How could the Maryland Jesuits baptize enslaved people one day and sell them the next?

4th June 1819 was Baptized Sylvester the Property of New Town born 12ᵗʰ Feby. 1819 of Joe + Easter lawfully married—Sponsors: Mrs Ann Meryman + Revᵈ. Peter Devos—
Test—Revᵈ. Petrus Joannes Priest

11

Fr. James Ryder, SJ, Criticizes Abolitionism, 1835

American Catholicism was hostile to abolitionism. On August 30, 1835, the Jesuit priest and Georgetown professor Fr. James Ryder, SJ, passionately criticized abolitionists during a meeting of Richmond's Catholic congregation. The sermon was published in the Richmond Examiner. *Years later, Ryder became president of Georgetown College; he founded the school's Philodemic Society (a debating club) and its medical school.*

Why was Fr. Ryder hostile toward abolitionism?

COMMUNICATED

Meeting of the Roman Catholic Congregation of the City of Richmond and County of Henrico.

In conformity with a Circular addressed to the clergy of the city of Richmond and county of Henrico, by the Committee of Correspondence of the Committee of Vigilance, a meeting of the Roman Catholics of said city and county was convened at their Church, after divine service, on Sunday evening, the 30th August, 1835:

The meeting was organized by calling Mr. John J. Chevallie to the Chair, and appointing Mr. James Heron, Secretary.

The circular, together with the Resolution to which it refers, being submitted to the meeting by the Rev. Pastor of the Church, were then read by the Secretary.

When, on motion of the Rev. T. O'Brien, a Committee of three was appointed by the venerable Chairman, to take the same into consideration, and to draft resolutions expressive of the views of this meeting on the momentous subject for which it was convened.

The Committee consisted of the Rev. T. O'Brien, Mr. G. Picot, and Mr. P. Devereux—who, after retiring for a short time, returned and reported the following resolutions; which were read seriatim, and unanimously adopted by the meeting:

1st. Resolved, By the members of this congregation, individually, and collectively, that we view with abhorrence, the unholy and unprincipled interference of some Northern Fanatics and their associates, between the masters and their slaves in these Southern States.

2nd. Resolved, That such interference is condemned by the Constitution, under which we live, and cannot be otherwise than injurious to the slave and to his master.

3rd. Resolved, That we approve the determination of our Southern brethren, in not condescending to discuss the question of slavery with those fanatics.

4th. Resolved, That we hold as an enemy to this Commonwealth, any and every individual, who directly or indirectly, aids in this unholy crusade against the rights of property and the sanctity of social order.

5th. Resolved, That while we view slavery in the abstract, as an evil, we hold it to be our first duty as Christians and citizens, to support the civil institutions of our country.

6th. Resolved, That copies of these resolutions be sent to the Editors of the Courier, the Enquirer and the Richmond Whig, with a request that they would publish them in their respective papers, as containing the sentiments of the Roman Catholics of the City of Richmond and the county of Henrico.

(signed) J. A. Chevallie, Chairman.

Jas. Herron, Secretary.

The following remarks embrace the substance of a very eloquent address delivered by the Rev. James Ryder. The orator yielded with great reluctance to their publication, induced thereto by the urgent solicitations of the venerable Chairman and others, who heard him.

Mr. Chairman; Although a stranger in the Capital of the Old Dominion, I am no stranger to the doctrines of the Old Religion, and may therefore be allowed, on an occasion like the present, to express my entire approval of the spirit and object of the resolutions which have just been read. I consider this meeting a Catholic meeting, convened in obedience to the Circular addressed by "the Committee of Vigilance" to the respected pastor of this

Congregation; and as the doctrines it now gives utterance to are those of the Catholics throughout the wide extent of the Union, on a subject involving the dearest interests of this community, I am happy, opposed as I should otherwise be to take any part in political discussions, in having the opportunity of assuring my fellow citizens of the South, that the Catholic body, both clergy and laity, North of the Potomac, will go heart and hand with them in defence of the Constitution, for the maintenance of social order, and in resistance to the unholy efforts of incendiary fanatics to mar the peace and happiness of this distinguished portion of our common country. The fidelity of Catholics to the laws of the land cannot be misunderstood. For centuries, they have bled under the lash of imperial tyrants, without one expression of resistance to constituted authorities; for centuries their creed has been outlawed and persecuted, and its professors subjected to every species of oppression and injustice by the British government; and yet the fidelity of Catholics has been proof against every temptation to ameliorate their condition by revolt against their oppressors. When but last year the fires of fanaticism were lighted up from the dismantled Convent of pious and accomplished Virgins[1]—on that spot where the fires of the Revolution were first enkindled to give us the light and warmth of Civil and Religious liberty, twenty-five thousand able bodied sons of St. Patrick; whose nerve and prowess no one can doubt; burned with holy indignation, as became men, at the outrage offered to helpless females, and to the creed which they professed; but because they valued more the preservation of order and due submission to the laws, they raised not a hand to avenge their wrongs, patiently awaiting the dispensations of justice at the hands of their country. And when the mockery of law was superadded to the other outrages, they still continued faithful to their duty, sacrificing the dearest feelings of nature to the dictates of religion.

If then the Catholic in the North, despite of such powerful provocation, has baffled the malignity of designing fanatics, who, under the cloak of religious zeal, brandished the torch of persecution, how can the Catholics of the South be other than faithful in defending the rights and property of that chivalrous people, always distinguished for their love of liberty, and their high-minded liberality, amongst whom he enjoys all the blessings of our happy Constitution? He has too long been the victim of persecution, not to feel an intense interest in the preservation of that order of things, under which he enjoys religious and civil liberty. The Catholic feels his obligations to his country, and is willing to prove his gratitude whenever an occasion occurs. He knows that love of country is a sacred and holy passion, which reason and religion approve; that his altars and his country's rights are identified; and that he cannot be faithful to his God, if deficient in fidelity to his country, which "embraces all the charities of all." He is convinced, too, that the day which shall witness the overthrow of our glorious system of national independence, will date the persecution of catholicity. It is for this reason that he hates bigotry in every shape and color.

The wicked interference of some would be philanthropists, who are jeoparding the peace of our flourishing country, in order to carry out their visionary schemes of emancipation, is too alarming to the liberty and prosperity of our national institutions; to be looked upon with indifference by the friend of his country. The Catholic that could countenance such conduct, would be looked upon by his brethren as a madman or a traitor. They never will join in fellowship with the miscreant that would sacrifice his country to his wild speculations, however they may be graced by the names of religion and philanthropy. They will shrink from shaking the polluted hand that would sow the seeds of confusion and horror in the fair fields of the South, rifling the domestic happiness of the master and his slave. It is not religion—it is not piety—it is a profanation of the gospel of peace and charity to allow so fell a spirit to be called religious!

God is a God of order—his religion secures order, and the ministers of that religion should be the ministers of order. How horrifying is the spectacle of a man clothed in the garb, or speaking the language, of religion, prowling about the humble habitations of our unsuspecting slaves, and, in the name of God, seducing them into rebellion and murder; and by intoxicating their minds with the poison of religious fanaticism, make them renew the scenes of Southampton, as beneficial to themselves and pleasing to heaven!

Could my feeble voice reach these misguided abettors of disorder, I would ask them, what possible advantage they can anticipate from the spread of their favorite system of Abolition? Can they hope to better the condition of the slave? Let them look to the disgusting state of morals among the colored free in the Northern Cities—where they are, for the greater part, a nuisance to the white population in almost every department of life; and then let them look to the peaceful, and contented, and secure condition of the Southern slave, under the gentle sway of an upright master. Here the slave has a home—he is clothed, maintained, and protected by his master, who looks upon him as a portion of his family—in sickness he is attended with medical aid, and frequently solace by the maternal kindness of his compassionate mistress.

His sickness and sufferings are a loss to his owners, and it is their interest to relieve him if they can. Nothing of this falls to the lot of the freed man of color, who must depend on his own resources for the sustenance of life. Where, then, is the humanity of driving the slave to seek for misery by a change of condition?

Mr. Chairman, I need not go more fully into the subject. My object in appearing before this respectable meeting, was only to second the resolutions of my Catholic brethren; and I now conclude, with a hope that the united expressions of their fidelity to their country, may be received with the same feelings of cordiality by their brethren of every denomination, with which it is made by the Catholics of Richmond.

Note

1. Here Ryder is referencing the Ursuline Convent Riots. These riots occurred in Charlestown, Massachusetts, on August 11 and 12, 1834, when a mob of Protestant men incited by rumors of abuse within the convent, anti-Catholic sermons, and nativism pillaged and burned to the ground the Ursuline convent and school. —Eds.

12

The Society of Jesus Sets Conditions
on the Sale of the Maryland Slaves, 1836

The Maryland Jesuits had to get approval from Jesuit leaders in Rome, before selling the people they owned. In 1836 Fr. General Jan Roothaan wrote this letter to the Maryland Jesuits approving the sale of their enslaved community, but he imposed several conditions. The buyers would have to allow the slaves to practice Catholicism; husbands and wives should be kept together; and the proceeds should not be used to liquidate debts. Two years after Fr. Roothaan's approval, the Maryland Jesuits sold their human property to Senator Henry Johnson, former governor of Louisiana, and Jesse Batey. The transaction violated several conditions set by Roothaan. This document has been translated from Latin.

Why did Fr. Roothaan place these conditions on the sale of the Maryland Jesuits' human property?

Reverend in Christ Provincial Father
Pax Christi Rome, 27 December 1836
. . . . . .

About the ~~slaves~~ negroes, already Father Vespre who set out the matter clearly for us, has written back to Your Reverence that we are persuaded, that they can be sold and should be sold, whenever the opportunity should present itself; I confirm this and I entrust this whole business to Your Reverence, on the following conditions.

    1. In order to satisfy the gravest debt of conscience, every care should be taken that they be sold in such a way that they have free exercise of the catholic religion, and they have the opportunity for exercising it. And so

1. They must not be sold except to planters, lest by chance the person who buys them from ours, afterwards may carelessly separate the slaves he has purchased and sell them to others.
2. It must be stipulated in selling that the benefit of exercising religion be given to the negroes, and the assistance of a priest.
3. Husbands and wives, ~~parents and children~~, in no way must be separated, nor, I should say, parents from the children, as much as is possible.
4. If any slave male or female of ours, should have a wife or husband in somebody else's possession, they ought to be joined together with all effort, otherwise they absolutely should not be sold with the intention of taking them to a far away region.

About these things, the conscience of Your Reverence is burdened, which I affirm, but not because I have doubts on the concern of Your Reverence in this matter, but so that I may satisfy my own conscience.

It also will be in keeping with charity and justice, to provide carefully for those negroes, who on account of burdensome age or incurable illnesses, cannot be sold and transferred elsewhere.

2. The money, which will be raised from this sale, absolutely must not be spent on making expenditures, nor in paying off debts, but it is <u>capital</u> which <u>ought to be invested</u> so that it may grow. The best way perhaps would be "<u>groundrent</u>," especially in the states of Pennsylvania and New York—but about this a plan must be initiated with upright and careful men, knowledgable in things of this kind, our own people, outsiders too.

Finally, about everything else which will be done in this business, may Your Reverence inform us, since the survival of this Province depends to a large degree on this being done well, clearly for the benefit of the Novitiate and the school. Consider therefore what is to be done, and deliberate, and pray, so that it may turn out for the good of the Province and the glory of God.

May God bless Your Reverence in all things, and pour new strength on him in the new year. I truly hope Your Reverence has recovered from his indisposition. Finally I recommend again and again that he <u>write, write, write</u> with more care and that he remember me in His Most Holy Sacrifices.

I am sincerely

To Your Reverence

A Slave in Christ

Ioannes Roothaan

To Father McSherry, Provincial in the Society of Jesus

13

Articles of Agreement between
Thomas Mulledy, Henry Johnson,
and Jesse Batey, 1838

On June 19, 1838, Fr. Thomas F. Mulledy, SJ, provincial of the Maryland Jesuits, signed a contract to sell 272 men, women, and children (known today as the GU272) to Jesse Batey and Henry S. Johnson, a US congressman and former governor of Louisiana. The contract identifies the people who were sold by name and age, often by their family connections. The Jesuits would receive $115,000 in five annual installments of $18,000, with a $25,000 down payment delivered upon the buyers' receipt in Alexandria of fifty-one persons named in the contract. Over the years, the payments were renegotiated because of the buyers' financial difficulties, subsequent sales, and death. The Jesuits did not receive the last payment until 1862.

What did it mean for the men, women, and children named in this contract to be treated as property?

19th June
1838.

Articles of agreement between Thomas F. Mulledy, of George Town, District of Columbia, of one part, and Jesse Beatty and Henry Johnson, of the State of Louisiana, of the other part.

Thomas F. Mulledy sells to Jesse Beatty and Henry Johnson two hundred and seventy two negroes, to wit:—Isaac, a man sixty five years of age, Charles, his eldest son, forty years of age, Nelly his daughter, thirty eight years of age, Henny, a girl thirteen years of age, Cecilia, a girl eight years of age, Ruthy, a girl six years of age, Patrick a man thirty five years of age, Letty, his wife, thirty years of age, Cornelius, thirteen years of age, Francis, a boy twelve years of age, Susan, a girl ten, Gabriel, a boy eight, Peter a boy five, Jackson a boy three, Elizabeth, a child one, James a man twenty eight, Delia a woman twenty two, Susan a girl three, George a boy one, Isaac a man twenty six, Kitty his wife, twenty eight, Austin a boy six, Isaac a boy four, Elias a boy about one and a half, Sally a woman sixty five, Ned a man forty five, Rachel a woman forty three, Simon their son twenty, Anderson a boy eighteen, Louisa a girl fourteen, Ned a boy ten, Billy a man forty, Nelly a woman thirty eight, John a boy five, John a man thirty Nancy a woman twenty four, Patrick a boy three, Charles a man forty five, Sally a woman forty four, Nancy a woman seventeen, Margaret a girl fifteen, David a boy fourteen, Eliza a girl twelve, Martha a girl five, Thomas a boy five, Sarah Anne a child one, Nelly a woman sixty Joseph a man forty, Nell a girl sixteen, Kitty a woman twenty two, Mary a girl six, Sam a boy four, Elizabeth a child one, Polly a woman sixty, Sally a woman fifty, William a man twenty one, Mary Anne a woman eighteen, Robert an idiot twelve, Henry eight, Harriett forty three Elizabeth twenty three, Isaiah a man twenty one, Mary Ellen seventeen, Nancy fifteen, Martha ten, Jemmy one, Betsy a woman thirty two, Austin her son thirteen, Adolph ten, Henrietta seven, Harriett Anne four, Richard thirty six, Nancy [Margy - crossed out] a woman thirty four, Margery sixty, Len sickly a man thirty eight Minty a woman thirty six, Nancy five Mary eighteen months, Charles sixty, James fifty, Tom forty five, Eliza twenty six, Reverdy seven, Noble five Edward three, William one Bill an idiot forty two Maria twenty six, Mary her daughter five, William six months, Charles [illegible] five, Benedict sixty five, Len Queen fifty, Sam [illegible] John Butler thirty five, John Coyles twenty one, [illegible] sixty five, Len Sweden fifty Daniel eighty, Nace fifty five Bernard thirty five, William eighteen, Tom sixteen, Jim twelve, Henry ten, Francis eight, Stephen lame sixty, Anne Len Queen's wife, two sons and a daughter, Betsy [wife?] of Sam, and her two daughters, Matilda and her three daughters, Kitty wife of George, her son + daughter Margaret + her daughter, Ginny wife of Charles, and her daughter, Crissy, her two sons + two daughters, Celestia, Henry (not married) Louisa, Teresa, Mary, - all the women except Ginny, Kitty and the last three of last mentioned are under fifty, and over twenty years of age, the children attended to are from one to seven years of age, Harry sixty five, Dina his wife sixty Joe fifty seven, Esther his wife fifty four, Bill twenty nine, Peter fifty seven, Stephen forty-nine, Sarah his wife forty eight, Bibiana forty nine, Mary fifty nine, Betty forty six, Bennet forty five, Clair his wife fortytwo, John thirty one, Abraham twenty seven, Susan twenty six, Priscilla seven, Perry twenty six, Jarred twenty four, Rose Anne his wife, twenty four, Charlotte twenty three, Mary twenty three, Julianne twenty two, Dick twenty seven, Greenfield twenty five, James twenty one, Ferdinand nineteen, Sylvester nineteen, Christianna eighteen, Harriette seventeen, Emmeline sixteen, Elenora fifteen, Mary twelve, Susanna fourteen, Ritta thirteen, Remus a man seventeen, Milly thirteen, Lucy eleven, Sall ten, Dina eight, Esther eight, Alexis thirteen, two children of one and two years of age, Nace fifty, Nace twenty, Biby forty five, Suzy twenty one, Bridget seventeen, Caroline fourteen, Basil thirteen, Martha eleven, Anne ten, Gabe eight, Biby seven, Henry six, Thomas five, Mary three, a child eighteen months old, Henry twenty eight, Emeline ten, Amanda eight, Elizabeth seven, Billy six, Biby five, Harriett five, Robert forty three, Mary thirty eight, Abraham sixteen, Robert fourteen, James twelve, Bridget eleven, Mary Jane ten, Susan eight, Sally Anne seven, Nelly six, Charles five, a child two, Bill Cush twenty eight, Phil fifty five, Nelly his wife, fifty three, Louis ten, Gusty eight, George thirty, Joseph twenty two, Harry seventy five, Anne seventy, Harry forty, Nelly thirty eight, Gabe twenty three, Daniel twenty five, Louise twenty three, Arnold thirty eight, Anna his wife, twenty seven, Arnold seven, Louisa five, Betsy thirty eight, Barney twelve Lucinda ten, Greenfield five, Daniel four, Watt forty five, Teresa forty two, Frank twenty, Sam fourteen, Rachel eleven, Alexander ten, Charlotte seven, Emeline six, Watt three, a child one, Dick forty, Adeline thirty two, Matt ten, Ginny seven, Catherine four, a child six months, Nelly forty five, Eliza twenty two, Regis twenty eight, Kitty fifty three, Peter thirty seven, James sixty nine, Michael thirty three, Ned thirty, Sally fifty six, Alexis thirty six, Henney twenty two, Frederick twenty, Jenny nine, her child two, Zeke thirty two, Nathan sixty four, Henny his wife, sixty, James sixty years of age, it being understood, that if there be any children on either of the places where the said slaves now reside, belonging to any of the women herein named, that they are to be included in this sale. It is understood that the said negroes are to be delivered at Alexandria in the District of Columbia, as follows. Fifty one contained in the list annexed, as soon as practicable, and all the others at such time as may be designated by the purchasers, between the 15th October & the 15th November next, with their [?] beds [?]:

Jesse Beatty & Henry Johnson agree on their part to pay to Thomas F. Mulledy for the said negroes, the sum of one hundred & fifteen thousand dollars, to wit: - Twenty five thousand dollars on the delivery of the fifty one negroes if they shall be considered worth, agreeably to the average price of the whole, that sum, but if they should not be worth that amount agreeably to the said average, their estimated value is to be paid on their delivery, but the balance required to make up the amount of twenty five thousand dollars, shall be paid on the delivery of the other slaves in the fall. For the remaining sum of ninety thousand dollars, which J. Beatty & H. Johnson agree to pay, they are to have a credit of ten years, paying interest at the rate of six percent annually thereon; it being agreed and understood, that at the end of five years from the delivery of the said slaves at Alexandria, in the fall, as stipulated, the payments are to be made in five equal annual installments of eighteen thousand dollars each, from that time; that is, the first payment is to be made in the month of March next after the said time thus designated, and the other installments annually thereafter. It is distinctly understood, however, that the interest is to be paid from the time of the delivery of the slaves, as aforesaid, and that the first payment of interest will commence from the time of said delivery, and be calculated up to the period of payment, and that the interest thereafter is to be annually paid to T. F. Mulledy, at George Town College, District Columbia.—

It is further agreed, that on the delivery of the slaves in the fall, they are to be divided between Jesse Beatty and Henry Johnson, each agreeing to place his portion on a tract or tracts of land in the State of Louisiana, of the value of one thousand dollars, and to mortgage the said tract lands, together with the said negroes, (except those first to be delivered) to secure the payment of the said sum stipulated to be paid by him for his portion of the said slaves. And it also understood, that besides the said mortgages, the said J. Beatty + H. Johnson are to give their joint + several notes, or notes drawn in favor of one and endorsed by the other, for the amount stipulated to be paid for the negroes, and to cause each to be sub-[signed?] by some responsible person as security.—

It is further stipulated, that if the said negroes herein named shall be of different ages from that affixed to their names, and their value thereby impaired, or shall be unhealthy, or in any manner unsound, a fair deduction shall be made for such difference in age, or for such defects as shall lessen their value; and if the parties shall not agree as to the amount to be deducted, the question shall be submitted for decision to two arbitrators to be chosen by the parties. It is further understood, that the fifty one negroes herein before alluded to, contained in the annexed list, are considered to be of the value of twenty five thousand dollars, and that the part of the contract relating to those to be immediately delivered, will be fulfilled when they are received, and the amount paid.

City of Washington, June 19th 1838.—

Thomas F. Mulledy
J. Batey
H. Johnson

———

A list of fifty one negroes referred to in the foregoing contract.
From White Marsh.—

Ned age 45
Rachel " 43
Simon " 20
Anderson " 18
Louisa " 14
Ned " 10
Charles " 45
Elizabeth " 23
Isaiah " 21
Mary Ellen " 17
Nancy " 15
Martha " 12
Jim " 1
Sally " 44
Nancy " 17
Margaret " 15
David " 14
Eliza " 12
Martha " 5
Sarah Anne " 1
Thomas " 5
Emeline—age—6
Watt " 3
Robert " 45
Mary " 38
Abraham " 16
Robert " 14
James " 12—
Bridget " 11

Harriett age 43
James " 28
Delia " 22
Susan " 3
George " 9
From St. Inigoes
Ned age 30
Fred " 20
Henry " 22
Bill Cush not mar. 28
[crossed out]
George " 30
Bill not mard 23
~~Joseph~~ " 22
Watt " 45
Teresa " 44
Frank " 20
Sam " 14
Rachel " 11
Alexander " 10
Charlotte " 7
Mary Anne age—10
Louisa " 8
Sally " 7
Nelly " 6
Charles " 5
Child " 2

51

Signed duplicates each party retaining a copy.
June 19th 1838.—
Thomas F. Mulledy
J. Batey
H. Johnson

14

A Jesuit Priest Witnesses Anguish at Newtown, 1838

Fr. Peter Havermans, SJ, the superior at Newtown plantation, was an eyewitness to the deportation of the slave community in the fall of 1838. In a letter to the Jesuit Father General in Rome, the priest told of the despair of one unnamed pregnant woman who pleaded with him, "What will become of me? Why do I deserve this?" This letter is one of few in the Jesuit archives in which the words, thoughts, and feelings of the enslaved community can be heard, even if indirectly. This excerpt from the letter has been translated from Latin.

Why did the enslaved woman quoted in this letter feel despair at the prospect of being sold to Louisiana?

———————————

Nevertheless about an especially important thing, about the slaves of course, who all as I was then anticipating, have been sold, I will not now say much. When I consider the affair as now it has been brought to an end and after the fact, I will say only so much, that, inasmuch as I am able to apprehend, they were sold to infidels, living in places of infidelity, at a distance of five thousand English miles. The affair gave many here a reason for speaking badly about us. "No one does this but bad people, as they are dealers of Negroes, who care for nothing except money, or also by those who by necessity, e.g. from misfortunate, or of paying contracted debts, are driven toward it." Others [^even Protestants] consider this forbidden.[1] And I also will say that this thing was especially grim and displeasing to me, and still is, even more because the slaves who were under my care conducted themselves well, and, as long as they were beneath me, they were of great use for the Society, and would have been of greater use still, and for the rest, if they did need to be sold, they could have been sold without scandal and clear danger of losing their souls ....

... From the residence at Newtown 12th November 1838
When I had already finished this letter, Provincial Father Mulledy arrived with Johnson, the ex-governor of the state of Louisiana, the master to whom our slaves were sold, around evening on the day of Saturday, intending on the following day, the day of our Lord around noon, to put them all on a boat, but since the laws require so many formalities, this luckily was rendered impossible. I ought, as the provincial father was saying to me, to have sent for the *prolictor*, commonly known as Sheriff, who was here for two days. In which time they had the opportunity to wash their clothes and of preparing themselves a bit for such a long journey. How these sad days passed I am not able to say. The slaves with heroic fortitude were giving themselves to fate and with Christian resignation relinquishing themselves to God. One woman more pious than the others, and at that time pregnant most demanded my compassion. She was coming toward me so that for the last time she could greet me and seek benediction, and she observed as she was genuflecting: "If ever someone should have reason for despair, do I not now have it? I do not know on what day the birth will come, whether on the road or sea. What will become of me? Why do I deserve this?" I was saying "Trust in God." So it was, she agreed, I offered myself totally to her. All were coming to me seeking rosaries, medals, a cross or something so that they would remember me. And with how much obedience they went to the boat. Only one tried to run away. And the official was not compelled to bind him. This day for a long time here [?] ...

The encumbered slaves remain here so that either their wives or husbands might be bought, or there might be an arrangement concerning them by said Johnson. For I wish that he would not separate them from their partners and children. For this would resound louder still and greatly hurt the faith ...

Note

1. The caret character signifies that the writer inserted more text between the margins. Using carets to insert text was fairly common in the 19th century. Usually, letter writers would use them to add text they omitted as they wrote or to further explain something.—Eds.

15

Bill of Sale for Len, 1843

Although the 1838 sale diminished the Maryland Jesuits' direct stake in slavery, the Province continued to own, buy, hire, rent, and sell enslaved people after 1838. Some members of the Jesuit enslaved community remained in Maryland, and the Jesuits purchased additional people. In 1843 Fr. Robert Woodley, SJ, bought a man named Len for $400 from Jane Smith, a business acquaintance who had rented two enslaved men to the Jesuits' Newtown plantation. Woodley's purchase was controversial in the mission as he proceeded without authorization from superiors.

Why did the Maryland Jesuits continue to buy and sell people after 1838?

Know all men by these presents that I Jane E Smith of Saint Mary's County and State of Maryland for and in consideration of the sum of four hundred dollars, current money to be to me paid by the Rvd. Mr. Woodley of the County & State aforesaid, the receipt whereof I do herewith acknowledge, have granted, bargained sold and delivered unto the said Rvd. Mr. Woodley (agent for the Jesuit Society at Newtown) my negro man "Len" (Slave). I will warrant and defend to the said Rvd. Mr. Woodley his successors and assigners against me my executors administrators and assigns, & against any other person whosoever. In witness whereof I have hereunto set my hand and offered my seale this 4th day of September, Eighteen hundred and Forty-Three.

Seale Jane E. Smith

Signed, sealed and delivered
in the presence of ———
Enoch Neale

16

A Jesuit Priest Reports on the Fate
of the Ex-Jesuit Enslaved Community
in Louisiana, 1848

The Jesuit priest Fr. James Van de Velde visited Chatham plantation ten years after the sale of the Maryland Jesuit enslaved community to Louisiana. Observing that the enslaved community had no access to a priest on their remote plantation, he requested $1,000 from the Maryland Jesuits to build a church for the community so that they could continue to practice Catholicism. There is no record that the Maryland Jesuits responded to Van de Velde's plea. After emancipation, a Catholic church was built in the area, and many of the descendants of the Maryland Jesuit enslaved community remained devout Catholics well into the twenty-first century. This letter has been translated from French.

What does Fr. Van de Velde's letter reveal about the conditions that the GU272 faced in bondage in Louisiana?

Fredericktown, 27 Nov. 1848
Rev. I. Brocard
My Reverend and very dear Father
I take the liberty of writing a word to you again in order to plead the cause of the poor negroes, who previously belonged to your Province, and who are now found destitute of nearly all religious succor in Louisiana.

I may be mistaken, but it appears to me that the Province of Maryland is obligated by conscience to procure them succor and to make some sacrifices in this matter. The text of the Holy Scripture, "Qui suorum, maxime domesticorum curam non agit &c" comes to my mind continually when I think of these poor people, particularly the children, who, bit by bit, lose religion.[1] It is an extreme case. If justice does not demand it (although I am of the opinion that it demands it in this case), at least security asks it. I am only asking it for those who find themselves on the plantation of Messrs. Johnson & Thomson. They are numerous enough. One of the inhabitants, Judge Duffield [Edward Duffel], would give a parcel of land to build a church there for all the persons of color in the neighborhood. Mr. Elder [John C. Elder, a native of Maryland] and the other neighbors would contribute freely to this good work and, two times per month, would visit from Donaldsonville and give the slaves instruction.

All that is asked is that the Province of Maryland contribute $1,000, the neighbors will contribute the rest; and what is a mere $1,000 for the province that has the income from so many farms, and which has already received so large a sum for these poor exiles? The Good Lord will compensate for it; will return it with interest, and who knows if the refusal of coming to their aid will not attract misfortune on the Province? I myself am very worried about this, and if I seem tiresome to you, I am sure that you will pardon me for it, since it is for the good of these poor abandoned children that I importune you.

In case you will decide this matter in their favor, correspond with Father Bouillier [John Boullier, C.M.], Lazarist priest of Donaldsonville, La., and send him the amount, or to start, a part of the amount, and be sure that it will truly be a pleasure to commence this good work right away.

In union of your S.S. S.S. I have the honor of being,

My Reverend and very dear Father,

Your devoted brother in Jesus Christ /s/

Van de Velde SJ.

Note

1. Van de Velde here is paraphrasing 1 Timothy 5:8: "But if any man have not care of his own, and especially of those of his house, he hath denied the faith, and is worse than an infidel." In the Latin Vulgate this verse reads, "Si quis autem suorum, et maxime domesticorum, curam non habet, fidem negavit, et est infideli deterior." —Eds.

17

Aaron Edmonson, the Last Enslaved Worker at Georgetown, 1859–62

Aaron Edmonson was the last enslaved worker at Georgetown. He arrived at the college in 1859 when his owner Ann Green rented him out for $12 a month. He cleaned dormitories, lugged coal in the winter, and painted hallways during the summer. He labored at Georgetown while the Union army occupied the school in the spring of 1861. Edmonson left the school in March 1862, one month before the enactment of the Compensated Emancipation Act of the District of Columbia freed him. His owner received $100 as compensation from the federal government. What happened to Edmonson after that is unknown.

What does Edmonson's account reveal about the use of enslaved labor at Georgetown College?

		Aaron Edmundston:— Dr Cr		
1859		A Colored man of Mrs. Ann Green		
Nov	3	Commen'd this afternoon to work in dormity @ $12 pr mo.		
"	"			
"	"			
Dec	7	To cash for 1 month's wages ending 3rd inst	12.00	
"	"	By 1 months wages ...... " "		12.00
"	"			

(continued)

1860 Jan	3	By 1 months wages ending this date at . . . $10.00		
Feb	3	By 1 mos wages ending this date @ . . . : 12.00		. . . . 22.00
"	4	To cash Pd Oceola Green for above wage . . .	22.00	
May	4	" chk " " " " 3 mos wages	36.00	
"	"	By 3 months wages ending 3d inst @ . 12.00		. . . . 36.00
"	"		58.00	58.00
July	3	By 2 mos wages ending this date		24.00
"	"	To cash Pd Oceola Green	24.00	
"	"		24.00	24.00
Sep	5	To cash Pd Do Do	24.00	
Nov	7	" " " " Do Do	24.00	
Dec	5	" 10 days absence at sundry times to date	4.00	
"	14	" 1 day absent	.40	
1861 Jan	3	By 6 months wages ending date . . .		. . . . 72.00
"	4	To cash Pd Oceola Green	19.60	
"	"		72.00	72.00
Feb	5	To cash Pd O. Green 9.20		
"	"	" absence from work 2.80	12.00	
Mar	6	" cash Pd O Green	12.00	
Apr	6	" cash $10.80 " " Absence $1.20	12.00	
"	"	Left May 4/61		
May	3	Cr By 4 months wages ending this date . . .		. . . . . . 48.00
"	"	Dr To cash	12.00	
"	"	Note, Aaron Left College this date	48.00	48.00
June	3	Returned this day @ $12. pr mo:-		
"	12	To 1 pr shoes 2.75 (15) 1 hat 1.25	4.00	
July	10	" 4 shovels @ 1.50 2 do. @ 2.00	10.00	
Aug	10	" 2 undershirts 2.00 2 Pr drawers 2.00 3 pr socks 75	4.75	
"	29	" mending shoes	1.25	
Nov	13	" 1 pr shoes	2.50	
Dec.	16	" 1 pr gloves 60 (19) 1 suit, 23.00 1 coat 10.00	33.60	

1862 Jan	16 " 1 pr shoes 2.75 + mending .75	3.50	
Feb	14 " 1 hat 3.00, absent time, 5.82	8.52	
Mar	3 Cr By 9 mos wages @ $12. pr mo		. . . . 108.00
Sep	26 Dr To cash paid Mrs Anne Green	39.58	
	Left College Mar 3/62	108.00	108.00

18

Labor Contract at West Oak Plantation,
Iberville Parish, Louisiana, 1865

Emancipation came to Iberville Parish, Louisiana, with the US Army during the Civil War. On April 3, 1865, the former Jesuit slaves at West Oak plantation, now newly freed people, entered into a contract for wages with their former owner, Emily Woolfolk. Sixty-seven people are named in the contract, ranging from twelve to sixty years old. The contract stipulated rations, clothing, quarters, medical attention, instruction, and a share of the crops' profits. The document reveals both change and continuity at the dawn of emancipation: The inhabitants of West Oak continued to work on the plantation where they had been enslaved, but now they would get paid for their labor. The site of West Oak is now the town of Maringouin.

What does this contract tell us about the meaning of freedom for newly emancipated people?

_____

No. 2
Agreement with freedmen,
on
West Oaks
Plantation,
Parish of
Iberville
Employed by
Mrs. Emily Woolfolk
Date of Agreement,
April 3 1865

Agreement with freedmen.

This Agreement, (in three parts) made and entered into this First day of April A.D. 1865, by and between Mrs. Emily Woolfolk of the Parish of Iberville and State of Louisiana of the first part, and the Sixty seven persons hereinafter named and undersigned. Freedmen of the same place, parties hereto of the second part, WITNESSETH:

THAT for the purpose of cultivating the plantation known as the West Oaks in the Parish aforesaid, during the year commencing on the First day of January A. D. 1865, and terminating on the first day of January, A.D. 1866, the said parties do hereby mutually agree that the Genl Orders No. 23 [illegible] Dep. Of the Gulf providing for the employment and general welfare of Freedmen, series 1865 and the local rules in pursuance thereof, all of which are hereto annexed (or separately supplied,) and are hereby incorporated in and made part of this agreement as fully as if here recited. The said Mrs. E Woolfolk for the considerations and on the conditions and stipulations hereinafter mentioned, agrees to pay to the said Laborers, the rates of monthly wages agreed upon and as specified opposite their respective names hereto: one half to be paid at the end of each quarter as prescribed by order. Said Mrs. E Woolfolk further agrees to furnish to the said Laborers and those rightfully dependent on them, free of charge, good and sufficient quarters, a separate tenement for each family, fuel and medical attendance; to see that the premises thus furnished are kept in a good sanitary condition; to allot from the lands of said plantation for garden, to each family or Labourer the unit of land presented by said orders; such allotment to include a reasonable use of tools and animals; to exact only ten hours work per day, and no labor whatever on Sundays Except in case of absolute necessity and if any labor in excess of ten hours per day is rendered, the same is to be paid as extra labor, upon such terms as may be agreed upon by the parties hereto; to grant to such Laborers one-half of each and every Saturday, to enable them to cultivate the portions of land allotted to them, also the Fourth Day of July; to co-operate in the establishment of any school for the education of the children of said Laborers; that she will furnish them a sufficient supply of wholesome food and proper clothing for themselves and their families; and finally the said Mrs. Emily Woolfolk agrees to comply in all respects with the rules and regulations above referred to and made part hereof.

AND IN CONSIDERATION of the faithful performance of the said Mrs. Emily Woolfolk of all the obligations assumed by her, and of the punctual payment by her of the wages agreed upon as aforesaid, the said Laborers do hereby severally, and each for himself, agree with the said Mrs. E Woolfolk

& her heirs and assigns to well and faithfully perform the labor herein stipulated for the term aforesaid, in a strict conformity with the conditions aforesaid; and they further agree to observe and comply with the rules and regulations above referred to.

And it is furthermore Agreed: That in case the said Mrs E Woolfolk shall fail, neglect or refuse to fulfill any of the obligations assumed by her, or shall furnish said parties of the second part with bad or insufficient food, or insufficient or unhealthy quarters, or shall be guilty of cruelty to them, he shall, besides the legal recourse left to the particular party or parties aggrieved, render this contract liable to annulment, at the option of the Superintendent of Freedmen.

AND in case any Laborer shall voluntarily absent himself from, or shall neglect or refuse to perform the labor herein contracted for, and the fact shall be proved to the satisfaction of the proper Superintendent, the one-half of the wages due to said party so offending, retained in the hands of the said Mrs Emily Woolfolk as aforesaid, shal be forfeited to the said Mrs. E Woolfolk and the party so offending may be discharged from said employment.

And it is furthermore mutually Agreed by the said Mrs Emily Woolfolk and the following named Laborers, to-wit Basil Butler, Lewis Merrick, Tom Butler, Wash Nelsen, Polk Hill, Frank Hawkins, Neely Hawkins, Bill Hill, Jim Pendleton, Alex Scott, Jordan Sisaw, Jim Scott, Jack Hawkins, Bill Alexander, Jim Broadman, Joe Waters, Geo Harris, Miley Waters, Cumby Scott, Pat Hawkins, Ben Scott, Chas Nilsen, Geo Nelsen, Rich Nelsen, Wm Harris, Nace Scott, Joe hill, Abr Butler, Bole Scott, John H. Butler, Abr Scott, Alf Hawkins, Caroline Scott, Mary Butler, Eliza West, Amos Scott, Susan Hawkins, Lydia Scott, Delphy Gray, Eliza Butler, Martha Hawkins, Agnes Butler, Lucy Scott, Betsy Harris, Louisa Harris Beby Hawkins, Ellen Harris, Sarah Harris, Sarah Hill, Clara Scott, Fanny Scott, Rosa Scott, Adeline Waters, Ellenda Hawkins, Bridget Butler, Henry Butler, Louisa Scott, Matilda Hawkins, Betsy Hill, Jean Nelsen, Mary Waters, Emmelin Butler, Ella Harris, Amanda Hawkins, Esther Woolfolk, Mary Scott, Charlotte Pendleton. That in addition to just treatment, wholesome rations, comfortable clothing, quarters, fuel, and medical attendance, and the opportunity for instruction of children, they shall receive the share and portions of the net profits of the crop respectively set opposite their names balance payable one half of the money wages due quarterly as follows, on the first day of May, August and November, and final payment of the entire amount then due, on or before the 31st day of January 1866.

That in lieu of the half wages to be paid to them at the end of the year, the said Laborers shall be entitled to, and agree to accept, the share of net profits of carrying on the plantation during the period aforesaid, respectively set opposite their name below.

And it is furthermore Agreed, That any wages or share of profits due the said Laborers under this agreement, shall constitute a first lien upon all crops or parts of crops produced on said plantation or tract of land by their labor. And no shipment of products shall be made until the Superintendent shall certify that all dues to Laborers are paid or satisfactorily arranged.

In Testimony Whereof, the said parties have affixed their names to this Agreement, at Parish of Iberville State of Louisiana on the day and date aforesaid.

No.	Names	Age	Sex	Interest in Profits	Remarks
1	Basil Butler	40	Male	1/10	
2	Lewis Merrick	40	"	1/10	
3	Tom Butler	30	"	1/10	
4	Wash Nelsen	42	"	1/10	
5	Polk Hill	20	"	1/10	
6	Frank Hawkins	35	"	1/10	
7	Neely Hawkins	37	"	1/10	
8	Bill Hill	50	"	1/10	
9	Jim Pendleton	60	"		Sickly
10	Alex Scott	30	"	1/10	
11	Jordan Sisaw	55	"	1/10	
12	Jim Scott	40	"	1/10	
13	Jack Hawkins	30	"	1/10	
14	Bill Alexder	40	"	1/10	
15	Jim Broadman	30	"	1/10	
16	Joe Waters	18	"	1/10	
17	Geo Harris	20	"	1/10	
18	Miley Waters	18	"	1/10	
19	Cumby Scott	45	"	1/10	
20	Pat Hawkins	50	"	1/10	
21	Ben Scott	15	"	1/10	
22	Chas Nilsen	13	"	1/10	
23	Geo Nelsen	13	"	1/10	
24	Rich Nelsen	18	"	1/10	
25	Wm Harris	18	"	1/10	
26	Nace Scott	15	"	1/10	
27	Joe Hill	15	"	1/10	
28	Abr Butler	13	"	1/10	
29	Bole Scott	13	"	1/10	
30	John H. Butler	18	"	1/10	
31	Abr Scott	14	"	1/10	

(continued)

No.	Names	Age	Sex	Interest in Profits	Remarks
32	Alf Hawkins	12	"	1/10	
33	Caroline Scott	40	Female	1/10	
34	Mary Butler	37	"	1/10	
35	Eliza West	30	"	1/10	
36	Anne Scott	32	"	1/10	
37	Susan Hawkins	32	"	1/10	
38	Lydia Scott	25	"	1/10	
39	Delphy Gray	30	"	1/10	
40	Eliza Butler	40	"	1/10	
41	Martha Hawkins	40	"	1/10	
42	Agnes Butler	28	"	1/10	
[column	2]				
43	Lucy Scott	30	Female	1/10	
44	Betsy Harris	45	"	1/10	
45	Louisa Harris	25	"	1/10	
46	Beby Hawkins	26	"	1/10	
47	Ellen Harris	25	"	1/10	
48	Sarah Harris	36	"	1/10	
49	Sarah Hill	25	"	1/10	
50	Clara Scott	60	"		cook for field hands
51	Fanny Scott	40	"	1/10	
52	Rosa Scott	30	"	1/10	
53	Adeline Waters	30	"	1/10	
54	Ellenda Hawkins	40	"		sickly
55	Bridget Butler	22	"	1/10	
56	Henry Butler	18	"	1/10	
57	Louisa Scott	16	"	1/10	
58	Matilda Hawkins	16	"	1/10	
59	Betsy Hill	16	"	1/10	
60	Jean Nelsen	22	"	1/10	
61	Mary Waters	18	"	1/10	
62	Emmelin Butler	16	"	1/10	
63	Ally Harris	15	"	1/10	
64	Amanda Hawkins	12	"	1/10	
65	Esther Woolfolk	60	"		Cook for field hands
66	Mary Scott	50	"		" " family
67	Charlotte Pendleton	50	"		

Executed in the presence of Mr. Maynard[;] Isaac Erwin Approved, Nelson [illegible] leased by P. Marshal Parish Iberville

Emily Woolfolk Planter

NOTE—This Contract will be made out in three parts—one to be kept by the planter, and one by the local Superintendent—one to be forwarded through the local officer to the General Superintendent. No Contract will be accepted which does not contain the family name of each Laborer. If the Laborer has not one, he must assume one. The "Interest in Profits" is only in lieu of the half wages to be reserved. The first half wages to be paid each month as prescribed.

19

Photograph of Frank Campbell, ca. 1900

Frank Campbell was born in 1820 at St. Inigoes plantation in Maryland. His parents, Watt and Theresa, were owned by the Maryland Jesuits. In 1838 when Campbell was twenty years old, the Jesuits sold the family to Henry S. Johnson, a US congressman and former governor of Louisiana, and shipped them to Johnson's plantation in Louisiana. Frank Campbell married Mary Jane Mahoney in Louisiana, another member of the GU272. Decades later, after emancipation, a photograph captured an elderly Frank Campbell with his granddaughter Mary Jane. This photograph was discovered in a scrapbook owned by Robert Ruffin Barrow Jr. in the archives at Nicholls State University in Louisiana.

What does this photograph of Frank Campbell show us that written sources cannot?

Photograph of Frank Campbell, ca. 1900. *Archives and Special Collections, Nicholls State University, Thibodaux, Louisiana*

PART II

MEMORY AND RECONCILIATION

ESSAYS

20

American Slavery in History and Memory and the Search for Social Justice

IRA BERLIN

Historian Ira Berlin explores the difference between the history and the memory of slavery, and the contribution that both historical research and memorialization can make to healing the wounds of slavery. This essay was first published in the Journal of American History *90, no. 4 (March 2004).*

Tho' de slave question am settled, de race question will be wid us always, 'til Jesus come de second time. It's in our politics, in our justice courts, on our highways, on our side walks, in our manners, in our 'ligion, and in our thoughts, all de day and every day.
                                        —Cornelius Holmes, Winnsboro, South Carolina, c. 1937

The ratification of the Thirteenth Amendment to the Constitution in December 1865 abolished slavery in the United States. In the years that followed, southern planters and their allies proved extraordinarily resourceful in inventing new forms of labor extraction and racial oppression, but try as they might, they could not resuscitate chattel bondage. Yet, almost a century and a half later, the question of slavery again roils the water of American life. Indeed, the last years of the twentieth century and the first years of the twenty-first have witnessed an extraordinary resurgence of popular interest in slavery, which has stimulated its study and provided the occasion for a rare conversation between historians and an interested public. Slavery has a greater presence in American life now than at any time since the Civil War ended. The intense engagement over the issue of slavery signals—as it did in the 1830s and the 1960s—a crisis in American race relations that necessarily elevates the significance of the study of the past in the search for social justice.

The new interest has been manifested in the success on the big screen of the movies *Glory*, *Amistad*, and *Adanggaman*, along with a blockbuster with Oprah Winfrey as producer and star, *Beloved*.[1] They have been followed on the small screen: The four-part TV series *Africans in America* traced the course of slavery's development from the forcible deportation of Africans to the celebration of an American emancipation; in a televised sojourn through Africa, the scholar Henry Louis Gates Jr. confronted the painful matter of African complicity in the transatlantic slave trade; and HBO's *Unchained Memories* explored the remembrances of slavery collected in the 1930s by the Works Progress Administration.[2] The television docudramas were paralleled by radio broadcasts and audiobooks, of which *Remembering Slavery*, a collaboration of scholars (including myself) at the University of Maryland, the Smithsonian Institution, and the Library of Congress, was but one. They come hard on the heels of John Michael Vlach's "The Back of the Big House" exhibition at the Library of Congress and the presentation of the famous Augustus Saint-Gaudens frieze of the Fifty-fourth Massachusetts Regiment at the National Gallery. Workers in Washington have but recently put the finishing touches on a monument to black Civil War soldiers. Styled after the Vietnam Veterans Memorial, it lists the names of more than two hundred thousand soldiers and sailors, most of them former slaves. The city of Windsor, Ontario, placed a monument to the Underground Railroad on the border between the United States and Canada.[3] A monument to the *Amistad* captives stands in front of city hall in New Haven, Connecticut. The *Amistad* itself has been reconstructed at Mystic Seaport in Connecticut, and the ship recently completed its journey of reconciliation down the east coast and began a new one around the Great Lakes. The National Slave Memorial Act (H.R. 196), introduced by the Republican representative Cliff Stearns of Florida (who was joined by an unusual coalition of congressmen that included representatives John Lewis and Dick Armey), acknowledges the "injustice, cruelty, brutality, and inhumanity of slavery in the United States and the 13 American colonies," proposing to memorialize slaves on a site to be recommended by the secretary of the interior (a position currently held by a woman who has publicly regretted that the defeat of the Confederacy undermined the doctrine of states' rights).[4]

Some of those monuments—and others—are connected to larger sites of remembrance. One such site, the multimillion-dollar National Underground Railroad Freedom Center, is nearing completion in Cincinnati, Ohio. Other museums of slavery are proposed for Fredericksburg, Virginia; Charleston,

South Carolina; and Washington. When those massive halls of slavery's history are completed, they will stand alongside dozens of smaller ones as well as scores of Underground Railroad safe houses, hundreds of roadside markers, and thousands of miles of freedom trails.[5]

Historic sites that had been the residences of slaveholders, such as Belle Grove, Montpelier, and Mount Vernon in Virginia; Drayton Hall and Middleton Place in South Carolina; the Hermitage in Tennessee; Shadows-on-the-Teche in Louisiana; and the Decatur and Octagon houses in Washington once told only the story of the great men and women who rambled through their hallways, ate from fine china, and slept in plump feather beds. The itinerary that greets visitors now includes the history of those who lodged in the basement, ate from wooden bowls, and slept in hammocks or on hard pallets. Such matters are not the concern of the estates' keepers only. At Antietam, Fort Sumter, Gettysburg, and other famed battlefields, congressional mandate requires that National Park Service rangers address the role of slavery in the coming of the Civil War. Federal law thus returns the nation's battlefield parks to their first purposes in order that these "sacred sites" become—in the words of one historian—places "of reconciliation and healing."[6]

In the past year, according to the Gilder Lehrman Institute for the Study of Slavery, Resistance, and Abolition at Yale University (itself evidence of the renewed interest in slavery), some sixty scholarly books on slavery and related subjects have been published. Those are apparently not enough, for the institute has established the twenty-five-thousand-dollar Frederick Douglass Prize for the best book on slavery, in part to encourage further work in the field.[7] To the scholarly books, numbers of novels, textbooks, children's books, chronologies, and genealogies can be added, as well as hundreds of Web sites, dozens of CDs, and at least two operas. Slavery has been on the cover of *Time* and *Newsweek*, above the fold in the *Washington Post*, and the lead story in the "Week in Review" section of the Sunday *New York Times*. And, if that was not enough, there is the continuing controversy over the paternity of Sally Hemings's children.[8]

That controversy provides a reminder of how much slavery has become part of contemporary American politics. Bill Clinton early recognized slavery's political significance, hence the debate or phantom debate over "the apology" that President Clinton eventually delivered at Gorée, a former slave factory on the west coast of Africa in 1998. Since the press reported the event so poorly, it is not clear what Clinton said at Gorée. But it soon became evident that Clinton had indeed apologized because conservative congressmen demanded he retract "the apology."[9]

Five years later, much has changed in American politics, but slavery, if anything, has grown in significance, as was suggested by the lack of controversy over President George W. Bush's visit to Gorée. There, amid references to Olaudah Equiano, Phillis Wheatley, Sojourner Truth, and Frederick Douglass, he denounced slavery as "one of the greatest crimes of history." Although Bush faced the ire of angry activists for not apologizing directly for the part the United States played in the slave trade, the American press greeted his condemnation of slavery as the conventional wisdom.[10] His visit suggests that presidential sojourns to African slave factories may become as much a part of the protocol of American politics as the once ritual Labor Day visits to Detroit's Cadillac Square.

Still, it remains easier for American leaders to address the question of slavery from the coast of Africa than from the heartland of the United States. Between the two presidential visits, controversy continued as President Clinton's National Advisory Panel on Race Relations—chaired by the distinguished historian John Hope Franklin and charged to initiate a national dialogue on race—hove into view. When it too flagged, a dispute over the placement of the Confederate banner atop South Carolina's capitol erupted, and like controversies respecting the Confederate flag soon spread to neighboring Georgia and Mississippi. In the latter state, a contentious plebiscite disturbed local politics.[11] A like dispute in Virginia over the naming of April as Confederate History Month embarrassed the governor and set loose another long controversy, as did Virginia's state song with its cheerful references to "darkies" and "ole massa." To avoid such strife, although perhaps also to prove that the Potomac River still divides the states that stood with the Union from those that joined the Confederacy, the District of Columbia officially reinitiated the commemoration of April 16 as Emancipation Day—the date Abraham Lincoln signed the legislation freeing slaves in the federal district—and Maryland has appointed a commission for the study and commemoration of slavery. It is the first in the nation, although doubtless not the last.[12]

As the twenty-first century is aborning, the press and the TV news daily present some new controversy over slavery—and not just in the states of the former Confederacy. Washingtonians have discovered that slaves built the national Capitol building. New Yorkers have found that the entire lower end of Manhattan Island is underlain with the bones of slaves. Philadelphians have learned that a proposed visitors' center to house the Liberty Bell sits directly on the ground where President George Washington housed his slaves.[13] Students at Yale University uncovered slave owners and slave traders among the university's most prominent founders and benefactors.[14]

Each discovery has generated its own controversies, whose political resonance has echoed on the hustings and, given the litigious nature of the American people, in the courts and legislatures. Thus the reduction of the size of the Confederate flag incorporated into the Georgia state flag allegedly contributed to the defeat of a sitting governor. A suit against the insurance company Aetna, Inc., for insuring slave property more than a century earlier has not only unleashed a host of similar legal actions but also prompted the California legislature to require all insurance companies doing business in the state to reveal whether they have insured slave property. And insurance companies are not the only corporate entities at risk. The accusations against Aetna encouraged the *Hartford Courant*, one of the oldest newspapers in the nation, to apologize for advertising the sale of slaves. Then, in one of the most remarkable events of recent American journalism, it reprised the history of slavery in Connecticut in a seventy-nine-page supplement to its Sunday edition.[15] While the *Hartford Courant* confesses, dozens of corporations—including some of the largest banks, railroads, and manufacturers—send their lawyers scrambling, issuing denials and preparing for their day in court. As such events resonate in the daily press and on the nightly news, their cumulative presence grows, for lurking behind them wait debates over thousands of schools named for Confederate generals and slaveholding politicians (including the most revered leaders in American history) and the vexed question of reparations, a subject that has already been the topic of congressional hearings, books, articles, Web sites, conferences, seminars, and talk shows.[16]

Although such matters seem to appear and disappear without reason, they reflect no fleeting engagement. A story on the front page of the *Washington Post* described a living history performance that disturbed the quiet of Colonial Williamsburg. The enactment began with a slave auction, an inescapable reality in seventeenth- and eighteenth-century Williamsburg. The local chapter of the National Association for the Advancement of Colored People (NAACP) objected to the performance as not only in bad taste but also insulting and harmful to people of African descent, a painful and unwanted reminder of a nightmarish past. The director of the project, Christy S. Coleman, now the president of Detroit's Charles H. Wright Museum of African-American History, refused to retreat, arguing that slavery was an essential part of the history of Colonial Williamsburg. The NAACP has since conceded Coleman's point. The results of the incorporation of the slave trade into the reenactments astounded observers, as visitors to Colonial Williamsburg became caught up in the presentation in all of the complicated ways that slavery and its memory touches Americans, black and white. Some have stepped forward to help "slaves" escape, others have offered to protect slaves from abusive masters, and some have even turned on the putative owners—and not merely to debate the issue. Indeed, several visitors have had to be physically restrained. Lest it be thought that it was only the visitors who forgot that they had witnessed an enactment, the actors themselves—mostly young black men and women—have been caught up in the drama as well. In playing slaves, they found that they were often treated as slaves, not merely by visitors but also by others, setting in motion depressing fantasies.[17]

It is rare for Americans to engage their history, especially with such intensity and persistence. The past has not been of great concern to the American people, especially its most painful aspects. For most of the twentieth century, slavery was excluded from public presentations of American history and played no visible role in American politics. It is useful to ask why the sudden and dramatic change. Surely part of the reason for the explosion of popular interest is related to the recognition of the sheer weight of slavery's importance. Simply put, American history cannot be understood without slavery. Slavery shaped the American economy, its politics, its culture, and its fundamental principles. For most of American history, the society of the mainland colonies and then the United States was one of slaveholders and slaves.

The American economy was founded on the production of slave-grown crops, the great staples of tobacco, rice, sugar, and finally cotton that slave owners sold on the international market to bring capital into the colonies and the young republic. That capital eventually funded the creation of an infrastructure on which rest three centuries of American economic success. The great wealth slavery produced allowed slave owners to secure a central role in the establishment of the new federal government in 1789, as they quickly transformed their economic power into political power. Between the founding of the Republic and the Civil War, the majority of the presidents—from George Washington, Thomas Jefferson, James Madison, James Monroe, and Andrew Jackson through John Tyler, James K. Polk, and Zachary Taylor—were slaveholders, and generally substantial ones. The same was true for the Supreme Court, where, for most of the period between the ratification of the Constitution and the Civil War, a slaveholding majority was ruled over by two successive slaveholding chief justices, John Marshall and Roger B. Taney. A similar pattern can be found in Congress, and antebellum politics revolved around the struggle between the slaveholding and nonslaveholding states for control of Congress.[18]

The power of the slave-owning class, represented by the predominance of slaveholders in the nation's leadership, gave it a large hand in shaping American culture and the values central to American society. It is no accident that a slaveholder penned the founding statement of American nationality and that freedom became central to the ideology of American nationhood. Men and women who drove slaves understood the meaning of chattel bondage, as most surely did the men and women who were chattel. And if it is no accident that Jefferson wrote that "all men are created equal," then it most certainly is no accident that some of the greatest spokesmen for that ideal, from Richard Allen and Frederick Douglass through W. E. B. Du Bois and Martin Luther King Jr., were former slaves and the descendants of slaves. The centrality of slavery to the American past is manifest.

It would be comforting—particularly for historians—to conclude that a recognition of slavery's importance has driven the American people to the history books. But there is more to it than that. There is also a recognition, often backhanded, sometimes subliminal or even subconscious, that the largest, most pervasive social problem of the United States—what Du Bois called the great problem of the twentieth century, which is fast becoming the great problem of the twenty-first century, that is, racism—is founded on the institution of slavery.[19] There is a general if inchoate understanding that any attempt to address the question of race in the present must also address slavery in the past. Indeed, Du Bois's racial imperative becomes all the more compelling as the United States becomes more racially segregated and more unequal and as a previous generation's remedies for segregation and inequality are discarded as politically unacceptable. In short, behind the interest in slavery is a crisis of race that returns Americans to the ground zero of race relations: chattel bondage.

The crisis in black and white is compounded by changes within black society. The great success of the Civil Rights Act of 1965—the substantial enlargement of the black middle class—has allowed some black men and women to enter more fully into American economic life and enjoy its benefits. The appearance of business leaders such as Kenneth I. Chenault of American Express, Robert Johnson of Black Entertainment Television (BET), and Richard Parsons of America Online (AOL) and of political figures such as Condoleezza Rice and Colin Powell can be regarded as evidence of the massive expansion of the black professional and managerial class. However fragile this new class, its members stand apart from those left behind in the "hood," whose children have a greater chance of going to jail than going to college. Such expanding class differences are further complicated by the fact that many of those left behind are new arrivals. The Immigration Act of 1965 may have had as much effect on black society as the Civil Rights Act of the same year. In time, it not only dethroned black people from their place as the nation's largest minority but also transformed the black population. In 1960 fewer than one in one hundred black Americans was an immigrant; in 2000 one in twenty black Americans was an immigrant, a proportion that is doubtless higher still in most American cities. In New York City, always an anomaly but often a harbinger of change, more than one-third of the people of African descent are immigrants.[20]

Post-1965 demographic changes have greatly expanded the range of the black experience, creating growing divisions within black society. The forebears of many contemporary black Americans did not share the experience of wartime emancipation, disfranchisement and segregation, and the long struggle and heroic triumph over Jim Crow. Many derive from places where, despite their African lineage, they were not considered black. Others identify themselves, not as black, but as Latin American or, more specifically, as Brazilian, Cuban, or some other nationality.[21] Their presence requires reimagining a black American nation and a return to the mainspring of the African American experience in the New World: chattel bondage. Small wonder that the diaspora has become the trope of choice in studying the black experience.

The confluence of the history of slavery and the politics of race—the political interactions both between black and white and among people of African descent—suggests that slavery has become a language, a way to talk about race in a society in which race is difficult to discuss. In slavery, Americans, black and white, have found a voice to address some of their deepest hurts, festering anger, and the all too depressing reality of how much of American life—access to jobs, housing, schools, medical care, justice, and even a taxi—is still controlled by race. The renaissance in the interest in slavery—the movies, TV docudramas, books, museum exhibits, monuments, and living history reenactments—has become an emblem, sign, and metaphor for the failure to deal directly with the question of race and the long legacy of chattel bondage.

For black people, the slave experience may offer common ground. Slavery is not the shared origin of black Americans only; that common travail also joins together all peoples of African descent touched by the transatlantic diaspora—Brazilians, Britons, Cubans, Haitians, and Africans of many nations. It provides a means to construct a sense of unity among men and women whose experience has become increasingly diverse and who, with the emergence of new minorities in the United States, are threatened with political marginalization.[22]

Of course, employing slavery to those ends does not always clarify matters. Take, for example, the dispute over John Vlach's "Back of the Big House" exhibition, an exemplary presentation of slave housing by a premier folklorist that was drawn from Vlach's fine book of the same title. Its placement in the Library of Congress angered employees of the library—mostly black and nonprofessional—who demanded its removal. They saw in the pictures of the slave quarters an all too perfect representation of the plantation metaphor that they employed to describe their stormy relationship with the library's administration. The librarian of Congress, a historian by training and trade, readily acceded to the demand. But no sooner had the exhibit been dismantled than the librarians at the District of Columbia's Martin Luther King Library welcomed it and made it a centerpiece of their Black History Month commemoration. A similar double take occurred when some black members of Savannah's City Council objected to the words to be inscribed on a proposed monument to enslaved Africans. "We lay back to belly in the holds of the slave ships in each others' excrement and urine together, sometimes died together, and our lifeless bodies thrown overboard together" seemed too graphic a representation of their ancestors' arrival in the New World. "I myself wouldn't want to be reminded of that every time I look at it. History's a hell of a thing. It can hurt," declared a black city councilman. And so it can.[23]

If slavery has emerged from the hidden recesses of the American past, it has not done so gracefully. Wherever the issue of slavery has appeared— whether in books, museums, monuments, or classroom discussions—there have been tense debates over how to present the topic, often accompanied by charges that interpreters have said too much (why do you dwell upon it?) or too little (why can't you face the truth?). Should slaves be portrayed as pitiful victims or resolute heroes? Is the new presence of slavery an incitement to racial conflict or the beginning of a healing process? Little wonder that the debate over "the apology" began with great fanfare and ended in muffled silence, or that the National Park Service has struggled with the congressional mandate, or that the white Jeffersons cannot come to terms with the black Jeffersons over access to Monticello's graveyard. The fact that some of the black Jeffersons are whiter—at least to the eye—than the white Jeffersons only reveals the knurled complexity of race relations in the United States and suggests that Karl Marx was right. History does repeat itself, first as tragedy, then as farce.[24]

Those troubled cases demonstrate that the discussion of slavery is not easy. Even as slavery serves as a surrogate for race, it too becomes tangled in the very same emotional brier patch. For slavery, like race, also carries with it deep anger, resentment, indignation, and bitterness for some and embarrassment, humiliation, and shame for others, along with large drafts of denial. Almost 140 years after slavery's demise, the question still sits on tender and sensitive ground. It is so sensitive that many Americans cannot even say the word. For some, it is "servants" or "servitude," a recognition of subordination, but an obfuscation of the slave's unique status as property; for others, it is "enslaved people," or more awkward still, "enslaved circumstance," a recognition of the slave's humanity and a pointed denial of the slave's consent to enslavement, but a similar beclouding of the unique meaning of property in man. As the struggle over nomenclature reveals, Americans feel the need to address the subject of slavery, to understand it, but they do not exactly know how.

A good deal of the difficulty lies in the confusion between the history of slavery and the memory of slavery and the ways they are similar and different. The similarities and differences reflect the way historians have addressed the history of slavery and the way Americans have confronted the memory of slavery.

Start with slavery's history in the United States. Scholars have detached slavery from its Civil War nexus and extended its reach across the Atlantic Ocean and around the world. From this perspective, chattel bondage in the United States has taken on a new look. What was once an appendage of the sectional conflict has become a fulcrum for understanding American history and the basis for teaching world history, as historians recognize the universality of slavery.[25] Slavery is no longer a southern institution or a peculiar institution; it is a global institution whose ubiquity belies peculiarity. Chattel bondage extended across the continents and into a primordial past. For most of world history, slavery was embraced—almost without question—by nearly everyone, often including the slaves themselves.

Slavery's universality makes it an ideal subject for comparative studies, and historians raced to create a new genre, comparing the slave trade in the United States with that in Brazil, manumission in New Orleans with that in Havana, slave insurrections in the eighteenth and nineteenth centuries, and emancipations in various nations at various times. Such studies proved remarkably revealing, but historians soon outgrew such static comparisons in favor of seeing the worldwide development of slavery as one piece. Emerging from the remnants of antiquity in the twelfth century, the modern plantation order—with slavery at its center—spread first across the Mediterranean Sea, then into the Atlantic, and finally to the most distant corners of earth. As it did, slavery created new connections between peoples unknown to one another, new economies, new social relationships, new cultures, and, of course, new histories.[26]

Historicization of slavery does not deny the exceptional character of the North American experience. Indeed, attention to the globalization of slavery revealed with ever greater precision what made slavery in the United States unique: the early emergence of an indigenous slave population, the rapid development of a Creole culture, the peculiar definitions of race, and the particularly bloody and destructive emancipation. But the historicization of slavery countered a vision of slavery as static and transhistorical. In the United States, as elsewhere, slavery was not made but constantly remade, taking a variety of forms that themselves have become a subject of enormous debate.[27]

The lives of slaves differed as much as those of free laborers differed across both time and space. During the seventeenth century, men and women of black America's charter generation—the Atlantic Creoles—lived in a world different from anything that could be imagined by those who followed them in the eighteenth and nineteenth centuries, when the plantation came to dominate much of mainland North America. Similarly, men and women who came of age at the end of the eighteenth century—the revolutionary generation—followed a very different course from that of those who escaped bondage during the American Civil War. While the Atlantic Creole Paulo d'Angola of New Amsterdam shared the status of slave with Phillis Wheatley of Boston, Frederick Douglass of Baltimore, and Harriet Jacobs of Edenton, North Carolina, their lives in bondage were as different from one another as from those of John Winthrop, George Washington, Harriet Beecher, and Abraham Lincoln in freedom. The historicization of slavery rests, as does the historicization of freedom, on the differences that emerge over time and are peculiar to different places.[28]

What is true of slavery is also true of slavery's modern companion, race. With the transformations of slavery came a transformation in the definition of race, as blackness and whiteness gained new meanings. European and European American masters denigrated Paulo d'Angola and other members of African America's charter generation as untrustworthy, manipulative, cunning, deceptive, and too smart by a half. Few European contemporaries thought to apply those epithets to the members of the plantation generation, whom they depicted as dull, dirty, stupid, indolent, libidinous creatures, whose lies could be easily detected and whose attempts to be clever revealed them as both witless and ignorant.

Uncovering how slavery and race were continually remade is central to the project of freeing slavery in the United States from the stereotypes that have bound it. Those are stereotypes that fixed the history of slavery exclusively to the master narrative of the Civil War; that connected it to the history of cotton, the black belt, and Afro-Christianity and to contemporary notions of race, which were read back into the past; that denied historical contingency and scorned historical agency. In their place has arisen a history in which slavery was made and remade by men and women on their own terms, if rarely to their own liking. It is a history that reminds all that once something was different, and that men and women made it so.

Like all history, this new history of slavery is a critical reconstruction of past events based on the belief that the past was different. It is not simply that the past was slow and the present is fast or that the eighteenth century was wooden and the twentieth century is plastic or that once there were quills and now there are personal computers. Rather, the fundamental assumptions that governed men and women in the past and the basic relationships that they created were different. The axiom is that the past is a foreign country and that it must not be studied with an eye on the present, not looking for precursors of nowadays or harbingers of the contemporary world. The past must be reconstructed on its own terms, with care not to weigh it down with anachronisms or to confuse it with the present.

Like all history, this new history of slavery rests on the careful, dispassionate reconstruction of lived experience. Whatever slavery became after the age of revolution and however it is viewed in the twenty-first century, it must be comprehended in its own time. For the historian, context is all, and to step outside the assumptions of the historical moment violates the fundamental canons of the craft.[29] This does not deny slavery's brutality, mute the violence on which slavery necessarily rested, or even make such brutal impositions more explicable. It simply provides the basis for understanding the actions of master and slave.

Finally, like all history, the new history of slavery is inclusive. However personal or unique the story, its connections to the larger narrative—as example or exception—make the history of slavery one piece. History is about seamless relationships that cannot be parsed. Whatever the convenience of dividing the study of the past into components—economic, social, or political history, for example—it must encompass all people. Universities may teach courses on workers, women, and gays, but the history of workers cannot be separated from the history of bosses, that of women from that of men, and that of gays from that of straights, any more than one can distinguish "political man" from "social man." Although historians rarely succeed, their aim is to be universal and to connect all.

Thus the new history of slavery is part of a continuing debate about the past, what happened and what it means. It is an ongoing debate because historians understand that the past can never be recovered in full. New evidence and new perspectives will inevitably shift interpretations. Likewise, it must be acknowledged that some aspects of the past will be known imperfectly and, sadly, that some things will never be known. By definition, the reconstructed past is contested terrain. The reconstruction proceeds with great skepticism. Nothing is taken for granted. Everything is contingent; the presumption is that everyone lied.

Such an understanding puts slavery's history on a collision course with popular understanding, which is prone to fix institutions in time and place and to see events marching inevitably forward to the present, thus accentuating aspects of the past that shape contemporary life. Searching for the present in the past, popular understanding almost always returns to the last years of the southern slave regime. Such a view emphasizes the slaves' labor in cotton and sugar, their residence in the black belt, and their worship in African-Christian churches. It ignores or denies slavery's long history, its near universality, its association on mainland North America with tobacco

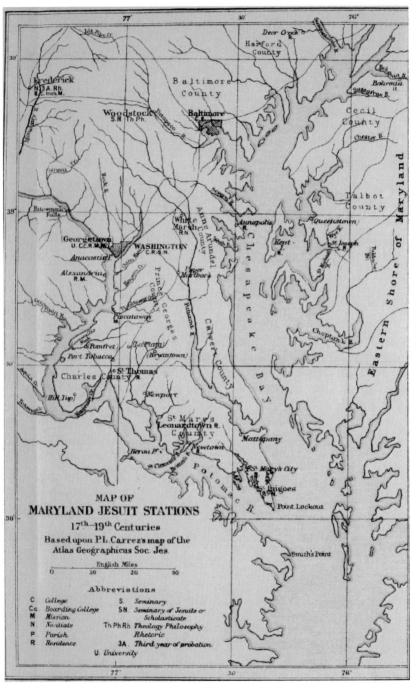

Map of the Maryland Stations. *From Thomas Hughes,* The History of the Society of Jesus in North America *(1907)*

Mary Land ſs.

Know all men. By these presents yt I William Hu
ter of yᵉ Charles County Gent for and in Consideration of the
summe of Tenn Shillings to me yᵉ sd William Hunter in hand
payd by Thomas Jamison Senʳ of Charles County Gent the receit
whereof I doe herby acknowledge and of every part thereof doe acer
quitt and discharge him yᵉ sd Thomas Jamison his Exeut.ᵗˢ Admʳˢ &
Assigns And for divers other good Causes and Considerations me there
 to moveing Have Given granted bargaind and sold and by these
presents dot give grant bargain and sell unto yᵉ sd Thomas Jam
all and every yᵉ Goods Church stuff Plate Houshold stuff Negros horses
mares Neat Cattle Hoggs Sheep Husbandry Impl'ments Tobacco Corn &
all other grain and all other things whatsoever now on or belonging to
Dwelling Plantation of Britton's head and yᵉ Quarter on yᵉ both
yᵉ sd head mentioned in a Schedule Presents annexed To Have an
hold all and every yᵉ sd Goods Church stuff Plate Houshold Stuff Negros
horses mares Neat Cattle Hoggs Sheep Husbandry Impl'ments Tobacco Co
and other grain and all other things in yᵉ sd Schedule mentiond unto
sd Thomas Jamison his Exeut.ᵗˢ Adminiſt.ʳˢ and Assigns for ever t
and their only Proffitt and proper use and Behoof. In witness wh
.. of I have herto sett my hand and seale this thirtieth of January
in yᵉ year of our Lord one thousand seven hundred and seventeen

Sign'd Seal'd & Delivered
in presence of us

Jonathan   his ✗ Walker
          mark

         William Hunter

Daniell   his ✗ Riordan
          mark

Memorandum the thirtieth day of January one thousand
seven hundred & seventeen in yᵉ presence of us the subscribe
yᵉ above named Wm Hunter delivered into yᵉ hands and posses
son of yᵉ above named Thomas Jamison one bay Gelding yᵉ sa
being one of yᵉ Geldings in yᵉ Schedule to this presents ann
mentiond and in part and leiu of yᵉ whole in yᵉ sd Schedule
mentiond & expressed and in token of possession of yᵉ whole

Jonathan   his ✗ Walker
           mark

Daniell   his ✗ Riordan
          mark

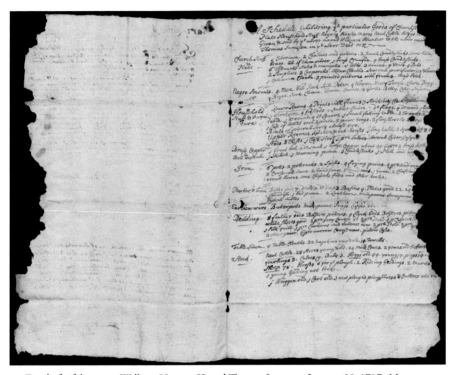

Deed of gift between William Hunter, SJ, and Thomas Jameson, January 30, 1717. *Maryland Province Archives*

THIRTY DOLLARS
REWARD.

Ranaway from Georgetown College, on Saturday night the 29th inst a Negro Man named ISAAC, about 23 years old, quite black complexion, about 5 feet 8 inches high; had on when he went away a short coat of drab cloth, pantaloons of the same kind, fur hat & great coat made of thick drab coating and bound with ferretting—he carried with him a pair of blue cloth trowsers, two Russia linen shirts, an old hat and other articles of clothing not recollected, it is probable he may change his clothing—he has learned to read tolerably well, and it is likely he may have procured a written pass. It is supposed that he is gone to Pennsylvania; he was raised at Mrs John-son's near Bryantown, Charles County. The above reward will be paid if secured in any Jail more than 50 miles from this District, and reasonable expences paid if brought home, or twenty dollars if a shorter distance, by the subscriber Clerk of Georgetown College, District of Columbia.

JOHN McELROY.

February 1—d1m

Runaway advertisement for Isaac, 1814. *Maryland State Archives*

Baptismal record for Sylvester Greenleaf, 1819. *Maryland Province Archives*

Student activists sit in at President DeGioia's office, 2015. *The Hoya*

Descendants at the dedication of Isaac Hawkins Hall, 2017.

Stained glass window from the Immaculate Heart of Mary Catholic Church, Maringouin, Louisiana, 2017. *Bernardine Poole*

Sandra Green Thomas during remarks at the Liturgy of Remembrance, Contrition, and Hope, April 17, 2017. *Georgetown University*

Fr. Timothy Kesicki, SJ, at the Liturgy of Remembrance, Contrition, and Hope, April 17, 2017. *Georgetown University*

Referendum chalk on campus, April 2019. *The Hoya*

and rice, its presence in the North as well as the South, and the centuries in which slaves rejected Christianity. Such popular understanding is often based on human recollections.

Those recollections, themselves contested, have taken a variety of forms, always maintaining the facade of truth and insisting on unchallenged allegiance. In the hands of former slaveholders and their apologists during the late nineteenth and much of the twentieth centuries, they yielded a vision of slavery as a benevolent institution that civilized the savage Africans and of masters as compassionate paternalists who prepared a benighted people for a distant freedom. Following World War II historians called into question slavery's benevolence and the slave masters' compassion. Their histories offered a radically different understanding in which slavery violated, rather than promoted, liberty and deprived men and women of their most basic human rights.

From this—now dominant, but still contested—perspective, the story of slavery has two large themes. The first is the physical and psychological imposition that slaves suffered. It is affirmed in the record of hideous, obscene violence: of murders, mutilations, beatings, and rapes; of the forcible separation of husbands and wives, parents and children; of husbands forced to see their wives abused, and of wives forced to do unspeakable things. Slavery is the story of power over liberty, of a people victimized and brutalized.

But there is a second theme, for the story of slavery is not only one of victimization, brutalization, and exclusion. If slavery was violence and imposition, if it was death, slavery was also life. Slaves did not surrender to the imposition, physical and psychological. They refused to be dehumanized by dehumanizing treatment. On the narrowest of grounds and in the most difficult of circumstances, they created and sustained life in the form of families, churches, and associations of all kinds. These organizations—often clandestine and fugitive, fragile and unrecognized by the larger society—became the sites of new languages, aesthetics, and philosophies as expressed in story, music, dance, and cuisine, worlds that were sacred and worlds that were profane. They produced leaders and ideas that continue to inform American life.

Appropriating the dual theme of imposition and resistance as it resonated in social movements and reverberated through popular understandings, the memory of slavery celebrates a cultural creativity that has its roots in the devastating rupture of the middle passage and the utter refusal of enslaved men and women to acquiesce in the abuse that followed. Necessitated by the threat of cultural annihilation and social disintegration, their ingenuity required innovation, as the world had to be conceived anew. While centuries of indignities, physical and psychological, marked slavery's victims—many of whom broke under its weight—the affronts did not define the society and culture that slaves produced. Slaves redirected the ridicule back at its source, transforming weakness into strength and denying the dispiriting message of inferiority. Indeed, if slavery is the bleakest element in the American past, it may also be the most creative. It is impossible to imagine American culture without the creative legacy of slavery.

Its mission of giving voice to the dual message of the dehumanizing force of slavery and the slaves' refusal to be dehumanized reveals how memory differs from history. For memory, unlike history, rejects a skeptical, detached reconstruction of the past. For the keepers of memory, it is unquestioned and reflexive, absolute, and instantaneous; not distant from the present but conjoined with today and contiguous with tomorrow. Memory speaks, not to a desire to understand the whole and to include all in the story, but to personal, individual understandings based on the most intimate experiences in families, churches, and communities. It is conveyed through symbols and rituals and knowing gestures, through often-repeated stories passed from grandparents who were too often ignored but never forgotten, and through kitchen table banter that was barely audible but always heard. Although scholarship may be incorporated into memory, the appropriated interpretations and perspectives are transformed, for they soon become emotively charged and morally freighted. Memories are anything but tentative, distant, contingent, or dispassionate. They are immediate, intense, and emotive. They do not evoke skepticism but command commitment; they demand loyalty, not controversy. Memories are not debated (except in the most trivial sense), they are embraced. If history is written with the presumption that everyone lied, memory presumes the truth. No one lied.[30]

The memory of slavery in the United States is constructed on different ground from its history. Rather than global, it is local. Memories generally derive from the particular rather than from a consideration of the larger context. Looking to the past for an understanding of the present, they are progressive, attending to aspects of the past that shaped current circumstances. Thus the memory of slavery rarely dwells on the *longue durée* and, indeed, often is oblivious to the existence of slavery at different times and places except as they too connect the past to the present.

Rather than dispassionate and boundless, the memory of slavery is immediate, emotive, and highly selective. In recent times, slavery's memories can be found in the picture of the slave ship Brooks, with its cargo of tightly packed men and women stuffed spoonlike into its hull, that has recently appeared on posters in college dormitories and on T-shirts, often emblazoned with the words "Never forget." They cluster around Thomas Jefferson's relationship with Sally Hemings and the refusal to recognize paternity—personal but also national.[31] They figure in the debates about naming high schools after Denmark Vesey, Nat Turner, and the slave rebel Gabriel and about removing the names of Robert E. Lee, Stonewall Jackson, and Jefferson Davis and, of course, the Confederate flag.[32]

If history is skeptical, contested, and universal, memory is certain, incontestable, and personal. If, at its best, history is a detached and disinterested weighing of all the evidence, memory is a selective recall of a portion of the past that makes no pretense of universality. If the history of slavery speaks to the world transformed, the memory of slavery addresses what was done to my people, to my family, to me. If history uses memory opportunistically and even parasitically, playing one memory against another in its search for some larger truth, memory adopts historical events, issues, and persons in order to condemn injustice and honor heroism.

Because it touches individual men and women with such power, memory becomes the driving force in the search for social justice, the mortar that bonds the violations of the past to the grievances of the present. The keepers of the memory of slavery reiterate that lives lost and mutilated should not be forgotten. The suffering and the sorrow, the pain and loss must be remembered. A rich legacy was created at great cost, and homage is owed to those who paid the price. The enemy must be identified, and crimes must be acknowledged. If the criminals can no longer be punished, at least they can be exposed and those who have benefited from the crime made to confess. The shibboleth of states' rights and a war fought only by brave white men and supported by true white women is no longer acceptable. The Confederacy and its symbols must be unmasked. The long complicity of the North must be unveiled. The memory of slavery demands that deniers be rooted out, dissemblers be exposed, that those who would forget be reminded. Never forget!

True enough, but such a formulation speaks against the skeptical, critical, and all-inclusive inspection of the past that is at the very heart of the historical enterprise. For those who draw on the remembered past, the study of slavery is not something that can be viewed dispassionately, questioned, inspected, and debated. Their truth is not one among many. Their understanding must be recognized, embraced, and celebrated, for the reality of slavery was absolute and undeniable.

But if this is so, what of the diverse worlds of Paulo d'Angola of seventeenth-century New Amsterdam and other Atlantic Creoles? How is their universe distinguished from that of Phillis Wheatley in eighteenth-century Boston or even more sharply from that of Frederick Douglass in nineteenth-century Baltimore? What of slavery's history, the unique experiences of Africans and African Americans in bondage, unique because they were Africans or descendants of Africa but also because of the diversity of the landscapes on which they lived, the economies in which they worked, the societies in which they were enmeshed, and, perhaps most important, the battles they won and lost and the identities they thereby created. For, if the memory of slavery is understood as fixed and undeniable, the history is contingent and endlessly debatable. How many slaves crossed the Atlantic Ocean? What was the nature of the slave family? Why were there so few slave rebellions, or so many? When did slaves become Christians; what did the slaves' Christianity mean? Those matters must be debatable because to deny the debate is to remove slaves from history, to separate them from the real world, and to mummify them in some transhistorical nether land of "social death" and "absolute aliens."[33] It too denies the undeniable.

History and memory both speak to the subject of slavery and the long experience of people of African descent in their American captivity, but they speak in different tongues. Not surprisingly, where history and memory meet, the results are often unpleasant. So it was at the conference to introduce the slave trade database in the summer of 1998 at the Omohundro Institute of Early American History and Culture in Colonial Williamsburg. An enormous machine-readable compilation of some twenty-seven thousand slaving voyages, the slave trade database, constructed under the leadership of David Eltis, Stephen D. Behrendt, David Richardson, and Herbert S. Klein with the support of the W. E. B. Du Bois Institute for African and African American Research at Harvard University, promised to revolutionize understanding of black life in the Atlantic world between the fifteenth and nineteenth centuries. The organizers of the conference expected to host several dozen historians, who would explore the initial findings and gain hands-on training in the use of the database.[34]

Even before the conference met, the organizers learned of their miscalculation. Rather than several dozen interested scholars, news of the database drew hundreds of people. Most were descendants of slaves with no particular academic or scholarly interest in the slave trade, but a desire to learn more about the enormous forced migration that had propelled their ancestors across the Atlantic. In haste, the conference was moved to a larger facility and a larger facility still. In the end, no venue could contain the growing number of interested parties, and buses full of would-be participants—many of them organized by church groups—rolled into Colonial Williamsburg.

As scholars presented their findings, the difference between history and memory manifested itself and the gap between scholars and the public grew into an unbridgeable cavern. In one particularly memorable session, historians debated the relationship between the size of slave ships and their construction and the mortality rates of the African captives packed in their holds while the majority of the audience pleaded for an understanding of the moral rupture that separated the slaves from their forebears. While technical aspects of the transport of Africans to the Americas are worthy of debate, nothing could convince the audience that historians were not wasting their time or, worse yet, obfuscating the critical moral issue. With tension rising, the differences between historians and the public dissolved into a mutual distrust founded on ignorance of one another.

Such is often the case when the question of slavery goes public. The problem is not confined to the subject of slavery, for it arises again and again whenever historians address a subject that, for whatever reason, engages "the people." While such differences are often—and rightly—blamed on poor writing, obscure jargon, or narrow conceptions, there is enough well-written and broadly conceived history to ask why the best scholarship is often viewed as irrelevant; why books that win prizes within the academy go unread by the public; why TV's History Channel has an audience in the millions and university presses publish books in the hundreds. At base, history and memory simply do not mix well. They speak past one another. Their dialogue is uncomfortable and rarely respectful.

And yet they desperately need one another. Consider the question of slavery. If memory is denied and history is allowed to trump memory, the past becomes irrelevant to the lives of all Americans at the beginning of the twenty-first century: their politics and their values, the kind of world they live in, the kind of world they would like to make. But if history is denied and memory is allowed to trump history, then the past becomes merely a reflection of the present with no real purpose other than wish fulfillment or, at best, myth with footnotes: a source of great satisfaction to some, but of little weight beyond assertion.

Slavery lives and will continue to live in both history and memory. But the time has come to join the two: to embrace slavery's complex history and the difficult realities of this extraordinary and extreme form of domination and subordination and to accept the force of slavery's memory and the passionate legacy it necessarily entails. Incorporating the emotions that accompany the memory with the uncomfortable realities of slavery's history just may produce a collective past that honors forebears and that acknowledges the connections between past and present. Indeed, only by testing memory against history's truths and infusing history into memory's passions can such a collective past be embraced, legitimated, and sustained. And perhaps by incorporating slavery's memory into slavery's history and vice versa, Americans—white and black—can have a past that is both memorable and, at last, past.

Notes

1. *Glory*, dir. Edward Zwick (TriStar Pictures, 1989); *Amistad*, dir. Steven Spielberg (DreamWorks SKG, 1997); *Adanggaman*, dir. Roger Gnoan M'Bala (Abyssa Film, 2000); *Beloved*, dir. Jonathan Demme (Clinica Estético Ltd., 1998).

2. Henry Louis Gates Jr., *Wonders of the African World* (New York, 1999); *Wonders of the African World* (Jan. 1, 2002), with subsequent discussion on H-AFRICA (Nov. 14, 2003); Peter Applebome, "Can Harvard's Powerhouse Alter the Course of Black Studies?," *New York Times*, Nov. 3, 1996, sec. 4A, p. 24; Lynn B. Elber, "PBS' Film 'Africans in America' Examines Roots of Slavery," Associated Press, Oct. 16, 1998; Michael O'Sullivan, "'Shadrach': A Museum Piece," *Washington Post*, Oct. 16, 1998, p. N49; "Unchained Memories: Readings from the Slave Narratives," dir. Ed Bell and Thomas Lennon, Home Box Office (HBO, Feb. 10, 2003). The last work became a book with contributions by Henry Louis Gates Jr. and by Spencer Crew and Cynthia Goodman: National Underground Railroad Freedom Center, *Unchained Memories: Readings from the Slave Narratives* (Boston, 2002). Many newspaper and wire service articles cited in this essay were read online and checked in fall 2003.

3. Ira Berlin, Steven F. Miller, and Mark Favreau, eds., *Remembering Slavery: African-Americans Talk about Their Personal Experiences in Slavery and Freedom* (New York, 1998). On the Library of Congress exhibit, see Hugh Davies, "Black Revolt Puts End to Exhibition of Old South," *London Daily Telegraph*, Dec. 21, 1995, international section; Linton Weeks, "The Continuing Hurt of History," *Washington Post*, Dec. 22, 1995; "A Library on Tiptoe," ibid.; and Linton Weeks, "Plantation Life Display Revived," ibid., Jan. 4, 1996. On the Civil War memorial, see Benjamin Forgey, "A Salute to Freedom's Soldiers," ibid., July 18, 1998; and David D. Kirkpatrick, "On Long-Lost Pages, a Female Slave's Voice," *New York Times*, Nov. 11, 2001.

4. On the *Amistad* monument, see Ken Ringle, "Sailor on History's Seas," *Washington Post*, March 23, 2000; and David M. Herszenhorn, "A Slave Ship Reborn into History," *New York Times*, March 26, 2000. Also see "*Amistad* Friendship Tour 2003" (Oct. 19, 2003). For the proposed legislation, see National Slave Memorial Act, H.R. 196, 108 Cong., 1 sess. (2003). Visiting a Confederate cemetery, Interior Secretary Gale Norton declared, "We lost too much. We lost the idea that the states were to stand against the federal government gaining too much power over their lives." See David W. Blight, "A Confederacy of Denial," *Washington Post*, Jan. 29, 2001, p. A19.

5. On the National Underground Railroad Freedom Center and other such museums, see Mark Fritz, "Chasing the Mystery of U.S.'s Secret Trail," *Los Angeles Times*, Feb. 5, 2000; and Anne Michaud, "Railroad History Put on Right Track," ibid. See also Peter Slevin, "Black History Museum Has Artifacts but No Building," *Washington Post*, Jan. 9, 2000; "Southern Almanac: A Civil War Legacy," *Atlanta Constitution*, Dec. 10, 2000; Steven Ginsberg, "Fredericksburg Prodded on Slavery Museum," *Washington Post*, Aug. 11, 2001; and Stephen Kinzer, "Planned Museum Would Lead Charleston to Its Past," *New York Times*, Aug. 14, 2001.

6. Jennifer L. Eichstedt and Stephen Small, *Representations of Slavery: Race and Ideology in Southern Plantation Museums* (Washington, 2002); Fath Davis Ruffins, "Revisiting the Old Plantation: Reparations, Reconciliation, and Museumizing American Slavery," 2003 (in Ira Berlin's possession), courtesy of the author. Linda Wheeler, "Civil War Tour Guides to Address Slavery," *Washington Post*, April 30, 2000; Patty Reinert, "New Battlefield," *Houston Chronicle*, May 14, 2000; Dwight T. Pitcaithley, "Barbara Kingsolver and the Challenge of Public History," *Public Historian*, 21 (Fall 1999), 9–18; David W. Blight, "Healing and History: Battlefields and the Problem of Memory," in *Rally on the High Ground: The National Park Service Symposium on the Civil War*, ed. Robert Kent Sutton (Fort Washington, Pa., 2001), 23–35, esp. 25.

7. That interest in slavery is not confined to the United States is suggested by the establishment of the Harriet Tubman Resource Center for the African Diaspora at York University in Ontario, the International Centre for the History of Slavery at the University of Nottingham in England, and the Slave Route Project of the United Nations Educational, Scientific, and

Cultural Organization (UNESCO). On the UNESCO slave trade project, see Douglas Farah, "Dahomey's Royal Legacy Slowly Crumbles," *Washington Post*, April 16, 2001. On the Frederick Douglass Prize for the best book on slavery, see "National Book Prizes," *The Gilder Lehrman Institute of American History* (Oct. 19, 2003).

8. David Brion Davis, "Free at Last: The Enduring Legacy of the South's Civil War Victory," *New York Times*, Aug. 26, 2001; Eugene Foster et al., "Jefferson Fathered Slaves Last Child," *Nature*, 396 (Nov. 1998), 27–28; Annette Gordon-Reed, *Thomas Jefferson and Sally Hemings: An American Controversy* (Charlottesville, 1997); Jan Ellen Lewis and Peter S. Onuf, eds., *Sally Hemings and Thomas Jefferson: History, Memory, and Civic Culture* (Charlottesville, 1999); "Forum: Thomas Jefferson and Sally Hemings Redux," *William and Mary Quarterly*, 57 (Jan. 2000), 121–210.

9. On Bill Clinton's apology, see William Douglas, "We Were Wrong," New York *Newsday*, March 25, 1998. On conservative reaction to it, see Leonard Pitts Jr., "Slavery Apology Fitting and Proper," *Baltimore Sun*, April 9, 1998.

10. For George W. Bush's speech at Gorée, see "President Bush Speaks at Gorée Island in Senegal" (Oct. 19, 2003).

11. White House Initiative on Race" (Oct. 19, 2003); "Race Panel's Lost Chance," *Los Angeles Times*, Sept. 21, 1998. On South Carolina, see Hamil R. Harris, "NAACP Issues Call for New Activism," *Washington Post*, Feb. 20, 2000; "Flag-Waving Controversy," *Houston Chronicle*, Feb. 24, 2000; Sue Anne Pressley, "SC Lowers Disputed Flag," *Washington Post*, July 2, 2000; and "Flag War Isn't Over at Carolina Statehouse," ibid., Jan. 15, 2001. On Georgia, see "Georgia Lawmakers OK New State Flag," *Associated Press*, Jan. 31, 2001. On Mississippi, see John Head, "Culture, Notes, and News," *Atlanta Constitution*, Oct. 29, 2000, "Dixie Living" section; Paul Duggan, "Mississippi Voters to Decide on Use of Confederate Emblem," *Washington Post*, March 25, 2001; and Dahleen Glanton, "In Mississippi, Flag Vote Shows Deep Divide," ibid., April 16, 2001.

12. R. H. Melton, "Va. Scraps Tribute to Confederacy," *Washington Post*, Nov. 21, 2001; "Slavery 'Abhorred,' Gilmore Says," ibid., April 10, 1998; Tyler Whitley, "More Criticism, Some Praise for Decree," *Richmond Times-Dispatch*, April 11, 1998; Peter Baker, "Va. House Votes to Repeal 'Old Virginia' as State Song," *Washington Post*, March 4, 1994; "'A Victim of History' As Virginia Retires the State Song, It Revives the Ambiguous Legacy of James Bland, Author of 'Carry Me Back to Old Virginia,'" *Roanoke Times*, Feb. 18, 1997. The District of Columbia Emancipation Day Foundation (Nov. 14, 2003); "The District of Columbia Emancipation Day: A Private Legal Holiday" (Oct. 19, 2003). Officially, the name is the Commission to Coordinate the Study, Commemoration, and Impact of Slavery's History and Legacy in Maryland (Oct. 19, 2003).

13. Darryl Fears, "The Capitol's Case of Slave Labor," *Washington Post*, July 19, 2000; Scott La Fee, "Grave Injustice," *San Diego Union-Tribune*, Sept. 15, 1999. See also Mel Tapley, "'Dem Dry Bones' Get Belated Respect," *Amsterdam News*, Oct. 19, 1991. Stephen Salisbury and Inga Saffron, "Echoes of Slavery at the Liberty Bell Site," *Philadelphia Inquirer*, March 24, 2002, p. A1; Stephen Salisbury, "Discussing Slavery at Liberty Bell Site," ibid., April 25, 2002, p. B1; Stephen Salisbury, "Liberty Bell's Symbolism Rings Hollow for Some," ibid., May 26, 2002, p. B1; "Liberty Bell Center Exhibit Preview Now on Independence National Historical Park Website" (Oct. 19, 2003).

14. See Brent Staples, "Wrestling with the Legacy of Slavery at Yale," *New York Times*, Aug. 14, 2001, p. 16; and the original report published by the Amistad Committee in New Haven: Antony Dugdale, J. J. Fueser, and J. Celso de Castro Alves, "Yale, Slavery, and Abolition," 2001 (Nov. 24, 2003).

15. See Jesse Leavenworth and Kevin Canfield, "To Be Sold," *Hartford Courant*, July 4, 2000; Ross Kerber, "Aetna Regrets Being Insurer to Slaveowners," *Boston Globe*, March 10, 2000; and Peter Slevin, "In Aetna's Past: Slave Owner Policies," *Washington Post*, March 9, 2000. Regarding California's actions, see Tamar Lewin, "Calls for Slavery Restitution Getting Louder," *New York Times*, June 4, 2001; *Slavery Era Insurance Registry Report to the California Legislature* (Oct. 20, 2003); and "California Identifies Slavery Insurers," *Washington Post*, May 2, 2002, p. A1. The Chicago City Council took similar action. "Chicago City Council Seeks Slavery Records," Reuters, Oct. 2, 2002. See Jesse Leavenworth and Kevin Canfield, "A Courant Complicity, an Old Wrong," *Hartford Courant*, July 4, 2000; "The Courant Apologizes for Ads Finding, Selling Slaves," *Greenwich [Connecticut] Times*, July 5, 2000.

16. For recent discussions of the reparations debate, see "Why We Did (or Didn't) Publish the Ad," *Washington Post*, April 1, 2001; Sophia A. Nelson, "We Need to Put Slavery in Its Place," ibid., June 10, 2001; and Jesse Leavenworth and Kevin Canfield, "The Reparations Debate," *Hartford Courant*, June 19, 2001. Also useful is Roy L. Brooks, ed., *When Sorry Isn't Enough: The Controversy over Apologies and Reparations for Human Injustice* (New York, 1999).

17. Leef Smith, "Williamsburg Slave Auction Rules Va. NAACP," *Washington Post*, Oct. 8, 1994, p. B1. See also Michael Janofsky, "Mock Auction of Slaves, Education or Outrage?," *New York Times*, Oct. 8, 1994; "Tears and Protest at Mock Slave Sale," ibid., Oct. 11, 1994; Dan Eggen, "A Taste of Slavery Has Tourists Up in Arms," *Washington Post*, July 7, 1999; Gail Russell Chaddock, "Williamsburg's Tale of Two Histories," *Christian Science Monitor*, Sept. 2, 1999. See also Eric Gable, Richard Handler, and Anna Lawson, "On the Uses of Relativism: Fact, Conjecture, and Black and White Histories at Colonial Williamsburg," *American Ethnologist*, 19 (Nov. 1992), 791–805; Curtis James, "To Live like a Slave," *Colonial Williamsburg Journal*, 16 (Autumn 1993), 14–24; the forum "Colonial Williamsburg: Planning and Public History," *Public Historian*, 20 (Summer 1998), 11–99; and James Oliver Horton, "Presenting Slavery: The Perils of Telling America's Racial Story," ibid., 21 (Fall 1999), 29–30.

18. Leonard L. Richards, *The Slave Power: The Free North and Southern Domination, 1780–1860* (Baton Rouge, 2000); Don E. Fehrenbacher with Ward M. McAfee, *The Slaveholding Republic: An Account of the United States Government's Relations to Slavery* (New York, 2001).

19. W. E. B. Du Bois, *The Souls of Black Folk: Essays and Sketches* (Chicago, 1903), 13; W. E. B. Du Bois, *The World and Africa: An Inquiry into the Part Which Africa Has Played in World History* (New York, 1947), 227, 236.

20. Computed from the U.S. census enumerations. Census 2000 Summary File 3 (SF-3) Population Tables—Sample Data (PDF 141.5KB); per 19 (Place of Birth for Foreign-Born Populations); PCT 63B (Place of Birth by Citizenship Status [Black or African Americans Alone]), U.S. Census Bureau (Oct. 19, 2003). Bart Landry, *The New Black Middle Class* (Berkeley, 1987).

21. See, for example, Philip Shenon, "An African Ambassador Battles Terror and Indifference," *New York Times*, June 5, 2000.

22. Felicia R. Lee, "New Topic in Black Studies Debate," ibid., Feb. 1, 2003.

23. See Davies, "Black Revolt Puts End to Exhibition of Old South," 11; Weeks, "Continuing Hurt of History"; "Library on Tiptoe"; "Library of Congress Scraps Plantation Life Exhibit," *Washington Post*, Dec. 25, 1995; and Weeks, "Plantation Life Display Revived." For Vlach's own account, see John Michael Vlach, "Confronting Slavery: One Example of the Perils and Promises of Difficult History," *History News*, 54 (Spring 1999), 12–15; and John Vlach interview by Charlayne Hunter-Gault, "Picturing Slavery," Feb. 5, 1996. For the book, see John Michael Vlach, *Back of the Big House: The Architecture of Plantation Slavery* (Chapel

Hill, 1993). Russ Bynam, "In Savannah, a Furor over Graphic Quote on Monument to Slaves," Associated Press, Feb. 10, 2001. The words are those of the poet Maya Angelou.

24. For background on the controversy, see Leef Smith, "Jeffersons Split over Hemings," *Washington Post*, May 17, 1999; Leef Smith, "Jefferson Paternity Called Likely," ibid., Jan. 27, 2000; and William Branigin, "Historians' Report Attacks Hemings Link to Jefferson," ibid., April 13, 2001.

25. David Brion Davis, "Looking at Slavery from Broader Perspectives," *American Historical Review*, 105 (April 2000), 452–66.

26. To grasp how comparative the study of slavery has become, see Joseph Miller, comp., *Slavery: A World Wide Bibliography* (White Plains, 1985). This work is updated annually in the journal *Slavery and Abolition*. For the distinction between direct comparison and transnational histories, see Jürgen Kocka, "Comparison and Beyond," *History and Theory*, 42 (Feb. 2003), 39–44. The most ambitious attempt to historicize the global history of slavery is Joseph C. Miller, "The Problem of Slavery in History," lectures delivered at the University of Virginia, March 2002 (in Berlin's possession), courtesy of the author. For the modern period, see Philip D. Curtin, *The Rise and Fall of the Plantation Complex: Essays in Atlantic History* (Cambridge, Eng., 1998); and David Eltis, *The Rise of African Slavery in the Americas* (Cambridge, Eng., 2000).

27. Ira Berlin, *Many Thousands Gone: The First Two Centuries of Slavery in North America* (Cambridge, Mass., 1998).

28. I trace some of these changes in greater detail in Ira Berlin, *Generations of Captivity: A History of African American Slaves* (Cambridge, Mass., 2003).

29. See especially Marc Bloch, *The Historian's Craft* (New York, 1953), 24–29.

30. For the modern discussion of memory, see Pierre Nora, "Between Memory and History: Les Lieux de Mémoire," *Representations*, 26 (Spring 1989), 7–24; and Pierre Nora, dir., *Realms of Memory: Rethinking the French Past*, trans. Arthur Goldhammer, ed. Lawrence D. Kritzman (3 vols., New York, 1996–1998). For discussions of the slave trade in history and memory that parallel my own, see Ralph A. Austen, "The Slave Trade as History and Memory: Confrontations of Slaving Voyage Documents and Communal Traditions," *William and Mary Quarterly*, 58 (Jan. 2001), 229–44; and Bernard Bailyn, "Considering the Slave Trade: History and Memory," ibid., 245–51.

31. On the slave ship Brooks, see Monica L. Haynes, "Escaped Slaves' Tales Remain Inspirational," *Pittsburgh Post-Gazette*, June 19, 1998. See Nora, "Between Memory and History," 9. On the controversy over Thomas Jefferson's involvement with Hemings, see n. 24 above.

32. On controversies over school names, see Ann O'Hanlon, "Racial History Fuels Growing Debate over School Names," *Washington Post*, Feb. 10, 1998; and "Black Begins Bid to Change School's Name," *New York Times*, Jan. 14, 1998.

33. On social death, see Orlando Patterson, *Slavery and Social Death: A Comparative Study* (Cambridge, Mass., 1982), 3–6. A defining property of slaves is their "insert[ion] as absolute aliens in the slave-owning host society," according to Claude Meillassoux, *The Anthropology of Slavery: The Womb of Iron and Gold*, trans. Alide Dasnois (Chicago, 1991), 99.

34. Some of the conference papers were published in a special issue, "New Perspectives on the Transatlantic Slave Trade," *William and Mary Quarterly*, 58 (Jan. 2001). David Eltis, Stephen D. Behrendt, David Richardson, and Herbert S. Klein, eds., *The Trans-Atlantic Slave Trade: A Database on CD-ROM* (Cambridge, Eng., 1999).

21

The Case for Reparations

TA-NEHISI COATES

Ta-Nehisi Coates's 2014 landmark essay in The Atlantic *sparked a new conversation on reparations and what forms they might take. Coates illustrates the extent to which the legacies of slavery and post-slavery forms of racism have had an impact on the lives of Black people. He focuses on how institutions and the national government have helped perpetuate inequality and emphasizes the need for national action on the issue to make amends.*

TWO HUNDRED FIFTY YEARS OF SLAVERY. NINETY YEARS OF JIM CROW. SIXTY YEARS OF SEPARATE BUT EQUAL. THIRTY-FIVE YEARS OF RACIST HOUSING POLICY. UNTIL WE RECKON WITH OUR COMPOUNDING MORAL DEBTS, AMERICA WILL NEVER BE WHOLE.

And if thy brother, a Hebrew man, or a Hebrew woman, be sold unto thee, and serve thee six years; then in the seventh year thou shalt let him go free from thee. And when thou sendest him out free from thee, thou shalt not let him go away empty: thou shalt furnish him liberally out of the flock, and out of thy floor, and out of thy winepress: of that wherewith the LORD thy God hath blessed thee thou shalt give unto him. And thou shalt remember that thou wast a bondman in the land of Egypt, and the LORD thy God redeemed thee: therefore I command thee this thing today.

—Deuteronomy 15: 12–15

Besides the crime which consists in violating the law, and varying from the right rule of reason, whereby a man so far becomes degenerate, and declares himself to quit the principles of human nature, and to be a noxious creature, there is commonly injury done to some person or other, and some other man receives damage by his transgression: in which case he who hath received any damage, has, besides the right of punishment common to him with other men, a particular right to seek reparation.

—John Locke, "Second Treatise"

By our unpaid labor and suffering, we have earned the right to the soil, many times over and over, and now we are determined to have it.

—Anonymous, 1861

I. "SO THAT'S JUST ONE OF MY LOSSES"

Clyde Ross was born in 1923, the seventh of 13 children, near Clarksdale, Mississippi, the home of the blues. Ross's parents owned and farmed a 40-acre tract of land, flush with cows, hogs, and mules. Ross's mother would drive to Clarksdale to do her shopping in a horse and buggy, in which she invested all the pride one might place in a Cadillac. The family owned another horse, with a red coat, which they gave to Clyde. The Ross family wanted for little, save that which all black families in the Deep South then desperately desired—the protection of the law.

In the 1920s, Jim Crow Mississippi was, in all facets of society, a kleptocracy. The majority of the people in the state were perpetually robbed of the vote—a hijacking engineered through the trickery of the poll tax and the muscle of the lynch mob. Between 1882 and 1968, more black people were lynched in Mississippi than in any other state. "You and I know what's the best way to keep the nigger from voting," blustered Theodore Bilbo, a Mississippi senator and a proud Klansman. "You do it the night before the election."

The state's regime partnered robbery of the franchise with robbery of the purse. Many of Mississippi's black farmers lived in debt peonage, under the sway of cotton kings who were at once their landlords, their employers, and their primary merchants. Tools and necessities were advanced against the return on the crop, which was determined by the employer. When farmers were deemed to be in debt—and they often were—the negative balance was then carried over to the next season. A man or woman who protested this arrangement did so at the risk of grave injury or death. Refusing to work meant arrest under vagrancy laws and forced labor under the state's penal system.

Well into the 20th century, black people spoke of their flight from Mississippi in much the same manner as their runagate ancestors had. In her 2010

book, *The Warmth of Other Suns*, Isabel Wilkerson tells the story of Eddie
Earvin, a spinach picker who fled Mississippi in 1963, after being made to
work at gunpoint. "You didn't talk about it or tell nobody," Earvin said. "You
had to sneak away."

When Clyde Ross was still a child, Mississippi authorities claimed his
father owed $3,000 in back taxes. The elder Ross could not read. He did not
have a lawyer. He did not know anyone at the local courthouse. He could
not expect the police to be impartial. Effectively, the Ross family had no way
to contest the claim and no protection under the law. The authorities seized
the land. They seized the buggy. They took the cows, hogs, and mules. And
so for the upkeep of separate but equal, the entire Ross family was reduced
to sharecropping.

This was hardly unusual. In 2001, the Associated Press published a three-
part investigation into the theft of black-owned land stretching back to the
antebellum period. The series documented some 406 victims and 24,000
acres of land valued at tens of millions of dollars. The land was taken through
means ranging from legal chicanery to terrorism. "Some of the land taken
from black families has become a country club in Virginia," the AP reported,
as well as "oil fields in Mississippi" and "a baseball spring training facility in
Florida."

Clyde Ross was a smart child. His teacher thought he should attend a
more challenging school. There was very little support for educating black
people in Mississippi. But Julius Rosenwald, a part owner of Sears, Roebuck,
had begun an ambitious effort to build schools for black children throughout the South. Ross's teacher believed he should attend the local Rosenwald
school. It was too far for Ross to walk and get back in time to work in the
fields. Local white children had a school bus. Clyde Ross did not, and thus
lost the chance to better his education.

Then, when Ross was 10 years old, a group of white men demanded his
only childhood possession—the horse with the red coat. "You can't have this
horse. We want it," one of the white men said. They gave Ross's father $17.

"I did everything for that horse," Ross told me. "Everything. And they
took him. Put him on the racetrack. I never did know what happened to
him after that, but I know they didn't bring him back. So that's just one of
my losses."

The losses mounted. As sharecroppers, the Ross family saw their wages
treated as the landlord's slush fund. Landowners were supposed to split the
profits from the cotton fields with sharecroppers. But bales would often disappear during the count, or the split might be altered on a whim. If cotton
was selling for 50 cents a pound, the Ross family might get 15 cents, or only
five. One year Ross's mother promised to buy him a $7 suit for a summer

program at their church. She ordered the suit by mail. But that year Ross's family was paid only five cents a pound for cotton. The mailman arrived with the suit. The Rosses could not pay. The suit was sent back. Clyde Ross did not go to the church program.

It was in these early years that Ross began to understand himself as an American—he did not live under the blind decree of justice, but under the heel of a regime that elevated armed robbery to a governing principle. He thought about fighting. "Just be quiet," his father told him. "Because they'll come and kill us all."

Clyde Ross grew. He was drafted into the Army. The draft officials offered him an exemption if he stayed home and worked. He preferred to take his chances with war. He was stationed in California. He found that he could go into stores without being bothered. He could walk the streets without being harassed. He could go into a restaurant and receive service.

Ross was shipped off to Guam. He fought in World War II to save the world from tyranny. But when he returned to Clarksdale, he found that tyranny had followed him home. This was 1947, eight years before Mississippi lynched Emmett Till and tossed his broken body into the Tallahatchie River. The Great Migration, a mass exodus of 6 million African Americans that spanned most of the 20th century, was now in its second wave. The black pilgrims did not journey north simply seeking better wages and work, or bright lights and big adventures. They were fleeing the acquisitive warlords of the South. They were seeking the protection of the law.

Clyde Ross was among them. He came to Chicago in 1947 and took a job as a taster at Campbell's Soup. He made a stable wage. He married. He had children. His paycheck was his own. No Klansmen stripped him of the vote. When he walked down the street, he did not have to move because a white man was walking past. He did not have to take off his hat or avert his gaze. His journey from peonage to full citizenship seemed near-complete. Only one item was missing—a home, that final badge of entry into the sacred order of the American middle class of the Eisenhower years.

In 1961, Ross and his wife bought a house in North Lawndale, a bustling community on Chicago's West Side. North Lawndale had long been a predominantly Jewish neighborhood, but a handful of middle-class African Americans had lived there starting in the '40s. The community was anchored by the sprawling Sears, Roebuck headquarters. North Lawndale's Jewish People's Institute actively encouraged blacks to move into the neighborhood, seeking to make it a "pilot community for interracial living." In the battle for integration then being fought around the country, North Lawndale seemed to offer promising terrain. But out in the tall grass, highwaymen, nefarious as any Clarksdale kleptocrat, were lying in wait.

Three months after Clyde Ross moved into his house, the boiler blew out. This would normally be a homeowner's responsibility, but in fact, Ross was not really a homeowner. His payments were made to the seller, not the bank. And Ross had not signed a normal mortgage. He'd bought "on contract": a predatory agreement that combined all the responsibilities of homeownership with all the disadvantages of renting—while offering the benefits of neither. Ross had bought his house for $27,500. The seller, not the previous homeowner but a new kind of middleman, had bought it for only $12,000 six months before selling it to Ross. In a contract sale, the seller kept the deed until the contract was paid in full—and, unlike with a normal mortgage, Ross would acquire no equity in the meantime. If he missed a single payment, he would immediately forfeit his $1,000 down payment, all his monthly payments, and the property itself.

The men who peddled contracts in North Lawndale would sell homes at inflated prices and then evict families who could not pay—taking their down payment and their monthly installments as profit. Then they'd bring in another black family, rinse, and repeat. "He loads them up with payments they can't meet," an office secretary told *The Chicago Daily News* of her boss, the speculator Lou Fushanis, in 1963. "Then he takes the property away from them. He's sold some of the buildings three or four times."

Ross had tried to get a legitimate mortgage in another neighborhood but was told by a loan officer that there was no financing available. The truth was that there was no financing for people like Clyde Ross. From the 1930s through the 1960s, black people across the country were largely cut out of the legitimate home-mortgage market through means both legal and extra-legal. Chicago whites employed every measure, from "restrictive covenants" to bombings, to keep their neighborhoods segregated.

Their efforts were buttressed by the federal government. In 1934, Congress created the Federal Housing Administration. The FHA insured private mortgages, causing a drop in interest rates and a decline in the size of the down payment required to buy a house. But an insured mortgage was not a possibility for Clyde Ross. The FHA had adopted a system of maps that rated neighborhoods according to their perceived stability. On the maps, green areas, rated "A," indicated "in demand" neighborhoods that, as one appraiser put it, lacked "a single foreigner or Negro." These neighborhoods were considered excellent prospects for insurance. Neighborhoods where black people lived were rated "D" and were usually considered ineligible for FHA backing. They were colored in red. Neither the percentage of black people living there nor their social class mattered. Black people were viewed as a contagion. Redlining went beyond FHA-backed loans and spread to the entire mortgage industry, which was already rife with racism, excluding black people from most legitimate means of obtaining a mortgage.

"A government offering such bounty to builders and lenders could have required compliance with a nondiscrimination policy," Charles Abrams, the urban-studies expert who helped create the New York City Housing Authority, wrote in 1955. "Instead, the FHA adopted a racial policy that could well have been culled from the Nuremberg laws."

The devastating effects are cogently outlined by Melvin L. Oliver and Thomas M. Shapiro in their 1995 book, *Black Wealth/White Wealth*:

> Locked out of the greatest mass-based opportunity for wealth accumulation in American history, African Americans who desired and were able to afford home ownership found themselves consigned to central-city communities where their investments were affected by the "self-fulfilling prophecies" of the FHA appraisers: cut off from sources of new investment[,] their homes and communities deteriorated and lost value in comparison to those homes and communities that FHA appraisers deemed desirable.

In Chicago and across the country, whites looking to achieve the American dream could rely on a legitimate credit system backed by the government. Blacks were herded into the sights of unscrupulous lenders who took them for money and for sport. "It was like people who like to go out and shoot lions in Africa. It was the same thrill," a housing attorney told the historian Beryl Satter in her 2009 book, *Family Properties*. "The thrill of the chase and the kill."

The kill was profitable. At the time of his death, Lou Fushanis owned more than 600 properties, many of them in North Lawndale, and his estate was estimated to be worth $3 million. He'd made much of this money by exploiting the frustrated hopes of black migrants like Clyde Ross. During this period, according to one estimate, 85 percent of all black home buyers who bought in Chicago bought on contract. "If anybody who is well established in this business in Chicago doesn't earn $100,000 a year," a contract seller told *The Saturday Evening Post* in 1962, "he is loafing."

Contract sellers became rich. North Lawndale became a ghetto.

Clyde Ross still lives there. He still owns his home. He is 91, and the emblems of survival are all around him—awards for service in his community, pictures of his children in cap and gown. But when I asked him about his home in North Lawndale, I heard only anarchy.

"We were ashamed. We did not want anyone to know that we were that ignorant," Ross told me. He was sitting at his dining-room table. His glasses were as thick as his Clarksdale drawl. "I'd come out of Mississippi where there was one mess, and come up here and got in another mess. So how dumb am I? I didn't want anyone to know how dumb I was.

"When I found myself caught up in it, I said, 'How? I just left this mess. I just left no laws. And no regard. And then I come here and get cheated wide open.' I would probably want to do some harm to some people, you know, if I had been violent like some of us. I thought, 'Man, I got caught up in this stuff. I can't even take care of my kids.' I didn't have enough for my kids. You could fall through the cracks easy fighting these white people. And no law."

But fight Clyde Ross did. In 1968 he joined the newly formed Contract Buyers League—a collection of black homeowners on Chicago's South and West Sides, all of whom had been locked into the same system of predation. There was Howell Collins, whose contract called for him to pay $25,500 for a house that a speculator had bought for $14,500. There was Ruth Wells, who'd managed to pay out half her contract, expecting a mortgage, only to suddenly see an insurance bill materialize out of thin air—a requirement the seller had added without Wells's knowledge. Contract sellers used every tool at their disposal to pilfer from their clients. They scared white residents into selling low. They lied about properties' compliance with building codes, then left the buyer responsible when city inspectors arrived. They presented themselves as real-estate brokers, when in fact they were the owners. They guided their clients to lawyers who were in on the scheme.

The Contract Buyers League fought back. Members—who would eventually number more than 500—went out to the posh suburbs where the speculators lived and embarrassed them by knocking on their neighbors' doors and informing them of the details of the contract-lending trade. They refused to pay their installments, instead holding monthly payments in an escrow account. Then they brought a suit against the contract sellers, accusing them of buying properties and reselling in such a manner "to reap from members of the Negro race large and unjust profits."

In return for the "deprivations of their rights and privileges under the Thirteenth and Fourteenth Amendments," the league demanded "prayers for relief"—payback of all moneys paid on contracts and all moneys paid for structural improvement of properties, at 6 percent interest minus a "fair, non-discriminatory" rental price for time of occupation. Moreover, the league asked the court to adjudge that the defendants had "acted willfully and maliciously and that malice is the gist of this action."

Ross and the Contract Buyers League were no longer appealing to the government simply for equality. They were no longer fleeing in hopes of a better deal elsewhere. They were charging society with a crime against their community. They wanted the crime publicly ruled as such. They wanted the crime's executors declared to be offensive to society. And they wanted restitution for the great injury brought upon them by said offenders. In 1968, Clyde Ross and the Contract Buyers League were no longer simply seeking the protection of the law. They were seeking reparations.

II. "A DIFFERENCE OF KIND, NOT DEGREE"

According to the most-recent statistics, North Lawndale is now on the wrong end of virtually every socioeconomic indicator. In 1930 its population was 112,000. Today it is 36,000. The halcyon talk of "interracial living" is dead. The neighborhood is 92 percent black. Its homicide rate is 45 per 100,000—triple the rate of the city as a whole. The infant-mortality rate is 14 per 1,000—more than twice the national average. Forty-three percent of the people in North Lawndale live below the poverty line—double Chicago's overall rate. Forty-five percent of all households are on food stamps—nearly three times the rate of the city at large. Sears, Roebuck left the neighborhood in 1987, taking 1,800 jobs with it. Kids in North Lawndale need not be confused about their prospects: Cook County's Juvenile Temporary Detention Center sits directly adjacent to the neighborhood.

North Lawndale is an extreme portrait of the trends that ail black Chicago. Such is the magnitude of these ailments that it can be said that blacks and whites do not inhabit the same city. The average per capita income of Chicago's white neighborhoods is almost three times that of its black neighborhoods. When the Harvard sociologist Robert J. Sampson examined incarceration rates in Chicago in his 2012 book, *Great American City*, he found that a black neighborhood with one of the highest incarceration rates (West Garfield Park) had a rate more than 40 times as high as the white neighborhood with the highest rate (Clearing). "This is a staggering differential, even for community-level comparisons," Sampson writes. "A difference of kind, not degree."

In other words, Chicago's impoverished black neighborhoods—characterized by high unemployment and households headed by single parents—are not simply poor; they are "ecologically distinct." This "is not simply the same thing as low economic status," writes Sampson. "In this pattern Chicago is not alone."

The lives of black Americans are better than they were half a century ago. The humiliation of WHITES ONLY signs are gone. Rates of black poverty have decreased. Black teen-pregnancy rates are at record lows—and the gap between black and white teen-pregnancy rates has shrunk significantly. But such progress rests on a shaky foundation, and fault lines are everywhere.

The income gap between black and white households is roughly the same today as it was in 1970. Patrick Sharkey, a sociologist at New York University, studied children born from 1955 through 1970 and found that 4 percent of whites and 62 percent of blacks across America had been raised in poor neighborhoods. A generation later, the same study showed, virtually nothing had changed. And whereas whites born into affluent neighborhoods tended to remain in affluent neighborhoods, blacks tended to fall out of them.

This is not surprising. Black families, regardless of income, are significantly less wealthy than white families. The Pew Research Center estimates that white households are worth roughly 20 times as much as black households, and that whereas only 15 percent of whites have zero or negative wealth, more than a third of blacks do. Effectively, the black family in America is working without a safety net. When financial calamity strikes—a medical emergency, divorce, job loss—the fall is precipitous.

And just as black families of all incomes remain handicapped by a lack of wealth, so too do they remain handicapped by their restricted choice of neighborhood. Black people with upper-middle-class incomes do not generally live in upper-middle-class neighborhoods. Sharkey's research shows that black families making $100,000 typically live in the kinds of neighborhoods inhabited by white families making $30,000. "Blacks and whites inhabit such different neighborhoods," Sharkey writes, "that it is not possible to compare the economic outcomes of black and white children."

The implications are chilling. As a rule, poor black people do not work their way out of the ghetto—and those who do often face the horror of watching their children and grandchildren tumble back.

Even seeming evidence of progress withers under harsh light. In 2012, the Manhattan Institute cheerily noted that segregation had declined since the 1960s. And yet African Americans still remained—by far—the most segregated ethnic group in the country.

With segregation, with the isolation of the injured and the robbed, comes the concentration of disadvantage. An unsegregated America might see poverty, and all its effects, spread across the country with no particular bias toward skin color. Instead, the concentration of poverty has been paired with a concentration of melanin. The resulting conflagration has been devastating.

One thread of thinking in the African American community holds that these depressing numbers partially stem from cultural pathologies that can be altered through individual grit and exceptionally good behavior. (In 2011, Philadelphia Mayor Michael Nutter, responding to violence among young black males, put the blame on the family: "Too many men making too many babies they don't want to take care of, and then we end up dealing with your children." Nutter turned to those presumably fatherless babies: "Pull your pants up and buy a belt, because no one wants to see your underwear or the crack of your butt.") The thread is as old as black politics itself. It is also wrong. The kind of trenchant racism to which black people have persistently been subjected can never be defeated by making its victims more respectable. The essence of American racism is disrespect. And in the wake of the grim numbers, we see the grim inheritance.

The Contract Buyers League's suit brought by Clyde Ross and his allies took direct aim at this inheritance. The suit was rooted in Chicago's long history of segregation, which had created two housing markets—one legitimate and backed by the government, the other lawless and patrolled by predators. The suit dragged on until 1976, when the league lost a jury trial. Securing the equal protection of the law proved hard; securing reparations proved impossible. If there were any doubts about the mood of the jury, the foreman removed them by saying, when asked about the verdict, that he hoped it would help end "the mess Earl Warren made with *Brown v. Board of Education* and all that nonsense."

The Supreme Court seems to share that sentiment. The past two decades have witnessed a rollback of the progressive legislation of the 1960s. Liberals have found themselves on the defensive. In 2008, when Barack Obama was a candidate for president, he was asked whether his daughters—Malia and Sasha—should benefit from affirmative action. He answered in the negative.

The exchange rested upon an erroneous comparison of the average American white family and the exceptional first family. In the contest of upward mobility, Barack and Michelle Obama have won. But they've won by being twice as good—and enduring twice as much. Malia and Sasha Obama enjoy privileges beyond the average white child's dreams. But that comparison is incomplete. The more telling question is how they compare with Jenna and Barbara Bush—the products of many generations of privilege, not just one. Whatever the Obama children achieve, it will be evidence of their family's singular perseverance, not of broad equality.

III. "WE INHERIT OUR AMPLE PATRIMONY"

In 1783, the freedwoman Belinda Royall petitioned the commonwealth of Massachusetts for reparations. Belinda had been born in modern-day Ghana. She was kidnapped as a child and sold into slavery. She endured the Middle Passage and 50 years of enslavement at the hands of Isaac Royall and his son. But the junior Royall, a British loyalist, fled the country during the Revolution. Belinda, now free after half a century of labor, beseeched the nascent Massachusetts legislature:

The face of your Petitioner, is now marked with the furrows of time, and her frame bending under the oppression of years, while she, by the Laws of the Land, is denied the employment of one morsel of that immense wealth, apart whereof hath been accumilated by her own industry, and the whole augmented by her servitude.

WHEREFORE, casting herself at your feet if your honours, as to a body of men, formed for the extirpation of vassalage, for the reward of Virtue, and the just return of honest industry—she prays, that such allowance may be made her out of the Estate of Colonel Royall, as will prevent her, and her more infirm daughter, from misery in the greatest extreme, and scatter comfort over the short and downward path of their lives.

Belinda Royall was granted a pension of 15 pounds and 12 shillings, to be paid out of the estate of Isaac Royall—one of the earliest successful attempts to petition for reparations. At the time, black people in America had endured more than 150 years of enslavement, and the idea that they might be owed something in return was, if not the national consensus, at least not outrageous.

"A heavy account lies against us as a civil society for oppressions committed against people who did not injure us," wrote the Quaker John Woolman in 1769, "and that if the particular case of many individuals were fairly stated, it would appear that there was considerable due to them."

As the historian Roy E. Finkenbine has documented, at the dawn of this country, black reparations were actively considered and often effected. Quakers in New York, New England, and Baltimore went so far as to make "membership contingent upon compensating one's former slaves." In 1782, the Quaker Robert Pleasants emancipated his 78 slaves, granted them 350 acres, and later built a school on their property and provided for their education. "The doing of this justice to the injured Africans," wrote Pleasants, "would be an acceptable offering to him who 'Rules in the kingdom of men.'"

Edward Coles, a protégé of Thomas Jefferson who became a slaveholder through inheritance, took many of his slaves north and granted them a plot of land in Illinois. John Randolph, a cousin of Jefferson's, willed that all his slaves be emancipated upon his death, and that all those older than 40 be given 10 acres of land. "I give and bequeath to all my slaves their freedom," Randolph wrote, "heartily regretting that I have been the owner of one."

In his book *Forever Free*, Eric Foner recounts the story of a disgruntled planter reprimanding a freedman loafing on the job:

Planter: "You lazy nigger, I am losing a whole day's labor by you."
Freedman: "Massa, how many days' labor have I lost by you?"

In the 20th century, the cause of reparations was taken up by a diverse cast that included the Confederate veteran Walter R. Vaughan, who believed that reparations would be a stimulus for the South; the black activist Callie House; black-nationalist leaders like "Queen Mother" Audley Moore; and the civil-rights activist James Forman. The movement coalesced in 1987 under an umbrella organization called the National Coalition of Blacks for Reparations in America (N'COBRA). The NAACP endorsed reparations in 1993. Charles J. Ogletree Jr., a professor at Harvard Law School, has pursued reparations claims in court.

But while the people advocating reparations have changed over time, the response from the country has remained virtually the same. "They have been taught to labor," the *Chicago Tribune* editorialized in 1891. "They have been taught Christian civilization, and to speak the noble English language instead of some African gibberish. The account is square with the exslaves."

Not exactly. Having been enslaved for 250 years, black people were not left to their own devices. They were terrorized. In the Deep South, a second slavery ruled. In the North, legislatures, mayors, civic associations, banks, and citizens all colluded to pin black people into ghettos, where they were overcrowded, overcharged, and undereducated. Businesses discriminated against them, awarding them the worst jobs and the worst wages. Police brutalized them in the streets. And the notion that black lives, black bodies, and black wealth were rightful targets remained deeply rooted in the broader society. Now we have half-stepped away from our long centuries of despoilment, promising, "Never again." But still we are haunted. It is as though we have run up a credit-card bill and, having pledged to charge no more, remain befuddled that the balance does not disappear. The effects of that balance, interest accruing daily, are all around us.

Broach the topic of reparations today and a barrage of questions inevitably follows: Who will be paid? How much will they be paid? Who will pay? But if the practicalities, not the justice, of reparations are the true sticking point, there has for some time been the beginnings of a solution. For the past 25 years, Congressman John Conyers Jr., who represents the Detroit area, has marked every session of Congress by introducing a bill calling for a congressional study of slavery and its lingering effects as well as recommendations for "appropriate remedies."

A country curious about how reparations might actually work has an easy solution in Conyers's bill, now called HR 40, the Commission to Study Reparation Proposals for African Americans Act. We would support this bill, submit the question to study, and then assess the possible solutions. But we are not interested.

"It's because it's black folks making the claim," Nkechi Taifa, who helped found N'COBRA, says. "People who talk about reparations are considered left lunatics. But all we are talking about is studying [reparations]. As John Conyers has said, we study everything. We study the water, the air. We can't even study the issue? This bill does not authorize one red cent to anyone."

That HR 40 has never—under either Democrats or Republicans—made it to the House floor suggests our concerns are rooted not in the impracticality of reparations but in something more existential. If we conclude that the conditions in North Lawndale and black America are not inexplicable but are instead precisely what you'd expect of a community that for centuries has lived in America's crosshairs, then what are we to make of the world's oldest democracy?

One cannot escape the question by hand-waving at the past, disavowing the acts of one's ancestors, nor by citing a recent date of ancestral immigration. The last slaveholder has been dead for a very long time. The last soldier to endure Valley Forge has been dead much longer. To proudly claim the veteran and disown the slaveholder is patriotism à la carte. A nation outlives its generations. We were not there when Washington crossed the Delaware, but Emanuel Gottlieb Leutze's rendering has meaning to us. We were not there when Woodrow Wilson took us into World War I, but we are still paying out the pensions. If Thomas Jefferson's genius matters, then so does his taking of Sally Hemings's body. If George Washington crossing the Delaware matters, so must his ruthless pursuit of the runagate Oney Judge.

In 1909, President William Howard Taft told the country that "intelligent" white southerners were ready to see blacks as "useful members of the community." A week later Joseph Gordon, a black man, was lynched outside Greenwood, Mississippi. The high point of the lynching era has passed. But the memories of those robbed of their lives still live on in the lingering effects. Indeed, in America there is a strange and powerful belief that if you stab a black person 10 times, the bleeding stops and the healing begins the moment the assailant drops the knife. We believe white dominance to be a fact of the inert past, a delinquent debt that can be made to disappear if only we don't look.

There has always been another way. "It is in vain to alledge, that *our ancestors* brought them hither, and not we," Yale President Timothy Dwight said in 1810.

We inherit our ample patrimony with all its incumbrances; and are bound to pay the debts of our ancestors. *This* debt, particularly, we are bound to discharge: and, when the righteous Judge of the Universe comes to reckon with his servants, he will rigidly exact the payment at our hands. To give them liberty, and stop here, is to entail upon them a curse.

IV. "THE ILLS THAT SLAVERY FREES US FROM"

America begins in black plunder and white democracy, two features that are not contradictory but complementary. "The men who came together to found the independent United States, dedicated to freedom and equality, either held slaves or were willing to join hands with those who did," the historian Edmund S. Morgan wrote. "None of them felt entirely comfortable about the fact, but neither did they feel responsible for it. Most of them had inherited both their slaves and their attachment to freedom from an earlier generation, and they knew the two were not unconnected."

When enslaved Africans, plundered of their bodies, plundered of their families, and plundered of their labor, were brought to the colony of Virginia in 1619, they did not initially endure the naked racism that would engulf their progeny. Some of them were freed. Some of them intermarried. Still others escaped with the white indentured servants who had suffered as they had. Some even rebelled together, allying under Nathaniel Bacon to torch Jamestown in 1676.

One hundred years later, the idea of slaves and poor whites joining forces would shock the senses, but in the early days of the English colonies, the two groups had much in common. English visitors to Virginia found that its masters "abuse their servantes with intollerable oppression and hard usage." White servants were flogged, tricked into serving beyond their contracts, and traded in much the same manner as slaves.

This "hard usage" originated in a simple fact of the New World—land was boundless but cheap labor was limited. As life spans increased in the colony, the Virginia planters found in the enslaved Africans an even more efficient source of cheap labor. Whereas indentured servants were still legal subjects of the English crown and thus entitled to certain protections, African slaves entered the colonies as aliens. Exempted from the protections of the crown, they became early America's indispensable working class—fit for maximum exploitation, capable of only minimal resistance.

For the next 250 years, American law worked to reduce black people to a class of untouchables and raise all white men to the level of citizens. In 1650, Virginia mandated that "all persons except Negroes" were to carry arms. In 1664, Maryland mandated that any Englishwoman who married a slave must live as a slave of her husband's master. In 1705, the Virginia assembly passed a law allowing for the dismemberment of unruly slaves—but forbidding masters from whipping "a Christian white servant naked, without an order from a justice of the peace." In that same law, the colony mandated that "all horses, cattle, and hogs, now belonging, or that hereafter shall belong to any slave" be seized and sold off by the local church, the profits used to support "the poor of the said parish." At that time, there would have still been people alive who could remember blacks and whites joining to burn down James-town only 29 years before. But at the beginning of the 18th century, two primary classes were enshrined in America.

"The two great divisions of society are not the rich and poor, but white and black," John C. Calhoun, South Carolina's senior senator, declared on the Senate floor in 1848. "And all the former, the poor as well as the rich, belong to the upper class, and are respected and treated as equals."

In 1860, the majority of people living in South Carolina and Mississippi, almost half of those living in Georgia, and about one-third of all Southerners were on the wrong side of Calhoun's line. The state with the largest number of enslaved Americans was Virginia, where in certain counties some 70 per-cent of all people labored in chains. Nearly one-fourth of all white Southern-ers owned slaves, and upon their backs the economic basis of America—and much of the Atlantic world—was erected. In the seven cotton states, one-third of all white income was derived from slavery. By 1840, cotton produced by slave labor constituted 59 percent of the country's exports. The web of this slave society extended north to the looms of New England, and across the Atlantic to Great Britain, where it powered a great economic transformation and altered the trajectory of world history. "Whoever says Industrial Revo-lution," wrote the historian Eric J. Hobsbawm, "says cotton."

The wealth accorded America by slavery was not just in what the slaves pulled from the land but in the slaves themselves. "In 1860, slaves as an asset were worth more than all of America's manufacturing, all of the railroads, all of the productive capacity of the United States put together," the Yale histo-rian David W. Blight has noted. "Slaves were the single largest, by far, financial asset of property in the entire American economy." The sale of these slaves— "in whose bodies that money congealed," writes Walter Johnson, a Harvard historian—generated even more ancillary wealth. Loans were taken out for purchase, to be repaid with interest. Insurance policies were drafted against the untimely death of a slave and the loss of potential profits. Slave sales were taxed and notarized. The vending of the black body and the sundering of the black family became an economy unto themselves, estimated to have brought in tens of millions of dollars to antebellum America. In 1860 there were more mil-lionaires per capita in the Mississippi Valley than anywhere else in the country.

Beneath the cold numbers lay lives divided. "I had a constant dread that Mrs. Moore, her mistress, would be in want of money and sell my dear wife," a freedman wrote, reflecting on his time in slavery. "We constantly dreaded a final separation. Our affection for each was very strong, and this made us always apprehensive of a cruel parting."

Forced partings were common in the antebellum South. A slave in some parts of the region stood a 30 percent chance of being sold in his or her lifetime. Twenty-five percent of interstate trades destroyed a first marriage and half of them destroyed a nuclear family.

When the wife and children of Henry Brown, a slave in Richmond, Virginia, were to be sold away, Brown searched for a white master who might buy his wife and children to keep the family together. He failed:

> The next day, I stationed myself by the side of the road, along which the slaves, amounting to three hundred and fifty, were to pass. The purchaser of my wife was a Methodist minister, who was about starting for North Carolina. Pretty soon five waggon-loads of little children passed, and looking at the foremost one, what should I see but a little child, pointing its tiny hand towards me, exclaiming, "There's my father; I knew he would come and bid me good-bye." It was my eldest child! Soon the gang approached in which my wife was chained. I looked, and beheld her familiar face; but O, reader, that glance of agony! may God spare me ever again enduring the excruciating horror of that moment! She passed, and came near to where I stood. I seized hold of her hand, intending to bid her farewell; but words failed me; the gift of utterance had fled, and I remained speechless. I followed her for some distance, with her hand grasped in mine, as if to save her from her fate, but I could not speak, and I was obliged to turn away in silence.

In a time when telecommunications were primitive and blacks lacked freedom of movement, the parting of black families was a kind of murder. Here we find the roots of American wealth and democracy—in the for-profit destruction of the most important asset available to any people, the family. The destruction was not incidental to America's rise; it facilitated that rise. By erecting a slave society, America created the economic foundation for its great experiment in democracy. The labor strife that seeded Bacon's rebellion was suppressed. America's indispensable working class existed as property beyond the realm of politics, leaving white Americans free to trumpet their love of freedom and democratic values. Assessing antebellum democracy in Virginia, a visitor from England observed that the state's natives "can profess an unbounded love of liberty and of democracy in consequence of the mass of the people, who in other countries might become mobs, being there nearly altogether composed of their own Negro slaves."

V. THE QUIET PLUNDER

The consequences of 250 years of enslavement, of war upon black families and black people, were profound. Like homeownership today, slave ownership was aspirational, attracting not just those who owned slaves but those who wished to. Much as homeowners today might discuss the addition of a patio or the painting of a living room, slaveholders traded tips on the best methods for breeding workers, exacting labor, and doling out punishment. Just as a homeowner today might subscribe to a magazine like *This Old House*, slaveholders had journals such as *De Bow's Review*, which recommended the best practices for wringing profits from slaves. By the dawn of the Civil War, the enslavement of black America was thought to be so foundational to the country that those who sought to end it were branded heretics worthy of death. Imagine what would happen if a president today came out in favor of taking all American homes from their owners: the reaction might well be violent.

"This country was formed for the *white*, not for the black man," John Wilkes Booth wrote, before killing Abraham Lincoln. "And looking upon *African slavery* from the same standpoint held by those noble framers of our Constitution, I for one have ever considered *it* one of the greatest blessings (both for themselves and us) that God ever bestowed upon a favored nation."

In the aftermath of the Civil War, Radical Republicans attempted to reconstruct the country upon something resembling universal equality—but they were beaten back by a campaign of "Redemption," led by White Liners, Red Shirts, and Klansmen bent on upholding a society "formed for the *white*, not for the black man." A wave of terrorism roiled the South. In his massive history *Reconstruction*, Eric Foner recounts incidents of black people being attacked for not removing their hats; for refusing to hand over a whiskey flask; for disobeying church procedures; for "using insolent language"; for disputing labor contracts; for refusing to be "tied like a slave." Sometimes the attacks were intended simply to "thin out the niggers a little."

Terrorism carried the day. Federal troops withdrew from the South in 1877. The dream of Reconstruction died. For the next century, political violence was visited upon blacks wantonly, with special treatment meted out toward black people of ambition. Black schools and churches were burned to the ground. Black voters and the political candidates who attempted to rally them were intimidated, and some were murdered. At the end of World War I, black veterans returning to their homes were assaulted for daring to wear the American uniform. The demobilization of soldiers after the war, which put white and black veterans into competition for scarce jobs, produced the Red Summer of 1919: a succession of racist pogroms against dozens of cities ranging from Longview, Texas, to Chicago to Washington, D.C. Organized white violence against blacks continued into the 1920s—in 1921 a white mob leveled Tulsa's "Black Wall Street," and in 1923 another one razed the black town of Rosewood, Florida—and virtually no one was punished.

The work of mobs was a rabid and violent rendition of prejudices that extended even into the upper reaches of American government. The New Deal is today remembered as a model for what progressive government should do—cast a broad social safety net that protects the poor and the afflicted while building the middle class. When progressives wish to express their disappointment with Barack Obama, they point to the accomplishments of Franklin Roosevelt. But these progressives rarely note that Roosevelt's New Deal, much like the democracy that produced it, rested on the foundation of Jim Crow.

"The Jim Crow South," writes Ira Katznelson, a history and political-science professor at Columbia, "was the one collaborator America's democracy could not do without." The marks of that collaboration are all over the New Deal. The omnibus programs passed under the Social Security Act in 1935 were crafted in such a way as to protect the southern way of life. Old-age insurance (Social Security proper) and unemployment insurance excluded farmworkers and domestics—jobs heavily occupied by blacks. When President Roosevelt signed Social Security into law in 1935, 65 percent of African Americans nationally and between 70 and 80 percent in the South were ineligible. The NAACP protested, calling the new American safety net "a sieve with holes just big enough for the majority of Negroes to fall through."

The oft-celebrated G.I. Bill similarly failed black Americans, by mirroring the broader country's insistence on a racist housing policy. Though ostensibly color-blind, Title III of the bill, which aimed to give veterans access to low-interest home loans, left black veterans to tangle with white officials at their local Veterans Administration as well as with the same banks that had, for years, refused to grant mortgages to blacks. The historian Kathleen J. Frydl observes in her 2009 book, *The GI Bill*, that so many blacks were disqualified from receiving Title III benefits "that it is more accurate simply to say that blacks could not use this particular title."

In Cold War America, homeownership was seen as a means of instilling patriotism, and as a civilizing and anti-radical force. "No man who owns his own house and lot can be a Communist," claimed William Levitt, who pioneered the modern suburb with the development of the various Levittowns, his famous planned communities. "He has too much to do."

But the Levittowns were, with Levitt's willing acquiescence, segregated throughout their early years. Daisy and Bill Myers, the first black family to move into Levittown, Pennsylvania, were greeted with protests and a burning cross. A neighbor who opposed the family said that Bill Myers was "probably a nice guy, but every time I look at him I see $2,000 drop off the value of my house."

The neighbor had good reason to be afraid. Bill and Daisy Myers were from the other side of John C. Calhoun's dual society. If they moved next door, housing policy almost guaranteed that their neighbors' property values would decline.

Whereas shortly before the New Deal, a typical mortgage required a large down payment and full repayment within about 10 years, the creation of the Home Owners' Loan Corporation in 1933 and then the Federal Housing Administration the following year allowed banks to offer loans requiring no more than 10 percent down, amortized over 20 to 30 years. "Without federal intervention in the housing market, massive suburbanization would have been impossible," writes Thomas J. Sugrue, a historian at the University of Pennsylvania. "In 1930, only 30 percent of Americans owned their own homes; by 1960, more than 60 percent were home owners. Home ownership became an emblem of American citizenship."

That emblem was not to be awarded to blacks. The American real-estate industry believed segregation to be a moral principle. As late as 1950, the National Association of Real Estate Boards' code of ethics warned that "a Realtor should never be instrumental in introducing into a neighborhood ... any race or nationality, or any individuals whose presence will clearly be detrimental to property values." A 1943 brochure specified that such potential undesirables might include madams, bootleggers, gangsters—and "a colored man of means who was giving his children a college education and thought they were entitled to live among whites."

The federal government concurred. It was the Home Owners' Loan Corporation, not a private trade association, that pioneered the practice of redlining, selectively granting loans and insisting that any property it insured be covered by a restrictive covenant—a clause in the deed forbidding the sale of the property to anyone other than whites. Millions of dollars flowed from tax coffers into segregated white neighborhoods.

"For perhaps the first time, the federal government embraced the discriminatory attitudes of the marketplace," the historian Kenneth T. Jackson wrote in his 1985 book, *Crabgrass Frontier*, a history of suburbanization. "Previously, prejudices were personalized and individualized; FHA exhorted segregation and enshrined it as public policy. Whole areas of cities were declared ineligible for loan guarantees." Redlining was not officially outlawed until

1968, by the Fair Housing Act. By then the damage was done—and reports of redlining by banks have continued.

The federal government is premised on equal fealty from all its citizens, who in return are to receive equal treatment. But as late as the mid-20th century, this bargain was not granted to black people, who repeatedly paid a higher price for citizenship and received less in return. Plunder had been the essential feature of slavery, of the society described by Calhoun. But practically a full century after the end of the Civil War and the abolition of slavery, the plunder—quiet, systemic, submerged—continued even amidst the aims and achievements of New Deal liberals.

VI. MAKING THE SECOND GHETTO

Today Chicago is one of the most segregated cities in the country, a fact that reflects assiduous planning. In the effort to uphold white supremacy at every level down to the neighborhood, Chicago—a city founded by the black fur trader Jean Baptiste Point du Sable—has long been a pioneer. The efforts began in earnest in 1917, when the Chicago Real Estate Board, horrified by the influx of southern blacks, lobbied to zone the entire city by race. But after the Supreme Court ruled against explicit racial zoning that year, the city was forced to pursue its agenda by more-discreet means.

Like the Home Owners' Loan Corporation, the Federal Housing Administration initially insisted on restrictive covenants, which helped bar blacks and other ethnic undesirables from receiving federally backed home loans. By the 1940s, Chicago led the nation in the use of these restrictive covenants, and about half of all residential neighborhoods in the city were effectively off-limits to blacks.

It is common today to become misty-eyed about the old black ghetto, where doctors and lawyers lived next door to meatpackers and steelworkers, who themselves lived next door to prostitutes and the unemployed. This segregationist nostalgia ignores the actual conditions endured by the people living there—vermin and arson, for instance—and ignores the fact that the old ghetto was premised on denying black people privileges enjoyed by white Americans.

In 1948, when the Supreme Court ruled that restrictive covenants, while permissible, were not enforceable by judicial action, Chicago had other weapons at the ready. The Illinois state legislature had already given Chicago's city council the right to approve—and thus to veto—any public housing in the city's wards. This came in handy in 1949, when a new federal housing act sent millions of tax dollars into Chicago and other cities around the country.

Beginning in 1950, site selection for public housing proceeded entirely on the grounds of segregation. By the 1960s, the city had created with its vast housing projects what the historian Arnold R. Hirsch calls a "second ghetto," one larger than the old Black Belt but just as impermeable. More than 98 percent of all the family public-housing units built in Chicago between 1950 and the mid-1960s were built in all-black neighborhoods.

Governmental embrace of segregation was driven by the virulent racism of Chicago's white citizens. White neighborhoods vulnerable to black encroachment formed block associations for the sole purpose of enforcing segregation. They lobbied fellow whites not to sell. They lobbied those blacks who did manage to buy to sell back. In 1949, a group of Englewood Catholics formed block associations intended to "keep up the neighborhood." Translation: keep black people out. And when civic engagement was not enough, when government failed, when private banks could no longer hold the line, Chicago turned to an old tool in the American repertoire—racial violence. "The pattern of terrorism is easily discernible," concluded a Chicago civic group in the 1940s. "It is at the seams of the black ghetto in all directions." On July 1 and 2 of 1946, a mob of thousands assembled in Chicago's Park Manor neighborhood, hoping to eject a black doctor who'd recently moved in. The mob pelted the house with rocks and set the garage on fire. The doctor moved away.

In 1947, after a few black veterans moved into the Fernwood section of Chicago, three nights of rioting broke out; gangs of whites yanked blacks off streetcars and beat them. Two years later, when a union meeting attended by blacks in Englewood triggered rumors that a home was being "sold to niggers," blacks (and whites thought to be sympathetic to them) were beaten in the streets. In 1951, thousands of whites in Cicero, 20 minutes or so west of downtown Chicago, attacked an apartment building that housed a single black family, throwing bricks and firebombs through the windows and setting the apartment on fire. A Cook County grand jury declined to charge the rioters—and instead indicted the family's NAACP attorney, the apartment's white owner, and the owner's attorney and rental agent, charging them with conspiring to lower property values. Two years after that, whites picketed and planted explosives in South Deering, about 30 minutes from downtown Chicago, to force blacks out.

When terrorism ultimately failed, white homeowners simply fled the neighborhood. The traditional terminology, *white flight*, implies a kind of natural expression of preference. In fact, white flight was a triumph of social engineering, orchestrated by the shared racist presumptions of America's public and private sectors. For should any nonracist white families decide that integration might not be so bad as a matter of principle or practicality, they still had to contend with the hard facts of American housing policy: When the mid-20th-century white homeowner claimed that the presence of a Bill and Daisy Myers decreased his property value, he was not merely engaging in racist dogma—he was accurately observing the impact of federal policy on market prices. Redlining destroyed the possibility of investment wherever black people lived.

VII. "A LOT OF PEOPLE FELL BY THE WAY"

Speculators in North Lawndale, and at the edge of the black ghettos, knew there was money to be made off white panic. They resorted to "block-busting"—spooking whites into selling cheap before the neighborhood became black. They would hire a black woman to walk up and down the street with a stroller. Or they'd hire someone to call a number in the neighborhood looking for "Johnny Mae." Then they'd cajole whites into selling at low prices, informing them that the more blacks who moved in, the more the value of their homes would decline, so better to sell now. With these white-fled homes in hand, speculators then turned to the masses of black people who had streamed northward as part of the Great Migration, or who were desperate to escape the ghettos: the speculators would take the houses they'd just bought cheap through block-busting and sell them to blacks on contract.

To keep up with his payments and keep his heat on, Clyde Ross took a second job at the post office and then a third job delivering pizza. His wife took a job working at Marshall Field. He had to take some of his children out of private school. He was not able to be at home to supervise his children or help them with their homework. Money and time that Ross wanted to give his children went instead to enrich white speculators.

"The problem was the money," Ross told me. "Without the money, you can't move. You can't educate your kids. You can't give them the right kind of food. Can't make the house look good. They think this neighborhood is where they supposed to be. It changes their outlook. My kids were going to the best schools in this neighborhood, and I couldn't keep them in there."

Mattie Lewis came to Chicago from her native Alabama in the mid-'40s, when she was 21, persuaded by a friend who told her she could get a job as a hairdresser. Instead she was hired by Western Electric, where she worked for 41 years. I met Lewis in the home of her neighbor Ethel Weatherspoon. Both had owned homes in North Lawndale for more than 50 years. Both had bought their houses on contract. Both had been active with Clyde Ross in the Contract Buyers League's effort to garner restitution from contract sellers who'd operated in North Lawndale, banks who'd backed the scheme, and even the Federal Housing Administration. We were joined by Jack Mac-namara, who'd been an organizing force in the Contract Buyers League when it was founded, in 1968. Our gathering had the feel of a reunion, because the writer James Alan McPherson had profiled the Contract Buyers League for *The Atlantic* back in 1972.

Weatherspoon bought her home in 1957. "Most of the whites started moving out," she told me. "'The blacks are coming. The blacks are coming.' They actually said that. They had signs up: don't sell to blacks."

Before moving to North Lawndale, Lewis and her husband tried moving to Cicero after seeing a house advertised for sale there. "Sorry, I just sold it today," the Realtor told Lewis's husband. "I told him, 'You know they don't want you in Cicero,'" Lewis recalls. "'They ain't going to let nobody black in Cicero.'"

In 1958, the couple bought a home in North Lawndale on contract. They were not blind to the unfairness. But Lewis, born in the teeth of Jim Crow, considered American piracy—black people keep on making it, white people keep on taking it—a fact of nature. "All I wanted was a house. And that was the only way I could get it. They weren't giving black people loans at that time," she said. "We thought, 'This is the way it is. We going to do it till we die, and they ain't never going to accept us. That's just the way it is.'

"The only way you were going to buy a home was to do it the way they wanted," she continued. "And I was determined to get me a house. If every-body else can have one, I want one too. I had worked for white people in the South. And I saw how these white people were living in the North and I thought, 'One day I'm going to live just like them.' I wanted cabinets and all these things these other people have."

Whenever she visited white co-workers at their homes, she saw the dif-ference. "I could see we were just getting ripped off," she said. "I would see things and I would say, 'I'd like to do this at my house.' And they would say, 'Do it,' but I would think, 'I can't, because it costs us so much more.'"

I asked Lewis and Weatherspoon how they kept up on payments.

"You paid it and kept working," Lewis said of the contract. "When that payment came up, you knew you had to pay it."

"You cut down on the light bill. Cut down on your food bill," Weather-spoon interjected.

"You cut down on things for your child, that was the main thing," said Lewis. "My oldest wanted to be an artist and my other wanted to be a dancer and my other wanted to take music."

Lewis and Weatherspoon, like Ross, were able to keep their homes. The suit did not win them any remuneration. But it forced contract sellers to the table, where they allowed some members of the Contract Buyers League to move into regular mortgages or simply take over their houses outright. By then they'd been bilked for thousands. In talking with Lewis and Weatherspoon, I was seeing only part of the picture—the tiny minority who'd managed to hold on to their homes. But for all our exceptional ones, for every Barack and Michelle Obama, for every Ethel Weatherspoon or Clyde Ross, for every black survivor, there are so many thousands gone.

"A lot of people fell by the way," Lewis told me. "One woman asked me if I would keep all her china. She said, 'They ain't going to set you out.'"

VIII. "NEGRO POVERTY IS NOT WHITE POVERTY"

On a recent spring afternoon in North Lawndale, I visited Billy Lamar Brooks Sr. Brooks has been an activist since his youth in the Black Panther Party, when he aided the Contract Buyers League. I met him in his office at the Better Boys Foundation, a staple of North Lawndale whose mission is to direct local kids off the streets and into jobs and college. Brooks's work is personal. On June 14, 1991, his 19-year-old son, Billy Jr., was shot and killed. "These guys tried to stick him up," Brooks told me. "I suspect he could have been involved in some things ... He's always on my mind. Every day."

Brooks was not raised in the streets, though in such a neighborhood it is impossible to avoid the influence. "I was in church three or four times a week. That's where the girls were," he said, laughing. "The stark reality is still there. There's no shield from life. You got to go to school. I lived here. I went to Marshall High School. Over here were the Egyptian Cobras. Over there were the Vice Lords."

Brooks has since moved away from Chicago's West Side. But he is still working in North Lawndale. If "you got a nice house, you live in a nice neighborhood, then you are less prone to violence, because your space is not deprived," Brooks said. "You got a security point. You don't need no protection." But if "you grow up in a place like this, housing sucks. When they tore down the projects here, they left the high-rises and came to the neighborhood with that gang mentality. You don't have nothing, so you going to take something, even if it's not real. You don't have no street, but in your mind it's yours."

We walked over to a window behind his desk. A group of young black men were hanging out in front of a giant mural memorializing two black men: IN LOVIN MEMORY QUENTIN AKA "Q," JULY 18, 1974 ♥ MARCH 2, 2012. The name and face of the other man had been spray-painted over by a rival group. The men drank beer. Occasionally a car would cruise past, slow to a crawl, then stop. One of the men would approach the car and make an exchange, then the car would drive off. Brooks had known all of these young men as boys.

"That's their corner," he said.

We watched another car roll through, pause briefly, then drive off. "No respect, no shame," Brooks said. "That's what they do. From that alley to that corner. They don't go no farther than that. See the big brother there? He almost died a couple of years ago. The one drinking the beer back there … I know all of them. And the reason they feel safe here is cause of this building, and because they too chickenshit to go anywhere. But that's their mentality. That's their block."

Brooks showed me a picture of a Little League team he had coached. He went down the row of kids, pointing out which ones were in jail, which ones were dead, and which ones were doing all right. And then he pointed out his son—"That's my boy, Billy," Brooks said. Then he wondered aloud if keeping his son with him while working in North Lawndale had hastened his death. "It's a definite connection, because he was part of what I did here. And I think maybe I shouldn't have exposed him. But then, I had to," he said, "because I wanted him with me."

From the White House on down, the myth holds that fatherhood is the great antidote to all that ails black people. But Billy Brooks Jr. had a father. Trayvon Martin had a father. Jordan Davis had a father. Adhering to middle-class norms has never shielded black people from plunder. Adhering to middle-class norms is what made Ethel Weatherspoon a lucrative target for rapacious speculators. Contract sellers did not target the very poor. They targeted black people who had worked hard enough to save a down payment and dreamed of the emblem of American citizenship—homeownership. It was not a tangle of pathology that put a target on Clyde Ross's back. It was not a culture of poverty that singled out Mattie Lewis for "the thrill of the chase and the kill." Some black people always will be twice as good. But they generally find white predation to be thrice as fast.

Liberals today mostly view racism not as an active, distinct evil but as a relative of white poverty and inequality. They ignore the long tradition of this country actively punishing black success—and the elevation of that punishment, in the mid-20th century, to federal policy. President Lyndon Johnson may have noted in his historic civil-rights speech at Howard University in 1965 that "Negro poverty is not white poverty." But his advisers and their successors were, and still are, loath to craft any policy that recognizes the difference.

After his speech, Johnson convened a group of civil-rights leaders, including the esteemed A. Philip Randolph and Bayard Rustin, to address the "ancient brutality." In a strategy paper, they agreed with the president that "Negro poverty is a special, and particularly destructive, form of American poverty." But when it came to specifically addressing the "particularly destructive," Rustin's group demurred, preferring to advance programs that addressed "all the poor, black and white."

The urge to use the moral force of the black struggle to address broader inequalities originates in both compassion and pragmatism. But it makes for ambiguous policy. Affirmative action's precise aims, for instance, have always proved elusive. Is it meant to make amends for the crimes heaped upon black people? Not according to the Supreme Court. In its 1978 ruling in *Regents of the University of California v. Bakke,* the Court rejected "societal discrimination" as "an amorphous concept of injury that may be ageless in its reach into the past." Is affirmative action meant to increase "diversity"? If so, it only tangentially relates to the specific problems of black people—the problem of what America has taken from them over several centuries.

This confusion about affirmative action's aims, along with our inability to face up to the particular history of white-imposed black disadvantage, dates back to the policy's origins. "There is no fixed and firm definition of affirmative action," an appointee in Johnson's Department of Labor declared. "Affirmative action is anything that you have to do to get results. But this does not necessarily include preferential treatment."

Yet America was built on the preferential treatment of white people—395 years of it. Vaguely endorsing a cuddly, feel-good diversity does very little to redress this.

Today, progressives are loath to invoke white supremacy as an explanation for anything. On a practical level, the hesitation comes from the dim view the Supreme Court has taken of the reforms of the 1960s. The Voting Rights Act has been gutted. The Fair Housing Act might well be next. Affirmative action is on its last legs. In substituting a broad class struggle for an anti-racist struggle, progressives hope to assemble a coalition by changing the subject.

The politics of racial evasion are seductive. But the record is mixed. Aid to Families With Dependent Children was originally written largely to exclude blacks—yet by the 1990s it was perceived as a giveaway to blacks. The Affordable Care Act makes no mention of race, but this did not keep Rush Limbaugh from denouncing it as reparations. Moreover, the act's expansion of Medicaid was effectively made optional, meaning that many poor blacks in the former Confederate states do not benefit from it. The Affordable Care Act, like Social Security, will eventually expand its reach to those left out; in the meantime, black people will be injured.

"All that it would take to sink a new WPA program would be some skillfully packaged footage of black men leaning on shovels smoking cigarettes," the sociologist Douglas S. Massey writes. "Papering over the issue of race makes for bad social theory, bad research, and bad public policy." To ignore the fact that one of the oldest republics in the world was erected on a foundation of white supremacy, to pretend that the problems of a dual society are the same as the problems of unregulated capitalism, is to cover the sin of national plunder with the sin of national lying. The lie ignores the fact that reducing American poverty and ending white supremacy are not the same. The lie ignores the fact that closing the "achievement gap" will do nothing to close the "injury gap," in which black college graduates still suffer higher unemployment rates than white college graduates, and black job applicants without criminal records enjoy roughly the same chance of getting hired as white applicants *with* criminal records.

Chicago, like the country at large, embraced policies that placed black America's most energetic, ambitious, and thrifty countrymen beyond the pale of society and marked them as rightful targets for legal theft. The effects reverberate beyond the families who were robbed to the community that beholds the spectacle. Don't just picture Clyde Ross working three jobs so he could hold on to his home. Think of his North Lawndale neighbors—their children, their nephews and nieces—and consider how watching this affects them. Imagine yourself as a young black child watching your elders play by all the rules only to have their possessions tossed out in the street and to have their most sacred possession—their home—taken from them.

The message the young black boy receives from his country, Billy Brooks says, is "'You ain't shit. You not no good. The only thing you are worth is working for us. You will never own anything. You not going to get an education. We are sending your ass to the penitentiary.' They're telling you no matter how hard you struggle, no matter what you put down, you ain't shit. 'We're going to take what you got. You will never own anything, nigger.'"

IX. TOWARD A NEW COUNTRY

When Clyde Ross was a child, his older brother Winter had a seizure. He was picked up by the authorities and delivered to Parchman Farm, a 20,000-acre state prison in the Mississippi Delta region.

"He was a gentle person," Clyde Ross says of his brother. "You know, he was good to everybody. And he started having spells, and he couldn't control himself. And they had him picked up, because they thought he was dangerous."

Built at the turn of the century, Parchman was supposed to be a progressive and reformist response to the problem of "Negro crime." In fact it was the gulag of Mississippi, an object of terror to African Americans in the Delta. In the early years of the 20th century, Mississippi Governor James K.

Vardaman used to amuse himself by releasing black convicts into the surrounding wilderness and hunting them down with bloodhounds. "Throughout the American South," writes David M. Oshinsky in his book *Worse Than Slavery*, "Parchman Farm is synonymous with punishment and brutality, as well it should be . . . Parchman is the quintessential penal farm, the closest thing to slavery that survived the Civil War."

When the Ross family went to retrieve Winter, the authorities told them that Winter had died. When the Ross family asked for his body, the authorities at Parchman said they had buried him. The family never saw Winter's body.

And this was just one of their losses.

Scholars have long discussed methods by which America might make reparations to those on whose labor and exclusion the country was built. In the 1970s, the Yale Law professor Boris Bittker argued in *The Case for Black Reparations* that a rough price tag for reparations could be determined by multiplying the number of African Americans in the population by the difference in white and black per capita income. That number—$34 billion in 1973, when Bittker wrote his book—could be added to a reparations program each year for a decade or two. Today Charles Ogletree, the Harvard Law School professor, argues for something broader: a program of job training and public works that takes racial justice as its mission but includes the poor of all races.

To celebrate freedom and democracy while forgetting America's origins in a slavery economy is patriotism à la carte.

Perhaps no statistic better illustrates the enduring legacy of our country's shameful history of treating black people as sub-citizens, sub-Americans, and sub-humans than the wealth gap. Reparations would seek to close this chasm. But as surely as the creation of the wealth gap required the cooperation of every aspect of the society, bridging it will require the same.

Perhaps after a serious discussion and debate—the kind that HR 40 proposes—we may find that the country can never fully repay African Americans. But we stand to discover much about ourselves in such a discussion—and that is perhaps what scares us. The idea of reparations is frightening not simply because we might lack the ability to pay. The idea of reparations threatens something much deeper—America's heritage, history, and standing in the world.

The early American economy was built on slave labor. The Capitol and the White House were built by slaves. President James K. Polk traded slaves from the Oval Office. The laments about "black pathology," the criticism of black family structures by pundits and intellectuals, ring hollow in a country whose existence was predicated on the torture of black fathers, on the rape of black mothers, on the sale of black children. An honest assessment of America's relationship to the black family reveals the country to be not its nurturer but its destroyer.

And this destruction did not end with slavery. Discriminatory laws joined the equal burden of citizenship to unequal distribution of its bounty. These laws reached their apex in the mid-20th century, when the federal government—through housing policies—engineered the wealth gap, which remains with us to this day. When we think of white supremacy, we picture colored only signs, but we should picture pirate flags.

On some level, we have always grasped this.

"Negro poverty is not white poverty," President Johnson said in his historic civil-rights speech.

> Many of its causes and many of its cures are the same. But there are differences—deep, corrosive, obstinate differences—radiating painful roots into the community and into the family, and the nature of the individual. These differences are not racial differences. They are solely and simply the consequence of ancient brutality, past injustice, and present prejudice.

We invoke the words of Jefferson and Lincoln because they say something about our legacy and our traditions. We do this because we recognize our links to the past—at least when they flatter us. But black history does not flatter American democracy; it chastens it. The popular mocking of reparations as a harebrained scheme authored by wild-eyed lefties and intellectually unserious black nationalists is fear masquerading as laughter. Black nationalists have always perceived something unmentionable about America that integrationists dare not acknowledge—that white supremacy is not merely the work of hotheaded demagogues, or a matter of false consciousness, but a force so fundamental to America that it is difficult to imagine the country without it.

And so we must imagine a new country. Reparations—by which I mean the full acceptance of our collective biography and its consequences—is the price we must pay to see ourselves squarely. The recovering alcoholic may well have to live with his illness for the rest of his life. But at least he is not living a drunken lie. Reparations beckons us to reject the intoxication of hubris and see America as it is—the work of fallible humans.

Won't reparations divide us? Not any more than we are already divided. The wealth gap merely puts a number on something we feel but cannot say—that American prosperity was ill-gotten and selective in its distribution. What is needed is an airing of family secrets, a settling with old ghosts.

What is needed is a healing of the American psyche and the banishment of white guilt.

What I'm talking about is more than recompense for past injustices—more than a handout, a payoff, hush money, or a reluctant bribe. What I'm talking about is a national reckoning that would lead to spiritual renewal. Reparations would mean the end of scarfing hot dogs on the Fourth of July while denying the facts of our heritage. Reparations would mean the end of yelling "patriotism" while waving a Confederate flag. Reparations would mean a revolution of the American consciousness, a reconciling of our self-image as the great democratizer with the facts of our history.

X. "THERE WILL BE NO 'REPARATIONS' FROM GERMANY"

We are not the first to be summoned to such a challenge.

In 1952, when West Germany began the process of making amends for the Holocaust, it did so under conditions that should be instructive to us. Resistance was violent. Very few Germans believed that Jews were entitled to anything. Only 5 percent of West Germans surveyed reported feeling guilty about the Holocaust, and only 29 percent believed that Jews were owed restitution from the German people.

"The rest," the historian Tony Judt wrote in his 2005 book, *Postwar*, "were divided between those (some two-fifths of respondents) who thought that only people 'who really committed something' were responsible and should pay, and those (21 percent) who thought 'that the Jews themselves were partly responsible for what happened to them during the Third Reich.'"

Germany's unwillingness to squarely face its history went beyond polls. Movies that suggested a societal responsibility for the Holocaust beyond Hitler were banned. "The German soldier fought bravely and honorably for his homeland," claimed President Eisenhower, endorsing the Teutonic national myth. Judt wrote, "Throughout the fifties West German officialdom encouraged a comfortable view of the German past in which the Wehrmacht was heroic, while Nazis were in a minority and properly punished."

Konrad Adenauer, the postwar German chancellor, was in favor of reparations, but his own party was divided, and he was able to get an agreement passed only with the votes of the Social Democratic opposition.

Among the Jews of Israel, reparations provoked violent and venomous reactions ranging from denunciation to assassination plots. On January 7, 1952, as the Knesset—the Israeli parliament—convened to discuss the prospect of a reparations agreement with West Germany, Menachem Begin, the future prime minister of Israel, stood in front of a large crowd, inveighing against the country that had plundered the lives, labor, and property of his people. Begin claimed that all Germans were Nazis and guilty of murder. His condemnations then spread to his own young state. He urged the crowd to stop paying taxes and claimed that the nascent Israeli nation characterized the fight over whether or not to accept reparations as a "war to the death." When alerted that the police watching the gathering were carrying tear gas, allegedly of German manufacture, Begin yelled, "The same gases that asphyxiated our parents!"

Begin then led the crowd in an oath to never forget the victims of the Shoah, lest "my right hand lose its cunning" and "my tongue cleave to the roof of my mouth." He took the crowd through the streets toward the Knesset. From the rooftops, police repelled the crowd with tear gas and smoke bombs. But the wind shifted, and the gas blew back toward the Knesset, billowing through windows shattered by rocks. In the chaos, Begin and Prime Minister David Ben-Gurion exchanged insults. Two hundred civilians and 140 police officers were wounded. Nearly 400 people were arrested. Knesset business was halted.

Begin then addressed the chamber with a fiery speech condemning the actions the legislature was about to take. "Today you arrested hundreds," he said. "Tomorrow you may arrest thousands. No matter, they will go, they will sit in prison. We will sit there with them. If necessary, we will be killed with them. But there will be no 'reparations' from Germany."

Survivors of the Holocaust feared laundering the reputation of Germany with money, and mortgaging the memory of their dead. Beyond that, there was a taste for revenge. "My soul would be at rest if I knew there would be 6 million German dead to match the 6 million Jews," said Meir Dworzecki, who'd survived the concentration camps of Estonia.

Ben-Gurion countered this sentiment, not by repudiating vengeance but with cold calculation: "If I could take German property without sitting down with them for even a minute but go in with jeeps and machine guns to the warehouses and take it, I would do that—if, for instance, we had the ability to send a hundred divisions and tell them, 'Take it.' But we can't do that."

The reparations conversation set off a wave of bomb attempts by Israeli militants. One was aimed at the foreign ministry in Tel Aviv. Another was aimed at Chancellor Adenauer himself. And one was aimed at the port of Haifa, where the goods bought with reparations money were arriving. West Germany ultimately agreed to pay Israel 3.45 billion deutsche marks, or more than $7 billion in today's dollars. Individual reparations claims followed— for psychological trauma, for offense to Jewish honor, for halting law careers, for life insurance, for time spent in concentration camps. Seventeen percent

of funds went toward purchasing ships. "By the end of 1961, these reparations vessels constituted two-thirds of the Israeli merchant fleet," writes the
Israeli historian Tom Segev in his book *The Seventh Million*. "From 1953 to
1963, the reparations money funded about a third of the total investment in
Israel's electrical system, which tripled its capacity, and nearly half the total
investment in the railways."

Israel's GNP tripled during the 12 years of the agreement. The Bank of
Israel attributed 15 percent of this growth, along with 45,000 jobs, to invest-
ments made with reparations money. But Segev argues that the impact went
far beyond that. Reparations "had indisputable psychological and political
importance," he writes.

Reparations could not make up for the murder perpetrated by the Nazis.
But they did launch Germany's reckoning with itself, and perhaps provided a
road map for how a great civilization might make itself worthy of the name.

Assessing the reparations agreement, David Ben-Gurion said:

> For the first time in the history of relations between people, a prece-
> dent has been created by which a great State, as a result of moral pres-
> sure alone, takes it upon itself to pay compensation to the victims of
> the government that preceded it. For the first time in the history of a
> people that has been persecuted, oppressed, plundered and despoiled
> for hundreds of years in the countries of Europe, a persecutor and
> despoiler has been obliged to return part of his spoils and has even
> undertaken to make collective reparation as partial compensation for
> material losses.

Something more than moral pressure calls America to reparations. We
cannot escape our history. All of our solutions to the great problems of
health care, education, housing, and economic inequality are troubled by
what must go unspoken. "The reason black people are so far behind now is
not because of now," Clyde Ross told me. "It's because of then." In the early
2000s, Charles Ogletree went to Tulsa, Oklahoma, to meet with the survivors of the 1921 race riot that had devastated "Black Wall Street." The past
was not the past to them. "It was amazing seeing these black women and
men who were crippled, blind, in wheelchairs," Ogletree told me. "I had no
idea who they were and why they wanted to see me. They said, 'We want you
to represent us in this lawsuit.'"

A commission authorized by the Oklahoma legislature produced a
report affirming that the riot, the knowledge of which had been suppressed
for years, had happened. But the lawsuit ultimately failed, in 2004. Similar
suits pushed against corporations such as Aetna (which insured slaves) and

Lehman Brothers (whose co-founding partner owned them) also have thus far failed. These results are dispiriting, but the crime with which reparations activists charge the country implicates more than just a few towns or corporations. The crime indicts the American people themselves, at every level, and in nearly every configuration. A crime that implicates the entire American people deserves its hearing in the legislative body that represents them.

John Conyers's HR 40 is the vehicle for that hearing. No one can know what would come out of such a debate. Perhaps no number can fully capture the multi-century plunder of black people in America. Perhaps the number is so large that it can't be imagined, let alone calculated and dispensed. But I believe that wrestling publicly with these questions matters as much as—if not more than—the specific answers that might be produced. An America that asks what it owes its most vulnerable citizens is improved and humane. An America that looks away is ignoring not just the sins of the past but the sins of the present and the certain sins of the future. More important than any single check cut to any African American, the payment of reparations would represent America's maturation out of the childhood myth of its innocence into a wisdom worthy of its founders.

In 2010, Jacob S. Rugh, then a doctoral candidate at Princeton, and the sociologist Douglas S. Massey published a study of the recent foreclosure crisis. Among its drivers, they found an old foe: segregation. Black home buyers—even after controlling for factors like creditworthiness—were still more likely than white home buyers to be steered toward subprime loans. Decades of racist housing policies by the American government, along with decades of racist housing practices by American businesses, had conspired to concentrate African Americans in the same neighborhoods. As in North Lawndale half a century earlier, these neighborhoods were filled with people who had been cut off from mainstream financial institutions. When subprime lenders went looking for prey, they found black people waiting like ducks in a pen.

"High levels of segregation create a natural market for subprime lending," Rugh and Massey write, "and cause riskier mortgages, and thus foreclosures, to accumulate disproportionately in racially segregated cities' minority neighborhoods."

Plunder in the past made plunder in the present efficient. The banks of America understood this. In 2005, Wells Fargo promoted a series of Wealth Building Strategies seminars. Dubbing itself "the nation's leading originator of home loans to ethnic minority customers," the bank enrolled black public figures in an ostensible effort to educate blacks on building "generational wealth." But the "wealth building" seminars were a front for wealth theft. In 2010, the Justice Department filed a discrimination suit against Wells Fargo alleging that the bank had shunted blacks into predatory loans regardless of their creditworthiness. This was not magic or coincidence or misfortune. It was racism reifying itself. According to *The New York Times*, affidavits found loan officers referring to their black customers as "mud people" and to their subprime products as "ghetto loans."

"We just went right after them," Beth Jacobson, a former Wells Fargo loan officer, told *The Times*. "Wells Fargo mortgage had an emerging-markets unit that specifically targeted black churches because it figured church leaders had a lot of influence and could convince congregants to take out subprime loans."

In 2011, Bank of America agreed to pay $355 million to settle charges of discrimination against its Countrywide unit. The following year, Wells Fargo settled its discrimination suit for more than $175 million. But the damage had been done. In 2009, half the properties in Baltimore whose owners had been granted loans by Wells Fargo between 2005 and 2008 were vacant; 71 percent of these properties were in predominantly black neighborhoods.

22

The Social Life of DNA:
Racial Reconciliation and Institutional
Morality after the Genome

ALONDRA NELSON

This 2017 lecture by sociologist Alondra Nelson draws on the case of the GU272 and their descendants to explore how genealogical research and direct-to-consumer DNA tests can be used for social repair. Nelson grapples with how these technologies can help people, families, and institutions repair the harms of the nation's slaveholding past and its many legacies. This lecture was first published in the British Journal of Sociology *69, no. 3 (September 2018).*

POSTGENOMIC

We can mark the start of the genomic era with the launch of the Human Genome Project (HGP) by the United States Department of Energy in 1990, during the administration of George H. W. Bush, or with the 2003 announcement of the successful completion of a full genome sequence and digital tools to analyse it, during the early months of the presidency of George W. Bush. *Post*genomic, therefore, may be both an institutional and a chronological indicator, suggesting the where and the when of the genome and its afterlives (Richardson 2013). Postgenomic may mark a range of socio-technical developments as well: Sarah S. Richardson and Hallam Stevens (2015) offer that the term captures "new methods and approaches" in life sciences research, including the "advent of whole-genome technologies as a shared platform for biological research across many fields," (3) "funding and investment" strategies premised on the anticipated efficacy of genomic analysis, and even an affect of humility, as techniques such as genome-wide association studies yield more questions and mysteries than answers (3–5). Evelyn Fox Keller further suggests that the postgenomic is characterized by a conceptual shift from the gene to the genome as the predominant unit of analysis, with a concomitant reckoning that the genome is "a dynamic and reactive system" and not merely a static structure (Keller 2015: 10).

A dynamism of use follows this re-conceptualization of structure. While the HGP has yet to live up to its booster's loftiest biomedical promises, it has certainly succeeded in broadening "the social life of DNA" (Nelson 2016). So much so that it can be said the postgenomic also concerns the move of genomics out of the formal biological sciences into a wider socio-technical ecology. Thus, as Jenny Reardon puts it, the postgenomic era should prompt further examination of "the uses, significance and value of the human genome sequence" (2013: 2). These include, for example, the panoply of "interests and agendas of commercial pharmaceutical, biotechnology and direct-to-consumer genetics enterprises . . . [that] apply human genomic data and technologies to locate variation in the human genome that may be marketable as a biomarker for disease, forensics, ancestry or human enhancement" (Richardson 2013: 208). Following from this, the postgenomic therefore also refers to the technical ability and the market desire to mine the minuscule veins of difference said to distinguish human groups.

The commercialization of genetics has launched possibilities for DNA that social theorists had not fully anticipated. Indeed, returning to Keller's insight about the transformation in our conceptual understanding of molecular biology, it is important to note that some early social science analysis assumed the gene as the unit of analysis, rather than the more cipher-like genome and, in so doing, left some of the pitfalls and the possibilities of the postgenomic era unexplored.

Keller describes the commercial uses of genetic science, and particularly as these products work to revive the "genetics of race," as one of the more problematic features of the postgenomic era (Keller 2015: 10). Yet, just as our notion of the gene has been transformed in the postgenomic era, so too must our understanding of what novel understandings of and uses for DNA mean for racial paradigms and politics. Long-standing ways of thinking about the relationship between race, genetics and heritability took up an appreciably new form in the last two decades in a process that Fullwiley (2017) calls the "molecularization of race."

There remains distinct evidence that the advent of genetic genealogy testing is a worrisome "backdoor to eugenics" (Duster 1990; Phelan, Link and Feldman 2013), new bottles for the old wine of racial essentialism. But this isn't all there is. Racism, then and now, has had many paradigms, including Jim Crow, laissez-faire (Bobo, Kluegel and Smith 1997), colour blind (Bonilla-Silva 2003; Brown et al. 2003), white nationalist (Daniels 1997), and digital (Daniels 2009). Race, too, is cross-cutting and experienced on "multiple dimensions" (Roth 2016), including identity, self-classification, ascription, phenotype, and ancestry. Race and racism, then and now, are also relational and site- or institutionally specific (Nelson 2016)—a "dynamic and reactive" system, much like Keller's genome.

RECONCILIATION PROJECTS

Bookended by two conservative US presidential administrations, the HGP emerged out of a colour-blind racial paradigm. Forgetting and masking are characteristic of this ideology. On the one hand, this paradigm frames racism as "a remnant of the past" and, therefore, something to be forgotten; on the other hand, the colour-blind paradigm obscures structural discrimination— "the deeply rooted institutional practices and long-term disaccumulation that sustains racial inequality" (Brown et al. 2003: 37). The commercialization of genomics activates and reinforces the pernicious dynamics of the genetics of race, privileging essentialist ways of knowing and being classified by Roth such as ascription and phenotype. At the same time, however, other, potentially benevolent "dimensions" of race are also given voice through the practice of genetic genealogy, such as self-classification and ancestral identity. It is in this heterodox milieu of a prevailing racial paradigm and racial multidimensionality, that the logic of using novel applications of genomics to recover, debate and reconcile accounts of the past takes shape.

At the intersection of postgenomics, the multiple dimensions of race, and colour-blind racism lie "reconciliation projects." Genetic analysis is today being applied in social endeavours in which DNA analysis is put to the use of repairing or reconciling the past. These are global social practices that take up genetic analyses in social, political and historical claims-making and may include reparations claims or campaigns to obtain apologies from the state for past atrocities. Reconciliation projects may be efforts to repair ruptures caused by fractious social and political struggles or efforts to (re)unite communities. They can be found in the courtroom, in the science laboratory, or within the practice of religious ceremonies, to name a few sites. Their aim is a desire to come to some mutual (if not consensual) understanding of the past with outcomes ranging the spectrum from unspecified endpoints to precise restitution. With the end uncertain, the endeavours themselves warrant our attention. Closure is not necessarily what is sought or can be accomplished, for as moral philosopher Susan Dwyer offers, "reconciliation is *fundamentally a process* whose aim is to lessen the sting of a tension: to make sense of injuries, new beliefs, and attitudes in the overall narrative context of personal or national life" (Dwyer 1999; emphasis added).

One of the appeals of genetic ancestry testing is its presumed ability to highlight the origins of not only root-seekers themselves but also social heredities of the contemporary moment. African Americans may use genetic ancestry testing to enter into a new political relationship with the past, one that foregrounds the fact and impact of racial slavery and makes this past a proximate, usable and, indeed, a living history, rather than something distant and, therefore, immaterial to the present (as colour-blind racism would have it).

In my book, *The Social Life of DNA: Race, Reparations and Reconciliation after the Genome* (Nelson 2016), I follow several reconciliation projects involving persons of African descent, including a West African religious ceremony or "sara" in which self-described "DNA Sierra Leoneans" sought and performed a psychic and spiritual reckoning with their ancestors, who had been trafficked as chattel. I also trace the use of genetic genealogy testing as a tactic to obtain legal restitution for the unpaid labour of enslaved Africans on the part of their descendants by attempting to demonstrate a genealogical kinship (and therefore also a legal relationship). In recent years, a notable reconciliation project has emerged in the US in which genetic genealogy is being engaged in efforts concerning elite institutions' foundational dependence on the slave trade.

EDIFICATION AND BONDAGE

Over the last twenty years, and accelerating in the last decade, US colleges and universities have increasingly uncovered and confronted their ties to racial slavery. During the 2000s, three graduate students at Yale University and a pioneering President of Brown University were among the first at educational institutions to highlight this issue. The 2013 publication of historian Craig Wilder's *Ebony and Ivy: Race, Slavery, and the Troubled History of America's Universities* represented a cresting wave of attention paid to how US institutions of higher education—including those most elite and venerable schools that evolved from British colonial learning academies—were literally built upon an edifice of structural racism. "[H]uman slavery," Wilder writes, "was the precondition for the rise of higher education in America" (Wilder 2013: 114), a central and emblematic feature.

Slaveholding and slave-trading were pervasive facts of life of higher education throughout the colonial and early American period, Wilder demonstrates. The full operation of colleges was supported by enslaved African labour, the dispossession of Native Americans, and the demonization of both. Wilder reveals how schools, such as Yale College and the College of William & Mary, were erected with and through slavery. Once built, bondsmen and bondwomen tended the grounds and staffed the kitchens of these institutions. In some instances, students brought enslaved people to campus with them as servants, with the privileged "establish[ing] their own intellectual freedom upon human bondage" (2013: 111). Similarly, the proceeds of chattel slavery donated by trustees or other benefactors endowed professorships and ensured the longevity of some institutions.

Slavery was not just an economic cornerstone of the colonial education system, but also an intellectual one. Wilder establishes that scientific racism, a pernicious ideology and methodology that "explained" the alleged inferiority of African and indigenous populations to justify their subjugation, was developed in the ivory towers and ivied halls of the first American colleges. These institutions, he argues, armed students with "theories of racial difference and scientific claims about the superiority of white people" (Wilder 2013: 3). The uniqueness of colonial and antebellum colleges as sites of slavery was this unique feedback loop: the slave trade provided the economic and social conditions necessary for the rise of higher education in the British colonies and later the United States, and these very same institutions played a part in perpetuating the ideology of white supremacy that concocted justifications for not just bondage, but a distinctive form of racial slavery. Wilder offers that these colleges also played a role in articulating a rationale for the new nation that would become the United States and that this rationale too relied in good measure on racial science that mythologized the inferiority of non-whites. Thus, more than some of the other social locations at which racism was embedded and institutionalized, its location in higher education was especially pernicious. It was both structure and epistemology; the emergence of the academy was enabled by both slave-trading *and* race-making via the scientism of biological racism that found succour in scholarly communities.

SLAVERY AND JUSTICE

In 2001, Ruth Simmons became the first African American and first woman leader of an Ivy League institution of higher education when she took the helm of Brown University as its eighteenth president. She took over leadership at a time when Brown was lagging behind its peers in both scholarly eminence and fiscal health.[1] After quickly putting herself to the work of improving the university's educational and fiscal profiles, Brown turned to its moral one. In 2003, she commissioned the Brown University Steering Committee on Slavery and Justice in order to investigate and address the institution's ties to the slave trade.

In this, she was in some way taking the lead of three graduate students at Yale, Antony Dugdale, J. J. Fueser, J. Celso de Castro Alves, who in 2001 published a detailed study of the university's connections to slavery (see Dugdale et al. 2001 and Zernike 2001). The resulting report, "Yale, Slavery and Abolition," demonstrated, among other things, that wealth resulting from the slave trade endowed the university's first scholarships and a professorship as well as funding the construction of one of the institution's first libraries. Well known today is the fact that several of Yale's residential colleges are named for men who owned men and women of African descent, including the avowed and unrepentant racist John C. Calhoun, a South Carolina congressman, and Bishop George Berkeley, who left his plantation and several enslaved persons to the institution, when he departed the colonies for England. (In 2017, the Yale University Board of Trustees voted to remove Calhoun's name from the residential college bearing it. Announcing the decision, Yale President Peter Salovey said, "Calhoun's principles and legacy as an ardent supporter of slavery as a positive good are at odds with the values of this university" [Megan 2017]).

While Yale's examination of the past was a grassroots effort carried out by student activists, the Brown endeavour was vouchsafed by the campus's most powerful figure. The Steering Committee on Slavery and Justice would be the first wholesale institutional-level self-study of ties between a university and the traffic in enslaved Africans.

Simmons cast the committee's work as a truth-seeking endeavour and, as such, aligned with the highest ideals of the liberal arts tradition and higher education and also her aspirations for the university's intellectual ascendancy. Simmons made the question of the history of slavery at Brown a matter for scholarship, a matter for intensive and comparative study, not a mandate with an expected political outcome. Despite this gatekeeping, the boldness of the endeavour and its potential implications was apparent to most.

Some feared that this road would lead inevitably to claims for restitution for slavery as intimated in some press accounts. As elaborated by *The New York Times*, the Simmons Committee was seen as "an unprecedented undertaking for a university: an exploration of reparations for slavery and specifically whether Brown should pay reparations or otherwise make amends for its past" (Belluck 2017). In other words, the Committee's report would prompt some action on the part of the institution, and this response might take the form of reparation. The concern about what future institutional choices might be propelled by the committee's findings was such that during this period, some Brown alumni made gifts to the university conditional on the agreement that they not be used to support the distribution of financial reparations to slave descendants. The debates at Brown over how (and how not) to respond to information emerging out of inquiries into ties between higher education and slavery would persist as other institutions embarked on similar excavation.

Simmons, for her part, would pen a *Boston Globe* op-ed seeking to clarify her aims, writing:

> The committee's work is not about whether or how we should pay reparations. That was never the intent nor will the payment of reparations be the outcome. This is an effort designed to involve the campus community in a discovery of the meaning of our past. (Simmons 2004)

The resulting report "Slavery and Justice" was released in 2006 (Brown University Steering Committee 2006). It placed at its centre the relationship between two Brown family members, siblings Moses and John, who were supporters of slavery and abolition, respectively. Steering Committee chair and then Brown professor, James Campbell, commented to *The New Yorker* that this difference between brothers "illustrated . . . moral choices within a historical context" (FitzGerald 2005). With this report, Brown too was making a moral choice. Brown's interrogation of the history of slavery in and on its campus was, from its beginnings, a distinctly ethical calculation.

Simmons' tenure at Brown lasted 11 years. The legacy of what she accomplished lives on there, in bricks and mortar, as the Center for the Study of Slavery and Justice. Her legacy also endures as the inspiration for what might be understood as a burgeoning institutional social movement (one that was, in many cases, spurred by student activism). Other institutions would follow suit over the next dozen years, sponsoring studies of their respective ties to racial slavery including the College of William and Mary, Harvard University, Emory University, the University of Maryland, Dartmouth College, the University of North Carolina at Chapel Hill, Columbia University, Princeton University, the University of Virginia, and Georgetown University. There is today a consortium of some 30 schools, established by the University of Virginia, called Universities Studying Slavery (USS) that enables "institutions to work together as they address both historical and contemporary issues dealing with race and inequality in higher education."[2] In now almost ritualized form, this new type of institutional self-study begins with a university course or commission for the undertaking of historical research into the institution's involvement in racial slavery. After a report is issued, the institution is faced with a choice of responses including: the placement (or removal) of plaques, artwork, statuary, or commemorative markers; public or academic convenings and discussions; the creation of websites containing documents that detail the school's role in facilitating or benefiting from slavery; the establishment of new research initiatives; calls for formal restitution to the descendants of persons enslaved by the institution's administration or by its faculty or students; and demands for racial equality on campus and in society.

In devoting a committee to the study of slavery and *justice*, Simmons supplied a new ethical valence to institutions of higher education. She insisted that the liberal arts tradition could and should be harnessed to better understand even the most deeply entrenched forms of inequality. Simmons also suggested that edification included attention to issues of justice. This was a framing that might be said to have drawn on one of two Rawlsian "moral powers" (Rawls 1996: 19)—having "a conception of the good" being the second after justice—and, in keeping with a recurrent touchstone in Rawls' "theory of justice," seeing equality from the perspective of the least advantaged (or in this case, enslaved persons and their descendants). Tellingly, none of the institutional self-studies of the last decade since have similarly invoked justice as a core framework in their titles. By contrast to Brown University's justice frame, there was "Yale, Slavery and Abolition" (Dugdale et al. 2001); *Harvard and Slavery: Seeking a Forgotten History* (Beckert et al. 2011); "Slavery and the University" (University of Virginia President's Commission 2018); and "The Princeton & Slavery Project" (Sandweiss and Hollander 2017), among others. These formulations leave the matter of slavery in the past. Closer to Brown's framing of the responsibilities that emerge out of the illumination of this past is William & Mary's "The Lemon Project: A Journey of Reconciliation" (2009) and the "Slavery, Memory, and Reconciliation" effort at Georgetown (Working Group on Slavery, Memory, and Reconciliation 2016).[3] Yet as Dwyer reminds us, the process of reconciliation is not one that necessarily results in a just social or economic outcome (1999).

Slavery, memory, and reconciliation

In 2015, Georgetown University President John J. DeGioia convened a Working Group on Slavery, Memory, and Reconciliation to explore the organization's ties to the peculiar institution. The report issued from this committee of students, faculty and alumni shone a brighter light on a historical episode already known to scholars of the period and to some in the Georgetown community. Namely, that in 1838, the Jesuit stewards of Georgetown College sold more than 200 enslaved persons of African descent (today known as the GU 272), residing in Maryland, to two purchasers in Louisiana. The transaction netted the college more than $3 million in today's currency and ensured the institution's existence into the future.

In response, following a practice that has been taken up on other campuses, the university renamed and rededicated two buildings on campus that previously honoured former presidents of the institution who had ties to the slave trade. One of these buildings now honours Isaac Hawkins, whose name was listed first on the 1838 bill of sale; and a second honours Anne Marie Becraft, a nineteenth-century educator and one of the first African American nuns.

However, Georgetown also engaged in forms of conciliatory practice that were novel among institutions of higher education and reflected its Jesuit roots. Referencing the institution's commitment to "racial justice" (Georgetown University 2016), its leadership issued an apology to the descendants of the GU 272; the apology was framed in religious language and was articulated during a campus mass of contrition. "We offer this apology for the sins against your ancestors," said Georgetown President John J. DeGioia (DeGioia 2017). In his remarks, DeGioia cited the writings of the Revd Bryan N. Massingale on racial justice and Catholicism. "The expression of contrition that we offer today 'guides … permeates … animates' our ongoing work for justice. We build a more just world with honest reflection on our past and a commitment to a faith that does justice," offered DeGioia. Although the Working Group's charge was not explicitly framed in the language of social justice, the presentation of its findings was unambiguous in drawing this connection.

Distinctively, the university has also extended "legacy status" for admissions consideration to GU 272 descendants, meaning that Georgetown offers preference for admission to these applicants as if they had a familial relationship to University alumni (Georgetown University 2016). The institution also vowed to work to improve the secondary education pipeline to provide "stronger pathways to higher education" (Georgetown University 2016). Another unique gesture was Georgetown's ambitious, but vaguely worded, promise to engage the "descendants" of those persons it enslaved "and members of our community in developing a shared understanding, determining priorities, and creating processes and structures" (Georgetown University 2016).

Georgetown alumnus Richard Cellini did not feel that the issue had been resolved with these gestures. Cellini is both a Georgetown loyalist and institutional firebrand. As a student, he was a member of the Stewards Society, a now disbanded secret club that was committed in part to preserving "campus traditions" (Feinberg 1988) and was accused of elitism. Yet, he later joined other alumni in a lawsuit against the university, demanding that the George-town alumni association remain independent of the institution (Carmody 1988). In the early 2000s, Cellini was on the executive team of a digital mar-keting company at which he advanced frameworks for business ethics. Today, he is an entrepreneur and software executive.

Cellini felt freighted down by the Working Group on Slavery, Memory, and Reconciliation report's revelations and the enormity of the university's debt to the descendants of enslaved men and women sold to Louisiana plan-tations. He thought this obligation might begin to be repaid through identi-fication of these descendants using genealogy and other means. "This is not a disembodied group of people, who are nameless and faceless . . . These are real people with real names and real descendants," Cellini would proclaim to *The New York Times* (Swarns 2016). In 2015, Cellini founded the non-profit Georgetown Memory Project (GMP) for this express purpose. Drawing on his own resources as well as contributions from Georgetown alumni and members of the wider public, Cellini commissioned a group of professional genealogists to work under the auspices of the GMP. Led by Judy Riffel, a specialist in Louisiana genealogical research, these family history researchers were tasked with identifying the full names of the GU 272 and locating their descendants. This work built on the extensive archival research of George-town's Working Group on Slavery, Memory, and Reconciliation as well as church and vital records (Swarns 2016).[4]

THE GENEALOGY OF THE "GU 272"

Soon after Georgetown Memory Project got underway, the services of a genetic ancestry testing company, AncestryDNA, were also incorporated into the work. A subsidiary of Ancestry.com, which was founded by two members of the Mormon Church in the 1990s, AncestryDNA was launched in 2012. Over the past two decades, Ancestry.com has entered into a series of contracts with the Mormon Church–owned company FamilySearch.org. In 2013, for example, Ancestry and FamilySearch signed a $60 million deal that granted the genealogy company extended access to its extensive digital records databases. Ancestry.com claims that to date it has enabled its seven million lifetime customers and two million regular subscribers to access a storehouse of more than 15 million digital records.[5]

AncestryDNA was a relative latecomer to the US direct-to-consumer (DTC) genetic market which arose in 2000; however, its parent company was a pioneer in the archiving, supply and visualization of vital records and other documents that are critical to genealogical research. More recently,

Ancestry developed a platform that allows consumers to federate archival and genetic data, creating a socially networked genealogical platform that combined genetic and conventional genealogy with relative ease, for the first time. The AncestryDNA service is virtually unique among DTC genetics companies in enabling consumers to integrate genetic test results with data about one's family tree generated through other sources of evidence. While a few companies have sold conventional family history tracing services alongside their DNA services, AncestryDNA leverages the interoperability of different types of genealogical data. This is the full datafication of genealogy, from the digitization of archival documents, to analysis of genetic data, to the combining of the two.

My earlier research explored how genealogists navigated and negotiated the differences between conventional and genetic genealogical data in the DTC genetics industry's early days (Nelson 2016). The AncestryDNA product seeks to smooth these distinctions. An individual can opt to be notified if their conventional or genetic genealogical information overlaps with others on the Ancestry platform, making myriad new (and sometimes surprising) connections possible. More specifically, after one receives their genetic ancestry inferences, AncestryDNA provides the consumer with "cousin matches" via its extensive databases. (Genealogists decide whether and what information they wish to share with potential kin).

For descendants of the GU 272 seeking to find others, this data integration proved helpful; knowledge of existing descendants could be leveraged in the Ancestry database to find more distant relationships. If an individual lacks one of the surnames common to the descendants of the GU 272 or archival evidence of a relationship to this group, the Georgetown Memory Project encourages them to use genetic testing to establish ties to the previously identified descendants.

A case in point is what occurred with Jeremy Alexander, who was coincidentally working as a Georgetown University employee when he discovered that he was a GU 272 descendant. Alexander had his genetic sample analysed by AncestryDNA in 2014 and also began to build a family tree on the Ancestry platform in that same year. (This was a year before both the completion of the Georgetown University Working Group's report and the establishment of the Georgetown Memory Project genealogy initiative.) Alexander subsequently was contacted by a "cousin" named Melissa Kemp, who told him that according to Ancestry they shared relatives in common, including Anna Mahoney Jones, who "was among the slaves sold to help Georgetown survive" (Burch 2017; see also Puno 2017).

AncestryDNA also played a role in the GMP's work with Mélisande Short-Colomb. GMP genealogist Riffel contacted Short-Colomb via a

Facebook message and asked if she might be related to a woman named Mary Ellen Queen. Although Short-Colomb had been raised with family oral history indicating that Queen, her great-grandmother, had been set free by a benevolent slaveholder, she would discover that she was in actuality a member of the enslaved cohort who had been sold down to Louisiana by Georgetown. Short-Colomb subsequently provided a saliva sample to AncestryDNA, and comparison of her genetic profile to others in the Ancestry .com descendant network indicated similarities high enough to suggest a biological relationship to GU 272 (McCoy 2017). Soon after, she "connected with the rest of the descendants" (McCoy 2017). In the fall of 2017, at the age of sixty-three, Short-Colomb enrolled as an undergraduate student at Georgetown (Sullivan 2017).

What of the family members who are not genetically related? What's at stake when genetics is used to gatekeep some from the GU 272 community, who may have legitimate, but non-biological, claims to membership in it? Genealogical kinship and DNA ancestry do not allot space for the families we choose or for the multifaceted ways families were constituted under the circumstance of slavery.

Compounding these challenges, genetics today plays a complex and even contradictory role in racial politics. For stigmatized and hyper-surveilled communities such as African Americans, the use of genetics in forms of social discovery and repair risk compounding the injury of their ancestors' enslavement with the capture of African American genetic samples into a commercial database over which they have little control. The desire to know more about one's tie to the historic GU 272 might prove somewhat coercive to those who would have otherwise opted out of DTC ancestry testing but may feel moved to do so by the strength of their desire to be reconciled with lost kin or to access proof of long-desired ancestral ties.

The risk is increasing. For example, DTC genetic ancestry testing data is being used in medical research. In 2015, Ancestry announced that it was in "initial conversations" to sell its "anonymized" genetic data and linked genealogical data to "large pharmaceutical and biotech companies" (Hernandez 2017). Notably, Ancestry.com's competitor 23andMe closed just such a deal with the British pharmaceutical company GlaxoSmithKline in 2018.

DTC genetic ancestry testing data is also being used in the criminal justice system. In one reported instance, genealogical data left open to all Ancestry.com users for the purpose of collectively sharing genealogical information—a Y-chromosome family surname project—was examined by police in an attempt to try to apprehend a murder suspect. As a consequence, a father and son who shared components of a Y-chromosome sample left at a crime scene were questioned by police. In the end, the men were cleared of any wrongdoing, but not before they were wrongly accused by criminal justice authorities (Mustian 2015). As the summer of 2018 further made clear, genetic genealogy databases and third-party applications such as GEDMatch are ripe for the culling by the criminal justice system, undermining trust in genealogical networks and subjecting genealogists to undue surveillance.

Because of "the social life of DNA"—genetic data's ability to find use across and between social and institutional domains (e.g., medical and forensic) despite original intent (e.g., genealogical)—the GU272 reconciliation project poses special risk for African American descendants of the unanticipated encroachment of clinical researchers or the criminal justice system. The growing number of African American samples in genetic databases and disproportionate racialized surveillance makes DNA genealogy databases, especially those like GEDMatch that operate with an ethic of openness, in order to facilitate genealogists' desire to locate the maximum number of matches, a risky proposition for African Americans. Although root-seekers can set privacy controls on the web-based platforms and applications they make use of, given the wider circulation of genealogical data, requiring genetic ancestry testing as a condition of inclusion in GU272 kinship networks is potentially coercive and dangerous.

INSTITUTIONAL MORALITY

The GU 272 reconciliation project is complex and contested for other reasons as well. The framing of Georgetown's initiative as a process of reconciliation has generated expectations among some stakeholders which have yet to be met. A group of descendants called the Legacy of GU272 Alliance, for example, protested that they were not consulted by the University before it announced its programmatic response to the report of the Working Group on Slavery, Memory, and Reconciliation (Mooney 2017). While a second group, the GU272 Descendants Association, has proposed to shift the scale of reconciliation from this single university to the Jesuit community more broadly. As descendant Karran Harper Royal explains, "it was not Georgetown who enslaved our ancestors, it was the Jesuits. It is the Jesuits who really have to reconcile the sale . . . [w]e know that Georgetown has put forth various recommendations for making amends, but we want to see what the Jesuits will do to mitigate the sale of our ancestors" (Jones 2017). In December 2017, two members of the international Jesuit leadership visited with GU 272 descendants in New Orleans and Maringouin, Louisiana. The descendant community's flyer for these meetings stated: "Listening is a core Jesuit virtue."

Eight months prior, Georgetown hosted a liturgy of "remembrance, contrition and hope" that included members of the descendant community, students, faculty, university administrators, community members and clergy. Revd Tim Kesicki, president of the Jesuit Conference of Canada and the United States, and one of the priests who would subsequently meet with the descendant communities in Louisiana, issued a public atonement at this mass, "Today the Society of Jesus, who helped to establish Georgetown University and whose leaders enslaved and mercilessly sold your ancestors, stand before you and say we have greatly sinned . . . With the pain that will never leave us, we resist moving on, but embrace moving forward with hope" (Zauzmer 2017). Kesicki's comments, and the earlier statements of President DeGioia, stressed that the reconciliation that was required had explicitly moral foundations—both the wanting morals that permitted the transatlantic enslavement of Africans and the contemporary institutional norms that now compelled a response.

Pace Schiller, today universities are emblematic moral institutions, with both parochial and secular organizations of higher education engaged in endeavours to come to terms with their role in racial slavery (Schiller 1959). In the climate of colour-blind racial ideology, these organizations may be among the last institutional possibilities for community- and national-scale discussions of contemporary racism and the after-effects of racial slavery. These may be the few remaining sites where light can be shined on structural racism. As Alex Carp wrote in the *New York Review of Books*, "[u]niversities are hardly the only American institutions to have grown from ties to slavery, but with this research they are among the first to acknowledge that their involvement was rarely recognized and poorly understood, and to mobilize the expertise and resources to change that" (Carp 2018).

But anthropologist Didier Fassin's (2015) important work reminds us of the difference between institutions in which moral rights and claims might be embedded and the institutional work of enacting these rights and claims. In other words, "institutional *morality*" is key. More than just an inversion of Schiller's terms, Fassin's interpretation suggests a dynamic process in which morality is in action. Whereas moral institutions might be said to have norms or principles that adhere an entity, with a sense of ethics or justice deemed to be inherent to an institution's structure or identity, institutional morality is a choice, or perhaps a calculation, in the face of *realpolitik*. In *At the Heart of the State*, Fassin offers that "moral economies . . . are connected in the daily activities of institutions through the values and affects which crystallize around social issues and the responses that are given in concrete situations" (Fassin 2015).

The GU 272 reconciliation project has yet to fully crystallize. But at Georgetown, we see institutional morality being ventured in a context in which a descendant community demands consultation in the process and in which genealogical and genetic data have been given constitutive roles in this group's identity. Genetic ancestry testing is a curious instrument of racial reconciliation at American universities because its deep roots lie in the racial science that took seed at these institutions. These tensions are the living toll of racial slavery.

Notes

1. FitzGerald, F. "Peculiar Institutions," *The New Yorker*, September 12, 2005. Available at https://www.newyorker.com/magazine/2005/09/12/peculiar-institutions [Accessed 26 February 2018].

2. https://slavery.virginia.edu/universities-studying-slavery/.

3. Lemon was the name of an enslaved man owned by the College of William & Mary. https://www.wm.edu/sites/lemonproject/.

4. In the *New York Review of Books*, Cellini is quoted thusly: "Believe me, for decades and decades people at Georgetown believed that the slaves didn't have surnames... It's because they didn't look hard enough. Basically all they did was look inside the four walls of their own institution.... It's not that you can't reach the conclusion that there is no documentation. It just takes a lot of hard work" (Carp 2018).

5. https://www.ancestry.com/corporate/about-ancestry/company-facts [Accessed on 23 March 2018].

Bibliography

Beckert, S., Stevens, K., and the students of the Harvard and Slavery Research Seminar 2011. *Harvard and Slavery: Seeking a Forgotten History*, Cambridge, MA: Harvard University.

Belluck, P. 2017. "Brown U. to Examine Debt to Slave Trade," *New York Times*. Available at: https://www.nytimes.com/2004/03/13/us/brown-u-to-examine-debt-to-slave-trade .html [Accessed on 14 August 2017].

Bobo, L., Kluegel, J. R., and Smith, R. A. 1997. "Laissez Faire Racism: The Crystallization of a Kinder, Gentler, Antiblack Ideology," in S. Tuch and J. K. Martin, (eds) *Racial Attitudes in the 1990s: Continuity and Change*, Westport, CT: Praeger, 15–42.

Bonilla-Silva, E. 2003. *Racism Without Racists: Color-blind Racism and the Persistence of Racial Inequality in America*, Lanham, MD: Rowman & Littlefield.

Brown, M. K., Carnoy, M., Currie, E., Duster, T., Oppenheimer, D. B., Shultz, M. M., et al. 2003. *White-washing Race: The Myth of a Color-blind Society*, Berkeley, CA: University of California Press.

Brown University Steering Committee on Slavery and Justice 2006. *Slavery and Justice: Report of the Brown University Steering Committee on Slavery and Justice*, Providence,

RI: Brown University. Available at https://brown.edu/Research/Slavery_Justice /documents/SlaveryAndJustice.pdf [Accessed on 12 January 2018].

Burch, A. D. S. 2017. "Tracing His Roots, Georgetown Employee Learns University Sold His Ancestor," *New York Times*. Available at: https://www.nytimes.com/2017/03/24/us/a -georgetown-employee-slavery.html [Accessed on 24 March 2017].

Carmody, D. 1988. "Education: Georgetown Redefines Alumni Role," *New York Times*. Available at: https://www.nytimes.com/1988/10/05/us/education-georgetown-redefines -alumni-role.html.

Carp, A. 2018. "Slavery and the American University," *New York Review of Books*. Available at: https://www.nybooks.com/daily/2018/02/07/slavery-and-the-american-university/.

Daniels, J. 1997. *White Lies: Race, Class, Gender and Sexuality in White Supremacist Discourse*, New York, NY: Routledge.

Daniels, J. 2009. *Cyber Racism: White Supremacy Online and the New Attack on Civil Rights*, Lanham, MD: Rowman & Littlefield.

DeGioia, J. J. 2017. "Remarks at the "Liturgy of Remembrance, Contrition, and Hope." Available at: https://president.georgetown.edu/liturgy-remembrance-contrition-hope -remarks-april-2017 [Accessed on 23 April 2017].

Dugdale, A., Fueser, J. J., and Alves, J. C. 2001. *Yale, Slavery and Abolition*, New Haven, CT: The Amistad Committee Inc.

Duster, T. 1990. *Backdoor to Eugenics*, New York, NY: Routledge.

Dwyer, S. 1999. "Reconciliation for Realists," *Ethics and International Affairs* 13(1), 81–98.

Fassin, D. 2015. *At the Heart of the State: Exploring the Moral World of Institutions*, London: Pluto Press.

Feinberg, L. 1988. "Secret Stewards Disbanded on Georgetown Campus," *Washington Post*. Available at: https://www.washingtonpost.com/archive/local/1988/02/28/secret-stewards -disbanded-on-georgetown-campus/333473d6-feb3-4181-aca1-7c20a3878838/?utm _term=.35e0c4a07a80 [Accessed on 24 February 2018].

FitzGerald, F. 2005. "Peculiar Institutions," *The New Yorker*. Available at: https://www .newyorker.com/magazine/2005/09/12/peculiar-institutions [Accessed on 13 August 2017].

Fullwiley, D. 2007. "The Molecularization of Race: Institutionalizing Racial Difference in Pharmacogenetics Practice," *Science as Culture* 16(1), 1–30.

Georgetown University. 2016. "Georgetown Shares Slavery, Memory, and Reconciliation Report, Racial Justice Steps." Available at: https://www.georgetown.edu/slavery -memory-reconciliiation-working-group-sept-2016.

Hernandez, D. 2017. "Ancestry. Com Is Quietly Transforming Itself into a Medical Research Juggernaut," *Fusion/Splinter*. Available at: https://splinternews.com/ancestry-com-is -quietly-transforming-itself-into-a-medi-1793846838 [Accessed on 1 October 2017].

Jones, T. L. 2017. "Georgetown slave descendants bring in legal team to help negotiate with university on reparations," *The Advocate*. Available at: https://www.theadvocate.com /baton_rouge/news/communities/westside/article_b221befe-0f26-11e7-8783-330932 e2f352. html [Accessed on 6 February 2018].

Keller, E. F. 2015. "The Postgenomic Genome," in S. S. Richardson and H. Stevens (eds) *Postgenomics: Perspectives on Biology after the Genome*, Durham, NC: Duke University Press, 9–31.

Mamdani, M. 2001. "A Diminished Truth," in W. James and L. van de Vijver (eds) *After the TRC: Reflections on Truth Reconciliation in South Africa*, Athens, GA: Ohio University Press, 58–62.

McCoy, T. 2017. "Her Ancestors Were Georgetown's Slaves. Now, at Age 63, She's Enrolled There—as a College Freshman," *The Washington Post*, 30 August.

Megan, K. 2017. "Calhoun's Principles and Legacy as an Ardent Supporter of Slavery as a Positive Good Are at Odds with the Values of this University," *Hartford Courant*, February 11, 2017. Available at https://www.courant.com/education/hc-yale-changing-calhounresidence-Hall-name-20170210-story.html [Accessed on 26 February 2018].

Mooney, A. 2017. "Descendants of 272 Recruit Legal Representation," *The Hoya*, March 31. Available at https://www.thehoya.com/descendants-of-272-recruit-legal-representation/ [Accessed on 6 February 2018].

Mustian, J. 2015. "New Orleans Filmmaker Cleared in Cold-case Murder; False Positive Highlights Limitations of Familial DNA Searching," *The New Orleans Advocate*. Available at: https://www.theadvocate.com/new_orleans/news/article_1b3a3f96-d574-59e0-9c6a-c3c7c0d2f166.html [Accessed on 29 June 2015].

Nelson, A. 2008. "Bio Science: Genetic Genealogy Testing and the Pursuit of African Ancestry," *Social Studies of Science* 38(5): 759–783.

Nelson, A. 2016. *The Social Life of DNA: Race, Reparations and Reconciliation after the Genome*, Boston, MA: Beacon Press.

Phelan, J. C., Link, B., and Feldman, N. M. 2013. "The Genomic Revolution and Beliefs about Essential Racial Differences: A Backdoor to Eugenics?," *American Sociological Review* 78(2), 167–191.

Puno, R. 2017. "How an AncestryDNA Test Led to a Mind-blowing Discovery about His History," *Upworthy*. Available at: https://www.upworthy.com/how-an-ancestrydna-test-led-to-a-mind-blowing-discoveryabout-his-history [Accessed on 13 July 2017].

Rawls, J. 1996. *Political Liberalism*, New York: Columbia University Press.

Richardson, S. 2013. *Sex Itself: The Search for Male and Female in the Human Genome*, Chicago, IL: University of Chicago Press.

Richardson, S. S., and Stevens, H. (eds) 2015. *Postgenomics: Perspectives on Biology after the Genome*, Durham, NC: Duke University Press.

Roth, W. D. 2016. "The Multiple Dimensions of Race," *Ethnic and Racial Studies* 39(8), 1310–1338.

Sandweiss, M. A., and Hollander, C. 2017. *Princeton & Slavery: Holding the Center*, Available at www.slavery.princeto. edu [Accessed on 6 November 2017].

Schiller, F. 1959. "The Stage Considered as a Moral Institution" (Die Schaubuhne al seine moralische Anstalt betrachtet)," in F. Schiller (ed) *An Anthology for Our Time*, New York: F. Ungarm.

Simmons, R. 2004. "Facing Up to Our Ties to Slavery," *Boston Globe*. Available at: https://archive.boston.com/news/globe/editorial_opinion/oped/articles/2004/04/28/facing_up_to_our_ties_to_slavery/ [Accessed on 14 August 2017].

Sullivan, K. 2017. "This Georgetown Freshman is 63, and Attending the School that Enslaved her Ancestors," *CNN.com*. Available at: https://www.cnn.com/2017/12/25/politics/georgetown-freshman/index.html [Accessed on 26 December 2017].

Swarns, R. 2016. "272 Slaves Were Sold by Georgetown. What Does It Owe Their Descendants?" *The New York Times*. Available at: https://www.nytimes.com/2016/04/17/us/georgetown-university-search-for-slave-descendants.html [Accessed on 17 April 2016].

Wilder, C. 2013. *Ebony and Ivy: Race, Slavery, and the Troubled History of America's Universities*, New York: Bloomsbury Press.

Zauzmer, J. 2017. "Grappling with Its History of Slavery, Georgetown Gathers Descendants for a Day of Repentance," *Washington Post*. Available at: https://www.washingtonpost.com

/news/acts-of-faith/wp/2017/04/18/georgetown-university-hosts-service-ofrepentance
-dedicates-building-to-slavesit-sold-in-1938-to-secure-schools-future/?tid=a_inl&utm
_term=.4272f9936e17 [Accessed on 18 April 2017].

Zernike, K. 2001. "Slave Traders in Yale's Past Fuel Debate on Restitution," *New York Times*.
Available at: https://www.nytimes.com/2001/08/13/nyregion/slave-traders-in-yale-s
-past-fuel-debate-on-restitution.html [Accessed on 24 February 2018].

THE WORKING GROUP

23

Slavery's Remnants, Buried and Overlooked

MATTHEW QUALLEN

This article was written by Georgetown University junior Matthew Quallen and originally published in the student newspaper The Hoya *on September 11, 2015. It introduced a new generation of Georgetown students to the history of the school's involvement with slavery. The following year, Quallen joined the Working Group on Slavery, Memory, and Reconciliation convened by Georgetown's president John J. DeGioia to examine the school's history of slavery. Several other students served on the working group too.*

Two weeks ago, the roughly 1,580 students comprising the Class of 2019 arrived on campus. Beginning with New Student Orientation and trailing into the first months of their time on campus, these thousand and a half eager freshmen will begin to learn the geography of our collective home. They will notice, no doubt, the canal, tracing the Potomac to the edge of the waterfront, where they'll find a park and a "harbor." They'll note, perhaps with surprise, the presence of a graveyard at the heart of our campus, or the trolley tracks still notched into the cobblestone streets. And these freshmen, like all of us, will come face to face with Mulledy Hall: imposing, stately and recently refurbished.

About a week before classes began, an email from University President John J. DeGioia reintroduced Mulledy Hall—one half of the Former Jesuit Residence—to all of us. Writing with reference to the tumult pouring out of Ferguson MO, Staten Island and elsewhere, DeGioia recognized the history behind Mulledy Hall. It was named for Thomas F. Mulledy, who twice served as president of Georgetown. In 1838, Mulledy sold 272 slaves, owned by the Maryland Jesuits, south to a future governor of Louisiana. He not only guaranteed their continued enslavement but set off a chain of events that separated families and destroyed lives.

Although this history is documented, the information contained in that email came as a surprise to many students. Why, they wondered, had such a name stood for so long? With students moving into the building, some have expressed a frustration that is almost achingly obvious: no student should have to occupy a building named in honor of someone who enslaved his ancestors.

It is troubling how many people were caught off guard by DeGioia's email. Many had never heard of Mulledy Hall. Until this year, it stood as a hulking red shell of a building. Passersby admired its elaborate balconies but largely paid the structure little mind. When a message from the president's office labeled "A Message Regarding Mulledy Hall" appeared in our inboxes, many of us felt like we were being introduced to the site and its history for the first time.

Mulledy isn't the only site to which Georgetown deserves a new introduction. Our campus environment is suffused with the legacy of slavery.

Take the waterfront and canal, for example. The canal, now a nice place for a light lunch or a stroll, exists because Georgetown was historically the last navigable site on the Potomac for seafaring vessels. The canal cuts deep into Maryland, Virginia and West Virginia, from which it used to ferry trade goods destined for the interior or for the port of Georgetown. Like most significant ports at the time, Georgetown was a slave hub. The community in Georgetown included hundreds of slaves and free blacks alike. In fact, the Georgetown of Thomas Mulledy's day was much blacker than the neighborhood we know today.

There's more. Roughly at the intersection of P Street and Wisconsin Avenue (think Thomas Sweet) a slave market took place. And a few dozen miles closer to the coast of Maryland, the Jesuits maintained vast plantations that relied on slave labor to support Jesuit education endeavors. Slavery built and supported Georgetown—all of it. Not just Mulledy Hall.

The signs are on campus too. Several slaves, although likely not many, worked on Georgetown's campus. Some of them are buried here. In 1821, a slave named Rachel, who worked in the "College Wash House," was buried in the Old College Ground—a cemetery that existed roughly where the Northeast Triangle is now being built. More slaves were likely buried in the area between Yates Field House and the Georgetown University Observatory, a garden now.

Slaveholding culture also infiltrated our campus. Georgetown, after all, was a southern institution. As many as one in five of our students during the first half of the 19th century were the children of planters. In the Civil War, our graduates overwhelmingly enlisted to fight for the Confederacy. They even participated in the Lincoln assassination, helping earn Georgetown the moniker "alma mater of the Confederacy." When Georgetown adopted Blue and Gray as its colors, it was as much out of necessity as magnanimity.

When we wander our campus, we are usually too self-assured in the present to interrogate Georgetown's sights and emblems. We often discuss the legacy of racial intolerance in the United States as if it is happening elsewhere. Ferguson, after all, is far away; it can be murky and fraught.

We would do better to take a lesson from the Class of 2019. Just as they introduce themselves to our campus for the first time, we should take this semester to reintroduce ourselves to our environment and its troubled history. If the dialogue on race DeGioia calls for is to be a success, Georgetown will need to come face to face with its history—now hidden, squirreled away in plain sight.

24

Student Activists Sit in outside DeGioia's Office

TOBY HUNG

In the fall of 2015, as the working group researched Georgetown's connections to slavery, Georgetown students organized to protest racism on campus. This article by student journalist Toby Hung in The Hoya *on November 13, 2015, describes a sit-in in President DeGioia's office, as the undergraduate community expressed frustration at the school's administration and demanded a set of reforms that included changing the names of the two buildings that honored the architects of the 1838 sale, the Jesuit priest and former presidents of Georgetown, Fr. Thomas F. Mulledy, SJ, and Fr. William McSherry, SJ.*

Student activists began staging a sit-in outside the office of University President John J. DeGioia today at 9 a.m. to pressure the administration into meeting a series of demands that address racial injustice at Georgetown.

As of press time, around 30 students remain seated outside DeGioia's office on the second floor of Healy Hall. The activists will continue the sit-in until 12 a.m., and expect to stage daily sit-ins until administrators meet the demands, which include changing the names of Mulledy Hall and McSherry Hall, revising university tours to include information on the history of campus sites, placing plaques on the known unmarked graves of slaves and establishing an annual program focused on education.

DeGioia interacted with the protesters briefly in the morning, and the Working Group on Slavery, Memory, and Reconciliation held a meeting at 12:30 p.m. At around 7 p.m. students from American University joined Georgetown students outside DeGioia's office.

The retention of Mulledy Hall's name sparked ire earlier this semester and drew attention to former University President Fr. Thomas Mulledy, S.J., who authorized the sale of 272 slaves to a Louisiana plantation in 1838. McSherry is named after former University President Fr. William McSherry, S.J., who served as Mulledy's lawyer during the sale. Student activists are using the hashtag #BuiltOn272—the number of slaves sold—on Twitter.

Other demands include creating an endowment for recruiting black professors—equivalent to the net present value of the profit from the 1838 sale—and mandatory training for professors on diversity and identity issues.

Black student activists announced the sit-in yesterday at a demonstration at Red Square, held in solidarity with students of color experiencing racism at the University of Missouri, Yale University and the University of the Western Cape. Multiple other universities, including Syracuse University, Howard University and the University of California, Los Angeles have held similar demonstrations in solidarity with these movements.

At the sit-in, students expressed their frustration with the university administration.

Alejandra Baez (SFS '16) said the ongoing struggle is important to the black community at Georgetown.

"The black student struggle is my struggle because this community, if we're not in it to support each other, is not a community. That's just the opposite of what a community means," Baez said.

Baez also criticized the retention of Mulledy Hall's name.

"Personally, I think that naming a building after someone who sold slaves to build up the institution is a disgrace," Baez said. "How can we build a legacy on an institution that disprivileged a huge portion of our country's people and that continues to disprivilege students at Georgetown, just in the aftermath of it?"

According to Latazia Carter (COL '17), a student participating in the sit-in, the movement began before the student demonstrations at Mizzou.

"As a black student at Georgetown, we frequently deal with micro-aggressions every day. This discussion didn't just start with Mizzou. . . . This has been an issue that we've been dealing with because, as black students, we don't feel comfortable with the name of that building," Carter said.

Carter said she hopes the administration will recognize the community's demands through the sit-in.

"I don't want this to seem like a new movement because it's not. But we've had to take this action because the university fails to hear us, and recognize our thoughts on the matter," Carter said.

Hoya *Staff Writer Ian Scoville contributed reporting.*

25

Report of the Working Group on Slavery,
Memory, and Reconciliation to the
President of Georgetown University

In August 2015 Georgetown president John J. DeGioia appointed and charged a Working Group on Slavery, Memory, and Reconciliation to study and guide the university's work related to slavery and its legacies. In the summer of 2016 the fifteen members, including faculty, staff, and students, presented a report to the office of the president. Their work was shared with the Georgetown community on September 1, 2016. These are the recommendations the working group proposed in its report.

RECOMMENDATIONS TO THE PRESIDENT

This section of the report presents the Working Group's recommendations to the president. Recommendations were proposed to the Working Group from many sources. Students, faculty, staff, administration, alumni, and friends of the University, sometimes individually, sometimes in groups, submitted ideas. These proposals were received by the Working Group in a variety of ways, including via the Working Group's webpage. Working Group members also proposed ideas, for themselves and on behalf of others. Proposals were reviewed by the full Working Group and distributed as appropriate to one or several committees for specific evaluation and further research, if needed.

At the Working Group's April 22 meeting, each committee presented and explained the recommendations it deemed most appropriate for the consideration of the full Working Group. The full Working Group deliberated on each recommendation and approved them one by one, consolidating, expanding, and amending them, as it deemed fit.

The full Working Group has approved all of the recommendations that follow. We first present a summary overview of the recommendations. That is followed by the reports of each of the five Working Group committees. These reports provide additional background and a fuller explanation of the recommendations being offered.

The Working Group makes these recommendations to the president of Georgetown University, pursuant to its mandate and for the University's continuing engagement with its history of slavery.

BUILDING NAMES

The Working Group recommends that:

- The building once known as Mulledy Hall and now called Freedom Hall should be permanently renamed Isaac Hall. Isaac is the first enslaved person named in the "Articles of Agreement" between Thomas Mulledy, S.J., and the Louisiana businessmen Henry Johnson and Jesse Batey.
- The building once known as McSherry Hall and now called Remembrance Hall should be permanently renamed Anne Marie Becraft Hall. Also known as Sister Aloysius, Anne Marie Becraft was a woman of color, a trailblazing educator, a person with deep family roots in the neighborhood of Georgetown, and a Catholic religious sister in the nineteenth century.

GENERAL RECOMMENDATIONS

The Working Group recommends the following:

- **An Apology**
  The University should offer a formal apology for the ways it participated in and benefited from slavery, especially through the sale of enslaved people in the 1830s.
- **Descendants**
  The University should engage the descendants of the enslaved whose labor and value benefited the University. In particular:
  - The University should develop an approach for engaging the descendants of the enslaved people owned by the Maryland Jesuits, especially those who were sold in 1838. This approach should be as expansive as possible and consider all the potential dimensions of

engagement, including the academic, the genealogical, and the personal. The University's engagement should be attentive to the interests of the descendants themselves, as well as respectful of the diversity of opinion and interest among them. Engagement could include, but not be limited to:

- *Meeting with descendant communities, here in Washington as well as in their home communities.*
- *Fostering genealogical research to help descendants explore their family histories. (This work could be housed in the new institute we recommend elsewhere in the report.)*
- *Commissioning an oral history project with descendant communities. Such a project might be pursued in collaboration with partner institutions.*
- *Exploring the feasibility of admission and financial aid initiatives that might be established for the descendant community.*
- *Holding public events to explore more deeply the story of Jesuit slaveholding and its legacies at Georgetown and beyond.*
- *Soliciting the input of the descendants as the University progresses in its engagement with this history, and especially as the University considers how it will memorialize the enslaved people sold in 1838.*

• **Memorialization: Ending Anonymity and Neglect**
The University should:
- Erect a public memorial to the enslaved persons and families outside the renamed halls.
- Preserve the names of the enslaved people either as part of the public memorial or as a display inside the renamed halls and associate the names of the enslaved with scholarships dedicated to correcting the legacy of racial injustice.
- Mark sites on our campus associated with the history of slavery with informative plaques.
- Fulfill its responsibilities to Holy Rood Cemetery and guarantee its good upkeep. The cemetery is the final resting place of many enslaved and free blacks of Georgetown, including family members of Anne Marie Becraft.

• **Research, Teaching, and Public History**
The University should:
- Create an Institute for the Study of Slavery and Its Legacies at Georgetown to coordinate scholarly research, curricular development, and public programs about the history of slavery and its legacies at Georgetown, in Washington, D.C., and its surroundings, and in Catholic America.

- Foster dialogue across departments and centers to address contemporary issues related to the history of slavery, such as our nation's system of mass incarceration, unlawful discrimination, unfair housing, unemployment, workers' rights, especially on campus, and health disparities, to name a few.
- Incorporate the Historical Walking Tour of Black Georgetown into programming for new students.
- Establish long-term displays of historical and archival materials at Lauinger; an interactive study installation; a website research portal; and support for future research projects, at all levels of study at the University.
- Continue the "Freedom and Remembrance" Grant Program to encourage grassroots efforts to understand and commemorate Georgetown's history with slavery.
- Encourage the work of the Working Group on Racial Injustice, especially in fostering diversity on campus in research and hiring.

♦ **Investment in Diversity**
The University should:
- Increase the diversity at Georgetown to a level commensurate, or surpassing, our peer institutions.
- Expand opportunities at all of Georgetown's schools in recognition of Georgetown's participation in slavery, especially for the descendants of the Maryland Jesuit slaves. For example, engagement could include, but not be limited to:
  - *Intensify outreach to prospective African American students, especially from Maryland, the District of Columbia, and Louisiana.*
  - *Grant the descendants of those owned by the Maryland Province an advantage in the admissions process.*
  - *Increase financial assistance to those who demonstrate need with the goal of eliminating financial barriers and making Georgetown more affordable, especially to eligible descendants of the Maryland Jesuit slaves.*
- Devote attention, funding, and resources to assessing and improving the racial climate on campus, including the use of racial and ethnic climate surveys and sensitivity training for all members of the community.

♦ **Engaging the Whole University**
The University should:
- Ensure that all schools of the University are fully engaged in the attempts to address slavery's direct and indirect legacy.
- Draw the Board of Directors fully and explicitly into this engagement, especially as it faces the serious challenge of ethically

fulfilling fiduciary responsibilities, a challenge which Frs. Mulledy and McSherry failed at.

- Broadcast the results of the Working Group through all communications channels at the University's disposal.
- Document for publication the University's process of self-examination.
- Create and maintain an enhanced interactive website to reflect all activities of the Working Group on Slavery, Memory, and Reconciliation.

THE FUTURE OF THE WORKING GROUP ON SLAVERY, MEMORY, AND RECONCILIATION

The president's charge to the Working Group expires with the conclusion of the 2015–16 academic year. The submission of this report completes the activities of the Working Group. The Working Group recommends that the president designate a Steering Committee to oversee implementation of the recommendations that he accepts. This Steering Committee could include, for example, representation from the descendant community in addition to students, faculty, and staff.

26

How Georgetown Is Coming to Terms with Slavery in Its Past

JAMES MARTIN, SJ

In the fall of 2016 Fr. James Martin, SJ, interviewed Fr. David J. Collins, SJ, a professor of history at Georgetown and the chair of Georgetown's Working Group on Slavery, Memory, and Reconciliation, for America *magazine. The conversation with Collins focused on the working group's mission, his experiences as its chair, and the impact that this process had on him as a Jesuit priest.*

In the past few months, the history of the slaves owned by the Jesuits who ran Georgetown University in its early years has been the source of intense discussion. The conversation generated articles that landed on the front page of the *New York Times* and in other newspapers. Central to the story was the historical evidence indicating that Jesuits had sold slaves in order to "save" Georgetown during a financial crisis. Less reported was that a group of faculty, students and members of the administration at the school had been studying the legacy of the slave-owning since the previous summer. Recently, I interviewed David Collins, S.J., chairman of the group, about the complex legacy of Georgetown's Jesuits. Father Collins is professor of history at Georgetown.

Father Collins, can you describe the genesis and the goals of the Working Group on Slavery, Memory, and Reconciliation?

A number of intersecting dynamics and motivations led Georgetown University's president, Dr. John J. DeGioia, to convene the Working Group (which I'll call the "W. G.") in late summer of 2015: the university's desire to more deeply and effectively address the abiding, systemic racial injustices and social inequalities in our nation; its desire to address the manifestations of such dynamics in its own community; its desire for a more complete understanding of the school's Jesuit history; and the example of other universities fruitfully undertaking an exploration of their own histories in this regard.

The immediate impetus behind the formation of the W. G. corresponded to the repurposing into a student residence of a building named after a Jesuit who organized the sale of the Jesuit slaves in 1838, Thomas Mulledy, S.J. Against the explicit instructions of the Jesuits' superior in Rome, Father Mulledy used some of the revenues from the sale to pay off the mounting, debilitating debt at Georgetown. The most well-known of the W. G.'s tasks was to evaluate whether the building should continue to be so named.

More broadly, we were asked to make recommendations on how best to acknowledge and recognize the university's historical relationship to the institution of slavery, to examine and interpret the history of certain sites on the campus (starting with Mulledy Hall) and to convene events and opportunities for dialogue on these issues.

Was this history well-known by the broader Georgetown community?

No. There were some who knew all of the history, some who knew parts of it and an awful lot who knew none of it. Knowing or not knowing the history also did not correlate to age or to status or length of time at the university.

I'll admit, this surprised me. The amount that's been written about Jesuit slaveholding in the United States is quite substantial. Some of it dates back more than a century. Most of the research in the last 50 years has come out of Georgetown. While some of the scholarship might be considered too technical for general readership, that scholarship inspired more accessible writings in newspapers. The information in the first *New York Times* article in April, for example, was largely drawn from the research of two Jesuit historians—R. Emmett Curran and Thomas Murphy—who published their findings in the 1980s and in the 2000s. The American Studies Program on campus also developed a fantastic online presence for the archival materials in the late '90s that was much accessed by teachers and genealogical researchers until last year. [It has since been supplanted by the Georgetown Slavery Archive.]

Two things are operative here. First, the population turnover on a university campus is both big and fast. Every four years we have an entirely new undergraduate population. The other factor is that it's hard to absorb ugly episodes in your own history. As Americans we're especially allergic to taking responsibility for the mistakes and crimes in our national history. Overcoming these two hurdles to getting the history known have occupied the W. G. a great deal.

Do you think Georgetown, or the Society of Jesus, owes something to the descendants of the slaves owned by the Jesuit community?

This is another issue that has occupied the W. G. over the last seven months. I think yes, and that was the clear consensus of the W. G.: Part of making amends must include the descendants. But how and what—that's the challenge. The most important component in figuring that challenge out is the participation of the descendants themselves. This is why, as you will see in the recommendations, the descendants are offered a privileged role in the ongoing process the university is undertaking.

What has been the involvement and reaction by the descendants of the slaves? Have you met many of them?

The outreach of the descendants to the university has been a moving part of the past year, at least for me. I certainly didn't anticipate it when I accepted the chairmanship of the W. G., and I am most grateful for it. At this point, I would also call their engagement preliminary. There's not much of a template for us—either for the university or for the descendants—to follow. We're figuring out how to proceed. It's important to keep in mind that "the descendants" are people, not an organization or an institution. Members of the W. G., and our lead historian Adam Rothman in particular, have had extensive contact with descendants. I myself have had contact with individual descendants since I was a Jesuit novice and was first introduced to the history about 30 years ago.

Some have argued that the focus on Georgetown has been unfair. Weren't there many other colleges and universities in the Deep South, for example, with ties to slavery? Even schools in the north, like Brown, were complicit. Have there been calls for reparations from these colleges as well? Why the focus, do you think, on Georgetown?

There are two books that I am particularly grateful to have read as part of the preparation for this Working Group. I recommend both to the people who have asked this question. The first is Craig Wilder's *Ebony and Ivy*, an outstanding investigation of the connections between the rise of higher education in the colonial and antebellum periods and the American slave economy and slave culture. It is meticulously researched and poignantly argued. It is especially disheartening for those of us who are passionate about our universities as a place where knowledge is increased and truth is pursued.

His thesis can be boiled down to this: The colonial and antebellum colleges and universities in the United States, both North and South, almost without exception, came into being because the slave economy supported them; and then the universities, especially in the 19th century, became greenhouses for the racism that still mars our social fabric.

The second book is a study and anthology of the ministry of reconciliation that St. John Paul II undertook in preparation for the millennium. The book is titled *When a Pope Asks Forgiveness* and was edited by Luigi Accattoli. It's a moving reminder that we make our examinations of conscience and offer our *mea culpas* because we ourselves need to, not because everyone else is, too.

Do you feel the coverage of this story so far has been fair and accurate? *The New York Times* **pieces seemed to give short shrift to the work already done by Georgetown, and might have made it seem as if the** *Times* **had discovered the story.**

Rachel Swarns's two pieces in the *New York Times* are outstanding; she deserves a Pulitzer. We're doing our work so that others can draw from it as she has. We want others to learn from our successes and failures in this process. If journalism like Ms. Swarns can get America to look more critically and self-reflectively at the ways in which we are still the beneficiaries of our slaveholding past and in which our current society is still scarred by it and its legacy, then I hardly feel a need to grumble about this or that initiative here on campus or this or that citation from careful historical scholarship being overlooked.

How has this process affected you as a Jesuit and a priest?

I've spent many years as a Jesuit in Germany. I remember a particularly jarring insight shared with me by a fellow scholastic [a Jesuit studying in preparation for ordination] with whom I was studying philosophy at the time. He remarked that as a German he had no right to claim Bach and Brahms as his own without doing the same for Birkenau and Bergen-Belsen.

That's certainly not how I was raised to think about my own American history. There's something dysfunctional about cherry-picking only the pride-worthy aspects of a community's past and saying these are things we will take credit for and the rest is not worth worrying about, as if the legacy of the good abides and that of the bad disappears, or is dismissed as someone else's problem.

Jesuit history runs a similar danger. We love our Jesuit history, and we readily point to our great heroes and accomplishments. They embolden us to imitation. We even have a range of stories about the great injustices inflicted against us by princes and prelates through the ages. But we do our history and ourselves a grave disservice if we pretend that there haven't been serious mistakes and deplorable crimes committed by us, as individuals, in governance and communally.

The participation of U.S. Jesuits in America's slaveholding and slave-trading past is a perfect example. I've had the honor to teach this history to Jesuit novices for nearly 20 years. I consider it one of the most important things I do as a priest, as a Jesuit and as a historian. In the final analysis, the goal is not to scapegoat the past or to pat ourselves on the back for having solved this problem, but rather to coach us in the hunt for our own moral blindness. Our generation is, after all, no less sin-scarred and sinful than theirs.

Along these lines, I recall Pope Francis's remarks on the opening of the Jubilee Year of Mercy. The year, he suggested, is not in the first instance about our running around and dispensing mercy to others. Rather, it is about taking the opportunity to understand how deeply we need God's mercy ourselves. So, too, in the Society of Jesus.

THE GU272 DESCENDANTS

27

272 Slaves Were Sold to Save Georgetown. What Does It Owe Their Descendants?

RACHEL L. SWARNS

This article by journalist Rachel L. Swarns was published by the New York Times *online on April 16, 2016, and appeared in the Sunday print edition the following day. Swarns's evocative reporting of the Jesuits' sale of 272 persons in 1838 and the genealogical research of the Georgetown Memory Project struck a chord with the public. The revelation that there were living descendants of the people sold by the Jesuits raised the issue of reparations in a new and dramatic way.*

The human cargo was loaded on ships at a bustling wharf in the nation's capital, destined for the plantations of the Deep South. Some slaves pleaded for rosaries as they were rounded up, praying for deliverance.

But on this day, in the fall of 1838, no one was spared: not the two-month-old baby and her mother, not the field hands, not the shoemaker and not Cornelius Hawkins, who was about 13 years old when he was forced onboard.

Their panic and desperation would be mostly forgotten for more than a century. But this was no ordinary slave sale. The enslaved African-Americans had belonged to the nation's most prominent Jesuit priests. And they were sold, along with scores of others, to help secure the future of the premier Catholic institution of higher learning at the time, known today as Georgetown University.

Now, with racial protests roiling college campuses, an unusual collection of Georgetown professors, students, alumni and genealogists is trying to find out what happened to those 272 men, women, and children. And they are confronting a particularly wrenching question: What, if anything, is owed to the descendants of slaves who were sold to help ensure the college's survival?

More than a dozen universities—including Brown, Columbia, Harvard and the University of Virginia—have publicly recognized their ties to slavery and the slave trade. But the 1838 slave sale organized by the Jesuits, who founded and ran Georgetown, stands out for its sheer size, historians say.

At Georgetown, slavery and scholarship were inextricably linked. The college relied on Jesuit plantations in Maryland to help finance its operations, university officials say. (Slaves were often donated by prosperous parishioners.) And the 1838 sale—worth about $3.3 million in today's dollars—was organized by two of Georgetown's early presidents, both Jesuit priests.

Some of that money helped to pay off the debts of the struggling college.

"The university itself owes its existence to this history," said Adam Rothman, a historian at Georgetown and a member of a university working group that is studying ways for the institution to acknowledge and try to make amends for its tangled roots in slavery.

Although the working group was established in August, it was student demonstrations at Georgetown in the fall that helped to galvanize alumni and gave new urgency to the administration's efforts.

The students organized a protest and a sit-in, using the hashtag #GU272 for the slaves who were sold. In November, the university agreed to remove the names of the Rev. Thomas F. Mulledy and the Rev. William McSherry, the college presidents involved in the sale, from two campus buildings.

An alumnus, following the protest from afar, wondered if more needed to be done.

That alumnus, Richard J. Cellini, the chief executive of a technology company and a practicing Catholic, was troubled that neither the Jesuits nor university officials had tried to trace the lives of the enslaved African-Americans or compensate their progeny.

Mr. Cellini is an unlikely racial crusader. A white man, he admitted that he had never spent much time thinking about slavery or African-American history.

But he said he could not stop thinking about the slaves, whose names had been in Georgetown's archives for decades.

"This is not a disembodied group of people, who are nameless and faceless," said Mr. Cellini, 52, whose company, Briefcase Analytics, is based in Cambridge, Mass. "These are real people with real names and real descendants."

Within two weeks, Mr. Cellini had set up a nonprofit, the Georgetown Memory Project, hired eight genealogists and raised more than $10,000 from fellow alumni to finance their research.

Dr. Rothman, the Georgetown historian, heard about Mr. Cellini's efforts and let him know that he and several of his students were also tracing the slaves. Soon, the two men and their teams were working on parallel tracks.

What has emerged from their research, and that of other scholars, is a glimpse of an insular world dominated by priests who required their slaves to attend Mass for the sake of their salvation, but also whipped and sold some of them. The records describe runaways, harsh plantation conditions and the anguish voiced by some Jesuits over their participation in a system of forced servitude.

"A microcosm of the whole history of American slavery," Dr. Rothman said.

The enslaved were grandmothers and grandfathers, carpenters and blacksmiths, pregnant women and anxious fathers, children and infants, who were fearful, bewildered and despairing as they saw their families and communities ripped apart by the sale of 1838.

The researchers have used archival records to follow their footsteps, from the Jesuit plantations in Maryland, to the docks of New Orleans, to three plantations west and south of Baton Rouge, La.

The hope was to eventually identify the slaves' descendants. By the end of December, one of Mr. Cellini's genealogists felt confident that she had found a strong test case: the family of the boy, Cornelius Hawkins.

BROKEN PROMISES

There are no surviving images of Cornelius, no letters or journals that offer a look into his last hours on a Jesuit plantation in Maryland.

He was not yet five feet tall when he sailed onboard the Katharine Jackson, one of several vessels that carried the slaves to the port of New Orleans.

An inspector scrutinized the cargo on Dec. 6, 1838. "Examined and found correct," he wrote of Cornelius and the 129 other people he found on the ship.

The notation betrayed no hint of the turmoil on board. But priests at the Jesuit plantations recounted the panic and fear they witnessed when the slaves departed.

Some children were sold without their parents, records show, and slaves were "dragged off by force to the ship," the Rev. Thomas Lilly reported. Others, including two of Cornelius's uncles, ran away before they could be captured.

But few were lucky enough to escape. The Rev. Peter Havermans wrote of an elderly woman who fell to her knees, begging to know what she had done to deserve such a fate, according to Robert Emmett Curran, a retired Georgetown historian who described eyewitness accounts of the sale in his research. Cornelius's extended family was split, with his aunt Nelly and her daughters shipped to one plantation, and his uncle James and his wife and children sent to another, records show.

At the time, the Catholic Church did not view slaveholding as immoral, said the Rev. Thomas R. Murphy, a historian at Seattle University who has written a book about the Jesuits and slavery.

The Jesuits had sold off individual slaves before. As early as the 1780s, Dr. Rothman found, they openly discussed the need to cull their stock of human beings.

But the decision to sell virtually all of their enslaved African-Americans in the 1830s left some priests deeply troubled.

They worried that new owners might not allow the slaves to practice their Catholic faith. They also knew that life on plantations in the Deep South was notoriously brutal, and feared that families might end up being separated and resold.

"It would be better to suffer financial disaster than suffer the loss of our souls with the sale of the slaves," wrote the Rev. Jan Roothaan, who headed the Jesuits' international organization from Rome and was initially reluctant to authorize the sale.

But he was persuaded to reconsider by several prominent Jesuits, including Father Mulledy, then the influential president of Georgetown who had overseen its expansion, and Father McSherry, who was in charge of the Jesuits' Maryland mission. (The two men would swap positions by 1838.)

Mismanaged and inefficient, the Maryland plantations no longer offered a reliable source of income for Georgetown College, which had been founded in 1789. It would not survive, Father Mulledy feared, without an influx of cash.

So in June 1838, he negotiated a deal with Henry Johnson, a member of the House of Representatives, and Jesse Batey, a landowner in Louisiana, to sell Cornelius and the others.

Father Mulledy promised his superiors that the slaves would continue to practice their religion. Families would not be separated. And the money raised by the sale would not be used to pay off debt or for operating expenses.

None of those conditions were met, university officials said.

Father Mulledy took most of the down payment he received from the sale—about $500,000 in today's dollars—and used it to help pay off the debts that Georgetown had incurred under his leadership.

In the uproar that followed, he was called to Rome and reassigned.

The next year, Pope Gregory XVI explicitly barred Catholics from engaging in "this traffic in Blacks . . . no matter what pretext or excuse."

But the pope's order, which did not explicitly address slave ownership or private sales like the one organized by the Jesuits, offered scant comfort to Cornelius and the other slaves.

By the 1840s, word was trickling back to Washington that the slaves' new owners had broken their promises. Some slaves suffered at the hands of a cruel overseer.

Roughly two-thirds of the Jesuits' former slaves—including Cornelius and his family—had been shipped to two plantations so distant from churches that "they never see a Catholic priest," the Rev. James Van de Velde, a Jesuit who visited Louisiana, wrote in a letter in 1848.

Father Van de Velde begged Jesuit leaders to send money for the construction of a church that would "provide for the salvation of those poor people, who are now utterly neglected."

He addressed his concerns to Father Mulledy, who three years earlier had returned to his post as president of Georgetown.

There is no indication that he received any response.

A FAMILIAR NAME

African-Americans are often a fleeting presence in the documents of the 1800s. Enslaved, marginalized and forced into illiteracy by laws that prohibited them from learning to read and write, many seem like ghosts who pass through this world without leaving a trace.

After the sale, Cornelius vanishes from the public record until 1851 when his trail finally picks back up on a cotton plantation near Maringouin, La.

His owner, Mr. Batey, had died, and Cornelius appeared on the plantation's inventory, which included 27 mules and horses, 32 hogs, two ox carts and scores of other slaves. He was valued at $900. ("Valuable Plantation and Negroes for Sale," read one newspaper advertisement in 1852.)

The plantation would be sold again and again and again, records show, but Cornelius's family remained intact. In 1870, he appeared in the census for the first time. He was about 48 then, a father, a husband, a farm laborer and, finally, a free man.

He might have disappeared from view again for a time, save for something few could have counted on: his deep, abiding faith. It was his Catholicism, born on the Jesuit plantations of his childhood, that would provide researchers with a road map to his descendants.

Cornelius had originally been shipped to a plantation so far from a church that he had married in a civil ceremony. But six years after he appeared in the census, and about three decades after the birth of his first child, he renewed his wedding vows with the blessing of a priest.

His children and grandchildren also embraced the Catholic church. So Judy Riffel, one of the genealogists hired by Mr. Cellini, began following a chain of weddings and births, baptisms and burials. The church records helped lead to a 69-year-old woman in Baton Rouge named Maxine Crump.

Ms. Crump, a retired television news anchor, was driving to Maringouin, her hometown, in early February when her cellphone rang. Mr. Cellini was on the line.

She listened, stunned, as he told her about her great-great-grandfather, Cornelius Hawkins, who had labored on a plantation just a few miles from where she grew up.

She found out about the Jesuits and Georgetown and the sea voyage to Louisiana. And she learned that Cornelius had worked the soil of a 2,800-acre estate that straddled the Bayou Maringouin.

All of this was new to Ms. Crump, except for the name Cornelius—or Neely, as Cornelius was known.

The name had been passed down from generation to generation in her family. Her great-uncle had the name, as did one of her cousins. Now, for the first time, Ms. Crump understood its origins.

"Oh my God," she said. "Oh my God."

Ms. Crump is a familiar figure in Baton Rouge. She was the city's first black woman television anchor. She runs a nonprofit, Dialogue on Race Louisiana, that offers educational programs on institutional racism and ways to combat it.

She prides herself on being unflappable. But the revelations about her lineage—and the church she grew up in—have unleashed a swirl of emotions.

She is outraged that the church's leaders sanctioned the buying and selling of slaves, and that Georgetown profited from the sale of her ancestors. She feels great sadness as she envisions Cornelius as a young boy, torn from everything he knew.

"NOW THEY ARE REAL TO ME"

Mr. Cellini, whose genealogists have already traced more than 200 of the slaves from Maryland to Louisiana, believes there may be thousands of living descendants. He has contacted a few, including Patricia Bayonne-Johnson, president of the Eastern Washington Genealogical Society in Spokane, who is helping to track the Jesuit slaves with her group. (Ms. Bayonne-Johnson discovered her connection through an earlier effort by the university to publish records online about the Jesuit plantations.)

Meanwhile, Georgetown's working group has been weighing whether the university should apologize for profiting from slave labor, create a memorial to those enslaved and provide scholarships for their descendants, among other possibilities, said Dr. Rothman, the historian.

"It's hard to know what could possibly reconcile a history like this," he said. "What can you do to make amends?"

Ms. Crump, 69, has been asking herself that question, too. She does not put much stock in what she describes as "casual institutional apologies." But she would like to see a scholarship program that would bring the slaves' descendants to Georgetown as students.

And she would like to see Cornelius's name, and those of his parents and children, inscribed on a memorial on campus.

Her ancestors, once amorphous and invisible, are finally taking shape in her mind. There is joy in that, she said, exhilaration even.

"Now they are real to me," she said, "more real every day."

She still wants to know more about Cornelius's beginnings, and about his life as a free man. But when Ms. Riffel, the genealogist, told her where she thought he was buried, Ms. Crump knew exactly where to go.

The two women drove on the narrow roads that line the green, rippling sugar cane fields in Iberville Parish. There was no need for a map. They were heading to the only Catholic cemetery in Maringouin.

They found the last physical marker of Cornelius's journey at the Immaculate Heart of Mary cemetery, where Ms. Crump's father, grandmother and great-grandfather are also buried.

The worn gravestone had toppled, but the wording was plain: "Neely Hawkins Died April 16, 1902."

28

"A Million Questions" from Descendants of Slaves Sold to Aid Georgetown

RACHEL L. SWARNS AND SONA PATEL

Rachel L. Swarns continued to report on descendants of the Maryland Jesuit enslaved community. In a New York Times *story published on May 20, 2016, Swarns and Sona Patel highlighted the stories of several people who had just learned that the Jesuits had sold their ancestors. This painful knowledge was leading to new understandings of their family histories and diverse opinions about how Georgetown and the Jesuits should make amends.*

African-Americans have long lived with unanswered questions about their roots, missing branches in their family trees and stubborn silences from elders reluctant to delve into a painful past that extends back to slavery. This month, scores of readers wrote to us, saying they had finally found clues in an unexpected place: an article published in *The New York Times*.

The story described the sale of 272 slaves in 1838. The men, women, and children were owned by the nation's most prominent Jesuit priests. And they were sold—for about $3.3 million in today's dollars—to help the college now known as Georgetown University stay afloat. We asked readers to contact us if they suspected that their ancestors were among those slaves, who had labored on Jesuit plantations in Maryland before being sold to new owners in Louisiana.

With the help of Judy Riffel, a genealogist hired by the Georgetown Memory Project, a group dedicated to supporting and identifying the descendants of the slaves, we were able to confirm the ancestry of several respondents. Here are their stories, edited and condensed for clarity.

CHARLES HILL, 74

Great-great-grandson of Bill and Mary Ann Hill

My father always told me that we came out of Maryland, and that the name of the slave ship was Jackson. But that's all he would tell us.

So when my cousin called me about the story, I couldn't believe it. I couldn't believe it. I said that was why my father wouldn't tell us. He didn't want to disturb our Catholic faith. He didn't want to lose us.

That whole part of my family is Catholic. They didn't cuss. They didn't drink. They didn't smoke. I'm the middle kid. I wanted to be a bad boy, and my father wasn't going to have that.

I'm still Catholic today, Knights of Columbus, fourth degree.

You know, that's pretty much what saved me. I grew up with all those renegades and hoodlums, but I'm 74 years old and haven't been to prison. I believe in my rosary. I believe in my prayers. I believe in my candles. I'm not angry at the church. I love my church. What happened with slavery, that was back in the day.

I feel good about knowing more about my family's history. My uncle Abraham was a carpenter like my great-great-grandfather. He thought he was Noah, he could make boats so smooth. Peter Hill, the grandson of Bill Hill, a slave, was a blacksmith. And you can't beat me with sheet metal and a hammer. I owned my own body shop in Santa Monica, Calif.

What should Georgetown do? Put up a monument with our forefathers' names on there. Give some scholarships to the kids. I'm 74. I'm on my way out of this world. If I could leave something behind to educate my grandkids, that's what I would like to do.

SANDRA GREEN THOMAS, 54

Great-great-granddaughter of Sam Harris and Betsy Ware Harris

I thought that we were from Louisiana. It never occurred to me that we were from any place else because we were so Catholic. We are an extremely close-knit family. Growing up, there were always discussions about the family and the family history.

William Harris was my great-grandfather. I knew that. I knew that he was born around 1850, and I knew that he was born a slave. That's why we talked about him so much, because of what he and his family were able to accomplish.

After the Civil War, they amassed property as a family. They founded St. Mary's Chapel, and there was a school for colored children of the same name. I knew all about my great-grandfather. But I didn't know the details about his parents or the Catholic Church or Georgetown. In the mid-1990s, I lived within walking distance of Georgetown. I was pushing my babies around in a stroller, going on campus, without knowing anything about the connection.

I read *The New York Times*, and I saw the story there. I saw the photo of the cemetery, and I saw Maringouin, La. I went to the website of Georgetown's slavery archive and saw the names of my relatives.

I am still processing it. I find it somewhat comforting and amazing that the immediate family remained intact after being sold. But there's some sadness, too. When I first read it, I was just looking at the facts. But when you start thinking about it, it is really horrific.

My great-great-grandmother had a 5-month-old child when she was forced onto that ship. That means she was pregnant or just giving birth when she was sold. When I realized that, my heart just broke for her.

I don't think that my family wanted to focus on that aspect of our history. I don't think they wanted to discuss those unpleasant details. You must understand that the older members of my family were very deferential to members of the clergy. Priests were always intimate associates of my family. They visited members of my family on a daily basis. We even had a family priest who every Christmas played Santa Claus—highball in hand—and distributed our toys.

There's a lot of hand-wringing, a lot of, "Oh my goodness, that was terrible. What can we possibly do?" But there's a lot Georgetown can do. The most obvious beginning is some sort of formal acknowledgment and apology from Georgetown officials to the descendants.

Next, since the Jesuits took away these individuals' right to freedom and self-determination, it follows that a Georgetown education should be offered to all descendants who wish it. One of the values espoused in this nation is that a good education is the best way to achieve personal liberty and self-determination. Of course, there are going to be people who aren't interested in that, so for them there would have to be other remedies.

It's complicated, but not insurmountable. It's actually pretty clear-cut in a situation like this. There's so much continuity from generation to generation. Our families are still here.

ORLANDO WARD, 55

Great-great-great-grandson of Bill and Mary Ann Hill

I remember, when I was younger, I would ask my grandfather Remus Hill where we were from, and he would say Maringouin. When I asked, "What about before that?" he would get hesitant and very solemn and say, "I could take you back as far as Maryland, but it would make your toes curl." He was upset by the memory. So I didn't push him. That was not a place he wanted to go.

It didn't knock me off my chair when I was reading the story. But I did sit up straight. I had to process it. How do you reconcile this with a faith that brought you into adolescence and one that you're still tied to through your mom and the memory of your grandfather? That's kind of where I am: putting the pieces together, trying to look at all sides of the equation.

Let's jump ahead and talk about reparations. How do you really value the damage that was done in a way that's straightforward and fair? Everybody should have scholarships, yes. But not everybody wants to go to Georgetown. The more important thing to me is to memorialize the 272 and, at the same time, the people who sold them and the people who brought the slaves to Louisiana. What do their descendants have to say about it? I don't know all the emotions they would go through; I can't fully get into their shoes. But I think it's important for both sides to be pointed out and memorialized, not villainized, to begin to build a model for healthy dialogue.

I have a 12-year-old son, and we live in a fairly diverse community where African-Americans are in the minority. He had a history project not too long ago where kids were asked to trace their families. Many of his European-American classmates could go all the way back to Ireland, England, and Spain. I could take him to Louisiana, and that's as far as I could go. As African-Americans, we've grown to accept that. But we've also known there's another door there that we didn't have a key to.

Now there's a chance to go back as far as we can so that my son can understand the circle of life. And his children will understand even more. I don't have to watch "Roots" 150 times anymore to imagine how we could come from there to here. I have a road now that I can look at. The ultimate goal now is, gosh, can we get across the Atlantic and figure out what port in Africa we were shipped from? That's where my curiosity has started to take me.

ROCHELL SANDERS PRATER, 55

Great-granddaughter of Jackson Hawkins,
who was about 3 when his family was sold

I'm going to be honest. This came to me at the right time in my life. It's a blessing from above for me. I'm at an age where I'm hungry to know where I came from. My grandma had always told us we were from the Eastern Shore of Maryland. But nobody ever talked about slavery in our family.

I was born in 1960. We were raised Catholic, and when I was coming up, blacks sat on one side of the church and whites sat on the other. A rebel spirit inside me said that something was wrong with that picture. How could a priest talk about Jesus' love and split up the congregation like that? I knew something was wrong. But I didn't know the history.

A young lady I know posted that photo of the headstone that ran with the story on Facebook. All my family is buried in that graveyard: my mom, my dad, my sister, my brother. I thought, "That might be my family." I couldn't believe it. I'm still actually in shock. I have a million questions for my ancestors now.

I know some things about slavery. I know that the deeper south you went the harder it was. I did not know that my family was used as leverage to help Georgetown. I did not know that. The priests sold human beings like they sold china. That's sinking in right now. But I'm not angry.

I trust that this is a divine intervention. It's a gift from God that can help heal this nation. I've been going to meetings with a white friend of mine; we're talking about racism and trying to bring blacks and whites together. The South African truth and reconciliation process is a model we may want to explore. I don't want to talk anymore. I don't want to have a dialogue about it. I want us to do something.

29

Louisiana Families Dig into Their History, Find They Are Descendants of Slaves Sold by Georgetown University

TERRY L. JONES

The GU272 descendant community grew as the news spread. Terry L. Jones, a reporter in Baton Rouge, Louisiana, spoke with descendants in the area who had researched their family histories. Published in The Advocate on Juneteenth, June 19, 2016, Jones's article sheds light on the close-knit community that grew out of the GU272 in Maringouin, Louisiana.

Growing up in tiny Maringouin, Jessica Tilson often heard that everyone in town was somehow related.

The 34-year-old Southern University student brushed off the statements as just a colloquial expression for the kinship residents living in the quaint Iberville Parish town felt toward one another.

However, Tilson recently learned more than just geography and skin color bonds her to many neighbors, classmates and fellow church members. She shares blood connections with them as well.

She also now understands her family's long connection to the Catholic faith and the tale that one of her ancestors implored family members to retain ownership of more than 60 acres of farmland near La. 76 in Maringouin that he purchased in 1898.

It all traces back to the sale of 272 slaves in 1838 by the Jesuit priests running the institution of higher learning known today as Georgetown

University. The group of men, women and children ended up in Louisiana, mostly working plantations in Iberville and Ascension parishes.

Tilson recently discovered she is the descendant of at least eight slaves the Jesuits sold to pay off mounting debts that could have forced the school to shut down.

Her family tree—populated by marriages between the children of the Georgetown slaves—gives researchers of the sale keen insight into how the slaves tried to maintain a sense of community and hold onto traditions dear to them despite the harsh realities they faced as the forced labor for wealthy, white plantation owners.

"They used to tell us we need to stick together with the people we grew up with in Maringouin, but I didn't know why," said Tilson, who now lives in Baton Rouge with her two children. "I see now it's because we're basically related somehow."

Over the past school year, students, alumni and professors at George-town have examined the slave sale, coming to terms with its financial impor-tance to the Catholic university and figuring out how the modern institution should honor people once deemed to be mere property.

The sale has gotten national prominence with articles published by *The New York Times*, including one in April that chronicled the sale and the cir-cumstances of the slaves' subsequent lives on rural plantations in Iberville, Ascension, and Terrebonne parishes. The article also revealed that Maxine Crump, a former Baton Rouge television news anchorwoman turned com-munity activist, was a descendant of Cornelius Hawkins, a 13-year-old boy named in the sale documents.

But it was an article also featuring Crump, published by *The Advocate* in May, that sent Tilson on a fact-finding mission of her own.

Tilson has spent hours upon hours over the past month tracing her family's origins as far back as she could, making connections to 1838 sale.

She admits digging into her family's past is both exciting and frustrating.

Reading some of the written statements that have been uncovered from priests involved in the sale struck several emotional chords for her.

"As a human being, how can you listen to someone begging—pleading—for their lives and family? And their cries and pleas fell on deaf ears," she said. "They were enslaved in Maryland already, but they didn't want to go Loui-siana. It pissed me off extremely when (the priests) decided that educating white children meant more to them than my family's well-being.

"I wish I could ask them, 'Was it really worth it?'"

Tilson's research unearthed the intricate—and sometimes confusing—web linking her family to many others who share her native roots in Mar-ingouin. But it also has led to the discovery of family she never knew she had—like the husband and children of Karran Harper Royal, who are her distant cousins.

"In Louisiana, there is zero degrees of separation," said Harper Royal, a 52-year-old education advocate living in New Orleans. "I sit up late at night researching all this ancestry stuff. My husband calls my research 'poking dead people.'"

Like Tilson, the news coverage of the Georgetown sale sent her on a hunt into the past. Both women found themselves making frequent trips to the Louisiana State Archives building, where one day, they met while searching for the faint footprints their ancestors left behind through historic documents.

"I go to the Louisiana Archives building about 25 hours a week. They know me by name now," Tilson said joking. "What was supposed to be this one-day thing for me turned into something more."

Crump learned about her connection to the 1838 slaves from the founder of the Georgetown Memory Project, a nonprofit dedicated to finding the descendants of the slaves.

The nonprofit hired Baton Rouge genealogist Judy Riffel, who had knowledge and experience investigating the lives of the Georgetown slaves, as she had done this work a decade earlier for a woman whose family tree also extended back to the sale.

Like she has done for many others who now suspect they could be the descendants of the Georgetown slaves because of the attention from *The New York Times* article, Riffel also helped Tilson and Harper Royal on their journeys to become the budding genealogists for their families.

"A lot of descendants are descendants from many of (the slaves) because they intermarried," Riffel said. "They had limited people in the area they could marry. I've got brothers and sisters marrying sisters and brothers of other families. You see a lot of Hawkins marrying Butlers, Harrises, and the Scotts."

One of Tilson's first discoveries was her blood relation to Crump.

"A lot of my family members were shocked when I told them that we were related to Maxine," she said.

"To us, calling each other 'cuz' was no different from black people calling each other 'brother' and 'sister' in the '70s," adds Tilson's 54-year-old mother, Debra Tilson. "'Cuz' was our way of saying, 'Hey, friend' and that we all get along."

Jessica Tilson said Crump is the great-granddaughter to one of two sons Cornelius Hawkins had in his marriage to Eleanor Scott, the daughter of Bennet and Clare Scott, who also were aboard the same ship as Cornelius and his parents, Patrick and Letty Hawkins.

Tilson said the Scotts lived next door to the Hawkins in Maringouin on West Oak Plantation—where the Georgetown slaves shipped to Iberville Parish ended up.

Tilson's family members are direct descendants of Matilda Hawkins, Cornelius and Eleanor's daughter.

Harper Royal has discovered her husband is a descendant of Francis Hawkins, Cornelius Hawkins' brother, who also was a part of the 1838 sale.

"I'm so into this genealogy stuff. I'm doing this for my children," Harper Royal said. "I want to make sure there is something for my children so they understand what their family history is when we're dead and gone. We have to tell our own story."

Besides her family tree, Tilson's research also has led to the discovery of a bill of sale detailing how her great-great-great-grandfather James Henry Hicks in 1898 purchased land where West Oak Plantation had been located.

According to the faded document, Hicks paid $698 for 69 acres, which he did through annual installments of $118.68.

Tilson said the family assumed Hicks had acquired the land through sharecropping. It wasn't until recently that the property, which has been subdivided through the years to various family members who use it for farming, took on a more significant meaning as part of their family's legacy.

"We own something they actually worked for," Tilson said. "Now we see the history behind it."

Tilson is organizing her research into a binder she hopes will become her family's tome, detailing their history through documents and an extensive family tree.

"The story hasn't ended. We're still doing some digging," Tilson's mother said. "We want to try and make this one of the largest family trees anyone has ever seen."

The marriages between the families of the Georgetown slaves is something history professor Adam Rothman suspected happened as he and his colleagues began piecing together what they could find about the lives of some of the 272 slaves after they were sold.

The university has found baptismal and marriage records, ship manifests, and bills of sale they have posted online at the Georgetown Slavery Archive.

"It wasn't until I saw the family tree Jessica has constructed did I see just how extensive all those ties are," said Rothman, a member of Georgetown University's Working Group on Slavery, Memory, and Reconciliation, which has delved into this history. "It's not shocking. We know that community was very close knit. They maintained these connections to each other through slavery and the emancipation.

"We now just have a much better picture of their community."

Rothman said recent discoveries by the university of baptismal records from a church in Newtown, Maryland, will help Tilson and other descendants trace their family roots to as far back as the early 1800s.

"It's just a register of slaves baptized on this one particular plantation. It lists the baptism of children from Bennett and Clare Scott," he said. "Since the fall, we've been going through our archives to digitize material relevant to people. In Louisiana and other Catholic areas, you have these sacramental records which are meaningful. In them, the slaves are represented as people with souls and not just property."

The university's Working Group is still exploring Georgetown's history and involvement with the slave trade. Many of the descendants, like Harper Royal, are anxiously waiting to see if the university will attempt to make amends for the sale, possibly through scholarships to the descendants to attend the prestigious university.

"At the very least, there should be some type of memorial," Harper Royal said. "After all, the blood, sweat and tears of these people that kept this university afloat. Scholarships would be nice."

30

My Family's Story in Georgetown's Slave Past

CHERYLLYN BRANCHE

Cheryllyn Branche's ancestors were sold by the Maryland Jesuits in 1838. In this essay published in the New York Times *on September 2, 2016, Branche shares how she learned of her family history and the impact that this knowledge had on her faith and identity. The retired principal of a Catholic school, Branche went on to become the president of the GU272 Descendants Association.*

One fall day in 1838, Jesuit priests from Georgetown University assembled enslaved people and walked them to a ship at a wharf south of Washington. The boat was not filled with silver or wood or cotton, but with 56 people, some of the 272 enslaved humans kept by the university.

The 56 people were unaware of the life of terror that awaited them when the boat docked in New Orleans. Georgetown was in debt and needed cash; so its priests forced the African-Americans they had enslaved onto the ship and sold them down the river.

My relatives—Hillary Ford, Henny Ford, their infant Basil and others—were on that ship. Hillary and Henny were my maternal grandmother's grandparents; their son Basil was my grandmother's father. They didn't live that long ago: I knew family members who had known them. They were real people with real names. They loved their child and would have done anything to escape the nightmare of their reality.

Hillary, Henny, and Basil were sold together to the Ascension Plantation, later called Chatham Plantation, in Ascension Parish, Louisiana. Henry Johnson, the former governor of the state, owned it; he bought my ancestors.

This is family history that I just learned in May, when I got a call from a Georgetown alumnus, Richard Cellini, who was working to make sure the school reckoned with its past. The Catholic Church, central to my life and the life of my family, had been involved in the sale of my ancestors.

Several months after learning this news, I remain rooted in my faith: Early on I was taught that faith is in God, not in man. If I had found out as a child what Georgetown and the Jesuits did to my family, I don't know if I would have been able to separate my faith from the actions of the church.

Georgetown announced this week that it will offer descendants of the enslaved preferential status in applying to the school, the same as it would treat legacy applicants. I listened to Georgetown's president, John J. DeGioia, speak eloquently Thursday about the school's plans to address the stain of slavery, and to help our nation to heal.

The school will offer a formal apology, build a memorial, and create an institute for the study of slavery. I wonder if my grandmother's story will have a place there.

My maternal grandmother, Louise Ford Rogers, granddaughter of two people sold by Georgetown, lived a block and a half from her church and just a short distance from the Catholic school she attended and where my mother, her daughter, eventually worked. It amazed me to watch my grandmother. She had a lot of pride in her faith and she practiced it fervently. She was so involved in the church I thought she was a saint. She worked in the rectory; she brought food to the elderly. She went to mass every day and gave money to the church.

She wasn't dull, though; she was fun. She loved church music and her family. I spent every day after school at her house, learning from her and watching her cook. Memere, as she was known in the neighborhood, was a good cook and always had something to offer, a meal, advice, a prayer or plums from her tree or mint from her garden.

What we never talked about was slavery, and our family history. She spoke of the Depression and how she and my grandfather survived, but she did not go further back in time to acknowledge her previously enslaved father, whose own parents had been enslaved and sold by the Jesuits.

I think she must have done what I do, and what many other African-Americans do, which is compartmentalize. We all know we are descendants of slaves. There are very few African-American people in this country who can say that they come from free people of color; yet so much is still unknown.

I dismissed the unknowns as lost. Now there is more to know—and if I don't pursue this there will be an ache in my heart. Not knowing who you are and where you came from leaves you without a sense of your true identity. Being able to access documents and information and connect with family has brought both joy and pain: the joy of discovery and the pain of accepting the realities of what my ancestors experienced.

Georgetown and the Jesuits buried my family's truth in institutional archives for almost two centuries. We need the truth to be shared. Our Catholic faith demands truth.

My mother and her sisters were the first generation to go to college in the Ford family, even though their mother, Louise Ford Rogers, with only an eighth grade education, taught neighborhood children to read. I wonder how the lives of my ancestors would have changed if opportunities presented to others were available to them, three and four generations ago, if my ancestors hadn't been enslaved for generations.

The Catholicism that the Jesuits and the Catholic Church taught my enslaved forefathers was rooted in discrimination. When I was a little girl, it was just a fact of life that Catholic schools and churches were segregated. It never dawned on me that my church was complicit in the slave trade; that's part of the painful process of discovery.

The eldest living descendant of the Ford family, my first cousin Maryann, was raised in a Catholic orphanage and became a nun, working directly with the archbishop of Detroit. Our family was as proud as any Catholic family, white or black, that had a relative belonging to a Catholic order, nuns or priests. As a child, I remember thinking how beautiful she was and wondering how Maryann had chosen her path.

I've been to the Georgetown campus once, around 20 years ago. I was working as a guidance counselor in Michigan, and I chaperoned a college trip for the students.

Back then I had no idea about my own family's connection to that school. Now, when I think about that beautiful, historic campus, I think about other prospective college students. Maybe it's where some of my relatives, descendants of the people sold by the school nearly 180 years ago, will come to learn.

31

Many in Slave Sale Cited by Georgetown Toiled in Southern Md.

RICK BOYD

Not everyone owned by the Maryland Jesuits in 1838 was sold to Louisiana. Some remained in Maryland. This article by Rick Boyd, published in the Southern Maryland Enterprise *on September 30, 2016, tells the story of Louisa Mahoney Mason and her children, the last people held in bondage by the Maryland Jesuits. Some of Mason's descendants continued to work for the Jesuits after emancipation and through the twentieth century. Their family history showcases the challenges of reconciliation in a community bound by a shared history and faith.*

Louisa Mahoney Mason had been warned what was about to happen, so on a fall day in 1838, she and her mother were hiding in the woods as most of the other slaves on the St. Inigoes plantation in southern St. Mary's County were rounded up and taken to Alexandria, Va.

From there they were herded onto ships headed to the Deep South.

The Jesuits, who owned and operated three plantations in Southern Maryland, and three more elsewhere in the state, had decided to sell 272 men, women and children to Louisiana slave owners, where they ended up working on sugar and cotton plantations.

The list of 93 slaves from St. Inigoes to be sold included a family of 10, including Watt, 45, Teresa, 42, and their eight children, ranging in age from 1 to 20.

The 44 slaves to be sold from Newtown, a Jesuit plantation near Leonard-town, included Harry, 65, and his wife, Dina, 68. Others were Susan, 20, and her daughter, 7. There were also two unnamed children, ages 1 and 2.

The 49 people at St. Thomas Manor in Charles County to be sold down the river included Charles, age 75. Also listed are seven women—Anny, Betsy, Matilda, Kitty, Margaret, Crissy and Jinny—and their 19 children, who are unnamed in the document.

Louisa Mason was among a number of slaves who were warned of the sale, likely by sympathetic Jesuits. They ran away and thus escaped the jour-ney south. When the danger was past, Mason returned to the plantation at St. Inigoes, where she continued in slavery until 1864, when slaves in Mary-land were emancipated. She remained with the Jesuits after that as well.

Melissa Kemp is the great-great-great-great-granddaughter of Louisa Mason. Her family has always known about their connection to the Jesuits and slavery in Southern Maryland, she said this week. Now she and other descendants of those held in bondage on the Jesuit plantations are learning more, and connecting with each other, spurred by Georgetown University's efforts to atone for its past.

It has long been known by historians that the Jesuits used slave labor on its plantations in Maryland, but the sale that Louisa Mason escaped has gained new attention as Georgetown, which was founded in 1789 and run by Jesuit priests, has undertaken to confront its historical connections to slavery.

Some of the proceeds from the 1838 sale of 272 human beings for $115,000—about $3.3 million in today's dollars—went to Georgetown to help keep the university afloat.

Early this month, Georgetown's president, John J. DeGioia, announced that he would offer a formal apology, and that the university would give pref-erence in admissions to the descendants of slaves whose labor benefitted the university.

This applies not just to the descendants of those sold and delivered to plantations in Louisiana, but to those in Southern Maryland and elsewhere whose ancestors lived and died on the Jesuit plantations before 1838, and to those who ran away to escape the sale that was intended to end the reliance on slave labor on the plantations. The admissions preference is intended to be the same as that given to the children of Georgetown alumni.

The university also will create an institute for the study of slavery and erect a memorial to the slaves whose work benefitted the university. Two uni-versity buildings that were originally named for two college presidents who were involved in the 1838 sale will be changed to Isaac Hall, the first name on the list of those to be sold to Louisiana, and Anne Marie Becraft Hall, to honor a free woman who founded a 19th-century school for black girls in Washington, D.C.

This attempt by the university to acknowledge nearly two centuries later that these black lives do matter attracted nationwide attention when it was announced.

However, most of the slaves sold in 1838 "were not at Georgetown," said the Rev. Thomas Clifford, a Jesuit priest who is currently the pastor of St. Ignatius Church at Chapel Point, the site of one of the Maryland plantations. Most of those enslaved by the Jesuits did not work for the university itself, but rather for the Jesuit plantations whose output was supposed to help support the university.

Georgetown's involvement was that some of its debts were paid through the sale of the slaves in 1838, Clifford said.

An 1838 list of the African American slaves that their owners intended to sell includes no last names, though the manifest of one of the ships that transported the slaves to Louisiana lists many of their surnames, including Butler, Harris, Hawkins, Plowden, Queen and Scott, according to a report prepared for Georgetown University.

Mason, Hill, Diggs, Dorsey, Greenfield, Mahoney and Merrick are among the other surnames of those enslaved by the Jesuits on their Maryland plantations, according to Adam Rothman, a history professor at Georgetown and also a member of the university's Working Group on Slavery, Memory, and Reconciliation, whose recommendations helped lead to the initiatives announced Sept. 1 by the university's president.

The report was unsparing of actions by the university and the Jesuit plantations before Maryland slaves were emancipated in 1864. Not all of the Jesuit slaves were sold to Louisiana in 1838—some escaped, some were elderly and some remained behind because they were married to spouses on other plantations and the Jesuits had promised not to separate families, Rothman said this week. "There are definitely families [descended from those slaves] still in Southern Maryland," he said.

Those who can demonstrate that their ancestors were enslaved by Jesuits on these plantations may be eligible for the preference in admission to the university, Rothman said.

Some of the families enslaved were split apart, as some family members, such as her own, escaped the sale, Melissa Kemp said. Some descendants in Louisiana and Maryland have taken DNA tests to re-establish these family connections, she said.

There is now a lot of information about the 272 slaves sold in 1838, she said, but little understanding of the others enslaved by the Jesuits. She encouraged their descendants to come forward. "Their ancestors also made contributions to Georgetown," Kemp said, "even if they were not part of the sale."

Kemp grew up in Woodstock in Baltimore County. Louisa Mason had two grandsons, Daniel and Gabriel Bennett, who were educated by the Jesuits at St. Inigoes and then offered jobs at Woodstock College, a Jesuit seminary from 1869 to 1974. Daniel Bennett was Kemp's great-great-grandfather. According to a 1958 article in the *Baltimore Afro-American*, Gabriel Bennett, Daniel's brother, was born at St. Inigoes in 1872 and arrived at Woodstock College as chief chef in 1898. He died in 1973 at age 100, and so was able to pass down family history to younger generations during his long life.

Kemp knows that members of the Butler, Barnes and Hawkins families from St. Mary's County also settled in Woodstock because of the Jesuit connection.

The Georgetown reconciliation project "is definitely a good move forward," Kemp said. The university's working group didn't include any descendants of Jesuit slaves, but has kept Kemp and others whose ancestors were slaves informed of its work, she said.

The group has "done tremendous work," she said, but Kemp and others want Georgetown's efforts to continue.

"Both sides need to be in continuing dialogue," she said.

Memorializing the lives of those who were enslaved is important, she said, because otherwise, "learning about slavery, you lose the human connection."

Some of the Louisiana and Maryland descendants are organizing the GU272 Foundation to promote education, racial healing and reconciliation, Kemp said, and hope to do that in partnership with Georgetown and the Maryland Province of Jesuits, which owned the slaves centuries ago.

The offer of preferential admission to Georgetown isn't of direct interest to Kemp, who has already earned a doctorate from Stanford and is now pursuing postdoctoral work in evolutionary biology at Harvard University. But she has encouraged her younger cousins to do well in school "because there is this university that may accept you."

Georgetown ties admission offers to financial aid packages based on family income, so aid would be available to these descendants. But the problem, Kemp said, is that some of the descendants of Jesuit slaves in Maryland and Louisiana live in "communities that are not very wealthy" and that don't offer schooling that would prepare them to meet Georgetown's admission standards.

As for the Jesuit plantations in Southern Maryland, much of the property has been sold by the Maryland Province of Jesuits to the state and federal governments. Part of St. Inigoes plantation is a now state forest, and part of it is occupied by the Navy facility at Webster Field.

Much of Newtown is now Newtowne Neck State Park, surrounded by Breton Bay in Compton.

Part of the Charles County plantation, listed in the 1838 records as St. Thomas's Manor, is now Chapel Point State Park near Port Tobacco, and part is the site of St. Ignatius Church, which is now celebrating its 375th anniversary.

Those plantations, which encompassed thousands of acres, were created largely by land grants shortly after the establishment of the Maryland colony in 1634. The labor on the Jesuit plantations was initially supplied by indentured servants, but around 1700, as the number of indentured servants dwindled, the Jesuit plantations, like many others in the region, turned to slavery.

The history of the Jesuit plantations is complex, covering as it does decades during which open Catholic worship was prohibited in the Maryland colony and a time when the Jesuits were suppressed by the pope, between 1773 and the early 19th century. The period when slaves were held by the Jesuits also includes the Revolutionary War and the War of 1812, both of which brought economic hardship to Southern Maryland.

During the years the Jesuits held people in bondage they justified it for various reasons, including the salvation of those they enslaved, as the Rev. Thomas Murphy makes clear in "Jesuit Slaveholding in Maryland, 1717–1838," published in 2001.

When the Jesuits decided to end the practice of slavery it was for purely economic reasons, said Mike Smolek, cultural resources manager at Patuxent River Naval Air Station, which includes Webster Field. In 1815, Brother James Mobberly, "a fairly brutal overseer" at St. Inigoes, Smolek said, wrote a justification for why the Jesuit plantations should get rid of their slaves, explaining that it was not profitable.

Mobberly argued that having free tenant farmers work the land would be less expensive—and less trouble—than keeping the slaves "because Blacks are more difficult to govern now, than formerly," he wrote in a letter to Georgetown's president.

In 1820, a priest named Peter Kenney visited the Jesuit plantations to report on conditions. At St. Inigoes those enslaved told him how much they disliked Brother Mobberly. He observed that the Jesuits were whipping slaves, and recommended that the practice of whipping pregnant women be prohibited. He said that tying up women in the parlors of priests to administer whippings was "indecorous" and should be stopped.

The 1838 sale was controversial within the Catholic church itself, according to the report of the Georgetown working group. Some Jesuits favored keeping the slaves, explaining it as a religious obligation. Others said the plantations and slaves should be sold and the money invested in Jesuit works.

A smaller group advocated for some form of emancipation. Jesuit authorities in Rome were inclined toward emancipation, but after lobbying by American Jesuits they agreed to the sale.

But the Jesuits in Rome placed conditions on the sale of slaves to Louisiana: Families were not to be divided. The continued practice of the Catholic faith by the slaves was to be ensured. The money raised from the sale of the slaves was to be used for endowment, not for operating expenses of the university or paying down the debt.

"In the end, none of these conditions was fulfilled," according to the report.

The terms of the sale were that the slaves were to be well treated, "but they weren't, really," said Clifford, the priest at St. Ignatius Church. Their new owners in Louisiana had money problems.

The slaves "labored under dreadful conditions on cotton and sugar plantations," according to the Georgetown report. "Many were sold again," some multiple times, breaking up families.

A Jesuit priest who visited the plantations where the slaves lived in 1848 reported that "their owners had neglected their religious instruction" and asked for funds to build a Catholic church for them.

"The University was party to a great harm that was inflicted over an extended period of time on a large number of people, whose human dignity was fundamentally disregarded for the sake of the University's balance sheet," the Georgetown report said.

Even in the context of the years before the Civil War, when slavery was widespread in Maryland there were "less shameful, even good alternatives that were rejected and moral resources that were neglected," the report added.

Julia King, professor of anthropology at St. Mary's College of Maryland, is preparing an archeological report based on research at Newtowne Neck State Park, a 776-acre property that was purchased by the state from the Maryland Jesuits in 1999.

The Newtown Manor House still stands near St. Francis Xavier Church in Compton and remains the property of the Catholic Archdiocese of Washington. It was built of brick in 1789, and the roof was raised in 1819. The Jesuits were building in a land of poverty, King said. "The craftsmanship of the brick work is extraordinary," she said. "It was the work of a skilled mason, who was very possibly enslaved." The bricks were made at the plantation, and the mortar was made of oyster shells.

At Newtown in 1717 there were 15 slaves, she said. In 1819 there were 43, and five years later there were 56 slaves. Some of them probably slept in the attic of the manor house, and some may have slept in the basement. King and students from the college investigated the archaeological remains of other sites where slaves lived and worked, many of which were abandoned in the years around the time of the 1838 slave sale.

The Jesuits kept records, but those who were enslaved are faceless, King said, often just first names on a census of men, women and children to be sold to plantations in Louisiana. "Their archives are these [archaeological] sites," she said.

Clifford told his parishioners at St. Ignatius Church that Georgetown's documents about its ties to slavery were coming out. Many knew about the past of the Jesuit plantations, "but some people didn't know that the church had slaves," he said.

These enslaved people were living in very poor conditions on the Maryland plantations, Clifford said, and the truly terrible thing was selling the slaves to Louisiana, which broke up families. It's valuable for the university and the church to recognize their past, he said, and Georgetown's initiatives provide a new opportunity for reconciliation. He's been involved in previous reconciliation endeavors to confront that past, but "it's always tricky to find people we can reconcile with . . . we don't know how to find them."

What's most interesting to him now, Clifford said, is that "we have descendants who have identified themselves. It makes it more tangible."

In some ways, reconciliation is more difficult and challenging because the descendants of those held in bondage by the church "are right in front of you," he said.

RECONCILIATION AND REPARATION

32

Remarks of Sandra Green Thomas
at Georgetown University's Liturgy
of Remembrance, Contrition, and Hope

Sandra Green Thomas, a descendant of the Harris and Ware families, spoke at the liturgy on April 18, 2017, about the courage and pain of her ancestors. She emphasized the importance of Catholicism in their lives, the meaning of forgiveness, and penance. Thomas's call for justice offered a poignant reminder of the continuing legacies of slavery and their impact on the lives of descendants.

I have been away from Georgetown for a long time. I have been away from the faith of my forefathers and foremothers—the Catholic faith—for an even longer time. But it is funny how the things you were taught as a child, and then thought you abandoned, all at once and without warning come back. Many days, in small and sometimes great ways, they emerge. These teachings from youth inform our decisions, color our perceptions, guide our steps, and sometimes trip us up. I have found the Tennessee Williams quote, "I tried to leave you behind me but I am more faithful than I intended to be," as true a representation of my residual religious education as any.

I return to this place, the Georgetown community, a place that filled my imagination as a girl and where I was lucky enough as a newly married woman to spend some of the happiest days of my life. I return different, aged, not filled with a sense of excitement and anticipation for the life that I am beginning but reflecting on the life I have lived and questioning its ultimate purpose.

Reflecting on my life naturally leads to musings about those who came before me. My people were humble and basically good. They provided for their families and they tried to protect their children, as best they could, from the cruelties of this world. But given what the world is and what people can be, they were not always as successful as they would have hoped.

I am also keenly aware of the steep obstacles that my immediate family and ancestors encountered. I know that the pain and suffering endured by African Americans has been lessened with each generation. Our disappointments and the fortitude needed for daily survival are both dwarfed by the experiences and the strength of those stalwart people who were ripped from their home place and sent to Louisiana. There is no comparison to be made between the enslaved of the Americas and any other group today or in history.

Their pain was unparalleled. Their pain is still here. It burns in the soul of every person of African descent in the United States. It lives in people, some of whom have no knowledge of its origins, but who cope with the ever-present longing and lack it causes.

All African Americans have hungered and thirsted for the bounty or promise that is America. The promise of the equality of man, the pursuit of happiness—those God given and unalienable rights.

But for so many of us it has only offered the meager scraps of:

+ You could not survive without the stewardship of the white race.
+ Pull yourself up by your boot straps.
+ Be patient, now is not the time for civil rights.
+ If only you would learn some personal responsibility.
+ And your reward for your sufferings and sacrifices will be in heaven.

What group in this country has demonstrated more faith, more belief in the American promise, more faith in heaven and the final communion with God and the saints than African Americans?

We all know that faith can be transcendent. Real faith, deep abiding faith in the face of indignities and systematic genocide must be transcendent. My race was taught that heaven, the place of peace where milk and honey flowed, was only attainable through faith. The ability to transcend the realities of life in this country has been a necessary tool in the survival kit of my people.

For the 272, I believe that their Catholic faith enabled them to transcend. No matter how incongruous their existence was with the gospel of God's love and protection, they clung to their faith. And even when they were deprived of the opportunity to practice it, they remained faithful and passed their faith to subsequent generations.

But we also know that there are realities in this world, realities that come with life. And I am speaking of life not as mere existence but something that has a quality to it that edifies the mind, enriches the soul, and enables the body.

We, African Americans, are flesh just as Jesus was the word made flesh. To be denied those things that rightly come from the labor of our bodies, to have our minds deprived of the tools to develop to their potential, to live under soul-crushing injustice, stress, and deprivation. Surely, these are sins against the word of God and therefore, God himself.

These people—the 272 men, women, and children we remember today—endured all of these. Their descendants are still experiencing them today.

Now, I may be making some of you uncomfortable. The Bible says, "Judge not, lest ye be judged." It also says, "If we discerned ourselves, we would not be under judgment." In fact, God has given us the tools to judge, our hearts and minds.

I know that it is difficult to honestly look at yourself, the way you operate in the world and your true motivations and priorities. Very few people ever experience one moment of self-revelation, and even fewer are courageous enough to reveal that secret part of themselves to another.

To truly look at yourself is to see the beautiful face of God with all its imperfections and possibilities too. This applies to others not like you, all races and all peoples. As you hold that mirror before you and see the face of God, know that when you gaze at another, they are the image and embodiment of God as well. And if you have wronged them, you must seek forgiveness.

Forgiveness is a major pillar of the Catholic faith. The certainty of forgiveness upon an act of contrition is one of the most hopeful and joyful aspects of the faith and its sacrament of penance.

Penance is very important. Penance is required when you have violated God's law. Penance, although personal and sometimes private, is not self-determined. Penance is not easy. Penance is not self-serving. Penance is not for public show, but penance is necessary.

So, I return. No, we the descendants, return to the home place, to our ancestors' home place acknowledging contrition, offering forgiveness, hoping for penance, and more importantly seeking justice for them and ourselves.

33

Remarks of Fr. Timothy Kesicki, SJ, at Georgetown University's Liturgy of Remembrance, Contrition, and Hope

On April 18, 2017, Georgetown University held a Liturgy of Remembrance, Contrition, and Hope in honor of the 272 persons sold by the Maryland Jesuits in 1838 and their descendants. Fr. Timothy Kesicki, SJ, the president of the Jesuit Conference of Canada and the United States, apologized on behalf of the Jesuits for the society's participation in the slave trade. President DeGioia apologized on behalf of the university. Nearly one-hundred descendants attended the event in Georgetown's Gaston Hall. This is the text of Kesicki's apology.

Sisters and Brothers—most especially the upwards of 100 descendants who have traveled so far to pray with us—today the Society of Jesus, which helped to establish Georgetown University and whose leaders enslaved and mercilessly sold your ancestors, stands before you to say that we have greatly sinned, in our thoughts and in our words, in what we have done, and in what we have failed to do.

Saint Ignatius Loyola mandates that each Jesuit pray for the grace to examine his conscience so that he might feel interior knowledge of his sins, feel the disorder of his actions, and, hating these, pray for the grace to correct himself.

We pray with you today because we have greatly sinned and because we are profoundly sorry.

The African American historian Fr. Cyprian Davis, of the Order of Saint Benedict, expresses our great sin when he wrote, "The tragic sin of Jesuit slaveholding reveals not only the harshness of slavery as it really existed, but the moral quicksand of expedience and inhumanity that sooner or later trapped everyone involved in the ownership, buying, and selling of human beings."

It is our very enslavement of another, our very ownership of another, culminating in the tragic sale of 272 men, women, and children, that remains with us to this day, trapping us in a historic truth for which we implore mercy and justice, hope and healing.

To think that together with those 272 souls we received the same sacraments, read from the same scriptures, prayed the same prayers, sang the same hymns, and praised the same God, how did we, the Society of Jesus, fail to see us all as one body in Christ? We betrayed the very name of Jesus for whom our least Society is named.

Now, nearly 200 years later, we know that we cannot heal from this tragic history alone. Many have confessed and labored to atone for this sin, mostly within the confines of our own religious houses and apostolic works. Because we are profoundly sorry, we stand before God and before you—the descendants of those whom we enslaved—and we apologize for what we have done and for what we have failed to do. Agreeing with poet and playwright Ntozake Shange that apologies "don't open doors or bring the sun back," we apologize nonetheless, hoping to imagine a new future. And with the pain that will never leave us, we resist moving on, but embrace moving forward with hope.

Attributed to Augustine, sainted son of Africa, and sainted son of the Church: "Hope has two beautiful daughters. Their names are Anger and Courage; anger at the way things are, and courage to see that they do not remain the way that they are."

Justly aggrieved sisters and brothers—having acknowledged our sin and sorrow and having tendered an apology, we make bold to ask on bended knee forgiveness. Though we think it right and just to ask, we have no right to it. Forgiveness is yours to bestow—only in your time and in your way. Until then, may we confront together with passion our past, present, and future, seeking the courage to see that things do not remain the way they are. And on this Easter Tuesday, fix our eyes on Jesus, confident that even with your great grief and right rage and our sin and sorrow, "All will be well and all will be well and every kind of thing will be well"—to help all God's children and God's greater glory. May it be so.

34

Her Ancestors Were Georgetown's Slaves. Now, at Age 63, She's Enrolled There— as a College Freshman

TERRENCE MCCOY

Mélisande Short-Colomb was one of the first GU272 descendants to matriculate at Georgetown after the school formally acknowledged its history. This August 30, 2017, Washington Post *profile by Terrence McCoy chronicles her decision to attend the school. Short-Colomb has also told her story in her own words in a TEDxGeorgetown talk called "Kingdom of Disruption," available on YouTube.*

On the first day of class at Georgetown University, the 63-year-old freshman left her dorm room in Copley Hall, carrying highlighters and a legal pad. Walking down the hallway, her gray-blond dreadlocks swinging, her heavy bracelets chiming, Mélisande Short-Colomb gave her schedule a quick look. Today she'd attend the "Problem of God," a course on the existence and nature of God. And tomorrow would bring the class she'd been waiting for: African American Studies.

It was a subject with which Short-Colomb had recently become more acquainted. The history of her own family was the history of African Americans, and, she has learned, proof of how deeply the roots of slavery go in America's most prominent institutions and universities.

At a time when the nation is undergoing a tumultuous reckoning with the darkest chapter of its past, when protests have turned deadly in Charlottesville and college students across the country are demanding the renaming of buildings linked to slavery, Short-Colomb was quietly coming to terms with her own place in that sweep of history.

Her ancestors were among the 272 slaves Georgetown priests had sold in 1838 to help pay off the university's debts during a financially turbulent time. Now it was nearly two centuries later, the truth of what happened was finally out in the open and here she was, a member of her family, again in Washington but under very different circumstances.

The university has granted legacy status to the slaves' descendants as part of an effort to atone for the sale of their ancestors. But only two have come so far. One is 20. The other, the oldest degree-seeking undergraduate at Georgetown, is Short-Colomb.

She had completed so much of life—she had become a mother, grandmother, professional chef—but increasingly she was feeling like a piece was missing. Did she owe something to the slaves who were sold and the children who followed, and would joining with the university that began it all bring some sense of resolution?

Hoping her experience at Georgetown would help answer this question, she walked into the Walsh Building. The elevators weren't working, so she climbed the steps beside scores of younger students—"kids," Short-Colomb described them—before stopping to catch her breath. "I'm not 18 anymore," she said.

She arrived at Room 496. Most of the students were already inside. She found a seat near the front, took out her legal pad and quietly waited for class to begin.

ORAL HISTORY, THEN THE TRUTH

Short-Colomb had heard the story her whole life, and in the summer of 1980, as she sat beside her grandmother in the family house in New Orleans, she listened once more. A local newspaper reporter was doing a story on the volunteer work of her maternal grandmother, Geneva Smith, who was saying their family wasn't from Louisiana but Baltimore. And they had been free.

"My great-grandmother was named Mary Ellen Queen," Smith told the reporter, according to the article. "She was beautiful, too. Even when she was old, she was a tall, beautiful, dark-skinned proud lady. Before the Civil War ended, the Queen family gave my great-grandparents their freedom, and they came down here to Terrebonne Parish because they heard that there was farmland. She told me how she came on a flatboat with a baby in her arms, and she remembered how the alligators would follow the boat all the way."

"I heard all the stories," is how Smith explained it.

But the stories never made much sense to Short-Colomb. Why had her family been freed? And why would they, a recently emancipated black family, ever travel to Louisiana to work land that was dominated by slaveholders? For Short-Colomb, there had never been any way to answer those questions. It's unusually difficult for black families to trace their roots. African Americans weren't listed in census records until 1870. So Short-Colomb, who had recently dropped out of college and become a chef, reconciled herself to never knowing. She told her children the same story she had been told, always wondering which details were missing.

Decades would pass before the details started filling in last year. Her grandmother was dead now. So was her mother. It was just Short-Colomb that day last summer, reading a Facebook message, asking a simple question that would turn out to have a very complicated answer: Was she related to a woman named Mary Ellen Queen?

The woman writing the message was Judy Riffel, a genealogist who had been hired by something called the Georgetown Memory Project. Short-Colomb had read about it in an article in the *New York Times*, which told of the story of the Jesuit priests' sale of 272 slaves. She recalled feeling sad for the slaves. Now she was being told that her own family had been a part of that history, too.

She couldn't sleep that night. She felt nauseated, thinking about all of the stories her grandmother had told her that hadn't been true. Mary Ellen Queen hadn't been freed. She had been sold. And the people who did it were the same priests who helped make Georgetown one of the nation's most prestigious universities. She arose the next morning feeling better, with a purpose: She provided a DNA sample to the Georgetown Memory Project and connected with the rest of the descendants.

"I felt okay with the history of my family as I had it," she wrote last September to Richard Cellini, an alumnus of Georgetown University and the founder of the memory project, with whom she developed a quick rapport. "I had heard the story of... [ancestor] Abraham Mahoney and Mary Ellen Queen being sent south as young adults... So, that's my pedigree line as I know from familial oral histories."

There was now so much more to know. She wanted to know Washington and Georgetown and how her family had come to be owned by Catholic priests. But how could she find that out? She was all the way down in New Orleans, "extremely underemployed," as she put it, earning her keep at a friend's house by caring for the friend's elderly mother.

In January, Cellini sent her an opinion piece in the *New York Times*, describing Georgetown's decision to provide legacy status to descendants as "making reparations." The article angered Short-Colomb. Was that gesture meant to compensate for all that had happened?

"I don't like those people, and we have unfinished business," she said. "I might [be] ready to . . . exercise that 'preferential legacy status.' "

"Actually, I think you SHOULD go to Georgetown," Cellini said.

"I would," she said.

"Someone has to be the first," he said.

"I'm a million years out of school," she said. "We should have a test case from the descendant group. Perhaps it should be a brilliant 17-year-old!"

Suddenly unsure, she talked to her roommate, Marcia Dunmore, who encouraged Short-Colomb but was apprehensive nonetheless. "You're talking about a 60-plus-year-old person becoming a freshman, and just the idea of that is daunting, the social aspect of it," Dunmore recalled thinking at the time.

Cellini soon responded to Short-Colomb's note.

"It needs to be someone with wisdom, strength, imagination, intellect, vision, and courage. Does that sound like a 17-year-old to you?"

"It feels right," she said, finally agreeing. "I want to go back to the source of my family in America."

So she sat down and, feeling anxious and unsure, began an application to enroll as a freshman at Georgetown University.

"My story begins simply," she typed, and for the first time, began writing the real one. "My family was sold by the Society of Jesus of Maryland in 1838."

THE PURPOSE OF AN EDUCATION

Nearly 200 years later, Short-Colomb was sitting in the "Problem of God," looking around the classroom. There were young women with long black hair. There were young men in polos and leather shoes. There was the professor, a middle-aged white woman, who said, "Let me see here, who is here?" and started going through the roll call.

Short-Colomb wanted to be a resource to students like these, educate them on how slavery had shaped Georgetown, but she already knew there would be many with whom she would never completely bond. In her week on campus, there had already been times when she felt she didn't quite fit in. Like when a young white student disparaged Black Lives Matter in one of her orientation sessions, and she wondered what sort of household he had come from. Or when a young woman in her dorm had asked her, "And who are you?" and she had felt out of place, alone in her dorm room. Or when an English professor had given a tour of campus and mentioned the sale of the 272 slaves, but in her mind didn't probe its moral implications deeply enough.

A university spokesman said, "Slavery was discussed in depth."

But that was then, this was class and she wanted to do well, so she focused on what the professor was saying. She asked students to read a recent article in the *Atlantic* magazine titled, "Have Smartphones Destroyed a Generation?" which explored the ramifications technology has had on millennials.

"They're talking about you, and the answer is 'Yes,'" the professor joked, and the younger students laughed.

Other students started asking questions, but not Short-Colomb. She stayed quiet, trying to absorb an experience she didn't yet know how she would apply. She knew she wanted to study African-American history, but would that be her major? And if so, what would she do with it? She would be 67—past retirement age—when she finally graduated, and what would come next?

Maybe, she thought, she would stick around. Maybe she would go on to get a PhD. Maybe she would be one of those "career students" she sometimes heard of. Maybe this was it. Her family had finally returned to Georgetown, and she was home.

Class was ending, and Short-Colomb glanced at tomorrow's reading assignment, "The Death of Reading." She gathered her things and walked outside, seeing what the sale of her family had ultimately helped accomplish: the gothic buildings, the coiffed gardens, students walking in every direction.

"Look how beautiful this view is," she said quietly.

She reached her room on the fourth floor of the dormitory and noticed the time. It was already afternoon. The first day of class was over, but it wouldn't be long before tomorrow. She had so much reading to get through before then, and it was time to get to it.

35

A New Path to Atonement

MARC PARRY

After the national publicity over Georgetown's role in the slave trade had died down, reporter Marc Parry followed the negotiations between leaders of the university, the Jesuits, and the GU272 descendant community. More than two years after the national revelations of the Jesuits' participation in the slave trade, Parry's January 20, 2019, article in the Chronicle of Higher Education *examined the efforts to achieve an elusive reconciliation.*

CONFLICTS HAVE MIRED THE EFFORTS OF GEORGETOWN U. AND THE JESUITS TO MAKE AMENDS FOR THEIR INVOLVEMENT WITH SLAVERY. NOW A MORE LASTING RECONCILIATION MAY BE IN SIGHT.

In 1838, the Jesuit priests who managed Georgetown University rescued it from debt by selling the enslaved ancestors of people like Joseph M. Stewart. In 2016, Stewart sat down in an auditorium at Georgetown to watch its leaders tell the world how they planned to make amends. Their message left Stewart, a retired food-industry executive, feeling brushed aside.

For Georgetown's president, John J. DeGioia, the event was a chance to showcase his campus as a model of "the academy at its best." DeGioia had charged a committee with figuring out how to recognize Georgetown's slave roots. He now presented its embossed, dark-blue report as a call to arms for combating the legacies of slavery. "This is a moment to discover new ways of being a university," he said.

For Stewart, though, this moment should not have been happening. A devout Catholic, he was coming to grips with the reality that Jesuit priests had held his ancestors as chattel in Maryland and then shipped them to Louisiana in a mass sale. Stewart, now 76, and other descendants of the roughly 300 slaves involved in that transaction, known as the GU272, had not been represented on DeGioia's committee. They had implored the president's chief of staff to delay this event until they could be heard. When that failed, Stewart bought a last-minute plane ticket to Washington.

That afternoon, DeGioia vowed that the descendants would play a central role in Georgetown's reconciliation going forward. He laid out plans to rename buildings, establish an institute for the study of slavery, and erect a memorial to the GU272. Most notably, he announced that Georgetown would grant preferential admissions to descendants of those slaves, treating them akin to the children of alumni.

None of these steps, in Stewart's view, would significantly uplift descendants' lives. When DeGioia solicited questions, Stewart stepped to the front of the auditorium with a group of other descendants. They sought a partnership.

"Our attitude," Stewart told the Georgetown president, "is: Nothing about us, without us."

That confrontation captures the paradox of the university's reckoning. By opening a dialogue with descendants, Georgetown has won a reputation for going further than its peers in the national movement of colleges wrestling with their ties to slavery. But a gulf exists between Georgetown's rhetoric and the frustrating reality that descendants have faced over the two and a half years they have now been fighting to get Georgetown and the Jesuits to make a far bigger investment in mitigating the impact of slavery. The descendants' own conflicting agendas have only compounded the controversy.

The struggle has escalated to the top of the Roman Catholic Church. A year after Georgetown's announcement, an organization of descendants that Stewart helped establish sent a confidential petition to Rome. Its recipient: the Rev. Arturo Sosa, leader of the nearly 16,000-member order of Jesuit priests and brothers. The GU272 Descendants Association, whose membership has since climbed to about 1,300, pleaded with Sosa to resolve "a great and growing scandal in the church." Their 32-page petition, which has not been previously reported, can be read as a counterreport to the one that DeGioia unveiled at Georgetown.

In contrast with DeGioia's warm public embrace—a presidential visit to Louisiana, the ceremonial apology at Georgetown—the petition from the descendants' association detailed how the university and the Jesuits had privately obstructed their requests for "meaningful engagement." For over a year, the petitioners wrote, "we have literally been ignored." The descendants called on Sosa to send outside investigators to the United States. Those officials, they wrote, should study "the physical, social, educational, and economic harm and disadvantages that have resulted from the 1838 sale, continuing down into the present day." And they should help put together an agenda for "reparations and restorative justice" proportionate to that damage.

The descendants also demanded a full accounting of financial dealings connected with this history. Of particular interest: what seemed to have been a private reparations fund that the Jesuits had apparently liquidated around the time a public spotlight began to shine on the Georgetown slavery story.

And then a remarkable thing happened. Rome responded.

That letter from Sosa to Stewart is thought to be the first time since the 1800s that the Jesuits' leader has formally commented on the GU272 in writing. It has set in motion a series of talks whose outcome could be felt far beyond Georgetown. More than 150 years after slavery's abolition in the United States, many colleges and other institutions grope for answers to the dilemma of how to reconcile their complicity with America's original sin. What the descendants are negotiating might offer a way forward.

In Georgetown's case, the best place to begin thinking about that dilemma is not the university's hilltop campus in the nation's capital. Instead, it's 1,200 miles away, here in southern Louisiana, a half-hour's drive from Baton Rouge, in a rural farming community called Maringouin.

Maringouin is ground zero for the impact of the mass slave sale that saved Georgetown. About 900 of the town's 1,100 residents descend from the GU272, many of whom ended up enslaved on plantations in the area. The descendants in this region hold different opinions on how to redress that past. The more you talk with them, the more it can feel like stepping into a family quarrel.

On one hand, you will meet people like Maxine Crump. On a Sunday morning in late October, she leads a reporter to a narrow dirt road beside a dried-up bayou littered with tires.

"This was West Oak plantation," says Crump, a colleague of Stewart's on the board of the GU272 Descendants Association. "My ancestors have lived along this bayou since we came."

Crump, 72, was one of the first major figures to emerge in the current Georgetown drama. A trailblazer in Baton Rouge, she helped desegregate Louisiana State University and later became the first black reporter at a local CBS affiliate. She now runs a nonprofit group whose educational programs seek to eliminate racism.

The place she visits today does not have a white-columned manor for tourists to see. What it has, on both sides of the bayou, is fields of spear-like sugarcane plants, brown-stalked and green-leaved, each about seven feet tall. The land crawls with bugs—Maringouin means "mosquito" in French—and, hidden from sight, snakes. A breeze carries the sweet-and-sour smell of cane being harvested.

When Crump looks at seemingly benign scenes like this, what she thinks about is the forced laborers, deprived of education, working from sunup to sundown, who enriched the economy of Louisiana and the United States. And then, after slavery, all the ways that society conspired to keep her people from accessing what they had built. The swindling of their land. The sharecropping. The lynching. The subjugation within segregated libraries, hospitals, schools.

Crump also sees how people struggle to discuss all this, even today. People like Robert, an elderly farmer she strikes up a conversation with in a cane field this morning. He's fine talking about the machine that cuts the cane and the truck that hauls it away. But when a reporter brings up slavery, Crump spots his discomfort. She abruptly thanks him and walks away.

"Don't get him in trouble," she says. "It ain't changed, OK?"

Later, Crump explains that he might have been fired if she hadn't ended the conversation. She imagines the confrontation: *What are you doing talking about slavery? You don't like your job?*

The question of why any of this should matter to Georgetown was not something Crump had thought about until three years ago, when she got a call from an alumnus of the university, Richard J. Cellini. At Georgetown, black students had been protesting to change the names of two buildings that honored the Jesuit priests who had orchestrated the 1838 slave sale. Cellini, a technology-company executive and lawyer based in Cambridge, Mass., became curious about a different aspect of the story: What happened to the slaves?

In 2015, Cellini emailed a senior member of Georgetown's slavery committee to suggest that the university track down the slaves' descendants. Georgetown had tried, the official replied. But it appeared that all the slaves had "quickly succumbed to fever in the malodorous swamp world of Louisiana," he wrote, according to a copy of the email Cellini shared with *The Chronicle*. (The sender's name was redacted.) Unsatisfied, he founded the Georgetown Memory Project, an independent nonprofit group focused on tracing the lives of the GU272 and finding their descendants. As of this month, its genealogists have identified 7,712 direct descendants, about 4,000 of them living.

Crump, a resident of Baton Rouge, was driving to Maringouin to visit her mother on the afternoon that she first spoke with Cellini. She had always wondered how her family first came to Maringouin, and Cellini began to fill in the picture. She was descended from Cornelius Hawkins, a slave whom the Jesuits had sold to a Louisiana plantation at the age of 13. Hearing this, she felt as if her car was moving but she was standing still. She immediately felt love for her great-great-grandfather.

These days, that emotion mixes with frustration. Crump thinks George-town and the Jesuits have an obligation to rebuild this town. When the schools here desegregated in the 1960s, she points out, white people began fleeing, taking resources with them. Maringouin is now 86 percent black. The average household income is estimated to be $59,000 a year, according to the U.S. Census Bureau, compared with $81,000 nationwide. Nonfamily households—mostly individuals living on their own in Maringouin—fare worse, with an estimated average income of $24,000. The community's pub-lic high school shut down in 2009. In its place, the school district put in a STEM-oriented academy with selective admissions, which has struggled to attract students.

The solution to Maringouin's woes? Georgetown should build a private high school here, Crump says, and make it free for descendants. They should also set up a memorial or museum that would attract visitors.

"Anybody who learned how to sell people, must learn how to do what it takes to restore people," she says.

And yet others here see no such duty. Some resent Crump and her group for speaking on Maringouin's behalf. They take offense at visiting reporters who parachute in seeking scenes of poverty. Sure, Maringouin has people living in aluminum-skirted trailers. But it also has the retired chemist with the brick ranch house and an Audi in the garage.

If you ask Jessica "Millie" Tilson, another descendant, she will tell you that she feels satisfied with what Georgetown has done. Tilson, 37, appre-ciates the university's admission of wrongdoing and its faculty's engagement with the Louisiana descendants. She frequently shows around the journalists, Jesuits, and Georgetown folks who make pilgrimages here. She depicts Marin-gouin as a place more of community self-reliance than of systemic deprivation.

She points out what would have been one of the area's first local schools for black children: a tin-roofed structure, boarded up and tucked beside some woods. She speculates that some of the original GU272 may have built it for their grandkids. That's how she remembers it growing up around here: black people building what they needed—their own baseball field, their own bar. They hunted and shared the meat with their neighbors. They checked on the sick. They bartered.

Tilson, who now lives in Baton Rouge, does not have an easy life. This morning, she has just come off an overnight shift stocking groceries. She also works a day job at a uniform-cleaning company. She earns about $50,000 a year and owes $83,000 in student loans from the degree she earned at South-ern University and A&M College. She is a mother of two kids.

Still, she says, her whole family is against monetary reparations. She can't stomach putting a price on her ancestors' suffering, just as their enslavers did.

As for Georgetown's building a school in Maringouin, where she still has family, Tilson thinks the idea makes no sense. There aren't enough kids here. Plus, putting it here would be unfair to those, like her, who left.

Tilson cares deeply about the GU272 history. But much of Maringouin has lost interest in the story. That, anyway, is what you will hear from the mayor who ran the town until recently, Demi L. Vorise.

Tilson's mother, Debra, gets why. People, she says, have concluded that if Georgetown was going to do something for Maringouin, it would have done so by now. Georgetown, as they see it, is a mostly white college. Should Maringouin's residents depend on white people to save them?

"No," says Debra Tilson, "Maringouin wasn't built like that."

Within Georgetown and the Jesuit hierarchy, two key people are trying to negotiate a lasting reconciliation with the descendants, both of them 56-year-old white men. One is Joseph A. Ferrara, Georgetown's vice president and chief of staff. He is the guy behind the scenes who moves along projects that need management across different parts of the university. Raised in Charleston, S.C., he was a career civil servant before his arrival at Georgetown. He had never worked on racial-justice issues before the slavery project landed in his inbox.

The main Jesuit official collaborating with Ferrara, Rev. Timothy P. Kesicki, has kept a lower profile than Georgetown's leaders. His headquarters, located in a nondescript office building in downtown Washington, is less imposing than the arched hallways of polished stone that a visitor walks to reach Ferrara's space in the presidential suite at Georgetown's Healy Hall. But he may be more critical to whatever becomes of the descendants' ambitions.

To understand why, it helps to know a bit about the nearly 500-year-old order that Kesicki represents. The Jesuits are a centralized group divided into about 70 regions around the world, each run by a "provincial" appointed by the Rome-based leader, the superior general. As president of the Jesuit Conference of Canada and the United States, Kesicki coordinates the provincials' work in the U.S., including their ties to its 28 Jesuit colleges and universities.

Kesicki has worked with black communities in Detroit, teaching and pastoring in schools. He spent five summers at the Institute for Black Catholic Studies, at Xavier University of Louisiana, in New Orleans. The education at that institute aims to help priests like Kesicki minister to black Catholics, like Stewart, whose faith is often a legacy of church slaveholding.

"This touches at the core part of who I am," Kesicki says in an interview.

It was at Xavier years ago that Kesicki says he came to understand the 1838 slave sale that has lately occupied so much of Ferrara's time at Georgetown. Jesuit scholars had been publishing articles and books about that history long before the rise of an organized descendant community. They knew the Jesuits had been "among the biggest planters in Maryland," as Adam Rothman, a slavery historian at Georgetown, describes them in a 2017 article. By the 19th century, Rothman writes, those Jesuits owned about 300 slaves across a series of farms and plantations. "The profits from their labor subsidized the Jesuits' religious and educational activities," he writes, "including the Jesuits' flagship school, Georgetown College."

But the farms floundered, and the college faced crippling debt. In 1838, Rothman writes, the Rev. Thomas F. Mulledy, head of the Maryland Province and an ex-Georgetown president, arranged to sell the Jesuits' slaves en masse to two Louisiana planters for $115,000, or about $3.3 million today. Mulledy used part of the windfall to settle Georgetown's debts. "It's safe to say, and rather shocking to understand, that Georgetown really owes its existence to the sale of those slaves in 1838," Rothman, a member of its slavery committee, has said.

The sale that secured Georgetown's future was calamitous for the slaves themselves. The Jesuits' superior general in Rome at that time, Rev. Jan Roothaan, had acquiesced to it only under certain conditions: among them, that families would not be broken up, that the sick and elderly would be cared for, and that all the slaves would be able to continue practicing their faith. None of those conditions were fully met.

Fast forward to 2017. When the current holder of Roothaan's office, Father Sosa, received the GU272 descendants' petition in Rome, with its exasperated account of what they described as stonewalling by Georgetown and the American Jesuits, the document in his hands was different than reparations bids that had come before it in the United States. It was not a legal demand seeking individual monetary payments via the courts. It was a moral appeal for atonement by a church that had baptized their ancestors and then abandoned its pastoral obligations to care for them.

Sosa's reply was prompt and unequivocal. Jesuit enslavement and the 1838 sale "were a sin against God and a betrayal of the human dignity of your ancestors," he wrote to Stewart. He expressed deep concern for the legacy of that history. And he entrusted Kesicki and the U.S. provincials with figuring out a path toward reconciliation.

So how does Kesicki see reparations? Beyond an apology he offered, do the Jesuits owe any material debt to descendants?

Officials at Georgetown seem to think that *they* owe something. "While we acknowledge that the moral debt of slaveholding and the sale of the enslaved people can never be repaid," the slavery committee's 2016 report said, "we are convinced that reparative justice requires a meaningful financial commitment from the University."

When Ferrara is asked to explain that, he talks about two things. George-town, he says, will focus primarily on what it can "realistically and feasibly" do within its mission of teaching and research. Along those lines, he points to the admissions advantage for descendants and a free online archive of historical materials related to Jesuits and slavery. Ferrara also emphasizes Georgetown's racial-justice work writ large, such as its programs to study and solve problems like health disparities and mass incarceration.

But Kesicki, citing his continuing talks with descendants, prefers to avoid commenting on reparations, except for a general affirmation of his "absolute commitment" to reconciliation.

"The Jesuits have not formulated a statement like that," Kesicki says of the reparations remarks in Georgetown's slavery report. "We have to do some-thing," he adds. "Something has to come out of this."

His vague answer is notable because some evidence suggests that past Jesuit leaders not only recognized a debt, they also spent a lot of money try-ing to atone for it. They just didn't tell people.

The evidence comes from an unpublished thesis that has circulated at the highest levels of Georgetown and the Jesuit order. It was written in 2015 by a Jesuit seminarian, Sean Toole, who at the time was pursuing a master's degree in theology at Santa Clara University and who is now a priest teaching at a Jesuit high school in Baltimore. Toole's thesis, obtained by *The Chronicle*, describes how in the early 1960s the Maryland Jesuits sold property that had been part of a plantation where many of the GU272 were born. They knew the land's history. And so, Toole writes, the province wanted to use proceeds from the sale "to offer private and unrecognized restitution for its history of slave holding."

This so-called "secret apology"—Toole's words—took the form of an account called the Carroll Fund that was set aside to finance the education of poor, mostly black students in Jesuit schools. At the time Toole carried out his research, which drew on interviews with Jesuit officials in Maryland, the fund was worth about $10 million.

Here's how it worked. The province, Toole writes, gave lump-sum pay-ments to each of its 10 secondary and pre-secondary schools. The schools vowed to spend the money for needy students. The students who got the money could use it only for tuition. And neither the students nor the schools were made aware of the money's origins.

The Maryland Jesuits apparently liquidated the fund around the same general period that Georgetown's slavery committee and *The New York Times* began to focus public attention on the GU272 story. The province disbursed $1 million to each of its schools, according to the descendants' petition to Rome. The timing of that step has raised suspicions that the Jesuits may have cashed out to prevent the GU272 descendants from making claims on the money.

The Carroll Fund proves that the Jesuits felt a need "to try to reconcile themselves with the wrong that had been done," says Stewart, whose descendant association's petition sought access to the fund's records.

"Except that it had these ill elements of self-dealing," he says. "And it only served to strengthen their own institutions. And it did nothing to uplift descendants who had been those the harm had been done to."

Toole declined to be interviewed on the record, referring questions to Kesicki. Asked about the Carroll Fund, Kesicki provided *The Chronicle* with a written statement from the Maryland Province. It says the province has "no recorded statement describing the purpose for the founding of the Fund." But it notes that the Jesuits, in an era of national concern over civil rights and racial equality, used the money to make their schools "a viable option for racial minorities." That remains the aim of the fund under its current management by the individual schools, the statement says.

The Carroll Fund's 1960s-era creators would not have construed what they were doing as an explicit atonement for slavery, Kesicki says. And its modern-day stewards did not liquidate the fund to keep the money from the GU272 descendants, he says. They divided the money among the individual schools in the context of a national Jesuit restructuring process that will merge the Maryland Province with those of New York and New England in 2020.

The full extent of the Jesuits' entanglement with slavery is still emerging. Cellini's Georgetown Memory Project, drawing on scholarly research and its own archival sleuthing, estimates that the Maryland Jesuits owned about 1,000 enslaved people between the Jesuits' arrival in Maryland, in 1634, and the state's abolition of slavery, in 1864.

As Jesuit missions spread, so did slaves. The story directly and indirectly touches other colleges, including Saint Louis University, in Missouri, John Carroll University, in Ohio, and the College of the Holy Cross, in Massachusetts. Cellini contends that Jesuit slavery and slave-trading essentially "made possible the entire edifice of Jesuit higher education in America today."

Joseph Stewart thinks he knows a way to reconcile that history. It's a vision that goes back to that afternoon in 2016 when he and his fellow descendants appealed to Georgetown's president for a partnership. But the partnership that Stewart seeks today differs from the one he imagined then.

Stewart quickly realized, he says, that the GU272 Descendants Association was "barking up the wrong tree" at Georgetown. The university would be unlikely to play the marquee role in realizing descendants' ambitions. It wasn't just the unsatisfying slavery report. It was something more basic.

Georgetown, he saw, was governed by a board with a fiduciary duty to protect everything involved with its mission. That mission is not mitigating slavery. Georgetown, he says, has no responsibility to answer for the morality of the church.

"Georgetown is an institution—a fine institution—that needs to play a role in supporting the Jesuits," says Stewart, a former Kellogg Company executive, in an interview at his Florida home. "But the burden of this is not theirs. And so I want to stop pretending that it is."

No, the ultimate resolution would come from Rome. But Stewart also confronted another challenge: How could the descendants reach a resolution with Rome, when they themselves were divided?

The GU272 diaspora extends far beyond Stewart's native Maringouin. The opinions that Crump and Tilson expressed in that town only gesture at the breadth of descendants' views. In 2018 a collective of 200 descendants, calling itself the GU272 Isaac Hawkins Legacy Group, staged a news conference demanding that Georgetown pay them reparations. A third group of about 200 descendants, the Legacy of the GU272 Alliance, enlisted a team of seven lawyers in its own campaign to achieve an agenda of potential goals that included monuments, scholarships, monetary payments, and life-insurance policies.

Stewart's petition to Rome had accused the Jesuits and Georgetown of ignoring descendants. To Ferrara, though, it was the emergence of these different GU272 groups that delayed the university's response.

To break the stalemate, Stewart, Kesicki and Ferrara turned for help to the W.K. Kellogg Foundation, an $8-billion philanthropy whose board Stewart had once chaired. In August, with Kellogg's consultants acting as neutral facilitators, the GU272 descendant groups met privately in Baton Rouge for three days. They emerged, Stewart says, on a path to unification. In November, meanwhile, leaders from Georgetown and the Jesuit provinces gathered in New Orleans for their own private convening. They dug into social-science data on the legacies of slavery and segregation and aired their goals and anxieties. If the plan holds, all parties will face one another in a high-stakes meeting this year.

The outcome Stewart's side seeks: a $1-billion charitable foundation that would support the descendants of Jesuit slaves for generations while also working more broadly to mitigate the impact of slavery in America.

Under this proposal, the descendants would sacrifice direct personal gain in the present for community self-determination in the future. They would no longer have to plead with Georgetown or the Jesuits. Instead they would join with representatives of those institutions, along with other philanthropic investors, to run the new GU272 Foundation. Its work would be sustained by a trust fund that would grow from an initial commitment of up to $800 million from the Jesuits, the Roman Catholic Church, and Georgetown.

Descendants of the Jesuits' slaves could apply to the foundation for money to support their educations—not just at Georgetown, or in Maringouin, but anywhere. The destitute among them could turn to the foundation for help with food, shelter, and medical care.

The foundation, Stewart says, would also invest in wider projects of "truth, racial healing, and transformation." He won't specify details, saying those would be for the foundation's board to decide. But the spirit of what he has in mind aligns closely with a major Kellogg Foundation project devoted to uprooting the beliefs that sustain racism. Kellogg's work borrows from the many panels that have sprung up around the world to help countries reckon with systemic wrongs, such as the Truth and Reconciliation Commission that Desmond Tutu led to rehabilitate race relations in post-apartheid South Africa. Since the Ferguson, Mo., unrest in 2014, experts have argued that similar processes can help Americans heal the wound of slavery and face problems like police killings of black men.

Stewart hopes that universities beyond Georgetown would eventually support the GU272 Foundation. Their motivation, on one level, would be practical. All of America's oldest seats of higher learning were complicit in slavery. Harvard University and the University of Virginia, among others, face growing pressure to make amends for that history. By investing in the foundation, Stewart says, they could settle the matter once and for all, indemnifying themselves against future claims. More important, he says, they would show leadership in a cultural transformation that will take the next century to achieve. And they would do it together, with a measurable impact, rather than spending their money on memorials and other scattered projects.

Ferrara responds warmly to the general concept Stewart has laid out: the idea of advancing future generations rather than only looking backward at the past. For now, though, neither he nor Kesicki will say much more publicly about the descendants' foundation proposal. The outcome, Stewart expects, will most likely involve Pope Francis.

"This is a tough, hard journey," says Stewart, placing a hand on his chest. "We are dealing with one of the strongest and longest bureaucracies in the history of mankind, called the Catholic Church. And it is no pushover. And we understand that. But then, too, we believe in the concept of David and Goliath. There's got to be hope."

Dan Bauman contributed research to this article.

36

This Could Be the First Slavery
Reparations Policy in America

JESÚS A. RODRÍGUEZ

In the spring of 2019, Georgetown undergraduates voted on a referendum to establish a student activity fee to create a fund to benefit descendants of the GU272. Published in Politico *on April 9, 2019, this article by Georgetown student Jesús A. Rodríguez describes the campus debate over the referendum. Days after this article was published, Georgetown students voted overwhelmingly in favor of the fee in an election that featured the largest turnout in the history of Georgetown's student government. The university has not approved the fee.*

In September 2014, a Georgetown junior published a column in *The Hoya*, the student newspaper, with the headline: "Georgetown, Financed by Slave Trading." It unearthed a known but largely forgotten history: that the esteemed Jesuit university had saved itself from financial ruin in 1838 by selling 272 enslaved people. The sale had been orchestrated by one of the school's presidents, Thomas Mulledy, himself a Jesuit priest, and the namesake of a residence hall that was at the time of the article undergoing renovations. The author, Matthew Quallen, urged the administration to strip Mulledy's name from the building.

Quallen's demand was effectively the first shot in what has become a 4½-year debate over how the school should atone for its slave-holding past. In September 2015, Georgetown's president, John J. DeGioia, impaneled a working group of academics, administrators, and students to study the issue. Two months later, black students staged a sit-in in his office success-fully demanding the removal of names like Mulledy's, which still graced several prominent buildings on campus. In 2016, the university agreed to give admissions preference to descendants of the 272 slaves; and the first two descendants arrived in the fall of 2017. College officials and the Jesuits held a mass of contrition in the spring of 2017 as a formal mea culpa for the sale.

But the perception has grown among some of the approximately 7,000 undergraduates that the university has moved too slowly. There is still no public marker of that dark chapter of Georgetown's history. Most import-ant, the university still has not addressed what many saw as the most crucial element in the working group's report: financial compensation for the esti-mated 4,000 living descendants. In a word, reparations.

This week, Georgetown students are attempting to change that.

On April 11, undergraduates will vote on a referendum to create a $27.20 per semester student fee to create a fund that would benefit the descendants through education and health care initiatives in the Louisiana and Maryland locales where many of them still live. If the measure passes, and the univer-sity's board of directors approves, it will mark the first time a major Amer-ican institution has gone beyond the platitudes of "dialogue" and actually compensated the victims of slavery. And it comes at a moment, not entirely coincidentally, when the conversation about America's racial reckoning has suddenly emerged as a subject many progressives are using to winnow the sprawling field of Democrats in the 2020 presidential campaign.

"What is happening right now on Georgetown's campus is a reflection of a larger political climate, in which, I think, people are taking seriously what anti-racist action looks like," said Marcia Chatelain, a professor of his-tory and African-American studies and a member of the president's working group. "So it's not just being nice to each other or saying racism is a bad thing. It's about actually taking account and responsibility for the ways that these decisions and processes in the past shape contemporary life."

And while the Georgetown student fee, which would raise about $400,000 in the first year, does not come close to matching the multibillion-dollar price tags of the national reparations projects being discussed by pres-idential hopefuls, its mere existence indicates the degree to which an idea once thought to be impractically extreme has now moved into the main-stream. (On Monday, Senator Cory Booker introduced a bill to study racial reparations for African-Americans, a companion proposal to one offered in the House by Texas Democrat Sheila Jackson Lee.)

William Darity Jr., a professor of public policy at Duke University and one of the leading scholars on the economics of reparations, said he was "admiring" of the student efforts, while also pushing them to lay the groundwork for a nationwide effort that avoids "piecemeal" solutions. "We do need to move away from viewing this as a matter of individual guilt or individual responsibility that can be offset by individual payments, towards the recognition that this is a national responsibility and a national obligation that must be met by the federal government," he said.

Indeed, the debate on campus mirrors some of the wider discussion about the nature of collective responsibility and whether there is such a thing as a statute of limitations on a crime of such magnitude. Like the American public at large, Georgetown students are far from unanimous in their support for the reparations fee. For one, it puts the burden of paying on students instead of the university. It raises the cost of attendance for families, many already on shoestring budgets. Some black students wonder why, if they too are descended from slaves, they should pay reparations they feel entitled to themselves.

"That's the problem, people don't want to be uncomfortable," said Mélisande Short-Colomb, a sophomore and descendant who came to Georgetown at age 63. "Everything happens for students here on campus. If you can receive a benefit, are you not capable of extending a hand in service? . . . Are you capable of washing feet?"

Like many other top-tier American colleges, including Harvard, Yale, Brown and the University of Virginia, Georgetown's ties to slavery predate the Union. And in Georgetown's case, they persisted even after the sale splintered 40 families and shipped them to plantations in Maryland and Louisiana. Slaves continued to wash the clothes of white, wealthy students from landowning families until Emancipation. After the end of the Civil War, black people continued to work on campus as servants, and integration of the student body wouldn't happen until the first black undergraduate was admitted in 1950. To this day, the colors worn by Georgetown's basketball team, Blue and Gray, are an homage to Union and Confederate military uniforms.

"The story of Georgetown, the Jesuits and slavery is such a vivid microcosm of the entire history of American slavery, going back to the early origins, colonial settlement, all the way through Emancipation and beyond," said Adam Rothman, a professor of history and the curator of the Georgetown Slavery Archive. "You can tell the whole history of American slavery through this particular story."

Rothman takes no public stance on the referendum so as not to intrude in an initiative that he sees as belonging to the students. But he does encourage them to know their history. "A partial truth is not the truth," he told me on a recent morning in his office.

And that history continues to emerge in shocking ways.

Kuma Okoro, a junior studying international political economy, said he was moved to action when he learned that during construction of a residence hall in December 2014, workers had unearthed a human thigh bone in the site of a segregated cemetery that is known to have had remains of slaves and free blacks. The discovery was kept under wraps until August of last year. "For me, that was, like, crazy. But it also kind of showed that they don't really care, right? The university's goal is to keep the conversation controlled and keep everybody moving along." He reached out to Short-Colomb, and within a month they were having meetings with other advocates of color in what would become the group Students for the GU272.

Students were already frustrated by the administration's refusal to erect a memorial honoring the 272 slaves. A student proposal in September 2018 to construct a 5-foot-tall, illuminated, marble and granite block, free of cost, to be placed near the residence hall built on the segregated cemetery, was politely rebuffed. The president's office, a representative wrote in an email reviewed by POLITICO, was focused on "developing a framework for dialogue." It was committed to "engaging these important topics." "Patience and understanding" were appreciated.

Despite its inaction on the memorial proposal, the university has not totally ignored the recommendations that emerged from the working group's 104-page report. Senior administrators are in the middle of tightly guarded talks with descendants, mediated by the W. K. Kellogg Foundation, to figure out the right steps for atonement. A grant from the Andrew Mellon Foundation has funded faculty positions and fellowships to study slavery. Some professors have dedicated entire classes to discussing the conflict between the school's founding principles, rooted in Catholic beliefs, and the moral stain that sustained it.

Nevertheless, the pace of atonement has led to impatience. "What they were doing was more like kiss and hug babies . . . to handle the media attention that was present at the time," Shepard Thomas, a junior studying psychology and one of the first descendants to be admitted under the new admissions policy, told me. "Yeah, it's important to rename buildings. [But] what's legacy status if they can't go to high school? You know, what are you promising at the end of the day?"

Last summer, Thomas, who comes from New Orleans, visited Maringouin, a small town outside of Baton Rouge, Louisiana, whose 1,000 residents are overwhelmingly descended from the 1838 sale. What he saw there—a town with a dearth of jobs, an absence of quality secondary schools and a median income ($36,518) far below the national median ($57,617)—spurred him to action. (Not all of the descendants think Georgetown has the wherewithal to solve the real problems that beset places like Maringouin,

Chatham, and Terrebonne Parish. Jessica Tilson, a descendant from Baton Rouge, recently told me: "What Maringouin needs is something Georgetown students can't provide—and that's jobs.")

Last fall, instead of dwelling on what the university hadn't done, a group of students gathered repeatedly in Short-Colomb's dorm to brainstorm how they could empower the student body to do what the administration had declined to do. They studied the legal intricacies of nonprofits. They drafted a resolution to permit a vote on the fee and saw it through four sessions of debate in the student senate. Finally, on February 3, the resolution passed, setting up the vote for April 11.

The precedent-setting measure, which they have termed a "reconciliation fee," would create a nonprofit governed by a board of five descendants and five students who would allocate the funds collected from the $27.20 fee assessed each semester and funnel them into projects that help cover descendant needs. For instance, there's talk of providing eye exams free of cost and laying the groundwork for a scholarship foundation for descendants to attend college, not just Georgetown. But ultimately, students say, it is up to descendants to decide how best the money should be used.

The biggest and most popular argument in opposition to the referendum is not against reparations, but rather who should pay. Many students think that the university needs to make a full commitment to the report of the working group, which reads in part, "While we acknowledge that the moral debt of slaveholding and the sale of the enslaved people can never be repaid, we are convinced that reparative justice requires a meaningful financial commitment from the University."

"When you target undergraduates, to be quite frank, you're literally targeting the least financially successful subset of people who benefit from Georgetown," said sophomore and student senator Sam Dubke, an international economics major.

Many return to the question of who bears the true responsibility for righting the wrong. "While we agree that the Georgetown of today would not exist if not for the sale of 272 slaves in 1838, current students are not to blame for the past sins of the institution, and a financial contribution cannot reconcile this past debt on behalf of the university," Dubke and another student, Hayley Grande, wrote in an op-ed earlier this semester.

The problem, supporters of the fee say, is that the university doesn't seem to want to have anything to do with financial restitution—not even if it's paid for by students. Two days before the senate resolution was passed, administrators filed into a room with students and launched a last-ditch effort to oppose their efforts. The fee, they said, was "just not appropriate" and outside the bounds of what the student government could do. Even federal research grants to the school could be threatened by this fee, officials said, according to an audio recording made by students in the room. An email statement from Todd Olson, vice president for student affairs, to POLITICO reaffirmed the administration's position that the vote is primarily symbolic: "Student referendums help to express important student perspectives but do not create university policy and are not binding on the university."

This fight has turned personal for many, including Thomas. "At the end of the day, this is my history," he said.

Each year since 1989, former Representative John Conyers (D-Mich.) introduced a bill to form a commission that would study slavery in the colonies and early Union and recommend appropriate measures—but it has never been brought up for a vote. The explanation for its perennial failure might be as simple as the negligible amount of support for the idea of reparations in any form; at most, 26 percent of Americans favor the idea and that level drops to 6 percent when polling white adults.

It was in the face of that disinterest, that in mid-2014, Ta-Nehisi Coates published a piece in *The Atlantic* called "The Case for Reparations." In unsparing detail, Coates traced the crushing financial toll that slavery, and the pernicious segregation that followed, has wreaked on black citizens. "What I'm talking about is more than recompense for past injustices—more than a handout, a payoff, hush money, or a reluctant bribe," Coates wrote. "Reparations would mean a revolution of the American consciousness, a reconciling of our self-image as the great democratizer with the facts of our history."

For all the attention Coates' 15,000-word piece garnered, it did not entirely bring a reparations policy to the forefront. (Though its influence endures: The conservative columnist David Brooks last month changed his stance on the issue, citing Coates' essay.) Indeed, the 2016 presidential contest, driven by Donald Trump's obsession with illegal immigration, scarcely touched on how to move forward on racial injustice. That has changed dramatically this cycle. And this might be a function of a significant generational split: While reparations have net negative support of 39 percent among voters 45 and older, according to a 2018 poll, voters 45 and younger have a net positive of 2 percent, according to the left-leaning group Data for Progress.

In town halls and living rooms across the country, reparations has emerged alongside "Medicare for All" and climate change as a litmus test on the Democratic side. Almost every candidate has been asked whether they support reparations.

The answer is overwhelmingly yes, though not everyone agrees on exactly how. Julián Castro and Senators Elizabeth Warren and Kamala Harris generally support the idea that any reckoning with slavery must include some form of restitution. Booker has embraced a "baby bonds" proposal, very similar to one put forth by Darity, the economist at Duke, and Darrick Hamilton, an economist at the New School, which creates a public trust fund that allows children to access monies—determined on a graduated scale based on their parents' wealth position—at 18. (The measure, though not specifically targeted toward descendants of slaves, would effectively be aimed at closing the racial wealth gap.) Senator Bernie Sanders, the Vermont socialist, has been much slower to establish a position. After opposing it at first in 2016 and again this year, he announced April 5 he was throwing his support behind the Conyers bill.

The Conyers commission may be the first step. The reparations checks and formal apologies doled out in 1988 by Ronald Reagan to victims of Japanese-American internment camps during World War II were preceded by such a panel. (And it may not be that checks are the ideal solution—Darity and other scholars have argued that it could end up benefiting white business owners and doing little to ameliorate the racial wealth gap.)

But the one candidate who is furthest ahead on this issue is one you'll rarely see on television. Democrat Marianne Williamson, a spiritual adviser and best-selling author whose campaign seeks to "heal the soul of America," came out swinging with a $100 billion reparations plan that would create a board of "esteemed African American leaders" to disburse the money. After Darity called the dollar amount "paltry" in a *New York Times* article, she upped the ante to $200 billion to $500 billion.

"I don't believe the average American is a racist," Williamson told me over the phone. "I do believe the average American is vastly undereducated about the history.... When I actually draw the timeline—speak about it for five to 10 minutes—by the time I reach the end and say, 'Therefore, reparations are only reasonable,' I get a lot of affirmation."

At Georgetown, plenty of question marks hang over the upcoming referendum. Campus sentiment seems to be leaning in favor of the fee. A poll conducted by *The Hoya* in early February, soon after the referendum was passed in the student senate, showed that only 16.3 percent of the 615 students surveyed were against the measure. Nevertheless, roughly as many students in favor of the fee were also undecided. Members of the advocacy team are confident in their campaigning since then, and students are banking on the message that a positive vote would send to the university's board of directors, which has the final say. If the board strikes down the proposal, Okoro said, it will be "a horrible mistake.... Also, I think it would be a statement of Georgetown's values."

"Without us there is no Georgetown," he said. "Change in society always comes from activism from college students."

37

Changing Perceptions on the GU272 Referendum

JAVON PRICE

In April 2019, Georgetown students voted in favor of establishing a fee to create a fund for the benefit of the descendant community. Javon Price, then a sophomore in the School of Foreign Service, was initially opposed to the fee but changed his mind after hearing Mélisande Short-Colomb speak about it at a town hall. In this opinion editorial published in Georgetown's student newspaper, The Hoya, *Price traced the evolution of his view during the referendum campaign.*

On April 11, the Georgetown University undergraduate student body overwhelmingly voted "yes" to the referendum, establishing a board of trustees to "directly better the lives of the descendants of the GU272," the 272 enslaved people sold by the Maryland Province of the Society of Jesus in 1838 to financially sustain the university. Students would pay a semesterly fee of $27.20, which would then be collected and distributed throughout the community of the descendants of the GU272. Shamefully, I was initially against this idea, seeing no benefit in its passage, and I even worked to ensure its defeat. However, on the nights leading up to the vote, I had a change of heart and mind and decided that the referendum had not only earned my vote, but required it.

As a conservative, there is an ideological case to be made against reparations in general. On the federal level, large government programs, often proposed by liberals, rarely accomplish their goal and often succumb to unforeseen consequences.

My original fear was that this reconciliation fee would eventually go awry and fail to help those whom it was designed to aid from the beginning. Georgetown has far fewer resources than the federal government, and if the government could not amend this centuries-old wound of slavery, how was Georgetown supposed to? The difference, as I would soon learn, is that this fund is not and should not be considered reparations.

We the students voted "yes" to a reconciliation fee whose charter explicitly details the form and function of the proposed GU272 reconciliation board of trustees. I was particularly struck by the potential projects discussed in the charter. The initiatives, ranging from "[providing] medical care" to "[supplementing] the education" of the descendant community struck me as necessary and worthy of students' endorsement. This referendum is a genuine grassroots, bottom-up movement to try and reconcile with the university's past of slavery.

Furthermore, I opposed the referendum based on moral beliefs. Why should I, an African American student myself, pay for the sins committed by the university centuries before my time here on the Hilltop? When I asked this question at the Georgetown University Student Association-sponsored town hall event, I received several answers from those on the panel, but when Mélisande Short-Colomb (COL '21), a descendant of the GU272, stood up to speak, the room went silent.

It was then that she gave me a gift: the gift of understanding, of perspective, of recognizing what is right. As she addressed the crowd, I felt as if she was speaking directly to me when she said that the descendants of the GU272 are as much a part of Georgetown as are we, the students, ourselves. She spoke about how we have a moral obligation to try to reconcile our past history and that we owe a debt to those sold so many years ago, as they are the reason that we can call the Hilltop our home today. As beneficiaries of this university—regardless of political leanings, race or gender—we have a responsibility to "better the lives of the descendants of the GU272," as they had, against their will, done for us. As a conservative African American student at Georgetown, I was no exception.

I now recognize my initial opposition was ill-founded and part of the overall problem. If we hope to address the issue of reconciliation the right way, we must all be a part of the solution. The first step in that solution can be recognized by holding the university accountable, as although the referendum has passed, more work is left to do. We must ensure the administration does not drag its feet on this issue and work towards realizing the ideas espoused in the charter. We must ensure the university begins to establish a GU272 reconciliation board of trustees and carry out the rest of the proposals to which students voted "yes." After all, the referendum wasn't just an idea, or just a charter, or even just a plan. The GU272 referendum and its passage was the first step toward justice for those people wronged so many years ago.

We have the opportunity, as a community, to set an example nationwide on how to deal with the issue of reconciliation. I hope that all Hoyas will join me and many others in ensuring that the GU272 reconciliation board of trustees is erected and the proposals advocated for in the charter come to fruition. We must not tire, we must hold University President John J. DeGioia and the administration accountable, and we must carry out our duty and continue on the path for justice.

Epilogue

ELSA BARRAZA MENDOZA

I first learned about Sucky in a letter from 1836. The writer, a priest, recounts to his colleague a conversation with Sucky, an elderly enslaved woman. Mimicking her speech, he uses her voice to describe physical violence at the hands of a Jesuit at St. Inigoes plantation: "a dreadful whipping for my curiosity." It was one of the few times I found the voice of an enslaved woman represented in the archives. Even in this letter, Sucky's testimony is an act of ventriloquism. Her voice only reaches us through the letters of her enslavers. That is one of the countless tragedies of enslavement. Men, women, and children were robbed of their names and their voices. Their descendants and the rest of society have only scraps of information with which to recognize and understand their lives. Although Sucky's name survives, I fear that we will never know her story beyond one reductive account of trauma. The least we can do is to say her name and share what remains of her story.

This responsibility to remember enslaved persons drives the Slavery, Memory, and Reconciliation initiative at Georgetown University and the work of the Georgetown Slavery Archive. It also motivates my work and that of genealogists, researchers, and descendants who scour records for men, women, and children enslaved at the Jesuit plantations and Georgetown's campus. The letter describing Sucky's harrowing experience at St. Inigoes was my first contribution to the Georgetown Slavery Archive more than three years ago. Today the archive has more than four hundred documents naming more than twelve hundred people enslaved by the Jesuits. This book continues the work of remembrance, naming more than three hundred persons in its primary sources and academic articles.

Before Georgetown's slaveholding history became national news in 2016, most names of the enslaved individuals lay buried in the archives of the university and the Maryland Province of the Society of Jesus. Scholars had addressed Jesuit slaveholding, the school's relationship to Jesuit plantations, and the sale of 1838, but they had seldom identified enslaved people by name. This neglect obscured those who suffered and minimized their experiences. Tireless advocacy by descendants and their allies, as well as conversations like the ones in this book, will change how we write and think about Georgetown's slaveholding past.

Georgetown University's archives name women like Margaret Smallwood, who labored in slavery at the school and was buried in a cemetery that is now underneath the school's science building. They tell us about Charles Taylor, a man who was enslaved at Georgetown for seventeen years before he liberated himself by self-purchase. They document Martha Hawkins, Mary Ellen Butler, and Charles Queen, who were barely infants when they were sold by Jesuit leaders to save Georgetown in 1838. They include Aaron Edmonson, the last enslaved man to labor at Georgetown's campus in the 1860s. These individuals made Georgetown possible with their bodies, labor, and lives. Their past has been obscured from the university's history for too long.

At Georgetown and across the country, we are finally beginning to acknowledge the people whose forced labor helped build America's schools. While it is important to research these individuals, it is equally important to memorialize them. It is not enough to publish the names and stories of those who labored under slavery, only to have those names languish in a new medium. Instead, those names and stories must live with us just as visibly as the institutions live. With this book, we invite readers and the university community to think about the importance of this history and the ways to keep our collective memory alive.

It is our responsibility to recognize women like Sucky and Margaret Smallwood, men like Charles Taylor and Aaron Edmonson, and infants like Mary Ellen Butler, Charles Queen, and Martha Hawkins. We now know about some abusive and tragic events of their pasts. We sometimes even know about possibly joyous occasions such as marriages, baptisms, and births of children. We will never be able to tell their full stories. But they should not escape our memory. We should try to our fullest extent to say their names, to remember, recognize, and honor them. We have hidden too long in the safety of abstraction, focusing on institutions instead of the individuals. This book is a small step in a more personal—and personally responsible—direction. Only when we see and name those who suffered can we begin to pay our debts.

TIMELINE

SLAVERY, THE MARYLAND JESUITS, AND GEORGETOWN UNIVERSITY

1634   English Catholics establish the Maryland colony.

1642   Thirteen Africans are sold into slavery in St. Mary's City, Maryland.

1664   Maryland legalizes slavery.

1717   Fifteen persons are named as property in Jesuit records at Newtown Plantation.

1773   The Society of Jesus is suppressed by Pope Clement XIV.

1789   The Corporation of Roman Catholic Clergymen (CRCC) establishes Georgetown College.

1791   Edward Queen, a man enslaved by the CRCC, sues Fr. John Ashton for his freedom.

1792   Georgetown College begins operations.

1804   The Society of Jesus is partially restored.

1808   Slave trade to the United States is banned. A Black Code is enacted for the District of Columbia.

1814   The Society of Jesus is restored by Pope Pius VII.

1818   College Ground on Georgetown campus serves as cemetery for Holy Trinity Church until the 1830s.

1833   The Jesuits' Maryland mission becomes the first Jesuit Province in the United States.

1835   The Snow Riot in Washington, DC.

1838   The Maryland Jesuits sell 272 children, women, and men to Jesse Batey and Henry S. Johnson of Louisiana.

1839   The pope issues *In Supremo Apostolatus,* a bull denouncing the slave trade.

1861   The Civil War begins at Fort Sumter, South Carolina.
        The Sixty-Ninth Regiment from New York occupies the grounds of Georgetown College.

1862   Aaron Edmonson, the last man enslaved at Georgetown College, leaves campus.
        Congress abolishes slavery in Washington, DC.
        The Maryland Jesuits receive the last payment from the sale of 1838.

1863   President Lincoln issues the Emancipation Proclamation.

1864   Slavery is abolished in Maryland, emancipating Louisa Mason and her children.

1865   The Thirteenth Amendment abolishes slavery in the United States.

1874   Fr. Patrick Francis Healy, SJ, is named president of Georgetown.

MEMORY AND RECONCILIATION AT GEORGETOWN

August 2014	Michael Brown fatally shot in Ferguson, Missouri.
September 2014	Matthew Quallen begins a series of articles on Georgetown, the Jesuits, and slavery in Georgetown's student newspaper, *The Hoya*.
June 2015	Mass shooting at Emanuel AME Church in Charleston, South Carolina.
August 2015	Creation of Georgetown's Working Group on Slavery, Memory, and Reconciliation.
November 2015	Students stage a sit-in at the president's office at Georgetown University, championing the GU272.
February 2016	Launch of the Georgetown Slavery Archive website.
April 2016	The *New York Times* runs a major article on the GU272 descendants.
June 2016	Georgetown establishes the African American Studies Department. Georgetown's president John J. DeGioia meets with members of the GU272 descendant community.
September 2016	Publication of the *Report of the Working Group on Slavery Memory, and Reconciliation*.
March 2017	First visit of a group of Georgetown faculty and students to Maringouin, Louisiana.
April 2017	Renaming of Isaac Hawkins and Anne Marie Becraft Halls. President DeGioia and Fr. Timothy Kesicki, SJ, apologize for Georgetown and the Jesuits' historical involvement in slavery.
April 2019	Georgetown undergraduates vote to approve a student activity fee to create a "reconciliation fund" for descendants. The fee has not been approved by the University.
October 2019	In an email to the university community, Georgetown announces its "Next Steps on Slavery, Memory, and Reconciliation," which includes the creation of advisory groups on descendant and community engagement, academic and research initiatives, and public history.[1]

Note

1. John J. DeGioia, "Next Steps on Slavery, Memory, and Reconciliation," Georgetown University, October 29, 2019, https://president.georgetown.edu/next-steps-on-slavery-memory -and-reconciliation/.

FURTHER READING

AMERICAN SLAVERY

Baptist, Edward E. *The Half Has Never Been Told: Slavery and the Making of American Capitalism*. New York: Basic Books, 2014.

Berlin, Ira. *Generations of Captivity: A History of African-American Slaves*. New York: Belknap Press, 2003.

Berry, Daina Raimey. *The Price for Their Pound of Flesh: The Value of the Enslaved, from Womb to Grave, in the Building of a Nation*. Boston, MA: Beacon Press, 2017.

Fields, Barbara Jeanne, "Slavery, Race and Ideology in the United States of America," *New Left Review* 181 (1990): 95–118.

Harris, Leslie M. "Imperfect Archives and the Historical Imagination." *The Public Historian* 36, no. 1 (February 1, 2014): 77–80.

SLAVERY IN THE CHESAPEAKE

Brown, Kathleen M. *Good Wives, Nasty Wenches, and Anxious Patriarchs: Gender, Race, and Power in Colonial Virginia*. Chapel Hill: University of North Carolina Press, 1996.

Corrigan, Mary Beth. "Imaginary Cruelties: A History of the Slave Trade in the District of Columbia," *Washington History* 13, no. 2 (Fall/Winter 2002): 4–27.

———. "Making the Most of an Opportunity: Slaves and the Catholic Church in Early Washington," *Washington History* 12, no. 1 (Spring/Summer 2000): 90–101.

Douglass, Frederick. *Narrative of the Life of Frederick Douglass, An American Slave*. Boston, MA: Anti-Slavery Office, 1845.

Fields, Barbara Jeanne. *Slavery and Freedom on the Middle Ground: Maryland during the Nineteenth Century*. New Haven, CT: Yale University Press, 1984.

Finkelman, Paul, and Donald R. Kennon, eds. *In the Shadow of Freedom: The Politics of Slavery in the National Capital*. Athens: Ohio University Press, 2011.

Flanagan, Charles M. "The Sweets of Independence: A Reading of the 'James Carroll Day Book, 1714–1721.'" PhD diss., University of Maryland, College Park, 2005.

Grivno, Max. *Gleanings of Freedom: Free and Slave Labor along the Mason-Dixon Line, 1790–1860*. Champaign: University of Illinois Press, 2011.

Hardy, Beatriz Betancourt. "Papists in a Protestant Age: The Catholic Gentry and Community in Colonial Maryland, 1689–1776." PhD diss., University of Maryland, College Park, 1993.

Jackson, Maurice. "Washington, DC: From the Founding of a Slaveholding Capital to a Center of Abolitionism." *Journal of African Diaspora Archaeology and Heritage* 2, no. 1 (May 2013): 40–66.

Kulikoff, Allan. *Tobacco and Slaves: The Development of Southern Cultures in the Chesapeake, 1680–1800*. Chapel Hill: University of North Carolina Press, 1986.

Millward, Jessica. *Finding Charity's Folk: Enslaved and Free Black Women in Maryland*. Athens: University of Georgia Press, 2015.

Morgan, Edmund S. *American Slavery, American Freedom: The Ordeal of Colonial Virginia*. Reissue edition. New York: W. W. Norton and Company, 2003.

Morgan, Philip D. *Slave Counterpoint: Black Culture in the Eighteenth-Century Chesapeake and Lowcountry*. Chapel Hill: University of North Carolina Press, 1998.

Rockman, Seth. *Scraping By: Wage Labor, Slavery, and Survival in Early Baltimore*. Baltimore, MD: Johns Hopkins University Press, 2009.

Whitman, T. Stephen. *Challenging Slavery in the Chesapeake: Black and White Resistance to Human Bondage, 1775–1865*. Baltimore: The Maryland Historical Society, 2006.

THE DOMESTIC SLAVE TRADE

Deyle, Steven. *Carry Me Back: The Domestic Slave Trade in American Life*. New York: Oxford University Press, 2006.

Johnson, Walter. *Soul by Soul: Life inside the Antebellum Slave Market*. Cambridge, MA: Harvard University Press, 1999.

Pargas, Damian Alan. *Slavery and Forced Migration in the Antebellum South*. New York: Cambridge University Press, 2015.

Schermerhorn, Calvin. *The Business of Slavery and the Rise of American Capitalism, 1815–1860*. New Haven, CT: Yale University Press, 2015.

Williams, Heather Andrea. *Help Me to Find My People: The African American Search for Family Lost in Slavery*. Chapel Hill: University of North Carolina Press, 2012.

SLAVERY IN LOUISIANA

Johnson, Walter. *River of Dark Dreams: Slavery and Empire in the Cotton Kingdom*. Cambridge, MA: Harvard University Press, 2013.

Malone, Ann Patton. *Sweet Chariot: Slave Family and Household Structure in Nineteenth-Century Louisiana*. Chapel Hill: University of North Carolina Press, 1992.

Northup, Solomon. *Twelve Years a Slave: Narrative of Solomon Northup, a Citizen of New-York, Kidnapped in Washington City in 1841 and Rescued in 1853, from a Cotton Plantation Near the Red River in Louisiana*. Auburn, NY: Derby and Miller, 1853.

Rothman, Adam. *Slave Country: American Expansion and the Origins of the Deep South*. Cambridge, MA: Harvard University Press, 2005.

SLAVERY, THE SOCIETY OF JESUS, AND CATHOLICISM

Beckett, Edward F. "Listening to Our History: Inculturation and Jesuit Slaveholding." *Studies in the Spirituality of Jesuits* 28, no. 5 (1996).

Brown, Joseph A. *To Stand on the Rock: Meditations on Black Catholic Identity*. Eugene, OR: Wipf and Stock Publishers, 2011.

Curran, Robert Emmett. "'Splendid Poverty': Jesuit Slaveholding in Maryland, 1805–1838." In *Catholics in the Old South: Essays on Church and Culture*, edited by Jon L. Wakelyn and Randall M. Miller, 125–46. Macon, GA: Mercer University Press, 1999.

———. *Papist Devils: Catholics in British America, 1574–1783*. Washington, DC: Catholic University of America Press, 2014.

Farrelly, Maura Jane. "American Slavery, American Freedom, American Catholicism." *Early American Studies: An Interdisciplinary Journal* 10, no. 1 (2012): 69–100.

———. *Papist Patriots: The Making of an American Catholic Identity*. New York: Oxford University Press, 2012.

Finn, Peter C. "The Slaves of the Jesuits of Maryland." Master's thesis, Georgetown University, 1974.

Jesuits. "Slavery, History, Memory, and Reconciliation." Accessed November 17, 2020. https://www.jesuits.org/our-work/shmr/.

Judge, Robert K. "Foundation and First Administration of the Maryland Province," *Woodstock Letters* 88, no. 4 (1959): 376–406.

Leon, Sharon. "Re-presenting the Enslaved Community Sold by the Maryland Province Jesuits in 1838," *[bracket]*, September 30, 2016. http://www.6floors.org/bracket/2016/09/30/re-presenting-the-enslaved-community-sold-by-the-maryland-province-jesuits-in-1838/.

Maxwell, John Frances. *Slavery and the Catholic Church: The History of Catholic Teaching concerning the Moral Legitimacy of the Institution of Slavery*. London: Barry Rose Publishers, 1975.

Murphy, Thomas. *Jesuit Slaveholding in Maryland, 1717–1838*. Studies in African American History and Culture. New York: Routledge, 2001.

Rothman, Adam. "Georgetown University and the Business of Slavery." *Washington History* 29, no. 2 (Fall 2017): 18–22.

Schmidt, Kelly L. "Enslaved Faith Communities in the Jesuits' Missouri Mission." *U.S. Catholic Historian* 37, no. 2 (Spring 2019): 49–81.

St. Ignatius Church at Chapel Point: Sharing God's Word since 1641. Port Tobacco, MD: St. Ignatius Church, 2016.

Walsh, Francis. *A Pictorial History of Saint Inigoes Mission, 1634–1984*. Hollywood, MD: St. Mary's Press, 1984.

Zanca, Kenneth J., ed. *American Catholics and Slavery, 1789–1866: An Anthology of Primary Documents*. Lanham, MD: University Press of America, 1994.

Zwinge, Joseph. "The Jesuit Farms in Maryland: Facts and Anecdotes. The Negro Slaves," *Woodstock Letters* 41, no. 3 (1912): 276–91.

SLAVERY AND UNIVERSITIES

Brown University. *Slavery and Justice: Report of the Brown University Steering Committee on Slavery and Justice*. Providence, RI: Brown University, 2006. https://www.brown.edu/about/administration/institutional-diversity/resources-initiatives/slavery-justice-report.

Columbia University. "Columbia University and Slavery." Accessed October 28, 2020. https://columbiaandslavery.columbia.edu/.

Fuentes, Marisa J., and Deborah Gray White, eds. *Scarlet and Black: Slavery and Dispossession in Rutgers History*. Vol. 1. New Brunswick, NJ: Rutgers University Press, 2016.

Harvard University. "Harvard and Slavery." Accessed October 28, 2020. http://www.harvard.edu/slavery.

John Carroll University. *Final Report, Working Group: Slavery—Legacy and Reconciliation, Spring 2018*. University Heights, Ohio: John Carrol University, 2018. http://webmedia.jcu.edu/mission/files/2018/08/WGSLR-Final-Report-Spring-2018.pdf.

Oast, Jennifer. *Institutional Slavery: Slaveholding Churches, Schools, Colleges, and Businesses in Virginia, 1680–1860*. New York: Cambridge University Press, 2016.

University of Virginia. "Universities Studying Slavery." Slavery and the University. Accessed October 28, 2020. https://slavery.virginia.edu/universities-studying-slavery/.

Walters, Lindsey K. "Slavery and the American University: Discourses of Retrospective Justice at Harvard and Brown." *Slavery and Abolition* 38, no. 4 (December 2017): 719–44.

Wilder, Craig Steven. *Ebony and Ivy: Race, Slavery, and the Troubled History of America's Universities*. New York: Bloomsbury Press, 2013.

———. "War and Priests: Catholic Colleges and Slavery in the Age of Revolutions." In *Slavery's Capitalism: A New History of American Economic Development*. Edited by Sven Beckert and Seth Rockman. Philadelphia: University of Pennsylvania Press, 2016.

SLAVERY AND MEMORY

Araujo, Ana Lucia. *Shadows of the Slave Past: Memory, Heritage, and Slavery*. New York: Routledge, 2015.

Berry, Mary Frances. *My Face Is Black Is True: Callie House and the Struggle for Ex-Slave Reparations*. New York: Vintage Books, 2005.

Blight, David W. *Race and Reunion: The Civil War in American Memory*. Cambridge, MA: Harvard University Press, 2001.

Hartman, Saidiya. *Lose Your Mother: A Journey along the Atlantic Slave Route*. New York: Farrar, Straus, and Giroux, 2007.

Nelson, Alondra. *The Social Life of DNA: Race, Reparations, and Reconciliation after the Genome*. Boston, MA: Beacon Press, 2016.

Savage, Kirk. *Standing Soldiers, Kneeling Slaves: Race, War, and Monument in 19th-Century America*. Princeton, NJ: Princeton University Press, 1997.

SLAVERY, MEMORY, AND RECONCILIATION AT GEORGETOWN

Collins, David. "Georgetown, Jesuits, Slaveholding." *The Hoya*, February 9, 2015.

Curran, Robert Emmett. *The Bicentennial History of Georgetown University: From Academy to University, 1789–1889*. 3 vols. Washington, DC: Georgetown University Press, 1993.

Foley, Thomas. "Saving Souls and Selling Them: Jesuit Slaveholding and the Georgetown Slavery Archive." *Jesuit Higher Education: A Journal* 6, no. 1 (2017).

Georgetown University. *Report of the Working Group on Slavery, Memory, and Reconciliation to the President of Georgetown University*. Washington, DC: Georgetown University, 2016.

Lesko, Kathleen M., Valerie M. Babb, and Carroll R. Gibbs. *Black Georgetown Remembered: A History of Its Black Community from the Founding of "The Town of George" in 1751 to the Present Day*. Washington, DC: Georgetown University Press, 2016.

O'Toole, James M. *Passing for White: Race, Religion, and the Healy Family, 1820–1920*. Amherst: University of Massachusetts Press, 2003.

INDEX

Illustrations are indicated by page numbers in italics.